ADY 2461   4

A·N·N·U·A·L E·D·I·T·I·O·N·S

DYING, DEATH, AND BEREAVEMENT

00/01

Fifth Edition

Editors

George E. Dickinson
College of Charleston

George E. Dickinson is professor of sociology at the College of Charleston in Charleston, South Carolina. He received a B.A. in biology from Baylor University, an M.A. in sociology from Baylor, and a Ph.D. in sociology from Louisiana State University. His research and publications focus on physicians' treatment of terminally ill patients, children and death, physician-assisted suicide, and health treatment for the elderly.

Michael R. Leming
St. Olaf College

Michael R. Leming is professor of sociology and anthropology at St. Olaf College. He holds a B.A. degree from Westmont College, an M.A. degree from Marquette University, and a Ph.D. degree from the University of Utah, and he has done additional graduate study at the University of California in Santa Barbara. Dr. Leming serves on numerous boards of directors, and he serves as a hospice educator, volunteer, and grief counselor.

Alan C. Mermann
Yale University School of Medicine
Alan C. Mermann received an A.B. degree in biology from Lehigh University, an M.D. degree from Johns Hopkins University, and M.Div. and S.T.M. (Master of Sacred Theology) degrees from Yale University. Dr. Mermann is a clinical professor of pediatrics and a chaplain at Yale University School of Medicine. He counsels and teaches courses on homelessness, death and dying, and coping with chronic illness.

Dushkin/McGraw-Hill
Sluice Dock, Guilford, Connecticut 06437

Visit us on the Internet
http://www.dushkin.com/annualeditions/

DATE DUE	
~~MAY~~ JAN 2 9 2004	
GAYLORD	PRINTED IN U.S.A.

Copyright

Cataloging in Publication Data
Main entry under title: Annual Editions: Dying, death, and bereavement. 2000/2001.
1. Death—Psychological aspects—Periodicals. 2. Bereavement—Periodicals. I. Dickinson, George E., *comp.* II. Leming, Michael R., *comp.* III. Mermann, Alan C., *comp.* IV. Title: Dying, death, and bereavement.
ISBN 0-07-233374-X   155.937′05   BF789.D4   ISSN 1096-4223

© 2000 by Dushkin/McGraw-Hill, Guilford, CT 06437, A Division of The McGraw-Hill Companies.

Fifth Edition

Cover image © 1999 PhotoDisc, Inc.

Printed in the United States of America   1234567890BAHBAH543210   Printed on Recycled Paper

Members of the Advisory Board are instrumental in the final selection of articles for each edition of ANNUAL EDITIONS. Their review of articles for content, level, currentness, and appropriateness provides critical direction to the editor and staff. We think that you will find their careful consideration well reflected in this volume.

Staff

To the Reader

In publishing ANNUAL EDITIONS we recognize the enormous role played by the magazines, newspapers, and journals of the public press in providing current, first-rate educational information in a broad spectrum of interest areas. Many of these articles are appropriate for students, researchers, and professionals seeking accurate, current material to help bridge the gap between principles and theories and the real world. These articles, however, become more useful for study when those of lasting value are carefully collected, organized, indexed, and reproduced in a low-cost format, which provides easy and permanent access when the material is needed. That is the role played by ANNUAL EDITIONS.

New to ANNUAL EDITIONS is the inclusion of related World Wide Web sites. These sites have been selected by our editorial staff to represent some of the best resources found on the World Wide Web today. Through our carefully developed topic guide, we have linked these Web resources to the articles covered in this ANNUAL EDITIONS reader. We think that you will find this volume useful, and we hope that you will take a moment to visit us on the Web at *http://www.dushkin.com* to tell us what you think.

Though dying, death, and bereavement have been around for as long as humankind, as topics of discussion they have been "offstage" for decades in contemporary American public discourse. Indeed, dying in the United States currently takes place away from the arena of familiar surroundings of kin and friends, with approximately 70 percent of deaths occurring in institutional settings of hospitals and nursing homes. Americans have developed a paradoxical relationship with death: We know more about the causes and conditions surrounding death, but we have not equipped ourselves emotionally to cope with dying, death, and bereavement processes. The purpose of this anthology is to provide an understanding of dying, death, and bereavement that will assist individuals to better cope with and understand their own deaths and the deaths of others.

Articles in this volume are taken from professional publications, semiprofessional journals, and popular publications aimed at both special populations and a general readership. The selections are carefully reviewed for their currency and accuracy. On some issues, opposing viewpoints are presented. The current edition has changed through updating and responding to comments of reviewers.

The reader will note the tremendous range of approaches and styles of the writers from personal, first-hand accounts to more scientific and philosophical writings. Some are more practical and applied, while others are more technical and research-oriented. If "variety is the very spice of life," this volume should be a spicy venture for the reader.

As these articles are drawn from many different periodicals, they expose the reader to a diversity of publications in the library. With stimulated interest from a particular article, the student is encouraged to pursue other related articles in that particular journal.

This anthology is organized into six units to cover many of the important aspects of dying, death, and bereavement. Though the units are arranged in a way that has some logical order, one can determine from the brief summaries in the *table of contents* and the cross-references in the *topic guide* whether another arrangement would best fit a particular teaching situation. The first unit gives an overview of the American way of dying and death. Unit 2 takes a life-cycle approach and looks at the developmental aspects of dying and death at different age levels. The third unit concerns the process of dying. Unit 4 covers ethical issues of dying, death, and suicide. In the fifth unit, the articles deal with death rituals and funerals. Finally, unit 6 presents articles on bereavement.

Annual Editions: Dying, Death, and Bereavement 00/01 is intended for use in augmenting selected areas or chapters of regular textbooks on dying and death. The articles in this volume can also serve as a basis for class discussion about various related issues.

Annual Editions: Dying, Death, and Bereavement 00/01 is revised periodically to keep the materials timely as new social concerns about dying, death, and bereavement develop. Your assistance in the revision effort is always welcome. Please complete and return the postage-paid *article rating form* at the back of the book. We look forward to your input.

George E. Dickinson

Michael R. Leming

Alan C. Mermann
Editors

Contents

UNIT 1

The American Way of Dying and Death

Eight selections discuss definitions of death, focusing on the denial of death, various burial customs,

DATE DUE

WITHDRAWN

GAYLORD   PRINTED IN U.S.A.

The concepts in bold italics are developed in the article. For further expansion please refer to the Topic Guide and the Index.

UNIT 2

Developmental Aspects of Dying and Death

Five articles examine how the experience of watching friends and relatives die can affect individuals at various periods of their lives.

UNIT 3

The Dying Process

Seven articles examine the various stages of the dying process, how physicians view dying, spiritual needs of the dying, and the dynamics of hospice.

The concepts in bold italics are developed in the article. For further expansion please refer to the Topic Guide and the Index.

Overview   **122**

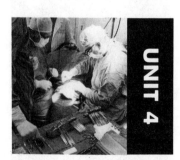

UNIT 4

Ethical Issues of Dying, Death, and Suicide

Six unit selections discuss active
euthanasia and assisted suicide.

The concepts in bold italics are developed in the article. For further expansion please refer to the Topic Guide and the Index.

UNIT 5

Funerals and Burial Rites

Seven articles discuss the
American funeral, cross-cultural
burial rites, and cremation.

The concepts in bold italics are developed in the article. For further expansion please refer to the Topic Guide and the Index.

The concepts in bold italics are developed in the article. For further expansion please refer to the Topic Guide and the Index.

UNIT 6

Bereavement

Eight articles discuss the grieving process of children and young people and the loss of a significant other.

The concepts in bold italics are developed in the article. For further expansion please refer to the Topic Guide and the Index.

The concepts in bold italics are developed in the article. For further expansion please refer to the Topic Guide and the Index.

This topic guide suggests how the selections and World Wide Web sites found in the next section of this book relate to topics of traditional concern to students and professionals involved with the study of dying, death, and bereavement. It is useful for locating interrelated articles and Web sites for reading and research. The guide is arranged alphabetically according to topic.

The relevant Web sites, which are numbered and annotated on pages 4 and 5, are easily identified by the Web icon (◎) under the topic articles. By linking the articles and the Web sites by topic, this ANNUAL EDITIONS reader becomes a powerful learning and research tool.

TOPIC AREA	TREATED IN	TOPIC AREA	TREATED IN
Assisting Grievers	5. At Your Disposal		12. Older Americans in the 1990s
	31. We Can Help Children Grieve		24. Conversation with My Mother
	32. Do-It-Yourself Funeral		◎ **1, 2, 3, 5, 7**
	33. Time to Mourn	**Euthanasia and**	4. Death Be Not Painful
	37. Increasing Prevalence of Complicated Mourning	**Physician-**	8. Is It Time to Abandon?
	38. Children Grieve Too	**Assisted Suicide**	14. Planning to Die
	39. Living with Loss		21. Doctor, I Want to Die
	40. Grief and Depression		22. Supreme Court
	41. GriefTips		23. Competent Care for the Dying
	◎ **1, 2, 36, 37, 38, 39**		24. Conversation with My Mother
Caregivers	4. Death Be Not Painful		25. Euthanasia
	15. Attitudes to Death		◎ **20, 21, 22, 23, 27**
	16. Spiritual Needs of the Dying	**Funerals**	3. Look at How Kentuckians in Knox County Once Treated the Dead
	20. Hospice Care for the 1990s		5. At Your Disposal
	23. Competent Care for the Dying		7. Putting Death on Ice
	24. Conversation with My Mother		9. Communication among Children
	◎ **13, 14, 15, 16, 17, 18, 19**		27. Contemporary American Funeral
Children	9. Communication among Children		30. Burying the Ungrateful Dead
	10. Children, Death, and Fairy Tales		31. We Can Help Children Grieve
	13. Schools Struggle to Teach		32. Do-It-Yourself Funeral
	31. We Can Help Children		33. Time to Mourn
	38. Children Grieve Too		◎ **32, 33, 34, 35**
	◎ **9, 10, 11, 12, 31**	**Grief and Bereavement**	3. Look at How Kentuckians in Knox County Once Treated the Dead
Communication	9. Communication among Children		5. At Your Disposal
	11. Failing to Discuss Dying		7. Putting Death on Ice
	13. Schools Struggle to Teach		31. We Can Help Children Grieve
	17. Request to Die		32. Do-It-Yourself Funeral
	21. Doctor, I Want to Die		33. Time to Mourn
	24. Conversation with My Mother		34. Grieving Process
	38. Children Grieve Too		35. Learning to Mourn
	39. Living with Loss		36. Disenfranchised Grief
	◎ **5, 9, 10, 11, 12**		37. Increasing Prevalence
Cremation	5. At Your Disposal		38. Children Grieve Too
	32. Do-It-Yourself Funeral		39. Living with Loss
	◎ **34**		40. Grief and Depression
Cultural Differences	2. Dealing with Death		41. GriefTips
	3. Look at How Kentuckians in Knox County Once Treated the Dead		◎ **5, 36, 37, 38, 39**
	5. At Your Disposal	**History**	1. Facts of Death
	12. Older Americans in the 1990s		3. Look at How Kentuckians in Knox County Once Treated the Dead
	15. Attitudes to Death		5. At Your Disposal
	25. Euthanasia		6. Death Poetry of Emily Dickinson
	◎ **3, 6, 7**		10. Children, Death, and Fairy Tales
Demography	1. Facts of Death		14. Planning to Die
	5. At Your Disposal		20. Hospice Care for the 1990s
	12. Older Americans in the 1990s		26. Attitudes toward Suicidal Behavior
	◎ **6, 7**		◎ **1, 2, 3**
Depression	17. Request to Die	**Hospice**	4. Death Be Not Painful
	18. Quality End-of-Life Care		20. Hospice Care for the 1990s
	21. Doctor, I Want to Die		32. Do-It-Yourself Funeral
	40. Grief and Depression		◎ **13, 16, 17, 18, 19**
	◎ **14, 15**		
Elderly Persons	5. At Your Disposal	**Institutional**	2. Dealing with Death
	11. Failing to Discuss Dying		

TOPIC AREA	TREATED IN	TOPIC AREA	TREATED IN
Policies	4. Death Be Not Painful 8. Is It Time to Abandon? 13. Schools Struggle to Teach ◎ *1, 2, 3, 4*		41. GriefTips ◎ *15, 36, 37, 38, 39*
Intervention	4. Death Be Not Painful 8. Is It Time to Abandon? 13. Schools Struggle to Teach 17. Request to Die 18. Quality End-of-Life Care 19. Maumee: My Walden Pond 24. Conversation with My Mother 32. Do-It-Yourself Funeral 38. Children Grieve Too 39. Living with Loss ◎ *21, 22, 23, 24, 28, 29*	**Palliative Care**	4. Death Be Not Painful 17. Request to Die 18. Quality End-of-Life Care 19. Maumee: My Walden Pond 20. Hospice Care for the 1990s 23. Competent Care for the Dying 24. Conversation with My Mother 32. Do-It-Yourself Funeral ◎ *1, 2, 3, 4, 5*
		Parents	9. Communication among Children 24. Conversation with My Mother ◎ *9, 36, 37*
Legal Issues	8. Is It Time to Abandon? 22. Supreme Court 23. Competent Care for the Dying 25. Euthanasia ◎ *21, 23, 25, 26*	**Patients**	4. Death Be Not Painful 8. Is It Time to Abandon? 11. Failing to Discuss Dying 14. Planning to Die 15. Attitudes to Death 16. Spiritual Needs of the Dying 20. Hospice Care for the 1990s 24. Conversation with My Mother 32. Do-It-Yourself Funeral ◎ *1, 2, 3, 5, 14, 17*
Life Expectancy	1. Facts of Death 8. Is It Time to Abandon? 12. Older Americans in the 1990s ◎ *1, 2, 3, 5*		
Literature	6. Death Poetry of Emily Dickinson 10. Children, Death, and Fairy Tales 26. Attitudes toward Suicidal Behavior ◎ *1, 2, 3*	**Prolonging/Terminating Life**	2. Dealing with Death 4. Death Be Not Painful 7. Putting Death on Ice 8. Is It Time to Abandon? 11. Failing to Discuss Dying 14. Planning to Die 21. Doctor, I Want to Die 24. Conversation with My Mother 32. Do-It-Yourself Funeral ◎ *20, 21, 22, 23, 27, 28*
Living Will	8. Is It Time to Abandon? 17. Request to Die 19. Maumee: My Walden Pond 24. Conversation with My Mother 26. Attitudes toward Suicidal Behavior ◎ *21, 25, 26*		
		Religion	15. Attitudes to Death 16. Spiritual Needs of the Dying 25. Euthanasia 29. How Different Religions
Meaning of Life/Death	2. Dealing with Death 4. Death Be Not Painful 6. Death Poetry of Emily Dickinson 7. Putting Death on Ice 8. Is It Time to Abandon? 16. Spiritual Needs of the Dying 32. Do-It-Yourself Funeral ◎ *4, 5, 21*	**Rituals**	3. Look at How Kentuckians in Knox County Treated the Dead 5. At Your Disposal 29. How Different Religions 30. Burying the Ungradeful Dead 31. We Can Help Children Grieve 32. Do-It-Yourself Funeral 41. GriefTips ◎ *1, 2, 3*
Medical Ethics	4. Death Be Not Painful 8. Is It Time to Abandon? 11. Failing to Discuss Dying 14. Planning to Die 17. Request to Die 18. Quality End-of-Life Care 19. Maumee: My Walden Pond 21. Doctor, I Want To Die 24. Conversation with My Mother 25. Euthanasia ◎ *20, 21, 22, 23, 24, 25, 26*	**Suicide**	13. Schools Struggle to Teach Lessons in Life and Death 26. Attitudes toward Suicidal Behavior ◎ *8, 11, 28, 29, 31*
		Timing of Death	4. Death Be Not Painful 6. Death Poetry of Emily Dickinson 7. Putting Death on Ice 8. Is It Time to Abandon? 14. Planning to Die 17. Request to Die 18. Quality End-of-Life Care 19. Maumee: My Walden Pond 21. Doctor, I Want to Die 24. Conversation with My Mother 32. Do-It-Yourself Funeral ◎ *1, 2, 3, 23, 24, 27, 28, 29*
Mourning	5. At Your Disposal 6. Death Poetry of Emily Dickinson 31. We Can Help Children Grieve 32. Do-It-Yourself Funeral 33. Time to Mourn 34. Grieving Process 35. Learning to Mourn 38. Children Grieve Too		

● AE: Dying, Death, and Bereavement

The following World Wide Web sites have been carefully researched and selected to support the articles found in this reader. If you are interested in learning more about specific topics found in this book, these Web sites are a good place to start. The sites are cross-referenced by number and appear in the topic guide on the previous two pages. Also, you can link to these Web sites through our DUSHKIN ONLINE support site at *http://www.dushkin.com/online/*.

The following sites were available at the time of publication. Visit our Web site—we update DUSHKIN ONLINE regularly to reflect any changes.

General Sites

1. Death, Dying, and Grief
http://www.emanon.net/~kcabell/death.html
There are many World Wide Web links to resources on death, dying, and bereavement at this site.

2. Death Related Weblinks
http://www.stolaf.edu/people/leming/death.html
This site contains links to some of the best Internet sites related to death and dying.

3. Yahoo: Society and Culture: Death
http://dir.yahoo.com/Society_and_Culture/Death_and_Dying
This Yahoo site has a very complete index to issues of dying and a search option.

The American Way of Dying and Death

4. Agency for Health Care Policy and Research
http://www.ahcpr.gov
Information on the dying process in the context of U.S. health policy is provided here, along with a search mechanism. The agency is part of the Department of Health and Human Services.

5. Growth House, Inc.
http://www.growthhouse.org
Growth House is a nonprofit organization working with grief, bereavement, Hospice, and end-of-life issues, as well as pain, AIDS/HIV, suicide, and palliative care issues.

6. Mortality Rates
http://www.Trinity.Edu/~mkearl/b&w-ineq.jpg
This site contains a graphic representation of the U.S. death rates of different social groups to ascertain social inequities.

7. WWW Virtual Library: Demography & Population Studies
http://coombs.anu.edu.au/ResFacilities/DemographyPage.html
A definitive guide to demography and population studies, with a multitude of important links, can be found here.

Developmental Aspects of Dying and Death

8. CDC Wonder on the Web—Prevention Guidelines
http://wonder.cdc.gov
At this site of the Center for Disease Control there are a number of papers on suicide prevention, particularly relating to American youth.

9. Children, Neonates, Family, Caregivers
http://www.katsden.com/death/child.html
Many sites aimed at the family, including such subjects as miscarriage, neonatal death, and children, may be accessed from this site.

10. Children with AIDS Project
http://www.aidskids.org
This organization's role is to develop fuller understanding of children with and at risk of AIDS, including medical, psychosocial, legal, and financial issues. The mission of the organization is to develop local and national adoptive, foster, and family-centered care programs that are effective and compassionate.

11. Light for Life Foundation
http://www.yellowribbon.org
The Yellow Ribbon Program of the Light for Life Foundation provides educational material for American youth aimed at preventing youth suicide through the provision of easy access to support services.

12. National SIDS Resource Center
http://www.circsol.com/SIDS/
The National Sudden Infant Death Syndrome Resource Center (NSRC) provides information services and technical assistance on SIDS and related topics.

The Dying Process

13. American Academy of Hospice and Palliative Medicine
http://www.aahpm.org
This is the only organization in the United States for physicians that is dedicated to the advancement of hospice/palliative medicine, its practice, research, and education. There are also links to other Web sites.

14. As Death Draws Near
http://www.emanon.net/~kcabell/signs.html
A list, *Death—What You Can Expect*, with the signs of death, is posted at this Web site.

15. Death in America, Project on: Death, Dying, Bereavement
http://www.soros.org/death.html
The goal of Project on Death in America is to help people understand and transform the dying experience in America. Headings include "Progress," "Issues in the News," and "Links."

16. Hospice Foundation of America
http://www.hospicefoundation.org
Everything you might need to know about Hospice and specific information on the Foundation is available at this Web site.

17. Hospice Hands
http://hospice-cares.com
An extensive collection of links to Hospice resources can be found at this site. Try "What's New" to access the *ACP Home Care Guide*, a book whose goal is to support an orderly problem-solving approach in managing care of the dying at home.

18. National Prison Hospice Association
http://www.npha.org
This prison Hospice association promotes care for terminally ill inmates and those facing the prospect of dying in prison.

19. The Zen Hospice Project
http://www.zenhospice.org

The Zen Hospice Project organizes programs dedicated to the care of people approaching death and to increasing the understanding of impermanence. The project also runs a small hospice in San Francisco. There are links here to related information on the Web.

Ethical Issues of Dying, Death, and Suicide

20. Articles on Euthanasia: Ethics
http://www.acusd.edu/ethics/euthanasia.html
This site covers biomedical ethics and issues of euthanasia in many ways, including recent articles, ancient concepts, legal and legislative information, selected philosophical literature, Web sites, and a search engine.

21. DeathNET
http://www.islandnet.com/~deathnet/open.html
Many Web links to biomedical topics, including living wills, "how to" suicide, euthanasia, mercy killing, and legislation regulating the care of the terminally ill can be accessed at this site.

22. Kearl's Guide to the Sociology of Death: Moral Debates
http://WWW.Trinity.Edu/~mkearl/death-5.html#eu
An Internet resource on the ethics of biomedical issues that includes issues of dying and death, such as euthanasia, is found here.

23. The Kevorkian File
http://www.rights.org/deathnet/KevorkianFile.html
This Internet resource archive is devoted entirely to Dr. Jack Kevorkian, inventor of the controversial "suicide machine."

24. Last Rites Journal
http://www.islandnet.com/~deathnet/lr_journal.html
The electronically published journal of the Last Rites group has the complete texts of many of the key legal documents about a patient's right to die.

25. The Living Will and Values History Project
http://www.euthanasia.org/lwvh.html
Set up in response to the growth and proliferation of living will documents, this project works on a nonprofit basis and attempts to collate, analyze, and apply research in this area.

26. Living Wills (Advance Directive)
http://www.mindspring.com/~scottr/will.html
The largest collection of links to living wills and other advance directive and living will information is available at this Web site.

27. Not Dead Yet
http://acils.com/NotDeadYet/
Americans with Disabilities organization uses this Web site to mobilize Americans against euthanasia and mercy killing. Information about the Hemlock Society is also available here.

28. Suicide Awareness: Voices of Education
http://www.save.org
This popular Internet suicide site provides information on suicide (both before and after), along with material from the organization's many education sessions.

29. Suicide Prevention Advocacy Network
http://www.spanusa.org
SPAN, a nonprofit organization, offers a more political site on suicide prevention. The aim is to have suicide treated as a national (and global) problem that must be solved as a priority.

30. UNOS: United Network for Organ Sharing
http://www.unos.org/frame_default.asp
This Web site of the United Network for Organ Sharing Transplantation includes facts and statistics, resources, and policy proposals.

31. Youth Suicide League
http://www.unicef.org/pon96/insuicid.htm
International suicide rates of young adults in selected countries are available on this UNESCO Web site.

Funerals and Burial Rites

32. Cryonics, Cryogenics, and the Alcor Foundation
http://www.alcor.org
This is the Web site of Alcor, the world's largest cryonics organization.

33. Funerals and Ripoffs
http://www.xroads.com/%7Efunerals/
Sponsored by the Interfaith Funeral Information Committee and Arizona Consumers Council, this Web site is very critical of the funeral industry and specializes in exposing funeral home financial fraud.

34. The Internet Cremation Society
http://www.cremation.org
The Internet Cremation Society provides statistics on cremations, links to funeral industry resources, and answers to frequently asked questions.

35. Funeral and Memorial Societies of America
http://www.funerals.org/famsa/
The Funeral Societies of America is the only group that monitors the funeral industry for consumers regarding funeral guides, planning, and issues of social concern.

Bereavement

36. Bereaved Families of Ontario Support Center
http://www.inforamp.net/~bfo/index.html
The Self-Help Resources Guide at this site indexes resources of the Center along with more than 300 listings of other resources and information that are useful to the bereaved.

37. The Compassionate Friends
http://www.compassionatefriends.org
This self-help organization for bereaved parents and siblings has hundreds of chapters worldwide.

38. GriefNet
http://rivendell.org
Produced by a nonprofit group, Rivendell Resources, this site provides many links to the Web on bereavement process, resources for grievers, and information concerning grief support groups.

39. Widow Net
http://www.fortnet.org/WidowNet/
Widow Net is an information and self-help resource for and by widows and widowers. The information is helpful to people of all ages, religious backgrounds, and sexual orientation who have experienced a loss of a spouse or life partner.

We highly recommend that you review our Web site for expanded information and our other product lines. We are continually updating and adding links to our Web site in order to offer you the most usable and useful information that will support and expand the value of your Annual Editions. You can reach us at: *http://www.dushkin.com/annualeditions/.*

www.dushkin.com/online/

Unit 1

Unit Selections

Key Points to Consider

❖ What can we learn from studying various cultures around the world as to how they relate to dying and death? Do you feel that Americans are really losing interest in memorialization of the dead?

❖ In a society where many people have limited resources, is it acceptable for some individuals to have access to better medical care than others? Defend your answer.

❖ Since socioeconomic status is related to death rates, should something be done to correct this inequity in our society? What do you suggest?

❖ Some health professionals argue that there simply is no room in the curriculum for thanatology. Yet, health professionals, especially physicians, have a high probability of relating to dying patients and their families. Should more emphasis be placed on presenting the topic of dying, death, and bereavement to health professionals? Why or why not?

❖ How can society help to reduce death anxiety? Do you personally see any relationship between religion and attitudes toward death? Explain.

 **Links** | **www.dushkin.com/online/**

4. **Agency for Health Care Policy and Research**
   http://www.ahcpr.gov
5. **Growth House**
   http://growthhouse.org
6. **Mortality Rates**
   http://www.Trinity.Edu/~mkearl/b&w-ineq.jpg
7. **WWW Virtual Library: Demography & Population Studies**
   http://coombs.anu.edu.au/ResFacilities/DemographyPage.html

These sites are annotated on pages 4 and 5.

Death, like sex, is a rather taboo topic. Socialization into the American way of life has not traditionally prepared us to cope with dying and death. Sex and death have "come out of the closet" in recent decades, however, and they now are issues discussed and presented in formal educational settings. Though these topics frequently make news headlines, we have a long way to go in educating the public about these rather "forbidden" subjects. Basically, the United States is a "death-denying" society, notes Stacey McArthur in her article, "Dealing with Death: A Culture in Denial."

We are beginning to recognize the importance of education at an earlier age on the subject of dying and death. Like sex education, death education is an approved topic for presentation in elementary and secondary school curricula in many states, but the topics (especially thanatology) are "optional" and therefore seldom receive high priorities with limited educational funds available. Death education in medical schools has also received limited exposure, though one might think that such instruction would be important for future doctors. In addition, medical schools have not traditionally emphasized pain control in dealing with patients, as is pointed out in Adam Marcus' article on palliative care.

The question of who dies in the United States and the "how, when, where" of death is discussed in the essay "The Facts of Death." What to do with the body after death? A rarely-chosen option is cryonics (body-freezing), which is discussed in "Putting Death on Ice." Concerning handling the body prior to final disposition, "At Your Disposal: The Funeral Industry Prepares for Boom Times" points out changes in the funeral industry in part because of aging baby boomers. The issue of determining when death has actually occurred is presented in "Is It Time to Abandon Brain Death?"

This section on the American way of dying and death includes a perspective on death customs in Appalachia, both past and present. Finally, the poetry of one of America's greatest poets is discussed as a way of examining death and is presented by William Cooney in "The Death Poetry of Emily Dickinson."

The American Way of Dying and Death

THE FACTS OF
DEATH

This tour of the average American's death says a lot about modern life. When and where we die is largely up to medicine. But trends in how we die and honor our dead depend more on social change, aging, and demographic diversity.

BY BRAD EDMONDSON

Death has a contract on everyone, but 20th-century Americans have renegotiated the deal. A baby girl born in the U.S. in 1900 could expect to live 49 years; in 2000, she will expect to live almost 80 years. Thanks to advances in medicine, sanitation, and basic nutrition, the annual age-adjusted death rate per 100,000 Americans will decline from 2,296 in 1900 to a projected 731 in 2000. If this decline had never occurred, half of Americans alive in 2000 would never have been born.

Still, no one gets out of the contract. Sooner or later, every American's life and death is summarized on a state certificate like the one reproduced here. And as our souls float toward the afterworld, our numbers go to the National Center for Health Statistics (NCHS). From the NCHS and other sources, here is what the average Americans death looked like at the end of the 20th century.

1-2. NAME AND SEX

Jane American Decedent is the average dead American. Her husband Joe, who died six years and six months before her, was almost as average. There were 2,278,994 deaths in the U.S. in 1994, and 51 percent of the dead were men. For most

of this century, 51 percent of babies born in the U.S. have been boys. But boys are more likely than girls to have accidents, work in dangerous jobs, and smoke cigarettes. They may also have shorter-lived genes than girls do. Whatever the reason, the median age at death in 1992 was about 73.2 years for men and about 79.7 years for women, for a national average of about 76.4. At age 75 to 84 about 51 percent of deaths are to women. After that, the gender gap widens fast. More than two-thirds of Americans who die at age 85 or older are women.

Because of the age difference, women are more likely than men to die of the lingering conditions that afflict the old. Heart disease is the leading cause of death in the U.S. for both sexes, followed by cancer. Together, these two causes account for 56 percent of deaths. The third most common cause of death for men is accidents; for women, it is cerebrovascular diseases (strokes). Human Immunodeficiency Virus infection (which causes AIDS) is seventh for men, suicide is eighth, and homicide is tenth, but none of these causes shows up on the top-ten list for women. Instead, women are more likely to face nephritis (kidney failure), septicemia (blood poisoning), and Alzheimer's disease.

These differences largely disappear with age, however. Among men and women aged 65 and older, the top-ten list

From *American Demographics*, April 1997, pp. 46-53. © 1997 by Brad Edmondson. Reprinted by permission.

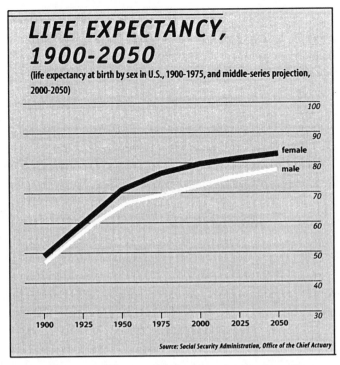

LIFE EXPECTANCY, 1900-2050

(life expectancy at birth by sex in U.S., 1900-1975, and middle-series projection, 2000-2050)

female
male

1900 1925 1950 1975 2000 2025 2050

Source: Social Security Administration, Office of the Chief Actuary

Since 1900, life expectancy at birth has increased by almost 30 years. By 2050, it could increase another 5 years.

is almost identical. As a result, increases in life expectancy for men will mean that fewer Americans will die suddenly, and that more will die in ways that consume a lot of health-care services.

3A. DATE OF DEATH

Winter is death's favorite season. In 1995, January had many more deaths than any other month (220,000). It was followed by March, April, and December. (February would have been second if it had had 31 days instead of 28). The month with the least deaths was September (178,000), followed by June, August, and May. The top day for death in 1992, the most recent year for which daily data are available, was January 3, when 7,422 Americans died. That is about 25 percent more than an average day in 1992. Death's slowest day was July 22, with just 5,347 deaths. That's about 10 percent below average.

There is less variation in death's weekly schedule. The most likely day to die in 1992 was either Wednesday, Thursday, or

> *For every person who dies in a modern hospital or nursing home, there are several healthy people who would have died without one.*

Saturday, but the day with the least deaths—Sunday—was less than 2 percent below the daily average.

4A. PLACE OF DEATH

Seventy-seven percent of U.S. deaths in 1992 took place in some kind of health-care facility. These include the 48 percent of U.S. residents who died as hospital inpatients, 9 percent who died in emergency rooms, 3 percent who were pronounced dead on arrival at a hospital, and 17 percent who expired in a nursing home. Just 20 percent of U.S. residents died in a private home, and 4 percent died in other places.

If your time comes prematurely, you're much more likely than average to die in a hospital. Ninety-one percent of infant deaths (under 1 year of age) were in hospitals in 1992. The proportion of hospital deaths was below average for only two age groups. Young people aged 15 to 24 are much more likely than the average American to die at the scene of a suicide, homicide, or motor-vehicle accident. Just 45 percent of deaths to those aged 85 and older took place in a hospital. But these very old were less likely than average to die at home, too, because 39 percent died in a nursing home.

Women are less likely than men to die in a hospital and more likely to depart from a nursing home. Only 56 percent of women died in hospitals in 1992, compared with 62 percent of men. Yet 23 percent of all deaths for women were in nursing homes, compared with just 12 percent for men. This is because men are more likely to die elsewhere, such as at home or at the scene of an accident.

Most Americans say that they would prefer to die at home than in a hospital. A lingering death in a nursing home is one of the biggest fears of the elderly. But the alternative to death in a medical setting would usually be a shorter life. In 1900, only a small fraction of Americans died in hospitals, and infectious diseases like influenza were among the leading killers. For every person who dies in a modern hospital or nursing home, there are several healthy people who would have died without one.

4B-C. IF FACILITY, DATE OF ADMISSION, NAME, ADDRESS

Jane happened to die in Bellevue, New York City's largest public hospital, along with 400 other inpatients in an average year. Among the 401 who died at Bellevue in 1994, the average length of stay before death was 19 days and 18 hours. But the length of stay before death varied from 1 day to more than 73 days.

In all of New York City, about 71,000 people die every year. Last year, for the first time since the early 1970s, fewer than 1,000 were murdered. In contrast, about 27,500 New Yorkers a year die of heart disease, and 15,300 die of cancer.

5. DATE OF BIRTH AND AGE

When Jane was born in 1919, hospitals and antiseptics were new to most Americans. In that year, life expectancy at birth was 54 years and 2 months for males, and 56 years and 5 months for females. But Jane's survival chances improved throughout her life. Medical advances caused mortality rates to decline steadily for most of this century, with the most rapid drops between 1936 and 1954 (due mainly to new drugs, such as antibiotics) and between 1968 and 1982 (due to further advances in medical technology). In the 1980s and 1990s, mortality rates have declined at a slower but steady pace. Life expectancy for Americans born in 1997 is 72 years and 7 months for males, and 79 years and 5 months for females.

In the first half of the 20th century, the most dramatic improvements in survival rates happened among children. In 1900, an infant had only an 80 percent chance of surviving to age 15. Today, that probability approaches 99 percent. A couple with three children in 1900 faced almost a 50-50 chance that one child would die before maturity. In the 1980s, the odds for this loss were 1 in 17, and even lower for some families.

Mortality declines since 1950 have been more evenly distributed throughout the life cycle. Since 1980, in particular, there have been significant improvements in the rates for heart disease and cancer. How low can mortality ultimately go? It's hard to say, because changes in mortality depend on things that can't be predicted. Medical breakthroughs, trends in pollution control, changes in health behavior, the rate of violent crime, legislation, and many other factors can all have a major impact on the number who die, how we die, and how much it all costs.

Charting trends in mortality is vital to the profitability of insurance companies. As a result, more than 15,000 actuaries in the United States have thriving professional careers. Actuaries for the nation's largest insurance fund, the Social Security Administration (SSA), make sets of demographic projections every year that show the effects of low, middle, and high mortality rates eight decades into the future.

In the SSA's current middle series, the moderate mortality declines of 1968-91 continue at about the same rate. Under these conditions, the age- and sex-adjusted death rate would decline from 750 per 100,000 U.S. residents in 1997 to 677 in 2010, 620 in 2025, 572 in 2040, and 529 in 2055. Life expectancy at birth increases to 74 years and 6 months for males, 80 years and 7 months for females in 2010. It then increases at the rate of about one year of extra life in every 15 calendar years, to reach 77 years and 6 months for men, 83 years and 3 months for women, in 2055.

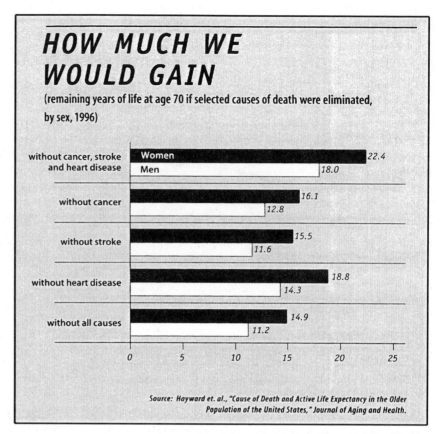

HOW MUCH WE WOULD GAIN
(remaining years of life at age 70 if selected causes of death were eliminated, by sex, 1996)

Source: Hayward et. al., "Cause of Death and Active Life Expectancy in the Older Population of the United States," Journal of Aging and Health.

If the three largest causes of death were eliminated, the average 70-year-old woman would live another 7.5 years before succumbing to something else.

7A. CITY AND STATE OF BIRTH

Like 58 percent of people who died in New York state in 1992, Jane was also born there. But the proportion of U.S. residents who are born and die in the same state varies widely, depending on prevailing migration flows and how long ago the state was settled. Among the ten largest states, Pennsylvania has the most who stay put: in 1992, 76 percent of deceased Pennsylvania residents were also born there. Georgia (70 percent) also does an unusually good job of holding on to its natives. The share is respectable in Texas (65 percent), Ohio (61 percent), Illinois (61 percent), and Michigan (56 percent). But it is lower in New Jersey (44 percent), which has absorbed large numbers of migrants from other states throughout the century. It is very low in California (23 percent), and it is rare for someone who dies in Florida (13 percent) to have been born there.

In retirement and tourist havens, there's a thriving business in shipping bodies up north to be buried. Most of the bodies packaged and shipped by Flite-Rite, Inc. of Fort Lauderdale are northern tourists. In fact, Flite-Rite does about twice as much business in January as it does in July.

"Assume that Jones comes down from New York and drops dead in Fort Lauderdale," says Hugh Allgood, president of Flite-Rite. "He doesn't know anybody here, and the funeral home up there wants his business." If Jones isn't embalmed in Florida, the law says that he must be sent home in a sealed container. If he is embalmed, he is legally allowed to travel home in a "combo box" made out of particle board with a foam-rubber mattress and pillow.

Although Flite-Rites volume comes from tourists, its best customers are retirees. "Your older person may have lived here for 15 years," says Allgood, "but as much as they like Florida, Mom and Dad are buried in New York, so that's where they want to lie. We'll build them a nice display-quality box for a memorial service down here, then they'll be sent up north and get a fancy metal casket there. It's the college students who come down for spring break who go back in combo boxes."

9. RACE

Jane Decedent was white, as were 86 percent of Americans who died in 1994; 12 percent were black. This is roughly equivalent to the way the races were once distributed. In 1997, an estimated 83 percent of living Americans are white and 13 percent are black.

White Americans dominate the dead for a simple reason: they are older. The median age of whites in 1995 was 35.3 years,

> In retirement and tourist havens, there's a thriving business in shipping bodies up north to be buried.

compared with 29.2 years for blacks. Because of this, the mortality rate for whites is substantially higher than the rate for blacks. But if you adjust the rate for age differences, black mortality rates become higher. In fact, age-adjusted black mortality rates are higher than white rates for all ten leading causes of death except for suicide and chronic obstructive pulmonary diseases, such as emphysema and bronchitis. The rate of death from strokes and diabetes is twice as high for blacks as it is for whites. The rate for conditions originating during the perinatal period (just before or after birth) is three times as high for blacks. For HIV infection, the black rate is four times as high. And blacks are almost seven times more likely than whites to be murdered.

The facts suggest that whites have benefited more than blacks from a variety of medical and social improvements that stave off death. This is especially true for childhood diseases and other forms of death that strike at younger ages. At birth, life expectancy is 7 years longer for whites than it is for blacks.

DEATH'S TOP TEN

(top-ten causes of death, U.S., 1985, 1995, and percent change 1985-1995)

	numbers of deaths 1995	numbers of deaths 1985	percent change 1985-95
All causes	2,312,203	2,086,440	10.8%
Diseases of heart	738,781	771,169	-4.2
Malignant neoplasms (cancer)	537,969	461,563	16.6
Cerebrovascular diseases (stroke)	158,061	153,050	3.3
Chronic obstructive pulmonary diseases	104,756	74,662	40.3
Accidents and adverse effects	89,703	93,457	-4.0
Pneumonia and influenza	83,528	67,615	23.5
Diabetes mellitus	59,085	36,969	59.8
HIV infection (AIDS)	42,506	n/a	n/a
Suicide	30,893	29,453	4.9
Chronic liver disease and cirrhosis	24,848	26,767	-7.2
Total top 10	1,870,130	1,714,705	9.1%
All other causes	442,073	347,809	27.1

Source: National Center for Health Statistics

More than eight in ten deaths in the U.S. are caused by these conditions. Old-age diseases are growing fastest.

At age 25, it is 5 years and 10 months longer. At age 55, life expectancy for whites is just 3 years longer than it is for blacks. And at age 85, it is 1 month longer.

10. HISPANIC ORIGIN

In 1994, 4 percent of U.S. deaths were to persons of Hispanic origin. This is notable because Hispanics made up more than 10 percent of the entire population in 1994. Because of heavy immigration of young adults from Mexico and other Latin countries since 1980, Hispanics are the youngest minority group. Their median age in 1995 was just 26.2 years.

Hispanics can be of any race, and researchers have found that people who fill out death certificates sometimes fail to note the Hispanic origin of the deceased. But Hispanics will become harder to miss in the future, as their share of the population will increase to 11 percent in 2000, 14 percent in 2010, and 16 percent in 2020. In the long run, this growing influence will change the focus of care for the dying.

Hispanics are less likely than non-Hispanic whites to die of cancer, heart disease, suicide, or motor-vehicle accidents. They are more likely to die of pneumonia, influenza, cirrhosis of the liver, diabetes, or homicide. Because cancer and heart disease claim so many lives, overall Hispanic death rates are lower than those for non-Hispanic whites, even after adjusting for age differences.

HOW MEN AND WOMEN DIE

(number of deaths and rate per 100,000 for top-ten causes of death by sex, 1994)

		male			female	
	rank	number	rate	rank	number	rate
All Causes		1,162,747	915		1,116,247	837.6
Diseases of heart........................1		361,276	284.3	1	371,133	278.5
Malignant neoplasms (cancer)...........2		280,465	220.7	2	253,845	190.5
Accidents and adverse effects...........3		60,509	47.6	7	30,928	23.2
Cerebrovascular diseases (stroke)........4		60,225	47.4	3	93,081	69.8
Chronic obstructive pulmonary diseases ..5		53,729	42.3	4	47,899	35.9
Pneumonia and influenza...............6		37,339	29.4	5	44,134	33.1
HIV infection (AIDS) 7		35,641	28.0		6,473	4.9
Suicide................................8		25,174	19.8		5,968	4.5
Diabetes mellitus 9		24,758	19.5	6	31,934	24.0
Homicide and legal intervention 10		19,707	15.5		5,219	3.9
Alzheimer's disease.....................		6,377	5.0	8	12,207	9.2
Nephritis (kidney failure)................		10,866	8.6	9	12,110	9.1
Septicemia (blood poisoning)		8,810	6.9	10	11,550	8.7

Source: National Center for Health Statistics

Men are more likely to die suddenly, while women succumb to the ills of old age.

Poverty does hurt the health of Hispanic Americans. Mexican Americans are three times as likely as the average American to have type II diabetes, and Hispanic children are more likely to catch diseases that are preventable by immunization. But something else gives a boost to Hispanic health, and it isn't just a diet of beans and rice. Researchers suggest that the strong social support networks in traditional Latin cultures may encourage Hispanics to recover from illness more quickly. And Hispanic mothers in southern California are less likely than non-Hispanic white mothers to have low birthweight babies, even though they are poorer and less likely to get regular medical care.

11. DECEDENT'S EDUCATION

Jane's children went to college, but she never did. The educational attainment of the dead lags behind that of the living. Among persons aged 15 and older who died in 1994, 24 percent had 8 or fewer years of formal education, 14 percent had 9 to 11 years, 40 percent had 12 years, 12 percent had 13 to 15 years, and 11 percent had 16 or more years. That is roughly similar to the educational attainment of the entire U.S. population aged 65 and older. Small wonder: 73 percent of deaths happen among this group.

The educational attainment of the elderly is increasing rapidly. About 64 percent of those aged 65 and older in 1995 had at least four years of high school; in 1980, only 41 percent did. And 30 percent have had some college experience, com-

pared with 17 percent in 1980. These gains will continue for several decades as baby boomers, more than half of whom have been to college, move toward old age. They should have a positive effect on the health and longevity of the elderly. The more education you have, the more likely you are to exercise for health, eat a lowfat diet, and stay away from tobacco.

13. MARITAL STATUS

Most women over age 15 (57 percent) die as widows, but only 18 percent of men outlive their spouses. Most men (57 percent) die as husbands, but only 26 percent of women die as wives. Only 9 percent of the dead are divorced, and only 11 percent of those aged 15 and older who die have never been married. Men are more likely than women to never marry, and the difference is most striking for blacks. Twenty-seven percent of black men die without marrying, compared with just 14 percent of black women.

The life expectancy of men has been gaining on women in recent years. If this trend continues, the proportion of deaths that create a widow should decrease. About 42 percent of deaths will result in a widowing in 1997. In the SSA's middle series projection, that share decreases to 41 percent in 2010, rises to 42 percent in 2030, and then drops to 37 percent in 2055.

> *Future reductions in mortality will continue to be most rapid among the diseases that strike children.*

20A. BURIAL, CREMATION, REMOVAL

Jane's family laid her to rest next to her departed husband. The vast majority of U.S. deaths are followed by a burial, but the trend is toward cremation. Between 1990 and 1995, the share of U.S. deaths handled by cremation increased from 17 percent to 21 percent, and the percentage of Americans who say they plan a cremation for themselves increased from 37 percent to 43 percent. Cremation is especially popular in trend-

38. HOUR OF DEATH

(number of deaths by hour of death for decedents in Fairfield County, CT, 1984-85)

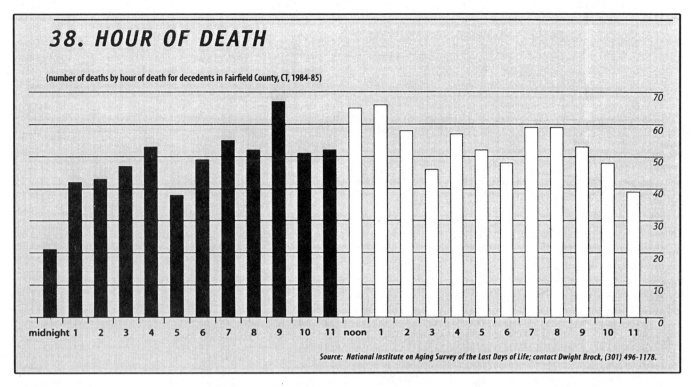

Source: National Institute on Aging Survey of the Last Days of Life; contact Dwight Brock, (301) 496-1178.

Of the 1,220 who died in one county in 1984–85, the fewest (21) died between midnight and 1 a.m. The most common hours of death were 9 a.m. (67), 1 p.m. (66), and noon (65).

setting states: 41 percent of deaths are cremations in California, where social trends are born, and 40 percent are cremated in Florida and Arizona, where death is almost as common as birth. Interest in cremation increases with age, education, and income. It is also popular with those who do not have big extended families, says Allgood of Flite-Rite, who also supplies cremation containers to Florida funeral homes.

Cremation is also a lot less expensive than a traditional funeral. The average U.S. funeral service cost more than $4,600 in 1996, according to the National Funeral Directors Association. This figure includes $2,100 for the casket, a $1,000 fee to the funeral director, $500 for embalming and other preparation, and about $1,000 in charges associated with the hearse and memorial service. That does not include the cost of a cemetery plot and marker, which usually adds another 25 to 40 percent. Compare that with the National Cremation Society. For about $500, depending on where you live, they will load the departed one into a Ford station wagon, drive the body to a walk-in freezer, put it in a cardboard box, cremate it, and dispose of the ashes. Ashes are returned to families in about 23 percent of cremations; 16 percent are buried or stored in a cemetary, and 6 percent are scattered over land or water. In most cases (54 percent), the cremator simply leaves the ashes with the funeral director.

Baby boomers, who love self-expression like a dog loves a bone, may cause a boom in creative cremations when they pass on. The trendsetters in this case are celebrities. Star Trek creator Gene Roddenberry's ashes are being carried into space on a rocket, along with those of hippie guru Timothy Leary. Rock star Kurt Cobain's ashes were molded into small sculp-

tures in a Buddhist monastery and sent to his friends. Union organizer Joe Hill's ashes were placed in envelopes and sent to union locals all over the world.

27. MANNER OF DEATH

About 93 out of 100 U.S. deaths are attributed to natural causes. Two are in motor-vehicle accidents, two are in other kinds of accidents, one is a suicide, one a homicide, and one is murkily attributed to "symptoms, signs, and ill-defined conditions." As you might expect, nonnatural deaths happen mostly to young people. A majority of the 91,437 accident victims in 1994 were under age 45. Forty-eight percent of the 31,142 suicides were people under age 45. Over two-thirds of the 24,926 homicide victims were under age 34. And one-fifth of the 25,245 "ill-defined" deaths were babies under age 1. Infant deaths are sometimes mysterious, and so are some deaths at the other end. About 38 percent of ill-defined deaths are people aged 75 or older.

29A. AUTOPSY

About 9 out of 100 deaths are followed by an autopsy. This includes virtually all murders, the majority of suicides, and almost half of accidents. It also includes some deaths with a murky cause: 1 in 8 from chronic liver disease and cirrhosis, and about 1 in 14 from Alzheimer's disease, blood poisoning, and heart disease.

30. CAUSE OF DEATH

Jane's immediate cause of death was heart disease, although she'd already been weakened by cancer and a stroke. These have been the top-three killers in the U.S. for several decades. Together, they account for 62 percent of all U.S. deaths. But deaths from heart disease declined 11 percent between 1985 and 1995, according to preliminary NCHS data, even as the total number of deaths from all causes increased 11 percent. Deaths from cerebrovascular diseases increased just 3.3 percent. And although the number of cancer deaths increased 17 percent, the age-adjusted mortality rate from cancer declined 17 percent between 1991 and 1995.

Demographic shifts, medical advances, and changes in behavior can create rapid growth or decline in specific causes of death. The number of deaths from accidents has declined in the last decade, and so have deaths from chronic liver disease. The number of suicides has increased only 50 percent. But deaths from pneumonia and influenza have increased 24 percent, deaths from chronic obstructive pulmonary disease are up 40 percent, and deaths from diabetes have increased almost 60 percent. Also, in 1985, there were no deaths directly attributed to AIDS. In 1995, there were 42,506.

Future reductions in mortality will continue to be most rapid among the diseases that strike children, according to the SSA's middle-series projections. The projections assume the most rapid declines will be in deaths ascribed to birth defects and infancy diseases, and in deaths from cancer, respiratory diseases, diabetes, and accidents/suicide/homicide among children aged 14 and younger. Among working-age Americans (aged 15 to 64), the most rapid declines will be in deaths from vascular diseases, digestive diseases, cirrhosis of the liver, and heart disease. Mortality declines will be slowest for those aged 65 and older, but the fastest declines within the group are assumed for elderly deaths caused by vascular disease, heart disease and congenital malformations.

Americans now take for granted that they will live to a ripe old age. Medicine's campaign against death has been so successful, in fact, that it may be almost over. Recently, a team of demographers asked what would happen to life expectancies if heart disease, cancer, and stroke deaths were totally eliminated. They found that the average 70-year-old American man would enjoy another 6.8 years of active life before succumbing to some other illness; the average 70-year-old woman, 7.5 years. The causes of death in an aging society are fragmenting, as dozens of smaller ailments move up to take the place of the big three. Sooner or later, death will collect on its contract.

Brad Edmondson is senior writer of American Demographics.

TAKING IT FURTHER

Here are the statistical sources cited in this article in order of appearance. **Introduction:** Life expectancy and age and sex-adjusted mortality rates are from Social Security Administration, *Social Security Area Population Projections: 1996,* Actuarial Study No. 110, from SSA Office of the Chief Actuary; telephone (410) 965-3015; fax (410) 965-6693. Effect of constant 1900 mortality rates: Kevin M. White and Samuel H. Preston, "How many Americans are active because of twentieth-century improvements in mortality?" *Population and Development Review,* Vol. 22, No. 3, September 1996; $8.00 from The Population Council, New York, New York; telephone (212) 339-0514; fax (212) 755-6052; e-mail pubinfo@popcouncil.org.

Name and sex: The most recent final mortality statistics are published in *Advance Report of Final Mortality Statistics,* 1994 Vol. 45, No. 3) supplement to the *Monthly Vital Statistics Report;* for a single copy or subscription, telephone the National Center for Health Statistics at (301) 436-8500 or send an e-mail to nchsquery@nch10a.em.cdc.gov. Causes of death in this report follow the Ninth Revision of the International Classification of Diseases; for more information, see the Report's technical appendix. **Date:** The most recent data are published in *Vital Statistics of the United States, 1992;* for sale by the Superintendent of Documents and on file at larger libraries. For more information and a locator service, telephone (202) 512-1800; fax (202) 512-2250; Internet http://www.access. gpo.gov/su_docs/index.html. **Place:** Vital Statistics; New York City Division of Vital Records; Bellevue Hospital Center. **Age:** Social Security Projections; "Death Takes a Holiday,"

American Demographics, April 1984, page 38. **Age:** Mortality and longevity statistics from Social Security Administration, plus 1996 membership in Society of Actuaries, Schaumburg, Illinois. **City and State:** *Vital Statistics.* **Race and Hispanic Origin:** *Advance Report,* 1994; Bureau of the Census; Sorlie, Backlund, Johnson, and Rogot, "Mortality by Hispanic Status in the United States," *Journal of the American Medical Association,* (Vol. 270, No. 20); reprints available from Paul D. Sorlie, National Heart, Lung, and Blood Institute, Room 3A10, Federal Building, Bethesda, MD 20892. **Education:** *Advance Report,* 1994; Bureau of the Census. **Marital Status:** *Advance Report,* 1994; SSA Projections. **Burial and Cremation:** Cremation Association of North America, Chicago, Illinois; National Funeral Directors Association, Milwaukee, Wisconsin; National Cremation Society, a division of SCI International, Houston, Texas. **Manner of Death:** *Advance Report,* 1994. **Autopsy:** *Advance Report,* 1994. **Cause of Death:** *Births and Deaths: United States, 1995, NCHS Monthly Vital Statistics Report* (Vol. 45, No. 3, Supp. 2); SSA Projections; Mark Hayward, Eileen Crimmins, and Yasuhiko Saito, "Cause of Death and Active Life Expectancy in the Older Population of the United States," Journal of Aging and Health (in press), copies available from Mark Hayward at Pennsylvania State University, telephone (814) 863-2938; fax (814) 863-8342; e-mail hayward@pop.psu.edu.

Dealing
with
death

Unwilling or unable to confront the realities of death, ours has become . . .

A culture *in* denial

Stacey McArthur
STAFF WRITER

Death. It robs us of spouses, parents, friends and children.

It steals futures and leaves hollow places in hearts.

It's an inevitable fate woven so tightly into the fabric of life that it can't be teased apart.

And it's so powerful it petrifies us.

"We talk about death as the Grim Reaper and depict him as someone with a long, black cloak," said Sister Ann Michele Kiefer, who works at the Damien Center, an organization specializing in helping people with AIDS.

That we fear death isn't surprising. It robs us of so much. Yet we often are ill-equipped to deal with it.

Death repeatedly has touched Shannon Dunkin's life, each time leaving her more and more devastated.

Her father committed suicide when she was 17, her boyfriend later was killed in a motorcycle accident, and then her mother died of colon cancer when Shannon was 18.

The 23-year-old has a rocky relationship with her extended family and no siblings—and therefore little emotional support.

"I feel very alone most of the time," Dunkin said.

"It's taken me a long time to pick up the pieces and want to go on every day."

We've evolved into a death-denying culture, says David W. Moller, who has extensively studied death and dying.

"People have been dealing with mortality since the beginning of time, and now we're the first culture that can't accept it."

Historically, Western people confronted death, said Moller, who teaches a class on death and dying at Indiana University-Purdue University at Indianapolis. The community gathered around loved ones with support and ritual.

"People were able to die their own deaths and bear mortality," he said. "Today, our folkways of life make death less bearable. It's hard for us in this day and age to witness our families suffering and accompany our loved ones through their dying."

That's because today, machines often keep people alive even when there is little chance for recovery, and many doctors see the deaths of their patients as personal failures.

Most people aren't surrounded by extended families. Their loved ones are scattered throughout the country—many times visiting only in time of crisis.

And terminally ill people often remain in hospitals because their loved ones don't know how to care for the dying. Or their harried lifestyles don't leave them time.

Once someone dies, people gather in a funeral home after strangers have prepared the body. Sometimes they have no idea what to say or do to comfort the grieving.

"With only some exceptions, the system today is failing dismally," Moller said.

A need to reform attitudes

He and others in the medical, sociology and teaching fields believe we are in desperate need of reform in our attitudes and practices surrounding death.

"Death is just a very uncomfortable thing to talk about with people that you love," said Judith Granbois, program associate for the Poynter Center in Bloomington. The Center, which studies ethics and American institutions, is working on a project in Paoli concerning attitudes about death.

Poynter's research has shown people are uncomfortable being around death—often because they aren't that familiar anymore with the death process and don't know what they should do.

People used to die at home. Today, they have a pretty good chance of dying alone and isolated in a hospital, being cared for by paid strangers, she said.

Nationally, groups are working to change current attitudes and practices.

The Project on Death in America is promoting better understanding of the experiences of dying and bereavement and ways to transform the culture surrounding death. The group includes representatives from national medical and law schools, cancer centers and health departments.

"In America, the land of perpetually young, growing older is an embarrassment, and dying is a failure. Death has replaced sex as the taboo subject of our times," George Soros, one of the founders of the national project, said in a recent speech at Columbia Presbyterian Medical Center in New York.

In addition, the American Medical Student Association organized a task force on death and dying in response to students' concern that medical schools don't prepare them to communicate with terminally ill patients.

The task force tries to provide guidance and resources for students who want to supplement their medical education in the areas of death and dying.

Technology as savior

Technology has been a savior to some, but a demon to others.

There's a growing concern among some patients and health care providers that technology keeps people alive past the point of futility.

They contend people spend millions of dollars on heroic lifesaving efforts only to exist connected to machines.

"Scientists are even starting to talk about the possibility of death being treated as a disease," Moller said.

Dr. Meg Gaffney, a physician active in ethics programs at Indiana University Medical Center, worries about this trend.

There is a view in Europe that the United States is the only country where death is an option, she said.

Some say that is evident in the extreme measures doctors take to keep patients alive when dying might be the more humane option.

"I almost quit nursing school because of that," said Debbie Pohle, who earned an associate's degree in nursing this year from Ivy Tech State College in Madison.

During her first working rotation at a nursing home in Osgood, Pohle met a late-stage Alzheimer's patient who couldn't chew or swallow food without choking.

The man had no living will, so doctors had no way of knowing his desires regarding medical treatment. So they put an artificial tube down his throat to feed him and hooked up a catheter and colostomy bag so he could relieve himself.

The man could not carry on a conversation. He couldn't walk and he couldn't even sit up without being restrained.

He didn't recognize his family, and his family didn't visit because they couldn't stand the sight of his suffering, Pohle said.

"He just laid there for years," she said.

We don't want to die

We're a society driven by living longer and better.

"It's not just the doctors," Granbois said. "A lot of times, patients, and patients' families, want everything done—even past the point of futility."

We're used to getting what we want, Gaffney said. And most of us don't want to die.

"There's a struggle for all of us to recognize that we are physical beings and we aren't going to live forever no matter how much we try or how much money we spend or how many organs we can transplant."

And if we think we're not supposed to die, we definitely think we're not supposed to suffer.

"When we look at our ability to face suffering and mortality, we learn about who we are individually and as a nation," Moller said.

In general, we are a greedy society; we don't recognize limits, Gaffney said.

For example, in the past people had to live with nature, which is unpredictable. It determined whether or not they would have crops every year.

Now, she said, we've taken control. We grow crops in environmentally controlled settings. We even control our temperature. If we're hot, we use air conditioning. If we're cold, we make heat.

But all of this control and technology takes its toll.

In the 20th century, we've lost the ability to care for the soul, Moller said.

Julie Niec, who has witnessed the deaths of many friends and even took one into her home to die, believes death has become depersonalized. Especially in the medical setting.

"So many machines, so many wires and monitors you can't get physical," she said.

Moller said doctors often see a "good death" as one in which everything was done medically—including hooking up a patient to machines—to let a person live longer.

In contrast, Moller sees a pleasant, peaceful death as someone dying in a familiar setting, surrounded by loved ones and having their physical and emotional needs addressed.

But that setting isn't possible when someone dies unexpectedly.

For Patti Hair, her husband Jesse's death was a combination of the two.

Technicians revived him at the scene of a car accident after he'd been dead 10 minutes. They took him to the hospital and hooked him up to life-supporting machines and kept him alive for 24 hours.

"It gave us time to gather everyone together," Hair said. Her two oldest children were away at college and the youngest was at baseball camp.

It gave the family a chance to say goodbye.

Sometimes, a person dying instantly can be a blessing for those left behind.

Amy Kotansky's brother drove down a country road in Illinois one fall night, headed toward his first semester of law school.

He died after his car hit a bull.

"I'm just glad he went quickly and didn't linger in the hospital for weeks," Kotanksy said.

His loss was hard enough on the family, but living and lingering could have caused a whole new set of dilemmas—like whether or not to keep him alive.

One of his college friends had been seriously hurt in an auto accident years before. The doctors said the girl would never wake up from her coma. Or breathe on her own without a ventilator.

Her family decided to keep her alive on machines.

Today, the girl leads an active life.

"She wrote my mom a letter and said, 'I'm glad you didn't have to go through that. I'm glad you didn't have to make those decisions,'" Kotansky said.

To heal, not comfort

It's a doctor's job to heal, and that creed sometimes gets in the way of comforting the dying.

"So what do we do? Sometimes we don't go to the room or we just sort of wave as we go by Mrs. So and So, who is dying," Gaffney said. "There's nothing we can do, so we go on to another Mrs. So and So who has something we can fix.

"The dying person gets deprived of human comfort that is very valuable to have."

Gaffney traces this mind-set back to medical school.

Most medical students are 22, healthy and, fortunately, haven't had a personal tragedy, she said.

On top of that, the premedical curriculum emphasizes science and healing, not humanities, arts and caring.

Discussions don't include mortality and finite lives. A doctor's achievement is measured by how quickly he or she can come up with a definition of what's wrong with a patient and fix it, Gaffney said.

Most medical students don't listen to a patient's heartbeat or diagnose symptoms until their third year of schooling.

Prior to that, they've worked with cadavers that don't bleed and don't ask questions.

"Part of the problem is their first exposure to death is the anatomy lesson," Moller said.

"Nobody teaches these doctors the telling of bad news. From my point of view of emphasizing personhood first, that's appalling."

But just a few generations ago, doctors sat at the bed of a dying patient.

"We did that pretty well because that is what we knew best," Gaffney said.

Still, the medical institution isn't the lone culprit in the conspiracy against death. Basically, we want to live, and sometimes doctors can grant that wish.

Talking about death

Americans didn't really talk about death until Elisabeth Kubler-Ross brought it to the forefront in the 1960s. Her five steps of grief—denial, anger, bargaining, depression and acceptance—were revolutionary because for the first time, the needs of dying patients and their loved ones were addressed.

Still, some thanatologists—people who study death—suggest that death and grief cannot be packaged so neatly.

But most people never even start talking about death.

Mary Z. Longstreth, a social worker for the Damien Center, has led workshops to help clients and loved ones prepare for death.

"The very first session I have is to gently lead people to go more in-depth—to get people to talk about it."

The problem usually goes back to childhood, when we begin to form opinions of death, Longstreth said.

It's very typical for families to not allow children to go to funerals, or children aren't allowed to ask questions or to talk about the death even when a family member has died, she said.

"We help adults go back to their childhood image and examine the subtle messages sent."

For example, one woman's first image of death as a child was walking into a room and seeing her uncle, who had hanged himself.

"They begin to realize the baggage they had all along," Longstreth said.

However, there are some people, such as Liz Cameron, who make sure young people learn about death early.

She has taken her grandson, Demarkis Clark, 4, to funerals since he was 6 months old. She lost count of how many he has attended.

Cameron explains to her grandson that death is final.

"We want him acquainted with it so he will not be looking for someone who won't be back," she said.

Few support systems

Death often hits people hard because they have few support systems.

We're a society that fiercely values individualism. In return, we often lack community.

We used to sit on large porches and chat with neighbors. Now, many of us live in apartment buildings, and even some homeowners might not know their next-door neighbor's name, Moller said.

We drive to work alone, sit in the office alone with a computer, and e-mail someone when we need to talk, instead of doing it face to face.

"We are isolated from each other," Gaffney said. "A lot of it is because of our lifestyle. The community is not there."

The creation of support groups for specific needs is a direct reflection of that, she added. Often, they replace relationships with neighbors and families.

Local shoe store co-owner Julia Sams gets most of her support from her church. When she's feeling well, she goes on Tuesday and Friday nights and twice on Sunday.

She has outlived six brothers, her only sister and her parents and grandparents.

"God has been my refuge and my help in times of trouble," she said.

Having most of these funerals at church also has helped comfort Sams because of the familiar, comforting environment.

"It helps when you have your church family with you."

Letting go

Yet, modern funerals are not always great sources of comfort.

Michael St. Pierre, an owner of Wilson St. Pierre Funeral Homes, described the traditional funeral as one that was religious and attended by the whole community.

Today, people are more concerned about convenience.

"If it's a rainy day, people aren't going to come to your funeral; or if it's snowing, they say they'll stop by the house instead and never do," St. Pierre said.

Sometimes, if a minister does give the eulogy, he doesn't even say the name of the deceased, St. Pierre said. That's because the minister didn't know the person because he or she did not attend church regularly.

Even when people do gather for a funeral, they avoid talking about death.

"When my mother died, the topic of conversation was snow-blowers," Moller said.

Accepting death

The realities of death can be difficult for the living.

St. Pierre recalls the funeral of a mother who was murdered in front of her two children.

He had a conversation with her 6-year-old son.

"The first words out of his mouth were, 'My mommy is going to be all right as soon as they get the bullet out.'

"I said, 'This isn't television. Your mom is not coming back.' "

When the funeral is over, the heartache doesn't subside.

Shannon Dunkin still misses her parents.

"It tears away a part of your soul, and it's hard to heal that," she said.

Death takes so much—but it also can give back.

It can challenge the soul and human spirit. It can encourage insight and teach strength.

It can also make people savor life more fully.

"It's life-impacting," Moller said.

"Death illuminates life and transforms life like no other experience."

A Look At How Kentuckians In Knox County Once Treated The Dead

Kentucky Burial Customs Have Changed Much During Recent Years

By David R. Helton—1997

The purpose of this article is to describe the death practices of our past as compared to the practices of today. The richness of our Appalachian culture, and that of Knox County, is not all that well-known to those who are not from the Appalachian areas and for some of the younger people that have grown up in the area. As we examine these practices we will look at several different aspects of a death in regard to the way the community and family were notified, how the community helped the family, preparing the body, digging the grave, the coffin, the wake, the funeral, burial, how the family dressed after a death, and superstitions surrounding death. I will make comparisons, from time to time, with what was once done when a death occurred in the Appalachian area, to the practices of today.

The hearty individuals that originally settled the Appalachian areas were truly a unique group of people, not as some misinformed individuals would have us believe. Most of the people who settled the Appalachian area were from Germany, Scotland, England, and some from Wales, France, Holland, Africa, and, of course, the Cherokees.

In today's world, things have changed a great deal. We no longer have vast amounts of space between ourselves and our closest neighbor. We no longer have to communicate with our families and friends in a pony express manner. In regard to funeral practices of the early Appalachian society, things have also changed greatly. The assistance of professions such as funeral homes, undertakers, and florists in today's time are considered necessary. In the early times of Appalachian history, things such as these were nonexistent.

When a member of the family died, the general rule was to notify the community in which you lived. The most commonly used method for this notification was the tolling of the bell, which was done most often by the caretaker of the church. Depending on which part of Appalachia you lived in the bell toll could be the age of the person or just to announce that there had been a death. Relatives who lived a great distance away were usually notified by mail. The letter would often be trimmed in black to alert the receiver of a death. Some families would send the word by a person on horseback if the death was of a parent or child. Later with the invention and widespread use of the telephone, the news quickly spread by word of mouth.

It was always the custom of the friends and family to gather at the house of the bereaved and offer any assistance that they could, as we do today. Because there were no funeral homes or undertakers until the late 1920's in Knox County, Kentucky, it became the role of friends and family to perform the necessary duties and services for the deceased. Everyone in the community did what they could to show their respect and help the bereaved family in their time of need. Women prepared food and brought it to the home of the deceased. Often, flowers were picked from the woods or garden to decorate the home. White blossoms were commonly picked in the spring. These blossoms became known as "service-berry," (pronounced as sahr-vice berry). Holly and cedar were often fashioned into wreaths or crosses with ribbons during the winter months. White and red roses with black ribbons and/or veils were placed on doors of some families homes. This practice is still done. Some families would, as did businesses, place a black or white card on the front door. This card told the person's name and date of birth and date of death and when and where the funeral would take place. We no longer place these cards on the front door but receive one at the funeral home to remember the service. Most businesses today still hang a wreath of flowers on the door with the person's name and relationship to the store owner on the card. This wreath is provided by the local business district of the town.

Preserving the body of the deceased was not customary. Since there were no undertakers, it was necessary for friends and family to prepare the body for the funeral and burial. First, the community people would wash the body of the deceased. Then the body would be dressed and laid on a board till the casket was finished. The body would be covered with a black sheet or coverlet. This had to be done soon after death occurred to prevent problems encountered from swelling and stiffening of the body. If too much time elapsed, it could become necessary to break bones while clothing the deceased.

A variety of clothing was traditionally used for burial purposes. In earlier centuries, it was customary for the people of Appalachia to dress the deceased in a shroud, or robe. Later, however, this practice became practically obsolete. Friends and family began to use more commonplace clothing. The best clothing of the deceased was chosen. If the deceased owned no good clothing, someone would sew a burial garment or donate one of their own. A variety of garments were used. However, there were some common practices that many people followed. Women were frequently dressed in long dresses that were black or white. Sometimes flowers were placed in their hands. Men were often dressed in white shirts with neckties and nice pants or a suit. Children were usually clothed in white. Many times the garments were split up the back to make them easier to dress the men, while the preacher's wife dressed the women.

In an attempt to improve the physical appearance of the dead, Appalachian people used several simple techniques. If the eyes of the deceased were open, massaging of the cheeks would aid in closing them. A silver coin was then placed on each eye to keep them shut. Silver was used rather than copper coins because copper had a tendency to turn the skin green. To help preserve the color of the face of the deceased, a washcloth soaked in soda water was placed on the face. Sometimes, aspirin was dissolved in this water. There were also some mountaineers who would place a saucer of salt on the chest or stomach during the preparation of the body. The salt was supposed to soak up moisture and keep the corpse from swelling and bursting.

While the women were busy preparing food, cleaning the house of the deceased and making sure the body was ready for burial, the men of the community also volunteered their time and skills. Many men, upon hearing of the death, would immediately begin digging the grave in the family grave yard. This, of course, was done by hand, using shovels and picks, unlike today when it is done with a backhoe. The grave was dug in vaults. The first two feet were dug wider than the next two and then the last two were even smaller, just large enough to accommodate the wooden box used as a vault for the casket, which would be placed inside. The grave's sides were smoothed by using a broad ax. After the vault and casket were placed in the grave, wood would be placed over the casket and then two feet of dirt, then more wood, and so on until the grave was covered. Others would aid in the preparation of the coffin.

Before the early 1930s everyone used homemade coffins on a regular basis and the makers charged a fee to supplement their income. Many coffins were made without charge as an act of kindness and respect. Usually the boards and other materials were donated by local men. Everyone would contribute any spare materials they happened to have at the time.

Since the coffins were fashioned by hand and made by various individuals, no two looked exactly alike. A variety of wood was used, including poplar, pine, oak, and chestnut. Sometimes the lumber was left unfinished. Other caskets were varnished, painted black or covered with black cloth. Usually the caskets were constructed in a design that followed the shape of the body. They were broad at the top, where the shoulders would lie, and became more narrow at the bottom where the feet would rest. The casket was made of four pieces of wood: the top, bottom, and sides. They were all constructed of one board per part. The side boards had to be bent at, or near, the top. To do this, one would take a handsaw and cut a series of small cuts across the width of the board. Then they would pour boiling water on the cuts and bend the wood. The cuts allowed the board to bend, and the water kept the board from bursting in the bending process. After the boards were bent, hot irons were placed on the cut area to dry the wood. One then planed the surface until it was smooth and put the casket together. The bottom and top were large boards which were cut at angles at the top and bottom. They were cut to match the sides, and when fitted together it was truly a work of art.

The insides of the coffins were as varied as the outsides. The interior padding was frequently made of cotton or shavings covered with cloth. Silk was often used when available. Carpet tacks were used to hold down the padding and cloth. Colors of casket linings were often symbolic of the individuals to be buried. Infants and children's caskets, which were much shorter than adults caskets, were usually lined in white. Coffins for adults were usually lined in black. Occasionally, blue or other colors were used, if available. After the inside and outside covering was placed on the casket a small piece of white lace was placed around the edge of the casket.

In the early 1930's one could, if they had the money, buy a ready made casket from a local store This casket was thought, by some, to be better than a homemade one. Others thought the homemade casket was better because they knew how it was made and what it was made of. Today we buy caskets and vaults made of steel.

Once the coffin was prepared, the body of the deceased was placed inside and was then ready to be viewed by family and friends. This visitation took place in the home of the deceased and was known as a wake, or sitting up with the dead. Food would be brought as people arrived to pay their respects to the deceased and to the bereaved family. This was a time for quiet socializing. Everyone would talk of memories of the deceased and try to comfort the family. It was also customary to have preaching during the wake. Many people would come and go, but there would always be some that would spend the entire night sitting up with the family and the body. Many songs were sung to pass the long hours.

There are many explanations to the etiology of the wake. Mountaineers, before preservation of the body, were concerned with making sure the body was actually dead. Sometimes people would be thought to be dead but would not be. One lady in Knox County, Kentucky, who was prepared for burial as described above, sat up during her funeral and scared the entire crowd to death.

In the summer, with the body decaying rapidly, friends and relatives had to maintain a twenty-four-hour vigil to keep insects and rodents away from the body. Protection of the corpse from cats was another concern. Folklore evidence indicates that one should never permit a cat near a corpse, because it will attack the face of the decedent, tear it with sharp claws, and feed on the flesh. Some people even believe that the cat will take the soul of the deceased. Another explanation for the mountain tradition of sitting up with dead was an ancient fear that the dead body might be carried off by some of the agents of the invisible world. Most caskets were draped with a black veil over the deceased. This helped keep insects off and also, if there was something wrong with the face, this helped hide blemishes on the person. Most people sat up at the home of the deceased so the family could rest, especially if the deceased had suffered with a long illness. This was the neighborly thing to do.

Since there is no longer a need to sit with the deceased to keep away the cats, insects, rats, and body snatchers, the contemporary wake is not an all-night affair, except when it is requested. The viewing today is still a social event, although it is usually held in a funeral home instead of at the deceased's home. Neighborliness is just as extensive as it was in previous years. Food is still provided for the bereaved. However, it is not brought to the site of the viewing and participants do not eat in the presence of the deceased.

In earlier days, the time between death and burial was generally about 24 hours, with an all-night wake and burial at about two o'clock the following afternoon. The gap between death and burial, as well as the determination of whether or not a wake was held, depended on a number of variables. If the death was the result of an incurable or contagious disease, burial was quick, but if disease was not a factor, the body was held until the family arrived. If the deceased died at night of a contagious disease that person would be buried as soon as death occurred. The home would be cleaned and the fur-

nishings burnt to keep the disease from spreading. Most of the time the family would be expecting the death, and the grave and casket would be prepared beforehand; the family would not be living in the home, but would take care of the sick person as best they could. Odor from the decaying body expedited disposal. Summer weather especially increased the need for rapid disposal of the body. In the early 1930's embalming started taking place in the Appalachian area and the embalmer would come to the house with his instruments and prepare the body there and the deceased would then be able to withstand a day or two's delay in the funeral. The embalmer brought with him in his bag embalming fluid, false teeth, eye patches, hair pens, and some makeup.

Nature provided a variety of obstacles to grave digging in this area. In the winter, mountain people had to deal with frozen ground that picks and shovels could not penetrate. They were sometimes able to build a fire on the ground at each step that the grave was dug, but this was very time consuming. On many occasions, the deceased was placed in a cold back room or wrapped in a sheet and placed in a outbuilding until the grave could eventually be dug. This practice was very seldom used in this area for fear of harm to the body. Graves could fill with water as the men were digging, so that it was impossible to place the deceased in the ground. One way in which the mountain people avoided water in the graves was to have their family cemetery on a hill. In Knox County, Kentucky, one will find over 80% of the cemeteries on small or large hills; this helps in keeping water out of the grave. This created major problems, especially in the summer, when there was accelerated decomposition. The major barrier to digging a grave in most mountain areas was rock. It was, at times, impossible to dig beyond a certain point.

Until the advent of coal mining in the area, sledge hammers and hand drills were the primary tools for breaking rock. Miners used dynamite to remove the rock, though care was needed to prevent the disturbances of other graves when the explosion occurred. Encountering rock generally meant a delay of a day or so before burial. In the past people tried to bury the dead at least six feet deep but now new state law requires only four feet. This is because of steel caskets and steel vaulting.

The funerals of the first people of Appalachia were conducted differently than those of more recent mountain people. This was partly due to the teaching of John Calvin, who influenced many Appalachian people. Calvin taught that burials should be done simply and should be held as soon after death as possible. Later, if everyone desired, friends and family could gather to pay their respects and socialize.

Early Appalachian people had to wait until certain seasons to conduct any services that large crowds could attend. Convenience was a factor that had to be considered. Funeral services were usually held during the fall after harvest, so there would be plenty of food for everyone. Weather was a variable that had to be considered. During rainy seasons, roads were often in such bad condition they could not be easily traveled. There were not many preachers in some areas, so it was necessary to schedule the services at a time when a preacher would be traveling through the area.

Therefore, when a death occurred, the burial immediately took place after the body and coffin were prepared. Usually a few people would gather at the grave site. Someone would sing a song, and a prayer would be uttered. Then the coffin would be lowered into the vault and covered with dirt and wood.

Later, sometimes as much as a year after the burial, funeral services would be held. The service would be for all who had died and were buried in the graveyard since the last funeral service.

The following is one account of such a service. In preparation for the funeral service, seats made of bark-covered logs were set up throughout the graveyard. A table, located in the center of the area, was covered with a cloth and supported a bucket of water and a gourd for drinking.

Three preachers came to this particular service to preach, or "funeralize" over the dead. Each preacher took turns delivering his message. In their sermons, they discussed the life and character of the deceased. They also focused on living right and pleasing God in order to be prepared to die. They were often very emotional, crying and using words that stirred up the emotions. Nearly everyone would be in tears before the sermon was over.

After approximately three hours of preaching, everyone would sing spiritual hymns. A handshake was conducted, so everyone could greet one another. Then they announced upcoming funerals to be held nearly a year later, and dismissed everyone to eat their meals and socialize.

As time passed and more people began to settle in the Appalachians, people began to drift away from the practice of delaying the funeral services. The wake, as previously discussed, was not held until all friends and family could arrive. The funeral service was then conducted. Some funerals were held at the home of the deceased, but most were held at a nearby church.

The coffin had to be hauled to the church in the back of a wagon. Usually, the church bell would begin to ring as soon as the wagon came into sight and would continue to ring until the body was inside the church building. In some communities the church bell will still be rung as the ambulance comes into the church lot. Often, very large crowds attended the services, sometimes more than the church could hold.

The length of the services varied. One account reported that they usually lasted thirty minutes to an hour. Another source said that most services lasted around four hours or longer, because several preachers attended and took turns preaching. Once the preaching was over,

everyone walked by the coffin to view the body. Neighbors and friends exited first, while family viewed the body last. Then the body was taken to the graveyard. These customs are still practiced today. Today some families no longer have preaching during the funeral but have friends and family members speak of the deceased.

At the graveyard the casket was carried from the wagon to the grave site, a song was usually sung, followed by prayer. The casket could be opened once more if the family or a friend requested it. Some families would place flowers on the closed casket before it was lowered into the grave. Then friends would take turns putting a shovelful of dirt on the grave, or some would put a handful of dirt on the grave. Each time a shovelful was dumped, they would say, "Ashes to ashes, dust to dust, sleep all night here, Brother." Then a tombstone, fashioned by hand of rock (or a temporary marker of wood) was placed at the head of the grave. The deceased's name and date of birth and death were etched on the tombstone. Following the burial, it was customary for the family and friends to gather at the family's home for socializing and to eat. Most families still practice this in the Appalachian region.

Today we use ambulances to transport the body from one place to another. Families can now travel with great ease for the wake, or viewing as we call it now, and for the funeral. After a death we usually have the funeral two days after the person has died. Some funerals now are changing to the night of the viewing instead of the day after.

Following the burial, it was customary for the family to dress in certain clothing to signify the death. Women and teenage girls usually dressed in black clothing for two to four weeks afterwards. Young girls wore white. Men wore two-inch black bands around their arms. If it was a child that had died, the mother would wear a veil for four to five months, also the woman may have worn a veil if it was a parent, brother or sister, older child or husband. She would also not wear any jewelry for this time.

If a woman's husband had died the men in the community helped her by taking on the responsibilities of farm work, handling legal matters, and other such work. Community women continued to cook and send food to the widow and her family. Today we still prepare food for the family and do what we can for them.

Cleanliness was a top priority, particularly following a death that was brought on by a contagious disease. The room where the body had rested, or sometimes the entire house, was disinfected. The walls and bed were scalded. Objects from the room were boiled, and the bed was taken outside to air out.

Since the people of Appalachia played such a direct role in matters related to death, it was perhaps only natural for them to fear death and try to avoid it. Over a period of many years, a wide range of superstitions that relate to death evolved. Some are as old as the first pioneers. Other came about later as people encountered the sometimes harsh life of the mountains.

The following is a list of superstitions that allow common events to foretell of death:

• If you sweep under the bed of a sick person, they will die.

• If you skip a line of quilting, someone in the family will die.

• Death will come if you take your old broom with you when you move into a new house.

• If coffee grounds in a cup form a coffin, death will come.

• If you sneeze at the table with your mouth full of food, you will die.

• Breaking a mirror brings death to the family.

• If two people look into a mirror at the same time, the younger will die within a year.

• Death will come if you dream of a wedding.

• If the weight of a clock falls, death will come.

• Death will come if you let a candle burn completely out.

• If you skip a row while planting corn, someone will die.

• Stretching dogs are measuring graves.

• Black honey bees foretell of death.

• When a bird flies in the house, it signals death.

In addition to believing in superstitions about the foretelling of death, many Appalachian people also believed in the special powers of the corpse and of graves. These beliefs often led to superstitions. Below are a few of these superstitions:

• Rubbing the hand of a corpse can remove birthmarks or cure eczema.

• Good luck comes to anyone who wears a bullet that has passed through a dead body.

• Carrying the bone of a corpse brings good luck.

• Touching a dead person's body will prevent him from haunting you.

• If you cut a corn with the same blade that shaved a dead man, the corn will heal.

• Walking in the same direction as a funeral possession will keep death away.

• When you shiver, someone is walking over the spot where your grave will be.

It becomes apparent that a large part of Appalachian life was in some way consumed by death. Entire funeral and burial procedures, from preparing the body and the coffin to conducting the funeral services and burying the body, rested solely in the hands of family members and neighbors. With this in mind, it is of no great surprise that many Appalachians developed superstitions about death.

Central Appalachians no longer look on death or treat dying in the same manner as their ancestors. As with all other traditions associated with death, within the last twenty to thirty years central Appalachian funerals have changed just as they have in the rest of the United States. The central Appalachian funeral has evolved into a private expression of grief from the social event so common to the settlers of the area. The focus now centers on the family, their wishes and feelings. Services are designed to accommodate the living rather than the dead.

David R. Helton, P.O. Box 653, Barbourville, KY 40906, has authored and co-authored several books on Knox County history and is very active in local history activities. The above is adapted from an upcoming book.

Death Be Not Painful

By Adam Marcus (MA'96)

Too many Americans spend their final days in the hospital and in unnecessary pain. Remedying that will mean changing the very way doctors and nurses are trained. At Hopkins, that process is already under way.

Medicine these days is enduring a highly publicized crisis of conscience. Patients in their final weeks of life seem more concerned about dying with dignity than extending their days. The notion almost has judicial fiat. When the Supreme Court in June upheld two state laws banning physician-assisted suicide, the justices raised the importance of palliative care, a testament to its increasing claim on the medical consciousness.

What's becoming increasingly clear, however, is how little we know about the dying process. In the past, doctors and nurses were educated with an almost warrior-like mentality: defeat disease before it defeats the body. Some are now re-examining such training and methods in an attempt to define the qualities needed to bring about the "good death." It's partly tilting at windmills. No death is good. But no death need be worse than another, and Johns Hopkins, a name for years synonymous with healing, has begun focusing on making its wards and wings a source of comfort to the dying.

Albert W. Wu's sixth-floor office at the School of Public Health overlooks the old Hopkins Hospital where, nearly a century ago, William Osler conducted the first study of pain in the final days of life. Wu's office may be more modern, but the associate professor of health policy and management is working on the same problem: trying to evaluate how patients die. Osler concluded that the majority of patients who died at Hopkins at the turn of the century did so without much "bodily pain or distress"—a finding most likely linked to the fact that infection, fever, and other complications did not give illnesses time to become chronic.

Indeed, Wu has turned up a much different picture. Wu collaborated with researchers from several other centers, including George Washington University and Beth Israel Hospital in Boston, on a study of some 9,000 individuals, known as SUPPORT (Study to Understand Prognoses and Preferences for Outcomes and Risks of Treatments). Their findings appeared last January in the *Annals of Internal Medicine*.

"The Death we fear most is the dying in pain, unnoticed and isolated from loved ones," the researchers noted in the *Annals* article. So it concerned the authors to learn that of the 46 percent of patients who died during the study, more than half spent their last moments in a hospital. Moreover, about 40 percent of those patients were in either severe or moderate pain for most or all of the last three days of life—pain, the authors argue, that could have been alleviated through medication.

SUPPORT, which was funded by the Robert Wood Johnson Foundation, began in the late 1980s in an attempt to describe the effects of Advance Directives (a terminal-care plan forged by patients in the event that they can't communicate their treatment wishes) and DNRs (a request not to be revived if their heart should stop). The data are so rich, however, that they are now throwing new light into nearly every corner of the dying process.

Patients qualified for the trials if they were over the age of 80, or had one of nine terminal illnesses—including certain cancers, congestive heart failure, coma, cirrhosis, and Multiple Organ System Failure. All patients in the five-center study were assigned nurse practitioners, whose role it was to give prognoses and improve communication among patients, families, and caregivers about end-stage care options.

Some of the participants had family members who agreed to be interviewed about their loved one's experience, and their thoughts formed the backbone of Wu's study. He found that most family members surveyed were pleased with the end-stage care their loved one received. Only one in 10 SUPPORT subjects received improper care, according to their families. Yet nearly half of the 4,100-some patients who died received "extraordinary measures" to keep them alive, including tube feeding, mechanical ventilation, and attempted resuscitation.

Here, according to Wu, arises a difficult paradox. Patient and family satisfaction might not be the most reliable measure of care in the case of terminal illness, he says. "That's part of this phenomenon of physicians and patients colluding in this vain attempt to defy death," he says. "They feel good about it because they did everything [they could]. The funny thing is, if we ask what a good death is, it's in a clean bed, with the family around, closing our eyes and drawing a last breath. And that's clearly not what's happening."

Although the nurse practitioners were specifically trained to be sensitive to end-of-life issues, including pain management, patient preferences about care, and how to convey patient wishes to physicians, their presence apparently did little to improve dialogue between the dying and their doctors, Wu says. Physician practices did not seem to change. In most cases, says Wu, patients and their loved ones should have been expecting death soon, but were not. Doctors continued to perform life-saving therapies even as their patients' prognoses worsened, sending the unrealistic message that survival was possible.

"I think that people did not understand that there were many things that they

 From *Johns Hopkins Magazine*, September 1997, pp. 46-51. © 1997 by Adam Marcus. Reprinted by permission.

should have been beginning to attend to," says Wu. Calling key relatives and friends to the hospital, for example, is something that too often comes too late, although it can make a tremendous positive difference in a person's final hours or days, he notes.

Sometimes families debate about whether to summon relatives. Delay is a way of blocking out the reality of the imminent death, says Wu. This sort of denial is unfortunate, Wu says, because it deprives the patient of emotional succor. Even worse, pretending optimistically that death is not at hand may lead to treatment decisions that compound pain. Says Wu of the families in SUPPORT, "People were thinking about doing everything possible to prolong life to the exclusion of thinking about what impact that might have on the patient's comfort both physically and emotionally."

Wu and his co-authors believe that end-stage care is not given the respect it deserves in medical training. "It's interesting how we use language," he says. "We talk about heroic measures, extraordinary measures, but most of those words don't have negative connotations. We don't say that people were tormented until they died, but if we're to believe the results of this study, people were in pain until the end."

On Stuart "Skip" Grossman's desk sits a computer—a computer that offers him and his colleagues in the Oncology Center a digital means of evaluating the pain of each patient they treat.

"We are making pain control much more of a priority," says Grossman, an associate professor of oncology, medicine and neurosurgery, and the director of Neurooncology. By the time Grossman meets his patients—adults who suffer from primary brain tumors—they are already dying, so pain control is often all he can offer.

Each morning, a nurse on the ward presents to patients a plastic strip with a 10-cm line on it. Patients draw their own line to match the level of pain they feel that day, with 0 being none and 10 being the worst imaginable. The rating is then entered into a computer, and, as Grossman says, "any day before noon I can sit down behind the computer and get the pain ratings of all of the patients in the Oncology Center. It allows us to figure out which patients need some further attention or further evaluation." Getting patients involved is crucial, Grossman has found, because apparently even doctors aren't so good at eyeballing pain. "We did

a study in the Oncology Center here looking at whether providers appreciated how much pain their patients had," says Grossman. "What you would hope is that the average of the pain rating from the providers would be similar to that of the patients, but it turns out that there is no statistical correlation between the two." In fact, the only time the estimates matched was when patients reported no pain at all.

Grossman says that one explanation for this finding is that patients tend to hide the severity of their pain from doctors and nurses, who in turn don't pry as deeply as they should. Patients often feel that cancer by definition is painful, so there's no reason to be making a big fuss. They are also concerned that more pain equals more severe disease, and they don't want to distract their caregivers from treating their disease. Still others worry that taking too much medication will render them incoherent.

There are other barriers to providing adequate pain relief. Some physicians, aware that they are under the watchful eye of government drug regulators, have concerns about overprescribing addictive medication—particularly opioids like morphine. Their fears aren't unwarranted. In 1991, the Pain and Policy Studies Group at the University of Wisconsin surveyed state medical boards on their attitudes about painkillers. The group concluded that boards worried too much about the dangers of addiction and too little about pain management—findings that can explain

why physicians have lost their licenses for prescribing narcotics to relieve pain in terminally ill patients.

Caregivers need to discuss with patients whether treating pain could bring death sooner, says Cindy Rushton, an assistant professor of nursing at Hopkins. "Many people are willing to accept that they may die sooner if they are able to die without pain. We know that one of the consequences of giving large doses of a pain medication is that life ends sooner, but in a terminally ill patient, that may be justified."

What's important, says Rushton, is knowing what a patient expects from palliative care, whether the goal is to obliterate pain completely, at the expense of lucidity, or simply manage it to the point of comfort.

Drugs today don't have to be incapacitating or mind-dulling, Wu notes, given recent advances in pain relief, such as patient-controlled anesthetics that can be self-titrated.

Grossman also pins some of the blame for poor pain relief on an institutional mindset that makes it a low priority. He finds a "gross imbalance" between the amount of attention devoted to palliative care in oncology, for example, and the attention given to the newest therapies. "It sends the message that it is more important to be researching a brand new drug than trying to make people more comfortable," he says.

Too often, the mental pain experienced by dying patients also goes unaddressed, Wu and his co-authors found. Dying patients frequently report feelings of intense sadness, depression, and anxiety—in fact, more than 60 percent of the SUPPORT participants had severe emotional symptoms like these, according to their family members. Wu says that those problems are readily treatable—as long as they are recognized.

Many people consider Hopkins's Debra Roter to be one of the nation's authorities on patient-provider communication. The professor of health policy and management at the School of Public Health has some ideas why the SUPPORT study uncovered muddled interactions between doctors and the dying. Crossed wires are especially troublesome with Advance Directives, she says.

Ideally, the process of working out an Advance Directive should allow a physician to explore what a patient is feeling about his or her imminent death, Roter says. Instead, physicians are often too un-

---

Comfort from a Different Source

"I've been holding hands as they've gone from warm to cold many times," says Matthew Lascalzo, director of the Ocology Center's social work service. He and his staff of six social workers are on call around-the-clock to help oncology patients and their families cope with the emotional anguish that comes with dying.

When dealing with families, Loscalzo says that pragmatic issues often take center stage—like making sense of confusing insurance forms or finding the means to pay mounting hospital bills. Today we're not seeing "the acute deaths that we were so used to seeing 50 years ago," he says. "The impact on the family has changed dramatically. It may sound cold and harsh, but these are things that families have to manage.

Loscalzo, who serves on a national panel on assisted suicide, has found that terminally ill patients—particularly the elderly—can feel a strong obligation to die. They worry about being abandoned, about medical costs and their family's suffering. "They feel they're such a burden to themselves and others," Loscalzo says. He is pleased with the Supreme Court's recent ruling against physician-assisted suicide, describing the ruling as "a good thing for the elderly and for the vulnerable people in the U.S."

comfortable to deal with the subject on an emotional level, so they resort to using a "legalistic script" with their patients. The result? Advance directives that don't accurately reflect patients' wishes, she says.

Roter is currently analyzing audio tapes of about 140 conversations between doctors and patients as part of a study to improve how the two parties communicate when death is imminent, so that patients will truly have informed consent when considering whether to terminate their own care.

"There certainly were a good number of [conversations] where it was clear that the doctor and patient were not on the same wavelength," she says. The physician end of the dialogue often consisted of overdoses of euphemism on the one hand and very technical medical jargon on the other. "It's confusing to patients," Roter says. "They're not sure what the doctor is telling them."

In her study, Roter hopes to identify the essential criteria of the end-stage-care discussion, a list that includes not only providing the cold facts (like what a defibrillator is), but how warm a physician's voice is in explaining what the device does. For, according to Roter, it's crucial that patients not only understand what their doctors are telling them, but that they feel comfortable hearing it. Early results of the study show that the most successful discussions of terminal care occur when doctors allow patients to express their fears, tell their stories, and explain their misgivings.

Part of the problem in communication can be linked to the fact that medical and nursing schools don't do enough to prepare their students to handle end-stage care issues, says Michael Williams, a neurologist and ethics committee member of the university's Bioethics Institute.

End-stage training ought to include hands-on experience, much the way students learn how to put in an IV or perform a surgical operation, Williams contends. He recently received a $200,000, two-year grant from the Kornfeld Foundation (to which the medical school added nearly $140,000 via the Bioethics Institute), to find out just how well he can teach good death etiquette. The study, which he plans to begin this fall with the help of other Hopkins colleagues, will look at two teaching paradigms for attending doctors and nurses: the traditional seminar model—the staple of Hopkins and other medical schools—and the more novel "standardized patient" technique, which uses realistic situations and role playing.

Williams gives an example of how the latter technique can work. Two students, a nurse and a physician, meet with an actress portraying the wife of a comatose patient. In their first consultation, the students "break the bad news" to the distraught spouse. In the second round, the patient's condition has worsened and death is imminent. In this scenario, the patient is a young man, perhaps in his early 30s, and therefore unlikely to have a living will. The students must try to find out whether he had ever discussed his wishes vis-à-vis life support. In the final phase, the patient is diagnosed as brain dead and unrecoverable. The students must now guide his wife to the realization, if it's not already clear, that her husband will not survive, and then discuss the possibility of organ donation.

The process demands sensitivity, says Williams, since when to admit the end "is the sort of decision that many, many [families] are really afraid of."

Patricia Grimm is doing her part to help students at the School of Nursing deal more successfully with end-stage patients. For the last five years, Grimm, an oncology nurse with a PhD in nursing, has taught an elective course on Death and Dying. The seven-week class introduces students to issues ranging from dying young to differences in handling loss. "We don't limit [the discussions] to people who have died—a job, a relationship, moving, these are also losses," says Grimm, whose course usually has a waiting list. "We do a lot of talking about our own losses so that we can understand how we're reacting and hopefully put that aside so that we can be there for the patient."

"Being there" can also include a more metaphysical approach to caregiving. The scientific community is increasingly recognizing links between faith and good health. Several recent studies have shown that strong religious conviction correlates with healthier living and longer life. Still, it has been almost an anathema to teach medical students about spirituality, says Thomas Corson '77 (MD'80, MPH'82), an assistant professor in Pediatrics and Medicine. Corson has spent most of the last 22 years at Hopkins. Training in Asia and Africa, he learned that "it's very hard to care for people unless you have a good sense of what their religious tradition is."

"Traditionally, in a lot of heritages, the concepts of healing the body and the soul were not dichotomized," he says. "Priests were healers. There was an angelic conjunction between divinity and physician." Ignoring this relationship today is poor medicine, says Corson, who has prayed and read Scripture with his dying patients throughout his career. "As we care for people there is still a significant overlap between matters of the soul and matters of the body."

With that in mind, Corson began the first Religion in Medicine course at Hopkins in 1995. Created with the help of the Templeton Foundation, the five-week course—a version of which has now become part of the required upper-level curriculum—encourages future physicians to incorporate their faith into their art. Students learn how to take a patient's spiritual history along with the physical one, how to call on clergy for help, and what science is showing us about the link between religious faith and well-being.

I F SUPPORT uncovered some distressing aspects of dying, it also suggested a few ways to ameliorate them. Foremost, says Wu, is to make hospice care an integral part of end-stage care. Where hospital deaths can be lonely, painful, and sterile, dying at home in private comfort and familiar surroundings can help ease the trauma of life's final passage—and the pain, according to two physicians in the SUPPORT study. They reported that hospices relieved pain in at least 98 percent of cases.

In 1982, Medicare began covering hospice care as a billable service. Since 1985, the number of hospice programs in the United States has jumped from 1,400 to more than 3,000. Today, 20 percent of those near death will choose hospice care, according to the National Hospice Organization. From a financial standpoint, hospice care makes sense: A recent study showed that in the last month of life, the average cost of hospice care for a cancer patient is $3,200 less than traditional hospital care would be.

At Hopkins, hospice care is the dominion of Hopkins Home Health Services (HHS), which was established in 1995 and is jointly owned by the health system and the university. HHS has three subsidiary companies: one for pediatrics care, one for pharmacological and equipment supply, and an in-home care arm for adults: Hopkins Home Care.

Amy Rader, senior director of operations and clinical services for HHS, notes that treatment is purely palliative and is planned and performed by an interdisciplinary team. Rader rattles off the list. "We do nursing, medical social services, spiritual care, social work, home health aid. There's a pharmacist on staff to do pain and symptom management. We have a physician to guide in palliative medicine." HHS usually has 25 caregivers serving 30 to 40 patients.

Hospice nurses visit each patient three to five times weekly. Visits can last anywhere from 45 minutes to several hours, during which time the patient gets hospital-quality care—except extraordinary measures to keep them alive—without a hospital-like atmosphere. Nor does care end when the patient dies. HHS follows families for up to two years afterward.

Since its inception, the hospice company has seen marked growth. It served 130 patients in the first half of 1997, compared to 163 for all of its first year. Rader says that patients and caregivers alike "see the reliability and validity of providing care at home."

Bill Kilgour, 67, will attest to that. His wife, Eleanor, died last January at the age of 65, the same week that the SUPPORT study was released. Her death, while drawn out, was in the end a model of what hospice care can offer.

The first time he saw her in the fall of 1995, Michael Carducci knew that Eleanor Kilgour would die from her disease. She had bladder cancer that had invaded the vagina and lymph nodes. Carducci, an assistant professor of oncology and urology, later discovered tumor cells in her lung and bone cancer in one knee. "At that time I told her that she had a lot of disease, but little, if any, chance of [our] curing it," recalls Carducci. Like every doctor with terminally ill patients, Carducci had to make a choice. He could treat Eleanor Kilgour's tumors, or he could treat Eleanor Kilgour. The choice was clear, he says: "I knew that we weren't going to be able to cure this," he says. "But hopefully we could improve her quality of life."

Eleanor's health deteriorated for a year, and in the fall of 1996 Carducci recommended hospice care—an admission that there was nothing left to do but ease her pain. Eleanor, however, remained adamant that she did not want it. Her husband, ever the faithful nurse, obeyed, though he found himself increasingly overwhelmed by the demands of her disease, which had turned their home into a makeshift infirmary. Eleanor deteriorated rapidly, and around New Year's Day she finally accepted what her doctor and her husband knew signaled the end. "She could have been helped by hospice earlier, but she was very much clinging to life," Carducci says.

Bill Kilgour arranged for a nurse from Hopkins Home Care Group to come to the house. Karen Trageser arrived. "Pain management was the biggest issue in that home," she recalled recently. Eleanor, she says, "had a lot of pain in her bones, so we got her a hospital bed and an air mattress. She was placed on pain medication and we made her comfortable enough to the point where she peacefully passed away." Her husband was at her bedside.

"Hospice nursing isn't a skill that's easily taught," according to Trageser. She herself was never introduced to any terminal care issues in nursing school, and would have been completely in the woods but for a personal tragedy—her father's death from thyroid cancer 14 years ago. "He was not in a hospice program, and I wish he had been," says Trageser, who since has taken courses in hospice care. "He died in the hospital in a great deal of pain. We didn't know what to do. We weren't prepared." Trageser has imported that experience to her practice. "I don't want to see people suffer," she says.

At the Kilgour home, Eleanor's hospital bed is gone now, and Bill Kilgour has turned the living room into something of a small office. The dining room table is covered with bills, the paper trail of Eleanor's passing. "She used to say that she knew she was very sick, and that she wasn't afraid to die," he says softly and through tears. "But then the last three weeks she started telling me that she was afraid, and that I had to be with her. She wanted me to hold her hand all the time. If I had to go to the bathroom she wouldn't let me go. I'd have to pry her fingers off."

Bill Kilgour has nothing but praise for the doctors and nurses at Johns Hopkins who helped him take care of his wife. "They were very honest with everything they did," he says. "Dr. Carducci never said how long she would live or when she would die. 'I'm not God,' he said. Eleanor was grateful because he was so honest. I couldn't do enough for those people," Kilgour says. "I couldn't do enough for them."

Adam Marcus (MA'96) is a freelance writer who lives in Washington D.C.

AT YOUR DISPOSAL

The funeral industry prepares for boom times

By Judith Newman

Show me the manner in which a nation or a community cares for its dead and I will measure with mathematical exactness the tender sympathies of its people, their respect for the law of the land and their loyalty to high ideals.

— Motto appearing on funeral-industry paraphernalia

Now, here's what you do if you've tied their mouths too tight, or they have no lips and the family's not happy," says Dina Ousley, placing a stencil over the mouth of an audience volunteer. Using an airbrush, she gently sprays on a full, lush pout in vermilion. "And these lips stay on, even when people are kissing their loved ones good-bye!" Ousley, the president of Dinair Airbrush Makeup Systems of Beverly Hills, California, is a makeup artist for Hollywood stars, but occasionally she takes clients who are, well, less fussy. She is here, at the 115th annual convention of the National Funeral Directors Association (NFDA) in Cincinnati, to sell her system of airbrushed makeup for glamorizing the deceased.

"Hmm, sort of like detailing a car," murmurs a man behind me, as Ousley, a cheerful, birdlike blonde, demonstrates how easy it is to cover bruises and restore a "natural" glow to skin. At the end of Ousley's demonstration comes the *pièce de résistance*: airbrushing, compared with the application of conventional cosmetics, makes it much

Judith Newman is a freelance writer living in New York City. This is her first article for Harper's Magazine.

easier to beautify the client who suffered from jaundice; apparently, when a jaundiced corpse is embalmed, the chemicals can turn it green. Grabbing another volunteer from the audience, Ousley first airbrushes him the color of Herman Munster, then attempts to restore him to his natural hue by spraying him white, as a primer, and applying an alabaster foundation. When I finally fled the room, the volunteer was the shade of a buttercup. He would have looked perfectly natural had he been not a human but a suburban kitchen circa 1950. Ousley did not look happy.

Here's the thing about death that's hard to grasp: It's going to happen to you. Whether you are embalmed and entombed or your ashes are shot out of a duck blind, your loved ones will be spending a small portion of the $7 billion that every year is poured into the U.S. funeral industry. Since the average funeral costs about $4,600—not including the expense of the cemetery or mausoleum, which can add thousands more—disposing of their dead is, for many families, one of the most expensive purchases they will ever make, right behind a house or a car.

No matter when you go, you'll be in good company; approximately 2.3 million people in the United States die each year. But if you're a baby boomer who pays attention to the actuarial tables and plans to go obediently to your final reward in twenty-five to forty-five years, you'll have to muscle others out of the way for a glimpse of that white light: by the year 2030, the annual death rate will have increased by about 30 percent. So naturally, funeral directors must be nodding somberly about this news, then retreating into

a small, quiet backroom office and doing the hora.

Well, not exactly. True, the nation's 22,000 funeral homes can look forward to a deluge of death—a certain consolation, since the average home handles about two deaths a week (fewer in sparsely populated rural areas). And since families have traditionally selected funeral homes based not on cost comparisons or value but on proximity—or, as Jim St. George, president and CEO of ConsumerCasket USA, a retail-coffin outlet, puts it, on "whoever can get Mama out of the living room fastest"—it would seem that the impending good fortune would be proportionally shared by all. But funeral directors are worried, because, as they see it, the baby boomers, who are now making decisions about how to dispose of their loved ones, are "under-ritualized." Religious observance is on a downswing, families are scattered around the country, and thus attendance at funerals has dropped significantly. "Baby boomers have developed a certain cynicism about what is traditional and what isn't," adds St. George. "And there's nothing traditional about getting ripped off."

On the other hand, this is also the Krups generation, a tidal wave of Americans who have had a passionate love affair with credit and a willingness to pay $3 for a cup of designer coffee. Many of us have ostentatiously lived the good life. Are we now going to choose—for ourselves and for our parents—the good death?

The funeral industry fervently hopes so. But, as I saw at the national convention last fall, they're not taking any chances.

My first seminar is entitled "Business Issues That Affect a Funeral Director's Bottom Line." "Service" is the buzzword in the industry, and speakers talk about the advantages—and profitability—of offering everything from catered lunches to grief therapy. Nobody could quite explain to me why I should be entrusting my mental health to guys whose favorite motto is "It ain't the dead who give you trouble, it's the living," but that's okay. Most directors are keenly aware that today's bereaved were raised on self-help books and support groups and are willing to pay a reasonable fee to unburden themselves to strangers.

The seminar quickly focuses around an ongoing source of anxiety: cremation, the increasingly popular and ostensibly inexpensive choice for disposal. (Fun fact: the average person takes an hour and a half to burn; the heavier you are, the hotter you burn, because fat acts as combustible fuel.) In 1963, only about 4 percent of the American population opted for the pyre; now, with cemetery space increasingly scarce and expensive, 21 percent nationwide prefer cremation, and more than 40 percent prefer it in such states as California and Arizona.

Of course, some segments of the population are still relatively unaffected by this disturbing trend toward cheap disposal. It's a not very well-kept secret that poorer families spend a disproportionate amount of their income on death. Dwayne Banks, an assistant professor of public policy at the University of California, Berkeley, who studies the economics of funerals and cemeteries, recently completed a paper on how the "Nike mentality" can afflict inner-city families making funeral arrangements. "In this society we're valued by our material possessions—not only by what we have but by our ability to purchase things," explains Banks. "So if you look at the cultural context of the inner cities, it makes sense: the way of showing you valued the deceased is by providing in death what you couldn't provide in life." And the fascinating thing, Banks adds, is that the community will rally around you. "You might not be able to get together the money for college, but death brings about this sense of communalism. For a funeral, a family will pull resources together and the church will contribute. It's what people dream of America being."

But even if poor and working-class families have not changed their spending habits in recent years, there remains the threat of middle-class baby boomers, who increasingly are opting for the simplicity of cremation. The emerging problem for the funeral directors is this: how to transform cremation from an event they dub "You call, we haul, that's all" to the payload of a full-blown ritual?

For years the industry line was that cremation was sacrilege, a cruel way to treat the body. Funeral directors lobbied state legislatures to ban ash scattering, painting pictures of a world where little Johnny out playing in a park would find recognizable bits of Grandma that had not been adequately incinerated. Despite the industry's campaign of disinformation, more and more citizens were taking matters into their own hands and scattering ashes of their loved ones out at sea or over Wrigley Field. After a couple of decades, the industry realized that cremation could be every bit as profitable as traditional burial; all it took was a little ingenuity and a good deal of manipulation.

Brian Joseph, who runs a funeral home in Grosse Pointe, Michigan, advises the audience to "educate yourself to the 'disaster family' who comes to you and says, 'We just want nothing.' " They may *think* they want nothing, explains Joseph, but you, the sympathetic funeral director, know better. The family just doesn't understand its options.

And what options there are! Later that day, I watch a sales tape produced by The York Group, one of the largest casket-and-urn manufacturers in the United States. Actors apparently plucked from the Infomercial School of Subtle Emoting play a family trying to decide what to do with Dad in a few years—because Dad, although crotchety, is still very much alive and is arguing with his family about the future ceremony. "Just put me in a pine box," he says. "Better still, cremate me! Throw my ashes in my garden, and maybe I can raise better tomatoes when I'm dead than I could when I was alive." Clearly, the funeral director (played here by an oil slick with legs) must make the family realize how important a service ($300 to $650) would be to his family and friends; how embalming Dad ($300 to $600) would make everyone at the memorial service more "comfortable." And after his loved ones pick up his "cremains," his wife could then place a portion in a solid bronze "Eden urn" with a lovely garland design (about $1,400), and his daughter could preserve a sprinkle of him in a lovely limited-edition keepsake urn depicting dolphins frolicking in the surf (about $1,300). Finally, the remainder of his ashes could be sprinkled not only on his tomatoes but also in a cemetery scattering garden ($150 to $400), so "that way you'll always know where your husband's cremated remains are located."

By the end of the tape, the Jones family is smiling delightedly at the thought of what a splashy exit Dad is going to make. Dad is delighted, too. From a degrading $400 direct cremation to a deeply meaningful $5,000-or-so ritual—it's so easy!

If only this scenario were fantasy. It's not. Cremations, although still often cheaper than traditional burials, are climbing ever higher in price. And since scattering remains requires a permit that funeral directors encourage people to think is more difficult to obtain than it actually is, the demand for urns, and for final resting places to put them, is also going through the roof, as the sudden boom of high-rise mausoleums in Los Angeles attests. "Don't forget about one additional product you can sell with cremation: the vault for the urn," says Brian Joseph at the end of his presentation. "We don't have some vault to put the vault in. We may someday," he adds wistfully.

A long habit of not thinking a thing wrong gives it a superficial appearance of being right.

—Thomas Paine.
Quoted by Bob Ninker, the
executive director of the
Funeral Ethics Association

Not until the late 1800s, when a more transient society began to require that someone other than the deceased's family or neighbors handle the body, was the funeral industry born. Undertakers originally were carpenters who built coffins on the side; sensing a profit center, they learned how to embalm. A typical late-nineteenth-century bill, quoted by Jessica Mitford in her 1963 ground-breaking indictment of the funeral industry, *The American Way of Death*, showed that embalming ran around $10; renting a hearse, $8 to $10; washing and dressing, $5. A few dollars were invariably thrown in for the embalmer being "in attendance." Embalming, the practice of replacing the body's blood with a chemical preservative became popular in the United States during the Civil War, when battlefield casualties had to be shipped home; before that, burials took place within a few days of death, and bodies were kept on ice, Arsenic was the embalming chemical of choice until the 1920s, when it became apparent that it was (a) carcinogenic and (b) confusing in murder cases: in several trials involving arsenic, guilt could not be proven because the chemical was already present in the embalmed body.

At any rate, embalming became perhaps the first service provided by the funeral industry that was almost always unnecessary and, because of its profitability, almost always performed. (In fact, modern embalming usually preserves the body only for a few weeks; the politico corpses that hang around for years—Marcos, Lenin, Evita—are preserved through careful climate control.) And thus began the industry's reputation for price gouging.

"People in the funeral industry have always had a bad rep," notes Mark Nonestied, a member of the Association for Gravestone Studies, who lectures on the history of the funeral industry. "First, you've got a group of people associated with death. There are some cultures where people who deal with dead bodies are shunned altogether, and in this culture there's certainly a stigma attached. Second, there's the fact that bad experiences are more memorable, because the average person connects with the funeral director at the time of his greatest vulnerability."

Such collective distaste is reinforced by stories like the one Nonestied tells next. "Did you hear about the guy in California? He wasn't even a funeral director, but *that's* what the public thinks of the funeral industry." Allan Vieira, a fifty-two-year-old pilot from Berkeley, had been contracted by local mortuaries to scatter the cremated remains of thousands of people at sea, for $50 to $100 a body. (That was the price fixed with the mortuaries; the bereaved paid hundreds, perhaps thousands, more.) Instead of scattering the ashes, however, Vieira stashed them in his airplane hanger and in a self-storage warehouse stuffed so full that the walls collapsed, which is how his duplicity was discovered. Several lawsuits have been filed against the pilot and the mortuaries that contracted him. (Vieira, however, has already paid the ultimate price. A few weeks after being caught, he drove to the woods and shot himself; his station wagon contained eleven more boxes of remains.) In 1988, a $31.1 million judgment was won against another pilot who had promised to scatter the ashes of 5,342 people but instead dumped them, in one nice big pile, on a ten-acre lot of land he owned in the foothills of the Sierra Nevadas.

What probably nettles the public more than such occasional tales of gross negligence is the velvet-pitbull tactics funeral directors routinely use to wear down traumatized consumers—not unkindly, not even with great calculation, but simply because this is the way the business has always been run.

"You see, there is usually only one thought going through the mind of a bereaved family when they walk through the doors of a funeral home, and that thought is, *Get me out of here*," says ConsumerCasket's St. George, who for ten years worked at a mortuary in Erie, Pennsylvania. "Of course, every funeral directors knows this. Which is why the most expensive merchandise is always brought to their attention first—and why, for example, the less expensive caskets are always shown in the ugliest possible colors."

Then there are the markups. In most businesses, a 100 to 150 percent markup is common; in the funeral industry, says St.

George, markups are 300 to 600 percent. "Where I worked, we'd sit around in meetings itemizing every single thing we used in the course of a funeral, right down to the ligature we needed per body to sew up incisions. Ligature—that's string for you laypeople. We'd triple the price of everything, including cold cream we used to rub on the deceased's hands. Naturally, we had to charge for the whole jar."

In part, markups are due to the way funeral costs are structured. Before 1984, the cost of a funeral was based on the price of a casket. There was all sorts of chicanery involved in getting a customer to purchase an expensive box, but in any case the cost of the coffin included the bare bones of a traditional funeral service: transportation of the deceased, embalming, staffing at the service, announcement cards, etc. In 1984, the Federal Trade Commission ruled that a funeral director had to agree to use caskets that the bereaved could buy from retailers such as ConsumerCaskets, but he could bill customers for allowing it into his mortuary—a practice the memorial societies refer to as a "corkage fee."[1] In 1994, the FTC again changed the rules and banned corkage fees. Yet what seemed like a slap on the wrist of the funeral industry has turned out to be a big wet kiss. Now all costs are billed separately, and although savvy consumers can find a cheaper casket, the funeral director can charge a "non-declinable fee," which is the cost of his overhead, however he chooses to define it.

At the Riverside Memorial Chapel in Mount Vernon, New York, for example (a home owned by the conglomerate Service Corporation International), the non-declinable fee is $1,495. The cheapest package costs $2,598; it covers moving the remains to the funeral home and an "alternative container" (read: cardboard box). Caskets, flowers, limos, embalming, cosmetology, announcement cards, flag cases, register books, shrouds, temporary grave markers, death notices in the newspapers, clergy—you name it, it's extra. (Did I mention the cost of refrigeration? If the body is in the funeral home for more than six hours, it costs an additional $550. At those rates it would be cheaper to put up your dear departed at The Plaza.)

In pursuit of profits, the funeral industry has demonstrated an unseemly propensity for capitalizing on public ignorance. In the 1980s, thousands of funeral homes started tacking on a $200 "handling fee"

---

[1] A number of cut-rate casket manufacturers have put up Web pages on the Internet; there's even a Web site (www.xroads.com/funerals) maintained by Father Henry Wasielewskil a semiretired parish priest and crusader in Tempe, Arizona, that details funeral-industry scams so that consumers can gauge their friendly neighborhood mortician's markup.

for people who had died of AIDS. When gay-rights groups complained, it was renamed a "contagious-disease fee"; then it was called a "protective-clothing fee," until, one by one, states began to enforce against the discriminatory fee.

"The thing is, the protective clothing embalmers have to wear is a throwaway 'moon suit' that costs ten bucks and surgical gloves that cost about ten cents a pair—and OSHA has declared this gear mandatory for every embalming," says Karen Leonard, the consumer representative for Funeral and Memorial Societies of America, an organization dedicated to providing dignified and affordable funeral services. "But lots of funeral directors justified the $200 to families by citing all the extra risk they were assuming." When the required safety procedures were followed, however, there was no extra risk. "Think about it for a minute," says Leonard. "If you were in mortal fear for your life would $200 make a difference?"

You know what I've decided? I don't want to be cremated. I used to, but now I think it sounds just a little too much like a blender speed. Now I've decided I want to be embalmed, and then I want a plastic surgeon to come put in silicone implants everywhere. Then I want to be laid out in the woods like Snow White, with a gravestone that reads Gotta Dance.

—Lorrie Moore, "Starving Again"

As expensive as funerals may seem, when adjusted for inflation the price of an average funeral has risen only a few percentage points in the last twenty-five years. It's the creative introduction of all sorts of new services and accoutrements, says Berkeley professor Dwayne Banks, that has increased the range of prices.

I got a little taste for all those delicious extras during a tour of the exhibitor's floor at the NFDA. First I spotted the mahogany casket my grandfather had unfortunately test-driven into eternity a few years earlier. At the time, the funeral director was keen on selling my family a model with a special seal to "protect" the body from wildlife; I seem to recall a speech that featured a Hitchcockian vision of marauding gophers. The memory made me a little nauseous: I had recently discovered that, far from protecting the body, the expensive protective seal is the best way to guarantee that anaerobic bacteria will turn the body into goo in record time.

Moving on, I strolled through row upon row of caskets, burial vaults, embalming chemicals to plump up dehydrated tissues (my favorite: a disinfectant called Mort-O-Cide), and restorative waxes to fill in those pesky irregularities left by, say, feeding tubes or gunshot wounds. Burial clothing consists of loose-fitting pastel nightgowns for ladies and pinstripe suits for the gents; apparently, in the afterlife, all women are napping and all men are taking meetings. The dominatrix in me almost sprang for an "extremities positioner," a rope gadget for the proper positioning of the arms over the chest. The Cincinnati College of Mortuary Science was trolling for students, proudly exhibiting a life-size model of Uncle Sam in restorative wax ("Careful, his limbs come off easily!"), and the American Funeral Service Museum in Houston exhibited Victorian mourning jewelry made from the hair of the deceased and memorial cards of the rich and famous (some jokester had placed Bobby Kennedy's next to Marilyn Monroe's).

These days, you can buy blowup digital "memory pictures" of the deceased to leave at the graveside and solar-powered memorial lights to keep those pictures backlit into eternity. For the pious, the NFDA exhibitors offered urns with portraits of Jesus and Mary; for the sportsman, there were urns shaped like deer, cowboy boots, and golfclub bags; and for Zsa Zsa Gabor impersonators, an Aurora, Illinois, mortician has created a line of cremation jewelry—gold-and-diamond hearts, teardrops, and cylinders (from $1,995 to $10,000) that can hold a few precious motes of Mom and Dad.

Batesville Casket Company, the largest manufacturer in the United States, was introducing a coffin with a special "memory drawer" for personal keepsakes. Marsellus Casket Company featured "the Rolls Royce of caskets," a hand-polished model of solid African mahogany lined with velvet (retail: about $10,000) that had been the final resting place for such stiff luminaries as Richard Nixon, Harry Truman, and John Kennedy. "And don't forget Jackie O.," said the salesman excitedly. Marsellus may have had presidential cachet, but The York Group was drawing crowds with a new casket model it calls "Expressions": the light, ash-wood exterior is treated with a veneer that allows the casket to be scrawled on in Magic Marker. "We see this as a big seller in the inner cities, for the teenage market," a York salesman told me. "You know, a kid goes, his homies can wish him well."

Companies whose primary source of business is in more lively industries were scavenging for scraps of the death market as well. GeneLink, a Margate, New Jersey, company that deals in DNA testing and storage, was offering the bereaved an opportunity to save a bit more of a loved one than mere dust. The mouth of the dead is swabbed for a cell sample, which is sent to GeneLink's lab in Fort Worth, Texas, where the DNA is extracted and stored for twenty-five years. A kit costs about $100,

and funeral directors will be charging about $295 for collecting a sample. I must admit, I never quite understood why anyone would want this service; after all, if you fear you are at increased risk for some genetically linked problem such as Alzheimer's, you could always test yourself.

Here's an idea that *does* make sense to me: cybergrieving. Jack Martin, president of Simplex Knowledge, an Internet production company in White Plains, New York, has come up with an idea that's bound to appeal to boomers too busy to hop halfway across the continent to weep over Aunt Martha's grave. Mourners will be issued a Website password; a camera will be set up at the funeral, and pictures of the service will be broadcast on the Internet every thirty seconds or so. "The family and funeral director can choose what will be highlighted," says Martin. "The grieving family, the body, the minister whatever." About half of the funeral directors who have learned about Martin's concept see it as a valuable marketing tool, a service they could offer families gratis. The other half see it strictly as profitable: fees could be collected not only from the families (about $200) but *also from the mourners.* "They imagined that someone, say, in New Jersey without Internet access could drop by their funeral home and witness a service going on in California," says Martin. "And then the funeral director could charge each mourner ten or twenty bucks. But frankly I don't think this concept will go over too well. Making people pay to mourn isn't such great publicity for the industry."

Of course, it's possible to bypass the traditional burial altogether. You might want to be put on ice until medical science figures out a cure for what ails you (the first cryonically frozen man, James H. Bedford, just celebrated his thirtieth anniversary of "de-animation," as cryonics enthusiasts call it). Then again, you might want to have yourself mummified. On its Web page, Summum, a New Age, quasi-religious organization in Salt Lake City that practices modern mummification, offers this sales pitch: "Unlike the mummification techniques used by ancient Egyptians, which left the dead shriveled, discolored, and ugly, Summum's method is designed to keep you looking healthy and robust for millennia. The appeal may be to anyone who has labored to stay in shape. Why spend thousands of dollars in health-club fees while you're alive, then let everything go to pot just because you've died?"

Why, indeed.

You know what's real tough about this business? No one's real happy to see you.

—Bob Jones, Jones Funeral Home, Altoona, Pennsylvania

At the end of the day, I was slumped at the hotel bar with a gin and tonic. The convention had no shortage of activities. I could have gone to hear Marvin Hamlisch give a command performance or had my picture taken with former astronaut Buzz Aldrin, who stood around in his flight suit looking a little confused; one funeral director solemnly shook his hand and murmured, "God bless America." But I wasn't up for merriment. I was exhausted. The worst thing about being at a funeral directors' convention was having to be around people who are so nice all the time; if I happened to be going through a door, four funeral directors would materialize from nowhere to open if for me. Despite their somber workaday attire, morticians are a jolly lot, and in a game effort to show they know how to have a good time, everyone wore his snappiest neckwear: I spotted a few screaming eagles, dozens of ball-team logos, and at least one portrait of Larry, Curly, and Moe.

I forgot about the entertainment and instead eavesdropped on war stories. Two guys were fretting about a recent "situation" in which someone had mistakenly cremated the wrong body. Another guy was complaining about a woman who had sued for injury and negligence after she passed out and gave herself a concussion; he had warned her that her mother was in no condition to be viewed, but she had insisted on one last look. Still others were relating a tale in which a colleague had forgotten to take out a pacemaker before cremation—a definite no-no, since batteries explode during incineration.

When the barflies ran out of conversation, they'd inevitably turn to the legend of Larry Titemore, a funeral director in Vermont. In 1995, in addition to embezzling over $75,000 in prepaid funeral funds that were supposed to be placed in an escrow account, Titemore stopped embalming the bodies entrusted to him and left them to ripen.[2] He also practiced a necrological bait

---

[2]*In his 1948 novel* The Loved One, *Evelyn Waugh satirized morticians' eagerness to lock people into prepaying for their own funeral: "Choose now, at leisure and in health, the form of final preparation you require, pay for it while you are best able to do so, shed all anxiety. Pass the buck, Mr. Barlow; Whispering Glades can take it." Recently, a number of lawsuits have been filed against companies refusing to honor preneed contracts. The money is supposed to go into a trust or escrow account, and the interest accrued will compensate for the rate of inflation. But there are two major problems: (1) although the funeral director gets to control the money you have to pay taxes on the interest you'll never see; and (2) governmental oversight varies wildly. In some states, says Sue Simon, publisher of* Preneed Perspective, *preneed trust funds are required and carefully monitored, and in others—such as Washington, D.C., and Alabama—"the funeral director can take your $5,000, go to Atlantic City, and put it on red."*

and switch, selling expensive caskets to families and then removing the bodies before burial and placing them in cheap models, or sometimes into no model at all: when investigators inspected his premises, they found the body of a local resident who had died earlier that winter stuffed into a broken-down hearse. After the service, Titemore had removed him from his pricey casket and then didn't seem quite sure what to do with him. Titemore's license was revoked. After completing his jail time, he found work as a used-car salesman.

A solidly built, bright-eyed man in a black polyester Elvis shirt and ruby jacket sits next to me, sipping Long Island iced teas with his wife. He notices me staring at his ensemble. "Don't get to wear this much around the home," he says. Ben Strickland's his name. Runs Seymour Funeral Home, sweet little operation in North Carolina. Knew he was right for the work when he embalmed a friend; knew nobody could do it better. "Don't want nobody to die, but I gotta eat," he says. Ben is a natural storyteller: we talk about gypsy funerals, where mourners throw money on top of the body; we talk about the fellow who was buried with his chihuahua's ashes. "He and his wife didn't have children. That was their baby," Ben explains. Ben loves everything about his business. Everything but the children. "Touches me real bad to have a child or infant die. Seventy-five, eighty, they lived their life. But a child?" Ben's eyes fill with tears.

Embarrassed, I look away; he thinks I'm looking at his watch. "Like that?" he says, playing with the thick gold band. "Took a lotta teeth to make this'un here."

I look up; Ben's still wiping his eyes, but he's grinning. "Gotcha!" he cries.

No question about it: Death care is becoming a hot career. According to the American Board of Funeral Service Education, since 1990 there has been a 45 percent increase in the number of students enrolled in mortuary-schools. And what used to be almost an entirely male-dominated industry is now increasingly estrogen-rich: in 1996, 33 percent of mortuary school grads were women. "There are several factors at work here," says Gordon Bigelow, ABFSE's executive director. "As we've gone through corporate downsizing, a number of adults looking for second and third careers have focused on funeral service as a recession-proof industry. And then, of course, there's the fact that the baby boom generation is beginning to, ah, terminate." According to the National Funeral Directors Association, the average funeral director makes about $49,000 a year (twice that in large, metropolitan firms). And considering that one needs no

more than two years of college to get a funeral director's license, the Grim Reaper offers a pretty promising and secure future.

"It's becoming cooler to be a funeral director than it once was," says one young buck, whose perfectly tailored sharkskin suit suggests one too many viewings of the movie *GoodFellas*. We are shouting at each other over the din of an oompah band; Wilbert Funeral Services is sponsoring an Oktoberfest, complete with knee-slapping dancers in Tyrolean hats and leder-hosen. Y. B. scans the room, a trace of a sneer on his blandly handsome face. "This is still a very clip-on-tie-and-polyester crowd, though."

Maybe, but the clip-on set is what made this country great. The vast majority of funeral directors are solid citizens in their communities, overwhelmingly conservative and Republican. Rotarians and Kiwanis Club members, they believe in boosterism and practice it too.

We whine about how much money they make, how they capitalize on grief and loss. Our irrationality about death leads us to believe that no one has a right to make a living from it. But let's look at it this way: It's 2:00 A.M., and after a long and debilitating illness Nana has shuffled off this mortal coil. In your house. In the summer. Your air conditioner has broken down. By the time you find her, Nana is beginning to leak.

Do you want their job? I didn't think so.

Underneath the lingering scent of lilies and formaldehyde, however, there lurks the unmistakable stench of money. Three months after the Cincinnati convention, I'm sitting in on a seminar called "Death Care IV: An Undertaking in New York." It's for financial analysts and investors who track the rapidly consolidating funeral industry; the tacit theme of the day is "Stiffs: They're a Growth Market!"

Thinking I'm also an analyst, an impeccably groomed brunette—one of only about five women in the packed room—leans over and proffers some helpful advice. "Projections for the next quarter are looking good," she whispers. "The strain of flu that's hit this season is *really* virulent."

Thirty years ago, when she wrote *The American Way of Death*, Jessica Mitford accurately predicted just about every trend that has since come to pass in the funeral industry—most significantly, the rise of the giant funeral chain. Together, the Houston-based Service Corporation International (SCI) and The Loewen Group, headquartered in Burnaby, British Columbia, own about 2,000, or 10 percent, of America's mortuaries. (Smaller chains such as Car-

riage Services and Stewart Enterprises account for another 300 or so.) Traditionally, funeral homes were the ultimate mom-and-pop operations, run by legions of slightly creepy moms and pops whose business acumen was usually not the soundest. Jim St. George recalls how the funeral home where he worked tried to compete with lower-priced mortuaries: "We only had one person standing around to say hello to strangers at the visitation instead of three or four. Oh, and we didn't put candy in the candy dishes, mourners weren't allowed to use the coffee room, and we didn't fold the first paper on the toilet roll into a little triangle, like they do in hotels."

With Pecksniffian economies like these commonplace, it's no wonder someone would start taking a McDonald's-like approach to marketing and service. Quietly, relentlessly, SCI and Loewen have been coming into town and buying up homes and cemeteries, leaving the current management in place—at least for a while. One funeral director compares the takeovers to the movie *Invasion of the Body Snatchers*. "You think you're dealing with the same people you've always known and trusted. But they're not. They're pods. The business has nothing to do with community values anymore. Everything about the way they run their business now has to be decided from a headquarters that knows nothing and cares nothing about the community."

The big chains don't see it this way. They say they're leaving the funeral directors to do what they do best—caretaking—and letting the suits make the business decisions. They wax poetic about economies of scale. SCI, for example, will go into an area, buy up five or six funeral homes, and pool their resources—with one centralized embalming site, a roving staff and a fleet of hearses that can float from one home to another, caskets bought in volume, and so forth.

But if you think consolidation means that the cost of dying is suddenly going to become more reasonable, think again. The *Seattle Times* found that in Washington State where 49 percent of the funeral homes are owned by chains, the cost of funerals has risen by as much as 65 percent since 1992—because the real client is no longer the family of the deceased but the stockholder.

In fact, so bullish is Wall Street on death care that this year saw the introduction of the Pauzé Tombstone Fund, a mutual fund diversified across the death-care industry. The fund's prospectus is filled with exciting bar charts and graphs, showing how, if Tombstone had been around since 1986, it would have soundly beaten the performances of the Dow Jones Industrial Average, Standard & Poor's, and the Russell 3000 Index: "Population demographics indicate that the death care industry will continue to experience long-term expansion due to the aging of the U.S. population and the estimated growing number of future annual deaths." In a quiet moment, you can almost hear the sound of investors hyperventilating.

Back at the seminar, the senior financial officer for Stewart Enterprises, Ronald Patron, confidently quotes predictions that his company will see a 20 percent growth. Someone raises his hand and asks Patron the question on everyone's mind. SCI's recent attempt at a hostile takeover of Loewen had failed, thus preventing what one industry critic said was "the equivalent to Pepsi and Coca-Cola merging." But the FTC made noises about regulating prices and launched antitrust investigations in eleven states. "We don't see any problems in either of those areas," Patron said soothingly. "The FTC recently renewed its rules about full disclosure of pricing, but there's no *regulation* of pricing."

Perhaps I just imagined I heard a collective sigh of relief. It was sort of appalling. Naturally, I went home and bought stock in SCI.

The public backlash against funeral monopolies is in its infancy, but it will die young without some government intervention. Like health care, the funeral industry can't be run solely as an enterprise that responds to market forces, because none of us have a choice in being part of it.

Or do we? Can we opt out of the system? In California, home of bizarre trends that eventually become mainstream, a group of community activists have started the Natural Death Care Project, which teaches the bereaved to care for and bury their loved ones. "In all but eight states in this country, you don't need a funeral director at all," says Lisa Carlson, author of *Caring for Your Own Dead: The Final Act of Love.* "You have to learn how to do the paperwork, but it's certainly not that hard." And the body itself? "Care for people when they're dead is the same as when they're alive, except you don't have to feed them," she says. In fact, it's not much more involved than that—especially if the body is kept cold and disposed of within a couple of days.

Before Jessica Mitford died of brain cancer last year, she made a last request to Karen Leonard, the consumer activist who was also Mitford's researcher. "Decca [Mitford's nickname] wanted me to send her funeral bill to SCI. 'After all,' she said to me, 'look how much fame I brought them!'" Leonard sent the bill, $475 for direct cremation, to CEO Robert Waldrip, pointing out how much more expensive it would have been if Mitford had been cremated at an SCI-affiliated funeral home. "I wanted him to know he was in Decca's thoughts at the end," Leonard says. "Oddly enough, we never heard from him."

Unlike Jessica Mitford, I think we are the victims not of the funeral industry but of ourselves. A friend of mine, a former flack at the public relations firm Hill and Knowlton, described a campaign for the National Funeral Directors Association she worked on a few years ago: "The idea was, we really had to create a cachet for death. You wouldn't cheap out on a wedding—why would you do it for a funeral?" The campaign never quite got off the ground, but it spoke eloquently to the guilt and desires of a generation that perhaps wasn't quite as kind to its elders as it should have been, a generation that trashed its parents' values and then tried desperately to acquire the things those values—respect, hard work, constancy, sacrifice—bought.

In some ways, we are more careful consumers than we used to be. But we are also terribly unsure of ourselves, unsure of our goodness, unsure of our souls. What a relief it is to be able to make up for our sins to the living by being generous to them after they're dead. When it comes to their future livelihoods, I'm quite sure the funeral directors of America may rest in peace.

THE DEATH POETRY OF EMILY DICKINSON*

WILLIAM COONEY, PH.D
Briar Cliff College, Sioux City, Iowa

ABSTRACT

The topic of death is an important theme in the work of Emily Dickinson, one of America's greatest poets. Dickinson scholars debate whether her focus on death (one quarter of all her poems) is an unhealthy and morbid obsession, or, rather, a courageous recognition that life itself cannot be understood fully except from the vantage point of the grave (just as light cannot be fully appreciated without the recognition of its opposite, i.e., darkness). Following the latter view, Dickinson's penetrating insights into death are examined. Some of her best known death poems are presented and briefly discussed (reference is also made to many other Dickinson poems, and insights are also drawn from her many letters). Brief comparisons of Dickinson's views to certain philosophers (for example, Nietzsche) are made, in order to provide a wider context of exploration into these important themes. In the end, Dickinson contends that affirmation of life is impossible without an examination of death—the article therefore ends with her famous poem about that affirmation.

Emily Dickinson (1830–1886) was an American poet of incontestable genius who, as Richard Sewall has said, "looked very deep and saw very clear" (1988). Her poems invite us to penetrate life itself, and death as a means toward understanding life. Some have said that she was obsessed with this topic (pointing to a fascination, for example, with death masks) (Benfey, 1984, p. 96). It is estimated that a quarter of all of Dickinson's poems deal with death. Conrad Aiken (1963) tells us that "she seems to have thought of it constantly—she died all her life, she probed death daily. 'That bareheaded life under grass worries one like a wasp', she wrote. Ultimately, the obsession became morbid" (p. 14). Henry Wells (1947) on the other hand, has argued that "there is remarkably little morbidity" in Dickinson's death poems. "Death," he continues, "became for Emily the supreme touchstone for life" (p. 93). Other scholars agree with Wells. Richard Wilbur (1963), for example, remarks that

---

From *Omega*, Vol. 37, No. 3, 1998, pp. 241-249. Reprinted by permission of Baywood Publishing Co., Inc.

Dickinson's contemplations on death are really an attempt to look at life "from the vantage of the grave" (p. 136). And Genevieve Taggard (1930) in her marvelous book about Dickinson's life, has said that "she saw Death's value. He should be her focus; not her woe" (p. 323).

According to this view, then, Dickinson should not be seen as obsessed with death but with life itself insofar as it can be understood from the grave. "A Death blow is a Life blow to Some," she writes (1955, #816). As Wells argues,

> Death becomes a gateway to vitality, lifelessness to life. The ultimate of the positive hinges upon the ultimate of the negative. . . . Emily outstares death: she looks so intently and piercingly upon it that its terrors vanish, as fog before the sun. . . . To Emily, death ceases to be a mere theme or problem and becomes the key to art, to beauty, and to life. . . . Death becomes for Emily the mountain of vision. Like the highest summit in a range, it commands the panorama of the whole. . . . Since for Emily, at least, death is symbol of reality, it becomes not the bitter dead-end of the grave—though on one level it remains that—but the gateway to reality and hence to life, joy, and ecstasy (pp. 95–96, 98).

And Emily Dickinson did find ecstasy in life. She once told T. W. Higginson (who later, along with Mabel Loomis Todd, became her first editor) that "I find ecstasy in living—the mere sense of living is joy enough" (1958, #342A). She begins a poem with "Water, is taught by thirst" (1955, #135); and in paraphrasing this we can argue that her contemplations on the mysteries of death were motivated by the belief also that life is taught by death. In a letter she writes that "Life is death we're lengthy at, death the hinge to life" (1958, #281). And we can imagine her speaking of life itself when she says in a poem, "I see the better—in the Dark— . . . /And in the Grave—I see Thee best—" (1955, #611). "This Consciousness that is aware" she also writes, " . . . Will be the one aware of Death" (1955, #822). Death, then, is not simply a terror to be feared; "So give me back to death/The Death I never feared . . ." (1955, #1632), it is also our teacher. Through this dark prism Emily Dickinson, in Sewall's (1988) words, "tells us again and again what it's like to be alive."

In this respect, Dickinson bears similarity to the German existentialist Martin Heidegger (1889–1976) who taught that the human being is a *"Sein sum Tode"*—a being toward death (1962, p. 306ff). But she is also like the French Christian existentialist Gabriel Marcel (1889–1973) in recognizing that it is the very essence of love, in reaching out toward the other, to deny death of our loved ones (1965, p. 147). She writes, for example, "Unable are the Loved to die/For Love is Immortality,/Nay it is Deity" (1955, #809).

And Emily Dickinson loved deeply. One need only look to her many letters wherein she expresses her love, and also her need to be loved. It is true that she became very reclusive, but she never stopped loving. Some would have it that it was an unrequited love that led to the seclusion. But for a more complete picture one has to dig deeper than this into Dickinson's tortured psyche. For she was a lonesome soul, like the Danish religious existentialist Soren Kierkegaard (1813–1855), who praised the need for solitude (1946, p. 363). "The Soul selects her own Society," she says in a famous poem (1955, #303). But like Friedrich Nietzsche (1844–1900), the German atheistic existentialist, she rejected the religious answers to life's mysteries (1961, pp. 52–53). She refused (to the frustration of her very prominent and Puritan family at Amherst, Massachusetts) to be among "the elect" of God (Sewall, 1988). And again like Nietzsche (who spent his last years in mental collapse), she lived near the boundaries of sanity and insanity. She seemed odd to many. Higginson referred to her as "partially cracked" (1958, p. 570). Upon meeting her face to face for the first time, he remarked that "I never was with any one who drained my nerve power so much. Without touching her, she drew from me" (1958, p. 476). And later, on recalling the meeting in the Atlantic Monthly, he writes "The impression made upon me was that of an excess of tension, and of abnormal life. . . . She was much too enigmatical a being for me to solve in an hour's interview . . ." (p. 476).

Dickinson was enigmatic. She exhibited strange behavior during this and the rest of her life as a recluse. Upon receiving guests she would rarely reveal herself face to face, preferring to converse between walls or in doorways hidden and half-hidden. In her letters she would ask for understanding. "Pardon my sanity," she says ironically, "in a world insane, and love me if you will, for I had rather be loved than to be called a king in earth, or a lord in Heaven" (#185). In 1862 she told Higginson of "a terror—since September—I could tell to none—and so I sing, as the Boy does by the Burying Ground—because I am afraid" (#261). In 1864 she writes of mental collapse in a poem: "I felt a Cleaving in my Mind—/As if my Brain had split—/I tried to match it—Seam by Seam—/But could not make them fit" (1955, #937). And there are many other references in her poetry, if they be taken as autobiography, to her mental troubles: "My Life had stood—a Loaded Gun—"(#754); "I lived on Dread—"

(#770); "I've dropped my Brain—My Soul is numb—" (#1046). In 1884 she suffered a nervous breakdown which was to trouble her during the last two years of her life (she died in 1886 of Bright's disease, a kidney ailment). But while these individual moments of mental darkness are no doubt important, still it is true that Emily had always been a troubled spirit. As early as 1852 she wrote "when nobody sees, I brush away big tears with the corner of my apron" (1958, #85).

It is that troubled spirit which seems to have given birth to her art. Nietzsche wrote that "one must still have chaos in oneself to be able to give birth to a dancing star" (p. 129). Dickinson spoke of the "Vesuvius at Home" (1955, #1705) to signal her own inner chaos. "On my volcano grows the Grass," she writes (#1677). According to Adrienne Rich, "Vesuvius at Home is how she perceived herself . . . It's the potential for chaos" (Sewall, 1988). Joyce Carol Oates agrees and adds that "It's also the Vesuvius that drives VanGogh insane. It's also the dark night of the soul" (1988). Dickinson seemed strangely attracted to darkness rather than to light. "Night is my favorite Day" she says in a letter (1958, #843). And many of her references to light reveal painful images (some have suggested an optical ailment as a possible cause for this) (Barker, 1987, p. 2).

Dickinson's inner chaos made her painfully aware of a potential danger to her soul. She remarked to Higginson that she had "no Monarch in my life, and cannot rule myself, and when I try to organize—my little Force explodes—and leaves me bare and charred" (1958, #271). And when he first suggested that she delay publishing her work, thinking it a little "wayward," she wrote "You think my gait 'spasmodic'—I am in danger—Sir—/You think me 'uncontrolled'—I have no Tribunal" (#265).

So Emily Dickinson faced the chaos within herself. In having no tribunal, as Sewall remarks, she was able to write "for herself, and therefore she was free" (1988). Only several of her poems were published in her lifetime; and then, only anonymously. She hid her poems away. No one, not even Higginson, was aware of the volumes of work she was stowing away in her private room. She instructed her sister Lavinia to destroy her papers after she died—the great Roman poet Virgil (70–19 B.C.) had given the same instructions regarding his classic *Aeneid* (1969, p. 18). And when "Vinnie" (as Dickinson preferred to call her) began to take up the task, she was overwhelmed with what she found. Thankfully for the world she disobeyed the dying wish. Dickinson's art soon became known to the world. No doubt this was her true desire. She once remarked to

Higginson that not publishing her work would be as "foreign to my thought, as Firmament to Fin—. If fame belonged to me, I could not escape her . . ." (1958, #265). It seems fitting that one who sought so much from death would receive fame only after she had passed through its door. We who are still alive are the benefactors. We who have not yet succumbed to the dark night stand ready to receive the truth from her art.

We begin with a poem which, in talking about death, links art and truth together in a style reminiscent of the romantic poet John Keats' (1795–1821) "Ode on a Grecian Urn"—"Beauty is truth, truth beauty,—that is all/Ye know on earth, and all ye need to know" (1968).

> I died for Beauty—but was scarce
> Adjusted in the Tomb
> When One who died for Truth, was lain
> In an adjoining Room—
>
> He questioned softly "Why I failed"?
> "For Beauty", I replied—
> "And I—for Truth—Themself are One—
> We Brethren, are", He said—
>
> And so, as Kinsmen, met a Night—
> We talked between the Rooms—
> Until the Moss had reached our lips—
> And covered up—our names—
> (1955, #449)

In reading this poem one can almost "feel" the act of dying. It is as if we are brought to death's door; it standing open and revealed with stark realism. One can only read with awe and wonder, and ask how anyone can have experienced the reality of death so crisply. And how is it that we, the living readers of this poem, are able to recognize these unmistakable ciphers of death? Is it because we, who still participate in life, are somehow aware of life's opposite? Is it because those still in the light are able to detect the nature and quality of darkness?

And what of the connections that Dickinson seems to be drawing between beauty and truth ("Themself are One")? The great philosopher Plato (428–348 B.C.), too, links beauty and truth (as well as goodness) together. Beauty and truth, he taught, must finally collapse into goodness as the ultimate reality (Kaplan, 1950, *The Republic*, Book VII).

Beside these philosophical conundrums, there lies the real value of the death poem—it brings us there to feel the truth for ourselves. It is an example of what Kierkegaard called "subjective truth": a truth to be passionately felt (pp. 210ff). And while the ultimate point may be to look more closely at life, still there is no reducing the real horrors of death. Dickinson faces death squarely and eye-to-eye.

> Safe in their Alabaster Chambers—
> Untouched by Morning—
> And untouched by Noon—
> Lie the meek members of the Resurrection—
> Rafter of Satin—and Roof of Stone!
> Grand go the Years—in the Crescent—above them—
> Worlds scoop their Arcs—
> And Firmaments—row—
> Diadems—drop—and Doges—surrender—
> Soundless as dots—on a Disc of Snow—
> (1955, #216, version of 1861)

One difference between this and poem #449 is that it is cast in the third person. In 449, Dickinson imagines the experience of death in the first person; in 216 she speaks about the death of others. Another difference is the introduction of the element of safety: "Safe in their Alabaster Chambers"—how ironic that true safety only comes when we are in the tomb. But safe from what? She seems to mean that we are safe from the daily troubles which life usually brings us—we are "untouched" by "Morning" and "Noon." A key similarity between the two poems is that both end with the unavoidable and undeniable reality of silence: "We talked between the Rooms—/Until the Moss had reached our lips—/And covered up—our names—" (449); and "Diadems drop—and Doges—surrender—/Soundless as dots—on a Disc of Snow" (216). Such reference to silence or stillness is a common theme found in Dickinson's death poems. "I heard a Fly buzz—when I died—" she writes, "The Stillness in the Room/Was like the Stillness in the Air—/Between the Heaves of Storm" (#465). But the silence in 216 brings a freedom: "Diadems drop,"—diadems comes from the Greek for "bound up" as with a rope. She seems to be saying that in death we are no longer bound up by the troubles of life. And it brings a surrender: "Doges surrender,"—doges comes from the Latin for "leaders." In death, there are no leaders except death itself, to which all must surrender. Even when we try to avoid death, it finds us, as she reveals in another poem: "Because I could not stop for Death—/He kindly stopped for me—" (#712).

> I felt a Funeral, in my Brain,
> And Mourners to and fro
> Kept treading—treading—till it seemed
> That Sense was breaking through—
>
> And when they all were seated,
> A Service, like a Drum—
> Kept beating—beating—till I thought
> My Mind was going numb—
>
> And then I heard them lift a Box
> And creak across my Soul
> With those same Boots of Lead, again,

> Then Space—began to toll,
> As all the Heavens were a Bell,
> And Being, but an Ear,
> And I, and Silence, some strange Race
> Wrecked, solitary, here—
>
> And then a Plank in Reason, broke,
> And I dropped down, and down—
> And hit a World, at every plunge,
> And Finished knowing—then—
> (#280)

Here we revert back to the first person. The focus is on the sensory experience of death itself, highlighting "Sense," "Mind," "Space," "Silence," "Reason," and "knowing." Dickinson feels the sensations of death, and she feels the silence of empty space as well. Paradoxically, she hears that silence: "Then Space—began to toll,/ As all the Heavens were a Bell,/ And Being, but an Ear." But the senses are breaking down, and so is reason: "And then a Plank in Reason, broke." And we are left not only in silence, as in poems 216 and 449, but with the end of knowledge: "And Finished knowing—then—." Dickinson does not attempt to disguise the realities of death. She seems to be saying here, like the philosopher Epicurus (341–271 B.C.), that death signals the end of the feeling, sensing, knowing subject (Epicurus, 1997, p. 78).

Is this not a view of death as unconquerable? Is there no hope for an afterlife? We have already seen Dickinson's rejections of her family's religion. And in another poem she hints at the failure of religion to overcome the finalities of death: "Much Gesture, from the Pulpit—/Strong Hallelujahs roll—/Narcotics cannot still the Tooth/That nibbles at the soul—" (1955, #501). She also writes that "No Drug for Consciousness—can be—/Alternative to die/Is Nature's only Pharmacy/For Being's Malady—" (#786).

But what do the death poems really teach us about life? How does this darkness cast light? The hint, perhaps, comes with the following poem:

> Of Death I try to think like this—
> The Well in which they lay us
> Is but the Likeness of the Brook
> That menaced not to slay us,
> But to invite by that Dismay
> Which is the Zest of sweetness
> To the same Flower Hesperian,
> Decoying but to greet us—
>
> I do remember when a Child
> With bolder Playmates straying
> To where a Brook that seemed a Sea
> Withheld us by its roaring
> From just a Purple Flower beyond
> Until constrained to clutch it
> If Doom itself were the result,
> The boldest leaped, and clutched it—
> (#1558)

Here death is seen not as the "menace," but rather as that which "invites" us. Invites us where and to do what? To the "Flower Hesperian" (the evening flower); to the "Zest of sweetness" (is this not life itself?). The "boldest" among us leap to clutch at the flower of life. Death disguised ("decoying") as a "roaring" "Sea," is there "to greet us" and to provide that obstacle to overcome.

Dickinson's ideas here resemble Nietzsche again. He wrote of the "overman" (*übermensch*)—the one who becomes the master over one's own life—the overman overcomes obstacles, and death is the ultimate obstacle (pp. 124ff). Dickinson's notion of death as the roaring sea is also reminiscent of Nietzsche's view that our lives lie before us like an open sea. "The sea, our sea, lies open again"; he wrote, "perhaps there has never yet been such an 'open sea'" (p. 448). The boldest ones are like Nietzsche's overman—they leap and clutch death. In doing so, they affirm life. And so we end with a poem about that affirmation.

The Props assist the House
Until the House is built
and then the Props withdraw
And adequate, erect,
The House support itself
And cease to recollect
The Auger and the Carpenter—
Just such a retrospect
Hath the perfected Life—
A past of Plank and Nail
And slowness—then the Scaffolds drop
Affirming it a Soul
(#1142)

This poem can be read within the context of the death poems we have examined. The "Props" which assist us in our self-development represent family, religion, society, culture—all that which nurtures us, but which also disguises, through various myths, the realities of death. Self realization and actualization ("The House support itself") require that we allow that the "Props withdraw" and "Scaffolds drop." In allowing this we do not reject them entirely, nor our love for them—there simply is no need to lean on them anymore. In facing death we affirm our own souls and stand "adequate, erect" toward life.

References

Aiken, C. (1963). Emily Dickinson. In R. Sewall (Ed.), *Emily Dickinson: A collection of critical essays* (pp. 9–15). Englewood Cliffs, NJ: Prentice Hall.

Barker, W. (1987). *Lunacy of light: Emily Dickinson and the experience of metaphor.* Carbondale: Southern Illinois University Press.

Benfey, C. E. G. (1984). *Emily Dickinson and the problem of others.* Amherst: University of Massachusetts Press.

Dickinson, E. (1955). *The complete poems of Emily Dickinson.* T. H. Johnson (Ed.). Boston: Little, Brown.

Dickinson, E. (1958). *The letters of Emily Dickinson.* T. H. Johnson (Ed.). Cambridge: Harvard University Press.

Epicurus. (1997). Letter to Menoeceus. In (W. T. Jones). *Approaches to Ethics.* New York: McGraw-Hill.

Heidegger, M. (1962). *Being and time* (J. Macqarrie & E. Robinson, Trans.). New York: Harper and Row.

Keats, J. (1968). Ode on a Grecian urn. In the *Norton anthology of English literature* (Vol. 2) p. 532. New York: W. W. Norton and Company.

Kierkegaard. (1946). *A Kierkegaard anthology.* R. Bretall (Ed.). New York: Modern Library.

Marcel, G. (1965). *Being and having* (K. Farrer, Trans.). New York: Harper Torchbooks.

Nietzsche. (1961). *The portable Nietzsche* (Walter Kaufmann, Trans.). New York: The Viking Press.

Plato. (1950). *Dialogues of Plato.* J. D. Kaplan (Ed.). New York: Pocket Books.

Sewall, R. (1988). *"Visions and Voices," episode 3: Emily Dickinson.* Annenberg/CPB project (PBS Video interviews with Joyce Carol Oates, Adrienne Rich, and Robert Sewall). New York: The Center for Visual History.

Taggard, G. (1930). *The life and mind of Emily Dickinson.* New York: Alfred A. Knopf.

Virgil. (1969). *Virgil's Aeneid* (J. Dryden, Trans.). Harvard Classics Volume 13, New York; Collier And Son.

Wilbur, R. (1963). Sumptuous destitution. In R. Sewall (Ed.), *Emily Dickinson: A collection of critical essays* (pp. 127–136). Englewood Cliffs: Prentice Hall.

Well, H. W. (1947). *Introduction to Emily Dickinson.* Chicago: Hendricks House.

Direct reprint requests to:

William Cooney, Ph.D.
Department of Philosophy
Briar Cliff College
Sioux City, IA 51104

Putting death on ice

Cryonicists preserving bodies for a possible thaw, second chance at life

By CLINT O'CONNOR
PLAIN DEALER REPORTER

Of all the fantastical, futuristic experiments of the '60s, none was stranger than what Robert Ettinger helped to do to James Bedford in 1967. He froze him.

Bedford, a 73-year-old psychology professor, had died of cancer. He agreed to be the first frozen human in the cold new world of cryonics–the practice of freezing and preserving a dead body in hopes of later reviving it. Thirty years later, he is frozen in, of all places, the desert. Bedford's body rests in liquid nitrogen at minus 320 degrees Fahrenheit inside the Alcor Life Extension Foundation in Scottsdale, Ariz.

If it works, if some day doctors can resuscitate Bedford's body, his name might be remembered like Christopher Columbus' or Neil Armstrong's. If it fails, if it is simply so much scientific fantasy, Bedford will just be another forgotten dead guy.

Cryonics was mostly the stuff of science fiction until Ettinger, a physics professor from Michigan, popularized the idea in his book, "The Prospect of Immortality" in 1964. Three years later came the Bedford freezing and the founding of three cryonics organizations, including Ettinger's Cryonics Society of Michigan (now the Immortalist Society). His society later opened a storage center and had its first freezing in 1977.

Today, there are only four such facilities in the world, all in the United States: Ettinger's Cryonics Institute, Alcor, and Trans-Time Inc. and Cryospan, both in California.

True believers have faith that technology will become so advanced in 50, 100, 200 years, that scientists will be able to awaken, or "reanimate" the frozen bodies and cure them of whatever they died of–old age, cancer, heart disease.

It is completely theoretical. No one has ever been unfrozen.

It also provokes a slew of legal, ethical and religious questions. Not to mention medical.

"Most people think of death as a yes or no. They assume you go out like a light," says Ettinger, 78, now semiretired and living in Scottsdale.

Cryonics was mostly the stuff of science fiction until Ettinger ... popularized the idea in his book "The Prospect of Immortality" in 1964.

"But in this country alone, thousands of people every year are revived after clinical death, even cessation of brain waves. How many drowning victims have been revived through basic CPR?"

Freezing a dead body in liquid nitrogen is vastly different, however, and Ettinger concedes that the strongest objections come from the medical profession.

"It strikes me as an unwillingness to come to terms with the reality of death," says Thomas Murray, director of the Center for Biomedical Ethics at Case Western Reserve University's School of Medicine. "It is almost certainly a waste of money on the part of people who are doing it."

Ettinger has been battling the naysayers for three decades. "The medical community says the damage by freezing is so great that it can't be done," he says. "That is arrogant. They have no basis or expertise for predicting the limits of future capabilities."

He notes that previous generations predicted man would never fly, reach the moon, cure polio or transplant a human heart. Anything is possible.

And some people are willing to spend as much as $150,000 hoping he is right.

The two Mrs. Ettingers

In a one-story, industrial park warehouse in Clinton Township, Mich., the Cryonics Institute maintains 22 frozen bodies.

They are tied up in sleeping bags, floating in liquid nitrogen, inside large, white fiberglass cryostats (cryonic storage units). Their bodies are kept at minus 320 degrees Fahrenheit.

The warehouse, a bland blend of cinder block and drywall, is the poplar opposite of high tech. Sally Bazan, the institute's executive director, points to one of the white containers and says, "That's the two Mrs. Ettingers."

Rhea Ettinger, Robert's mother, died in 1977 at age 78 and was frozen at the institute. Robert's first wife, Elaine, died and was frozen in 1987, at age 65.

"The only person we've lost in my family was my father," says Robert Ettinger, who along with his current wife, brother, son and other relatives, plans to be frozen. "He died and was buried. I was never able to persuade him to make arrangements."

Three other cryostats hold 20 bodies. They range in age from 42 to 92 and come from several states and countries, including France, Germany, Norway and Australia. They are lawyers, professors, an engineer and his wife. The people are not alone. There are also six frozen dogs and cats; the three cats share a short silver-colored cylinder called a catstat.

The dead bodies are called "patients"; a freezing is a "suspension." Arrangements for a suspension are elaborate. You must sign a contract well in advance, have your funding in place, fill out a Next Of Kin Agreement, and a Uniform Donor Form.

The latter states that you are making an "anatomical gift" to your cryonics center, and that upon your death you should be delivered there as soon as possible "without embalming or autopsy." The donor form buys cryonicists more cooperation from attending physicians and morticians.

At presstime, there were 73 suspended humans in America, and fewer than 1,000 people worldwide signed up for freezings.

One barrier is the cost. Trans-Time Inc. in San Leandro, Calif., charges the most: $150,000 for a suspension. Cryospan, in Rancho Cucamonga, Calif., and Alcor, a nonprofit foundation, charge about $120,000. At the Cryonics Institute, also nonprofit, it costs $28,000.

The payment covers the initial freezing; maintenance, which is largely adding liquid nitrogen to the storage tanks about once a week; and funding to support the center.

Financial stability is crucial. In 1976, the now-defunct Cryonics Society of California went broke and stopped pumping liquid nitrogen. Several frozen people thawed out.

"That rocked the cryonics industry. It set us back a good 10 years," says Jim Yount, chief operating officer of the American Cryonics Society in Mountain View, Calif. "We do a lot more fail-safing now to keep that

from ever happening again. And the organizations understand the importance of being financially sound."

Leaving the body behind

One method that uses less storage space is a "neuro-suspension"—freezing the head or brain only. Alcor will do a neuro for $50,000. It has 22 neuro-suspensions and 13 whole bodies. Why do the majority freeze only their heads?

"For one thing it's cheaper," says Brian Shock, Alcor's membership manager. "Also, their body may be old and worn out. The person may have died of cancer and the body is ravaged. What we're trying to do here is preserve a person's identity, memory. If you believe in cryonics, then you believe that whatever is you is encased in your brain."

A live, functioning brain is filled with identity and memories. Cryonicists are working with dead frozen brains.

"The question is can you freeze the brain and preserve it in a way that anything can come of it," says Case Western's Murray. "When you talk about an entire human brain, it seems the probability is pretty slim."

Thomas Donaldson was willing to test that probability in 1988. A California mathematics professor, Donaldson, then 45, was diagnosed with an inoperable brain tumor. He decided he wanted to be cryonically suspended before his brain deteriorated. But that would have been murder, or assisted suicide. Donaldson sued to be suspended while still alive, to have his head removed and frozen for some future revival date when his cancer might be cured.

In 1992, California's 2nd District Court of Appeal ruled that Donaldson had "no constitutional right to a state-assisted suicide," and that it could not prevent criminal prosecution of the cryonics company manager who performed the suspension.

Donaldson was furious, and became an outspoken advocate for cryonicists' rights. Then a funny thing happened. His cancer went into remission.

He is now enjoying better health as a computer consultant and author.

"It turned out I didn't need it, so here I am," says Donaldson from his home in Half Moon Bay, Calif. "I'm doing better. I've been very lucky."

The natural question is: Aren't you glad you didn't have your head cut off?

But Donaldson says it was more of a test case, that he may not have gone through with it after all.

"We will succeed eventually," he says. "It won't be me. But someday the law will allow someone to be cryonically suspended before they are legally dead."

If neuro-suspensions are ever successful, you would still need a new body.

Cryonicists mention as yet undiscovered technology for "growing bodies," or cloning.

"There's a wrinkle in that plan," says Murray, who is part of a team that prepared a report on cloning for President Clinton's National Bioethics Advisory Commission.

"If and when human cloning ever becomes possible, people who have frozen their heads and want a new body cloned would have to deal with a whole other body with a whole other head," he says. "It would be a baby that would have to grow up. Then, at a certain age, that person would have to consent to having its head ripped off and replaced by the frozen one."

Ettinger's institute does not do heads. "We think it's a public relations negative," he says.

The Michigan authorities might not warm up to it either.

"That would be considered a mutilation," says Bazan.

Rolling the ice dice

Most cryonicists are realistic about one thing: the unbelievable odds against revival. At the Cryonics Institute, the contract is clear about the experimental endeavor.

Under "Warranties," it says the institute does not guarantee that a pa-

---

How they do it

By CLINT O'CONNOR

PLAIN DEALER REPORTER

The Cryonics Institute in Michigan maintains 22 frozen bodies, called "patients." Here is the process they follow.

1. Once you have been declared dead, doctors or morticians will work to keep you cool (packing the head and chest with bags of ice). They inject you with heparin to prevent blood clots, hook you up to a heart-lung machine to keep oxygen and blood moving through your system artificially, and get you to the cryonics center as quickly as possible.

The optimum time from death to arrival at the center is less than an hour. Some patients have arrived as late as six hours after death.

2. At the center, your body is put on a table in the perfusion room. A team of three or four technicians work to drain the blood out of your body and inject a cryoprotective agent (a glycerin-based solution) to get as much moisture as possible out of the tissues, so the organs don't crack during freezing.

3. The body is then dried off and wrapped in a cotton sheet. It is placed, cocoonlike, into a standard sleeping bag, head first, with the open end by the feet tied off. The body is placed in a large brown box lined with styrofoam and packed with dry ice. It remains there for seven days to slowly bring the temperature down. By the time the body is removed, it is about minus 112 degrees Fahrenheit.

4. Next, the body is moved to another large brown box, the bottom lined with liquid nitrogen. For another week, it is slowly lowered, a little further each day, as more liquid nitrogen is added. Eventually it will be completely immersed in the liquid nitrogen at a temperature of minus 320 degrees Fahrenheit (or minus 196 Celsius).

5. The final step moves you to a cryostat to be stored with other bodies immersed in liquid nitrogen. The storage units are topped off with liquid nitrogen about once a week; excess air and gases are pumped out of the unit by a vacuum, weekly or monthly, to optimize insulation.

---

tient "can or shall ever be revived or rehabilitated, that the cause of the patient's death can be reversed, that future social institutions will permit the patient's revival, or that the methods used to cryonically suspend the patient will or can be successful."

It's a complete risk. So why do it?

"I just figured what have I got to lose?" says Randy Szabla, 55, an electronic technician from Farmington Hills, Mich.

"I have always questioned dying, and I don't want to die. This way, I could die and have a chance of coming back. I would just like to prolong my life as long as possible."

Szabla and his wife Dianne, 55, have both signed up to be frozen.

"I kind of laughed about the whole concept at first," says Dianne, who sells investments. "But then I decided, what do I have to lose? Most people think it's a little crazy. But now that

they're cloning sheep and so forth, this doesn't seem that far-fetched."

As bizarre as cryonics may seem, the related sciences have been in use for many years. Sir James Dewar liquified hydrogen in 1898; helium was liquified 10 years later. It was the beginning of cryogenics, the science of producing extremely low temperatures.

Cryogenics has since produced liquid oxygen and rocket fuel for space flight and improved the durability of everything from engine parts to violin strings. Cryosurgeons use the low temperatures to isolate and kill off tumors.

Cryobiologists use freezing methods to store sperm and eggs, and embryos for in vitro fertilization. They have also frozen red blood cells, corneas and skin for future use. But they have yet to successfully freeze large organs, such as hearts and livers, for future transplant.

Some cryobiologists have taken dogs, frogs and hamsters, as well as hearts from rabbits and rats, down to near-freezing temperatures, for a short time, then revived them.

But they were alive and cooled, not dead and frozen. Cryobiologists do not see much hope for frozen humans.

"Most scientists view the damage to the frozen tissue as insurmountable," says Ken Diller, director of the biomedical engineering program at the University of Texas. "In order to successfully reversibly freeze something, it is necessary to get the cryoprotective agent in and out of the system at the cellular level. We have not been able to do that successfully with individual organs, let alone a whole body. That is such a megajump forward based on our current scientific technology."

But it is the unknown technology that appeals to future freezees. Several cryonicists pin their hopes on nanotechnology, a potential microscopic manufacturing technique suggested at the Massachusetts Institute of Technology in the 1970s that is still in the developmental stage.

"Nanotechnology would allow us to manufacture products that are lighter, stronger, smarter, more precise and less expensive," says Ralph Merkle, a research scientist at the Xerox Palo Alto Research Center in California.

Merkle says nanotechnology, if successful, could rearrange atoms, the building blocks of matter.

The medical applications are astounding.

"It would completely alter the way we treat disease and illness," says Merkle, "by repairing damage at the molecular and cellular level."

Ettinger likens nanotechnology to the science fiction movie "Fantastic Voyage," when a team of scientists were made minuscule, then injected into a human. "The ultimate application," he says, "would be to build medical robots to penetrate your cells and repair you from the inside."

Merkle's prediction for the realization of nanotechnology: sometime next century.

Taking it with you

If you could wake up in 200 years, what would you want with you? Would you have money set aside? Gold? A detailed biography of your life?

The Cryonics Institute provides a safe, where some patients have left a few personal mementos, but several cryonicists have given little thought to needs at the other end. "The priority is setting up the freezing process as best as possible," says attorney David Ettinger, Robert's son and an institute member. "We haven't spent much time worrying about the details of revival."

John Besancon has.

A former accountant for General Motors, Besancon, 57, is funding his future freezing with an Individual Retirement Account, now worth about $30,000. He has three ways to prepare for financial viability, if and when he is revived.

"I thought I could go to garage sales and buy some junk. You never know what will be worth something–Barbie dolls, barbed wire, who knows. Then I'd take it to some state land, a state park, something that probably wouldn't be developed for a long time. Then I'd pack it in a capsule, get a post-hole digger and, when nobody's looking, dig a hole and bury the capsule in the ground. I'd have one of those devices [a global positioning satellite] where you can set your position by the stars, so I could always find it."

Besancon says it would be important to diversify. "I would also set aside something unique–jewelry, rare coins, artwork. The other way is you could set up a perpetual trust."

Such trusts have become the newest financial accouterment on the road to a second life.

"It is brand-new legal ground," says Yount. His American Cryonics Society has set up so-called "dynasty trusts"–legal in some states–for its members. Some have also named their cryonics center the beneficiaries of life insurance policies or trusts.

But like the mystery revival method, such trusts are largely untested. Would the IRS become a player? If your perpetual trust runs for a century, you may not want to wake up to your tax bill.

"The current tax structure could not accommodate something like that," says Bill Karnatz, a trusts expert with Thompson, Hine and Flory in Cleveland. "If you died today and were frozen and were later rejuvenated or whatever, it would be pretty difficult to determine how that would work."

The ultimate afterlife

Writer James L. Halperin just completed his second futuristic novel, "The First Immortal," about a reanimated suspension patient. Halperin, 44, who lives in Dallas, spent two years researching cryonics and nanotechnology. He was so impressed, he signed up to be frozen.

"It just seemed it was low risk and high reward," he says. "If it doesn't work, it will have the same result as if I was buried or cremated."

Joseph Kowalsky, 32, an attorney living outside Detroit, is also willing to risk it. "I hold a great value on life," he says, "but I'm also very afraid of dying."

Raised in a Jewish family, Kowalsky attended Jewish schools and learned that there is a world the soul goes to when you die. Now he says he is an agnostic.

"A lot of people say we're trying to be gods here, extending people's lives," he says. "But the alternative is that I'm put in the ground, where you have rain and worms and all of that."

Of course "all of that" also involves centuries of firmly held beliefs by millions regarding the rituals of dying.

"Part of the problem with cryonics is it's an attempt to deny death," says Rabbi Elliot Dorff, a professor of philosophy at the University of Judaism in Los Angeles.

"If you're Jewish and you die, we have certain mourning rites, the *shiva* period, which is a time to confront the fact that a loved one has died and how to deal with those feelings. It is a way to acknowledge death, not pretend it didn't happen."

The Rev. Don Dunson, who teaches moral theology and biomedical ethics at St. Mary's Seminary in Wickliffe, says Christians believe in the resurrection of the body and life everlasting.

"We believe there is a certain irrevocable nature to death," he says. "Indeed, you go to God. Science is really unable to close the door on this. The freezing of the body is in some sense denying our going to God."

Halperin was weighed the what-ifs. "There is no proof that there is an afterlife. That's just blind faith, and it's blind faith for people being suspended," he says. "If there is no afterlife and cryonics does work, then that's the big payoff."

It's also the $64,000 question for future freezees: What if you really are revived in 200 years? Will there still be a United States by then? Will it be a world you'll want to come back to?

Robert Ettinger would have to sort out the revival order of his family for one thing. Who gets reanimated first—him, his mother, his first wife, his second wife?

"Actually," says Ettinger, "the last person frozen will probably be the first revived because the technologies used would be the most compatible."

If the majority of scientists are right, all you'll have are frozen bodies and a big waste of time and money. If the cryonicists are right, there will be some amazing stories to tell at the other end of that icy highway through time.

If the religious people are right, and the soul or spirit has already moved on from the body, then what? What exactly is that person who gets defrosted and wakes up?

"Now," says Dunson, "you are steering into the real vast realm of the unknown."

Is It Time to Abandon Brain Death?

by Robert D. Truog

Despite its familiarity and widespread acceptance, the concept of "brain death" remains incoherent in theory and confused in practice. Moreover, the only purpose served by the concept is to facilitate the procurement of transplantable organs. By abandoning the concept of brain death and adopting different criteria for organ procurement, we may be able to increase both the supply of transplantable organs and clarity in our understanding of death.

Over the past several decades, the concept of brain death has become well entrenched within the practice of medicine. At a practical level, this concept has been successful in delineating widely accepted ethical and legal boundaries for the procurement of vital organs for transplantation. Despite this success, however, there have been persistent concerns over whether the concept is theoretically coherent and internally consistent.[1] Indeed, some have concluded that the concept is fundamentally flawed, and that it represents only a "superficial and fragile consensus."[2] In this analysis I will identify the sources of these inconsistencies, and suggest that the best resolution to these issues may be to abandon the concept of brain death altogether.

Definitions, Concepts, and Tests

In its seminal work "Defining Death," the President's Commission for the Study of Ethical Problems in Medicine and Biomedical and Behavioral Research articulated a formulation of brain death that has come to be known as the "whole-brain standard."[3] In the Uniform Determination of Death Act, the President's Commission specified two criteria for determining death: (1) irreversible cessation of circulatory and respiratory functions, or (2) irreversible cessation of all functions of the entire brain, including the brainstem.

Neurologist James Bernat has been influential in defending and refining this standard. Along with others, he has recognized that analysis of the concept of brain death must begin by differentiating between three distinct levels. At the most general level, the concept must involve a *definition*. Next, *criteria* must be specified to determine when the definition has been fulfilled. Finally, *tests* must be available for evaluating whether the criteria have been satisfied.[4] As clarified by Bernat and colleagues, therefore, the concept of death under the whole-brain formulation can be outlined as follows:[5]

Definition of Death: The "permanent cessation of functioning of the organism as a whole."
Criterion for Death: The "permanent cessation of functioning of the entire brain."
Tests for Death: Two distinct sets of tests are available and acceptable for determining that the criterion is fulfilled:

(1) The cardiorespiratory standard is the traditional approach for determining death and relies upon documenting the prolonged absence of circulation or respiration. These tests fulfill the criterion, according to Bernat, since the prolonged absence of these vital signs is diagnostic for the permanent loss of all brain function.

(2) The neurological standard consists of a battery of tests and procedures, including establishment of an etiology sufficient to account for the loss of all brain functions, diagnosing the presence of coma, documenting apnea and the absence of brainstem reflexes, excluding reversible conditions, and showing the persistence of these findings over a sufficient period of time.[6]

Critique of the Current Formulation of Brain Death

Is this a coherent account of the concept of brain death? To answer this question, one must determine whether each level of analysis is consistent with the others. In other words, individuals who fulfill the tests must also fulfill the criterion, and those who satisfy the criterion must also satisfy the definition.[7]

 From the *Hastings Center Report*, January/February 1997, pp. 29-37. © 1997 by The Hastings Center. Reproduced by permission.

First, regarding the tests-criterion relationship, there is evidence that many individuals who fulfill all of the tests for brain death do not have the "permanent cessation of functioning of the entire brain." In particular, many of these individuals retain clear evidence of integrated brain function at the level of the brainstem and midbrain, and may have evidence of cortical function.

For example, many patients who fulfill the tests for the diagnosis of brain death continue to exhibit intact neurohumoral function. Between 22 percent and 100 percent of brain-dead patients in different series have been found to retain free-water homeostasis through the neurologically medicated secretion of arginine vasopressin, as evidenced by serum hormonal levels and the absence of diabetes insipidus.[8] Since the brain is the only source of the regulated secretion of arginine vasopressin, patients without diabetes insipidus do not have the loss of all brain function. Neurologically regulated secretion of other hormones is also quite common.[9]

In addition, the tests for the diagnosis of brain death require the patient not to be hypothermic.[10] This caveat is a particularly confusing Catch-22, since the absence of hypothermia generally indicates the continuation of neurologically mediated temperature homeostasis. The circularity of this reasoning can be clinically problematic, since hypothermic patients cannot be diagnosed as brain-dead but the absence of hypothermia is itself evidence of brain function.

Furthermore, studies have shown that many patients (20 percent in one series) who fulfill the tests for brain death continue to show electrical activity on their electroencephalograms.[11] While there is no way to determine how often this electrical activity represents true "function" (which would be incompatible with the criterion for brain death), in at least some cases the activity observed seems fully compatible with function.[12]

Finally, clinicians have observed that patients who fulfill the tests for brain death frequently respond to surgical incision at the time of organ procurement with a significant rise in both heart rate and blood pressure. This suggests that integrated neurological function at a supraspinal level may be present in at least some patients diagnosed as brain-dead.[13] This evidence points to the conclusion that there is a significant disparity between the standard tests used to make the diagnosis of brain death and the criterion these tests are purported to fulfill. Faced with these facts, even supporters of the current statutes acknowledge that the criterion of "whole-brain" death is only an "approximation."[14]

Only 35 percent of physicians and nurses who were likely to be involved in organ procurement for transplantation correctly identified the legal and medical criteria for determining death.

If the tests for determining brain death are incompatible with the current criterion, then one way of solving the problem would be to require tests that always correlate with the "permanent cessation of functioning of the entire brain." Two options have been considered in this regard. The first would require tests that correlate with the actual destruction of the brain, since complete destruction would, of course, be incompatible with any degree of brain function. Only by satisfying these tests, some have argued, could we be assured that all functions of the entire brain have totally and permanently ceased.[15] But is there a constellation of clinical and laboratory tests that correlate with this degree of destruction? Unfortunately, a study of over 500 patients with both coma and apnea (including 146 autopsies for neuropathologic correlation) showed that "it was not possible to verify that a diagnosis made prior to cardiac arrest by any set or subset of criteria would invariably correlate with a diffusely destroyed brain."[16] On the basis of these data, a definition that required total brain destruction could only be confirmed at autopsy. Clearly, a condition that could only be determined after death could never be a requirement for declaring death.

Another way of modifying the tests to conform with the criterion would be to rely solely upon the cardiorespiratory standard for determining death. This standard would certainly identify the permanent cessation of all brain function (thereby fulfilling the criterion), since it is well established by common knowledge that prolonged absence of circulation and respiration results in the death of the entire brain (and every other organ). In addition, fulfillment of these tests would also convincingly demonstrate the cessation of function of the organism as a whole (thereby fulfilling the definition). Unfortunately, this approach for resolving the problem would also make it virtually impossible to obtain vital organs in a viable condition for transplantation, since under current laws it is generally necessary for these organs to be removed from a heart-beating donor.

These inconsistencies between the tests and the criterion are therefore not easily resolvable. In addition to these problems, there are also inconsistencies between the criterion and the definition. As outlined above, the whole-brain concept assumes that the "permanent cessation of functioning of the entire brain" (the criterion) necessarily implies the "permanent cessation of functioning of the organism as a whole" (the definition). Conceptually, this relationship assumes the principle that the brain is responsible for maintaining the body's homeostasis, and that without brain function the organism rapidly disintegrates. In the past, this relationship was demonstrated by showing that individuals who fulfilled the tests for the diagnosis of brain death inevitably had a cardiac arrest within a short period of time, even if they were provided with mechanical ventilation and intensive care.[17]

Indeed, this assumption had been considered one of the linchpins in the ethical justification for the concept of brain death.[18] For example, in the largest empirical study of brain death ever performed, a collaborative group working under the auspices of the National Institutes of Health sought to specify the necessary tests for diagnosing brain death by attempting to identify a constellation of neurological findings that would inevitably predict the development of a cardiac arrest within three months, regardless of the level or intensity of support provided.[19]

This approach to defining brain death in terms of neurological findings that predict the development of cardiac arrest is plagued by both logical and scientific problems, however. First, it confuses a prognosis with a diagnosis. Demonstrating that a certain class of patients will suffer a cardiac arrest within a defined period of time certainly proves that they are *dying,* but it says nothing about whether they are *dead.*[20] This conceptual mistake can be clearly appreciated if one considers individuals who are dying of conditions not associated with severe neurological impairment. If a constellation of tests could identify a subgroup of patients with metastatic cancer who invariably suffered a cardiac arrest within a short period of time, for example, we would certainly be comfortable in concluding that they were dying, but we clearly could not claim that they were already dead.

Second, this view relies upon the intuitive notion that the brain is the principal organ of the body, the "integrating" organ whose functions cannot be replaced by any other organ or by artificial means. Up through the early 1980s, this view was supported by numerous studies showing that almost all patients who fulfilled the usual battery of tests for brain death suffered a cardiac arrest within several weeks.[21]

The loss of homeostatic equilibrium that is empirically observed in brain-dead patients is almost certainly the result of their progressive loss of integrated neurohumoral and autonomic function. Over the past several decades, however, intensive care units (ICUs) have become increasingly sophisticated "surrogate brainstems," replacing both the respiratory functions as well as the hormonal and other regulatory activities of the damaged neuraxis.[22] This technology is presently utilized in those tragic cases in which a pregnant woman is diagnosed as brain-dead and an attempt is made to maintain her somatic existence until the fetus reaches a viable gestation, as well as for prolonging the organ viability of brain-dead patients awaiting organ procurement.[23] Although the functions of the brainstem are considerably more complex than those of the heart or the lungs, in theory (and increasingly in practice) they are entirely replaceable by modern technology. In terms of maintaining homeostatic functions, therefore,

the brain is no more irreplaceable than any of the other vital organs. A definition of death predicated upon the "inevitable" development of a cardiac arrest within a short period of time is therefore inadequate, since this empirical "fact" is no longer true. In other words, cardiac arrest is inevitable only if it is allowed to occur, just as respiratory arrest in brain-dead patients is inevitable only if they are not provided with mechanical ventilation. This gradual development in technical expertise has unwittingly undermined one of the central ethical justifications for the whole-brain criterion of death.

In summary, then, the whole-brain concept is plagued by internal inconsistencies in both the tests-criterion and the criterion-definition relationships, and these problems cannot be easily solved. In addition, there is evidence that this lack of conceptual clarity has contributed to misunderstandings about the concept among both clinicians and laypersons. For example, Stuart Youngner and colleagues found that only 35 percent of physicians and nurses who were likely to be involved in organ procurement for transplantation correctly identified the legal and medical criteria for determining death.[24] Indeed, most of the respondents used inconsistent concepts of death, and a substantial minority misunderstood the criterion to be the permanent loss of consciousness, which the President's Commission had specifically rejected, in part because it would have classified anencephalic newborns and patients in a vegetative state as dead. In other words, medical professionals who were otherwise knowledgeable and sophisticated were generally confused about the concept of brain death. In an editorial accompanying this study, Dan Wikler and Alan Weisbard claimed that this confusion was "appropriate," given the lack of philosophical coherence in the concept itself.[25] In another study, a survey of Swedes found that laypersons were more willing to consent to autopsies than to organ donation for themselves or a close relative. In seeking an explanation for these findings, the authors reported that "the fear of not being dead during the removal of organs, reported by 22 percent of those undecided toward organ donation, was related to the uncertainty surrounding brain death."[26]

On one hand, these difficulties with the concept might be deemed to be so

esoteric and theoretical that they should play no role in driving the policy debate about how to define death and procure organs for transplantation. This has certainly been the predominant view up to now. In many other circumstances, theoretical issues have taken a back seat to practical matters when it comes to determining public policy. For example, the question of whether tomatoes should be considered a vegetable or a fruit for purposes of taxation was said to hinge little upon the biological facts of the matter, but to turn primarily upon the political and economic issues at stake.[27] If this view is applied to the concept of brain death, then the best public policy would be that which best served the public's interest, regardless of theoretical concerns.

On the other hand, medicine has a long and respected history of continually seeking to refine the theoretical and conceptual underpinnings of its practice. While the impact of scientific and philosophical views upon social policy and public perception must be taken seriously, they cannot be the sole forces driving the debate. Given the evidence demonstrating a lack of coherence in the whole-brain death formulation and the confusion that is apparent among medical professionals, there is ample reason to prompt a look at alternatives to our current approach.

Alternative Approaches to the Whole-Brain Formulation

Alternatives to the whole-brain death formulation fall into two general categories. One approach is to emphasize the overriding importance of those functions of the brain that support the phenomenon of consciousness and to claim that individuals who have permanently suffered the loss of all consciousness are dead. This is known as the "higher-brain" criterion. The other approach is to return to the traditional tests for determining death, that is, the permanent loss of circulation and respiration. As noted above, this latter strategy could fit well with Bernat's formulation of the definition of death, since adoption of the cardiorespiratory standard as the test for determining death is consistent with both the criterion and the definition. The problem with this potential solution is that it would virtually eliminate the possibility of procuring vital organs from heart-beating donors under our present system of law and ethics, since current requirements insist that organs be removed only from individuals who have been declared dead (the "dead-donor rule").[28] Consideration of this latter view would therefore be feasible only if it could be linked to fundamental changes in the permissible limits of organ procurement.

The Higher-Brain Formulation. The higher-brain criterion for death holds that maintaining the potential for consciousness is the critical function of the brain relevant to questions of life and death. Under this definition, all individuals who are permanently unconscious would be considered to be dead. Included in this category would be (1) patients who fulfill the cardiorespiratory standard, (2) those who fulfill the current tests for whole-brain death, (3) those diagnosed as being in a permanent vegetative state, and (4) newborns with anencephaly. Various versions of this view have been defended by many philosophers, and arguments have been advanced from moral as well as ontological perspectives.[29] In addition, this view correlates very well with many commonsense opinions about personal identity. To take a stock philosophical illustration, for example, consider the typical reaction of a person who has undergone a hypothetical "brain switch" procedure, where one's brain is transplanted into another's body, and vice versa. Virtually anyone presented with this scenario will say that "what matters" for their existence now resides in the new body, even though an outside observer would insist that it is the person's old body that "appears" to be the original person. Thought experiments like this one illustrate that we typically identify ourselves with our experience of consciousness, and this observation forms the basis of the claim that the permanent absence of consciousness should be seen as representing the death of the person.

Implementation of this standard would present certain problems, however. First, is it possible to diagnose the state of permanent unconsciousness with the high level of certainty required for the determination of death? More specifically, is it currently possible to definitively diagnose the permanent vegetative state and anencephaly? A Multi-Society Task Force recently outlined guidelines for diagnosis of permanent vegetative state and claimed that

sufficient data are now available to make the diagnosis of permanent vegetative state in appropriate patients with a high degree of certainty.[30] On the other hand, case reports of patients who met these criteria but who later recovered a higher degree of neurological functioning suggests that use of the term "permanent" may be overstating the degree of diagnostic certainty that is currently possible. This would be an especially important issue in the context of diagnosing death, where false positive diagnoses would be particularly problematic.[31] Similarly, while the Medical Task Force on Anencephaly has concluded that most cases of anencephaly can be diagnosed by a competent clinician without significant uncertainty, others have emphasized the ambiguities inherent in evaluating this condition.[32]

Another line of criticism is that the higher-brain approach assumes the definition of death should reflect the death of the *person,* rather than the death of the *organism.*[33] By focusing on the person, this theory does not account for what is common to the death of all organisms, such as humans, frogs, or trees. Since we do not know what it would mean to talk about the permanent loss of consciousness of frogs or trees, then this approach to death may appear to be idiosyncratic. In response, higher-brain theorists believe that it is critical to define death within the context of the specific subject under consideration. For example, we may speak of the death of an ancient civilization, the death of a species, or the death of a particular system of belief. In each case, the definition of death will be different, and must be appropriate to the subject in order for the concept to make any sense. Following this line of reasoning, the higher-brain approach is correct precisely because it seeks to identify what is uniquely relevant to the death of a person.

Aside from these diagnostic and philosophical concerns, however, perhaps the greatest objections to the higher brain formulation emerge from the im-

plications of treating breathing patients as if they are dead. For example, if patients in a permanent vegetative state were considered to be dead, then they should logically be considered suitable for burial. Yet all of these patients

> Most people find it counterintuitive to perceive a breathing patient as "dead."

breathe, and some of them "live" for many years.[34] The thought of burying or cremating a breathing individual, even if unconscious, would be unthinkable for many people, creating a significant barrier to acceptance of this view into public policy.[35]

One way of avoiding this implication would be to utilize a "lethal injection" before cremation or burial to terminate cardiac and respiratory function. This would not be euthanasia, since the individual would be declared dead before the injection. The purpose of the injection would be purely "aesthetic." This practice could even be viewed as simply an extension of our current protocols, where the vital functions of patients diagnosed as brain-dead are terminated prior to burial, either by discontinuing mechanical ventilation or by discontinuing mechanical ventilation or by removing their heart and/or lungs during the process of organ procurement. While this line of argumentation has a certain logical persuasiveness, it nevertheless fails to address the central fact that most people find it counterintuitive to perceive a breathing patient as "dead." Wikler has suggested that this attitude is likely to change over time, and that eventually society will come to accept that the body of a patient in a permanent vegetative state is simply that person's "living remains."[36] This optimism about higher-brain death is reminiscent of the comments by the President's Commission regarding whole-brain death: "Although undeniably disconcerting for many people, the confusion created in personal perception by a determination of 'brain death' does not . . . provide a basis for an ethical objection to discontinuing medical measures on these dead bodies."[37] Nevertheless, at the present time any inclination toward a higher-brain death standard remains primarily in the realm of philosophers and not policymakers.

Return to the Traditional Cardiorespiratory Standard. In contrast to the higher-brain concept of death, the other main alternative to our current approach would involve moving in the opposite direction and abandoning the diagnosis of brain death altogether. This would involve returning to the traditional approach to determining death, that is, the cardiorespiratory standard. In evaluating the wisdom of "turning back the clock," it is helpful to retrace the development of the concept of brain death back to 1968 and the conclusions of the Ad Hoc Committee that developed the Harvard Criteria for the diagnosis of brain death. They began by claiming:

> There are two reasons why there is need for a definition [of brain death]: (1) Improvements in resuscitative and supportive measures have led to increased efforts to save those who are desperately injured. Sometimes these efforts have only partial success so that the result is an individual whose brain is irreversibly damaged. The burden is great on patients who suffer permanent loss of intellect, on their families, and on those in need of hospital beds already occupied by these comatose patients. (2) Obsolete criteria for the definition of death can lead to controversy in obtaining organs for transplantation.[38]

These two issues can be subdivided into at least four distinct questions:

1) When is it permissible to withdraw life support from patients with irreversible neurological damage for the benefit of the patient?

2) When is it permissible to withdraw life support from patients with irreversible neurological damage for the benefit of society, where the benefit is either in the form of economic savings or to make an ICU bed available for someone with a better prognosis?

3) When is it permissible to remove organs from a patient for transplantation?

4) When is a patient ready to be cremated or buried?

The Harvard Committee chose to address all of these questions with a single answer, that is, the determination of brain death. Each of these questions involves unique theoretical issues, however, and each raises a different set of concerns. By analyzing the concept of brain death in terms of the separate questions that led to its development, alternatives to brain death may be considered.

Withdrawal of life support. The Harvard Committee clearly viewed the diagnosis of brain death as a necessary condition for the withdrawal of life support: "It should be emphasized that we recommend the patient be declared dead before any effort is made to take him off a respirator . . . [since] otherwise, the physicians would be turning off the respirator on a person who is, in the present strict, technical application of law, still alive" (p. 339).

The ethical and legal mandates that surround the withdrawal of life support have changed dramatically since the recommendations of the Harvard Committee. Numerous court decisions and consensus statements have emphasized the rights of patients or their surrogates to demand the withdrawal of life-sustaining treatments, including mechanical ventilation. In the practice of critical care medicine today, patients are rarely diagnosed as brain-dead solely for the purpose of discontinuing mechanical ventilation. When patients are not candidates for organ transplantation, either because of medical contraindications or lack of consent, families are informed of the dismal prognosis, and artificial ventilation is withdrawn. While the diagnosis of brain death was once critical in allowing physicians to discontinue life-sustaining treatments, decisionmaking about these important questions is now appropriately centered around the patient's previously stated wishes and judgments about the patient's best interest. Questions about the definition of death have become virtually irrelevant to these deliberations.

Allocation of scarce resources. The Harvard Committee alluded to its concerns about having patients with a hopeless prognosis occupying ICU beds. In the years since that report, this issue has become even more pressing. The diagnosis of brain death, however, is of little significance in helping to resolve these issues. Even considering the unusual cases where families refuse to have the ventilator removed from a brain-dead patient, the overall impact of the diagnosis of brain death upon scarce ICU resources is minimal. Much more important to the current debate over the just allocation of ICU resources are patients with less severe degrees of neurological dysfunction, such as patients in a permanent vegetative state or individuals with advanced dementia. Again, the diagnosis of brain death is of little relevance to this central concern of the Harvard Committee.

Organ transplantation. Without question, the most important reason for the continued use of brain death criteria is the need for transplantable organs. Yet even here, the requirements for brain death may be doing more harm than good. The need for organs is expanding at an ever-increasing rate, while the number of available organs has essentially plateaued. In an effort to expand the limited pool of organs, several attempts have been made to circumvent the usual restrictions of brain death on organ procurement.

At the University of Pittsburgh, for example, a new protocol allows critically ill patients or their surrogates to offer their organs for donation after the withdrawal of life-support, even though the patients never meet brain death criteria.[39] Suitable patients are taken to the operating room, where intravascular monitors are placed and the patient is "prepped and draped" for surgical incision. Life-support is then withdrawn, and the patient is monitored for the development of cardiac arrest. Assuming this occurs within a short period of time, the attending physician waits until there

> The most difficult challenge for this proposal would be to gain acceptance of the view that killing may sometimes be a justifiable necessity for procuring transplantable organs.

has been two minutes of pulselessness, and then pronounces the patient dead. The transplant team then enters the operating room and immediately removes the organs for transplantation.

This novel approach has a number of problems when viewed from within the traditional framework. For example, after the patient is pronounced dead, why should the team rush to remove the organs? If the Pittsburgh team truly believes that the patient is dead, why not begin chest compressions and mechanical ventilation, insert cannulae to place the patient on full cardiopulmonary bypass, and remove the organs in a more controlled fashion? Presumably, this is not done because two minutes of pulselessness is almost certainly not long enough to ensure the development of brain death.[40] It is even conceivable that patients managed in this way could regain consciousness during the process of organ procurement while supported with cardiopulmonary bypass, despite having already been diagnosed as "dead." In other words, the reluctance of the Pittsburgh team to extend their protocol in ways that would be acceptable for dead patients could be an indication that the patients may really not be dead after all.

A similar attempt to circumvent the usual restrictions on organ procurement was recently attempted with anencephalic newborns at Loma Linda University. Again, the protocol involved manipulation of the dying process, with mechanical ventilation being instituted and maintained solely for the purpose of preserving the organs until criteria for brain death could be documented. The results were disappointing, and the investigators concluded that "it is usually not feasible, with the restrictions of current law, to procure solid organs for transplantation from anencephalic infants."[41]

Why do these protocols strike many commentators as contrived and even somewhat bizarre? The motives of the individuals involved are certainly commendable: they want to offer the benefits of transplantable organs to individuals who desperately need them. In addition, they are seeking to obtain organs only from individuals who cannot be harmed by the procurement and only in those situations where the patient or a surrogate requests the donation. The problem with these protocols lies not with the motive, but with the method and justification. By manipulating both the process and the definition of death,

these protocols give the appearance that the physicians involved are only too willing to draw the boundary between life and death wherever it happens to maximize the chances for organ procurement.

How can the legitimate desire to increase the supply of transplantable organs be reconciled with the need to maintain a clear and simple distinction between the living and the dead? One way would be to abandon the requirement for the death of the donor prior to organ procurement and, instead, focus upon alternative and perhaps more fundamental ethical criteria to constrain the procurement of organs, such as the principles of consent and nonmaleficence.[42]

For example, policies could be changed such that organ procurement would be permitted only with the consent of the donor or appropriate surrogate and only when doing so would not harm the donor. Individuals who could not be harmed by the procedure would include those who are permanently and irreversibly unconscious (patients in a persistent vegetative state or newborns with anencephaly) and those who are imminently and irreversibly dying.

The American Medical Association's Council on Ethical and Judicial Affairs recently proposed (but has subsequently retracted) a position consistent with this approach.[43] The council stated that, "It is ethically permissible to consider the anencephalic as a potential organ donor, although still alive under the current definition of death," if, among other requirements, the diagnosis is certain and the parents give their permission. The council concluded, "It is normally required that the donor be legally dead before removal of their life-necessary organs . . . The use of the anencephalic neonate as a live donor is a limited exception to the general standard because of the fact that the infant has never experienced, and will never experience, consciousness" (pp. 1617–18).

This alternative approach to organ procurement would require substantial changes in the law. The process of organ procurement would have to be legitimated as a form of justified killing, rather than just as the dissection of a corpse. There is certainly precedent in the law for recognizing instances of justified killing. The concept is also not an anathema to the public, as evidenced by the growing support for euthanasia, another practice that would have to be le-

gally construed as a form of justified killing. Even now, surveys show that one-third of physicians and nurses do not believe brain-dead patients are actually dead, but feel comfortable with the process of organ procurement because the patients are permanently unconscious and/or imminently dying.[44] In other words, many clinicians already seem to justify their actions on the basis of nonmaleficence and consent, rather than with the belief that the patients are actually dead.

This alternative approach would also eliminate the need for protocols like the one being used at the University of Pittsburgh, with its contrived and perhaps questionable approach to declaring death prior to organ procurement. Under the proposed system, qualified individuals who had given their consent could simply have their organs removed under general anesthesia, without first undergoing an orchestrated withdrawal of life support. Anencephalic newborns whose parents requested organ donation could likewise have the organs removed under general anesthesia without the need to wait for the diagnosis of brain death.

The diagnosis of death. Seen in this light, the concept of brain death may have become obsolete. Certainly the diagnosis of brain death has been extremely useful during the last several decades, as society has struggled with a myriad of issues that were never encountered before the era of mechanical ventilation and organ transplantation. As society emerges from this transitional period, and as many of these issues are more clearly understood as questions that are inherently unrelated to the distinction between life and death, then the concept of brain death may no longer be useful or relevant. If this is the case, then it may be preferable to return to the traditional standard and limit tests for the determination of death to those based solely upon the permanent cessation of respiration and circulation. Even today we uniformly regard the cessation of respiration and circulation as the standard for determining when patients are ready to be cremated or buried.

Another advantage of a return to the traditional approach is that it would represent a "common denominator" in the definition of death that virtually all cultural groups and religious traditions would find acceptable.[45] Recently both New Jersey and New York have enacted statutes that recognize the objections of particular religious views to the concept of brain death. In New Jersey, physicians are prohibited from declaring brain death in persons who come from religious traditions that do not accept the concept.[46] Return to a cardiorespiratory standard would eliminate problems with these objections.

Linda Emanuel recently proposed a "bounded zone" definition of death that shares some features with the approach outlined here.[47] Her proposal would adopt the cardiorespiratory standard as a "lower bound" for determining death that would apply to all cases, but would allow individuals to choose a definition of death that encompassed neurologic dysfunction up to the level of the permanent vegetative state (the "higher bound"). The practical implications of such a policy would be similar to some of those discussed here, in that it would (1) allow patients and surrogates to request organ donation when and if the patients were diagnosed with whole-brain death, permanent vegetative state, or anencephaly, and (2) it would permit rejection of the diagnosis of brain death by patients and surrogates opposed to the concept. Emanuel's proposal would not permit organ donation from terminal and imminently dying patients, however, prior to the diagnosis of death.

Despite these similarities, these two proposals differ markedly in the justifications used to support their conclusions. Emanuel follows the President's Commission in seeking to address several separate questions by reference to the diagnosis of death, whereas the approach suggested here would adopt a single and uniform definition of death, and then seek to resolve questions around organ donation on a different ethical and legal foundation.

Emanuel's proposal also provides another illustration of the problems encountered when a variety of diverse issues all hinge upon the definition of death. Under her scheme, some individuals would undoubtedly opt for a definition of death based on the "higher bound" of the permanent vegetative state in order to permit the donation of their vital organs if they should develop this condition. However, few of these individuals would probably agree to being cremated while still breathing, even if they were vegetative. Most likely, they would not want to be cremated until after they had sustained a cardiorespiratory arrest. Once again, this creates the awkward and confusing necessity of diagnosing death for one purpose (organ donation) but not for another (cremation). Only by abandoning the concept of brain death is it possible to adopt a definition of death that is valid for all purposes, while separating questions of organ donation from dependence upon the life/death dichotomy.

Turning Back

The tension between the need to maintain workable and practical standards for the procurement of transplantable organs and our desire to have a conceptually coherent account of death is an issue that must be given serious attention. Resolving these inconsistencies by moving toward a higher-brain definition of death would most likely create additional practical problems regarding accurate diagnosis as well as introduce concepts that are highly counterintuitive to the general public. Uncoupling the link between organ transplantation and brain death, on the other hand, offers a number of advantages. By shifting the ethical foundations for organ donation to the principles of nonmaleficence and consent, the pool of potential donors may be substantially increased. In addition, by reverting to a simpler and more traditional definition of death, the long-standing debate over fundamental inconsistencies in the concept of brain death may finally be resolved.

The most difficult challenge for this proposal would be to gain acceptance of the view that killing may sometimes be a justifiable necessity for procuring transplantable organs. Careful attention to the principles of consent and nonmaleficence should provide an adequate bulwark against slippery slope concerns that this practice would be extended in unforeseen and unacceptable ways. Just as the euthanasia debate often seems to turn less upon abstract theoretical concerns and more upon the empirical question of whether guidelines for assisted dying would be abused, so the success of this proposal could also rest upon factual questions of societal acceptance and whether this approach would erode respect for human life and the integrity of clinicians. While the answers to these questions are not known, the potential benefits of this proposal make it worthy of continued discussion and debate.

Acknowledgements

The author thanks numerous friends and colleagues for critical readings of the manuscript, with special acknowledgments to Dan Wikler and Linda Emanuel.

References

1. Some of the more notable critiques include Robert M. Veatch, "The Whole-Brain-Oriented Concept of Death. An Outmoded Philosophical Formulation," *Journal of Thanatology* 3 (1975): 13–30; Michael B. Green and Daniel Wikler, "Brain Death and Personal Identity," *Philosophy and Public Affairs* 9 (1980): 105–33; Stuart J. Youngner and Edward T. Bartlett, "Human Death and High Technology: The Failure of the Whole-Brain Formulations," *Annals of Internal Medicine* 99 (1983): 252–58; Amir Halevy and Baruch Brody, "Brain Death: Reconciling Definitions, Criteria, and Tests," *Annals of Internal Medicine* 119 (1993): 519–25.
2. Stuart J. Youngner, "Defining Death: A Superficial and Fragile Consensus," *Archives of Neurology* 49 (1992): 570–72.
3. President's Commission for the Study of Ethical Problems in Medicine and Biomedical and Behavioral Research, *Defining Death* (Washington, D.C.: Government Printing Office, 1981).
4. Karen Gervais has been especially articulate in defining these levels. See Karen G. Gervais, *Redefining Death* (New Haven: Yale University Press, 1986); "Advancing the Definition of Death: A Philosophical Essay," *Medical Humanities Review* 3, no. 2 (1989): 7–19.
5. James L. Bernat, Charles M. Culver, and Bernard Gert, "On the Definition and Criterion of Death," *Annals of Internal Medicine* 94 (1981): 389–94; James L. Bernat, "How Much of the Brain Must Die in Brain Death?" *Journal of Clinical Ethics* 3 (1992): 21–26.
6. Report of the Medical Consultants on the Diagnosis of Death, "Guidelines for the Determination of Death," *JAMA* 246 (1981): 2184–86.
7. Aspects of this analysis have been explored previously in, Robert D. Truog and James C. Fackler, "Rethinking Brain Death," *Critical Care Medicine* 20 (1992): 1705–13; Halevy and Brody, "Brain Death."
8. H. Schrader et al., "Changes of Pituitary Hormones in Brain Death," *Acta Neurochirurgica* 52 (1980): 239–48; Kristen M. Outwater and Mark A. Rockoff, "Diabetes Insipidus Accompanying Brain Death in Children," *Neurology* 34 (1984): 1243–46; James C. Fackler, Juan C. Troncoso, and Frank R. Gioia, "Age-Specific Characteristics of Brain Death in Children," *American Journal of Diseases of Childhood* 142 (1988): 999–1003.
9. Schrader et al., "Changes of Pituitary Hormones in Brain Death"; H. J. Gramm et al., "Acute Endocrine Failure after Brain Death," *Transplantation* 54 (1992): 851–57.
10. Report of Medical Consultants on the Diagnosis of Death, "Guidelines for the Determination of Death," p. 339.
11. Madeleine J. Grigg et al., "Electroencephalographic Activity after Brain Death," *Archives of Neurology* 44 (1987): 948–54; A. Earl Walker, *Cerebral Death*, 2nd ed. (Baltimore: Urban & Schwarzenberg, 1981), pp. 89–90;

and Christopher Pallis, "ABC of Brain Stem Death. The Arguments about the EEG," *British Medical Journal [Clinical Research]* 286 (1983): 284–87.

12. Ernst Rodin et al., "Brainstem Death," *Clinical Electroencephalography* 16 (1985): 63–71.

13. Randall C. Wetzel et al., "Hemodynamic Responses in Brain Dead Organ Donor Patients," *Anesthesia and Analgesia* 64 (1985): 125–28; S. H. Pennefather, J. H. Dark, and R. E. Bullock, "Haemodynamic Responses to Surgery in Brain-Dead Organ Donors," *Anaesthesia* 48 (1993): 1034–38; and D. J. Hill, R. Munglani, and D. Sapsford, "Haemodynamic Responses to Surgery in Brain-Dead Organ Donors," *Anaesthesia* 49 (1994): 835–36.

14. Bernat, "How Much of the Brain Must Die in Brain Death?"

15. Paul A. Byrne, Sean O'Reilly, and Paul M. Quay, "Brain Death—An Opposing Viewpoint," *JAMA* 242 (1979): 1985–90.

16. Gaetano F. Molinari, "The NINCDS Collaborative Study of Brain Death: A Historical Perspective," in U.S. Department of Health and Human Services, *NINCDS Monograph No. 24. NIH Publication No. 81–2286* (1980): 1–32.

17. Pallis, "ABC of Brain Stem Death," pp. 123–24; Bryan Jennett and Catherine Hessett, "Brain Death in Britain as Reflected in Renal Donors," *British Medical Journal* 283 (1981): 359–62; Peter M. Black, "Brain Death (first of two parts)," *NEJM* 299 (1978): 338–44.

18. President's Commission, *Defining Death.*

19. "An Appraisal of the Criteria of Cerebral Death, A Summary Statement: A Collaborative Study," *JAMA* 237 (1977): 982–86.

20. Green and Wikler, "Brain Death and Personal Identity."

21. President's Commission, *Defining Death.*

22. Green and Wikler, "Brain Death and Personal Identity"; Daniel Wikler, "Brain Death: A Durable Consensus?" *Bioethics* 7 (1993): 239–46.

23. David R. Field et al., "Maternal Brain Death During Pregnancy: Medical and Ethical issues," *JAMA* 260 (1988): 816–22; Masanobu Washida et al., "Beneficial Effect of Combined 3,5,3'-Triiodothyronine and Vasopressin Administration on Hepatic Energy Status and Systemic Hemodynamics after Brain Death," *Transplantation* 54 (1992): 44–49.

24. Stuart J. Youngner et al., " 'Brain Death' and Organ Retrieval: A Cross-Sectional Survey of Knowledge and Concepts among Health Pro-

fessionals," *JAMA* 261 (1989): 2205–10.

25. Daniel Wikler and Alan J. Weisbard, "Appropriate Confusion over 'Brain Death,' " *JAMA* 261 (1989): 2246.

26. Margareta Sanner, "A Comparison of Public Attitudes toward Autopsy, Organ Donation, and Anatomic Dissection: A Swedish Survey," *JAMA* 271 (1994): 284–88, at 287.

27. Green and Wikler, "Brain Death and Personal Identity."

28. Robert M. Arnold and Stuart J. Youngner, "The Dead Donor Rule: Should We Stretch It, Bend It, or Abandon It?" *Kennedy Institute of Ethics Journal* 3 (1993): 263–78.

29. Some of the many works defending this view include: Green and Wikler, "Brain Death and Personal Identity"; Gervais, *Redefining Death,* Truog and Fackler, "Rethinking Brain Death"; and Robert M. Veatch, *Death, Dying, and the Biological Revolution* (New Haven: Yale University Press, 1989).

30. The Multi-Society Task Force on PVS, "Medical Aspects of the Persistent Vegetative State," *NEJM* 330 (1994): 1499–1508 and 1572–79; D. Alan Shewmon, "Anencephaly: Selected Medical Aspects," *Hastings Center Report* 18, no. 5 (1988): 11–19.

31. Nancy L. Childs and Walt N. Mercer, "Brief Report: Late Improvement in Consciousness after Post-Traumatic Vegetative State," *NEJM* 334 (1996): 24–25; James L. Bernat, "The Boundaries of the Persistent Vegetative State," *Journal of Clinical Ethics* 3 (1992): 176–80.

32. Medical Task Force on Anencephaly, "The Infant with Anencephaly," *NEJM* 322 (1990): 669–74; Shewmon, "Anencephaly: Selected Medical Aspects."

33. Jeffrey R. Botkin and Stephen G. Post, "Confusion in the Determination of Death: Distinguishing Philosophy from Physiology," *Perspectives in Biology and Medicine* 36 (1993): 129–38.

34. The Multi-Society Task Force on PVS, "Medical Aspects of the Persistent Vegetative State."

35. Marcia Angell, "After Quinlan: The Dilemma of the Persistent Vegetative State," *NEJM* 330 (1994): 1524–25.

36. Wikler, "Brain Death: A Durable Consensus?"

37. President's Commission, *Defining Death,* p. 84.

38. Report of the Ad Hoc Committee of the Harvard Medical School to Examine the Definition of Brain Death, "A Definition of Irreversible Coma," *JAMA* 205 (1968): 337–40.

39. "University of Pittsburgh Medical Center Policy and Procedure Manual: Management of Terminally Ill Patients Who May Become Organ Donors after Death," *Kennedy Institute of Ethics Journal* 3 (1993): A1-A15; Stuart Youngner and Robert Arnold, "Ethical, Psychosocial, and Public Policy Implications of Procuring Organs from Non-Heart-Beating Cadaver Donors," *JAMA* 269 (1993): 2769–74. Of note, the June 1993 issue of the *Kennedy Institute of Ethics Journal* is devoted to this topic in its entirety.

40. Joanne Lynn, "Are the Patients Who Become Organ Donors Under the Pittsburgh Protocol for 'Non-Heart-Beating Donors' Really Dead?" *Kennedy Institute of Ethics Journal* 3 (1993): 167–78.

41. Joyce L. Peabody, Janet R. Emergy, and Stephen Ashwal, "Experience with Anencephalic Infants as Prospective Organ Donors," *NEJM* 321 (1989): 344–50.

42. See for example, Norman Fost, "The New Body Snatchers: On Scott's 'The Body as Property,' " *American Bar Foundation Research Journal* 3 (1983): 718–32; John A. Robertson, "Relaxing the Death Standard for Organ Donation in Pediatric Situations," in *Organ Substitution Technology: Ethical, Legal, and Public Policy Issues,* ed. D. Mathieu (Boulder, Col.: Westview Press, 1988), pp. 69–76; Arnold and Youngner, "The Dead Donor Rule."

43. AMA Council on Ethical and Judicial Affairs, "The Use of Anencephalic Neonates as Organ Donors," *JAMA* 273 (1995): 1614–18. After extensive debate among AMA members, the Council retracted this position statement. See Charles W. Plows, "Reconsideration of AMA Opinion on Anencephalic Neonates as Organ Donors," *JAMA* 275 (1996): 443–44.

44. Youngner et al., " 'Brain Death' and Organ Retrieval."

45. Jiro Nudeshima, "Obstacles to Brain Death and Organ Transplantation in Japan," *Lancet* 338 (1991): 1063–64.

46. Robert S. Olick, "Brain Death, Religious Freedom, and Public Policy: New Jersey's Landmark Legislative Initiative," *Kennedy Institute of Ethics Journal* 1 (1991): 275–88.

47. Linda L. Emanuel, "Reexamining Death: The Asymptotic Model and a Bounded Zone Definition," *Hastings Center Report* 25, no. 4 (1995): 27–35.

Unit Selections

Key Points to Consider

❖ Since children are experiencing death situations at an average age of 8 years, what societal steps can be taken to help children better cope with the death of a person or a pet?

❖ Are the elderly in America "warehoused" and put away to die? Can you present evidence of such "warehousing"? How might the image of the elderly be improved in our society? Is growing old really "the best is yet to be," or is growing old really "hell"?

❖ What do you recall from your own childhood experiences with fairy tales and death? Do you remember any death themes in children's literature and how you reacted at the time? Describe.

 **Links** **www.dushkin.com/online/**

8. **CDC Wonder on the Web—Prevention Guidelines**
   http://wonder.cdc.gov
9. **Children, Neonates, Family, Caregivers**
   http://www.kateden.com/death/child.html
10. **Children with AIDS Project**
    http://www.aidskids.org
11. **Light for Life Foundation**
    http://www.yellowribbon.org
12. **National SIDS Resource Center**
    http://www.circsol.com/SIDS/

These sites are annotated on pages 4 and 5.

Death is something we must accept, though no one really understands it. We can talk about death, learn from each other, and help each other. By better understanding death conceptualizations at various stages and in different relationships within the life cycle, we can better help each other. It is not our intent to suggest that age should be viewed as the sole determinant of one's death concept. Many other factors influence this cognitive development such as level of intelligence, physical and mental well-being, previous emotional reactions to various life experiences, religious background, other social and cultural forces, personal identity and self-worth appraisals, and exposure to or threats of death. Nonetheless, we will discuss death and death perceptions at various stages from the cradle to the grave or, as they say, the womb to the tomb.

Research on very young children's conceptions of death still does not reveal an adequate under- standing of their responses. A need exists to look more carefully at the dynamics of the young and to their families' relating to the concept of death. Adults, several decades later, recall vivid details about their first death experiences, and for many it was a traumatic event filled with fear, anger, and frustration.

In "Communication among Children, Parents, and Funeral Directors," Daniel Schaefer, a funeral director, encourages parents to talk to children about death. As parents, we need to recognize the insecurity often found in children at the time of a death and to deal with the situation accordingly. Children can generally accept a great deal of life experiences; the problem is that we adults are often inept in our dealing with dying and death, and thus we may practice avoidance in relating to children. We must remember that children, too, have feelings. They especially need emotional support during a crisis such as death.

Children's exposure to death may come through children's literature. In her essay, "Children, Death, and Fairy Tales," Elizabeth Lamers explores death themes in fairy tales and examines the evolution of these themes in children's literature.

Then, Esther Fein's "Failing to Discuss Dying Adds to Pain of Patient and Family" strongly urges better communication between adult children and elderly parents regarding wishes about the prolongation of life. As noted in "Older Americans in the 1990s and Beyond," the life expectancy tends to be extended more today than in the past.

Though children and teenagers do not have high death rates, suicide is a leading cause of death among adolescents. California schools are struggling to teach lessons in life and death and trying to reduce teenage suicides.

Developmental Aspects of Dying and Death

Communication Among Children, Parents, and Funeral Directors

Daniel J. Schaefer

Daniel J. Schaefer is a funeral director, Brooklyn, NY.

I have been a funeral director for the last twenty-five years. My family has been in the funeral service for one hundred and seven years. We have buried our friends; I have buried parents of my friends and children of my friends. Over the last ten years or so, I have found that something is missing: there have been fewer children attending funerals than I knew were in my friends' families. I began to ask parents, very simply, "What are you saying to your kids about this death in your family?" The replies of 1,800 sets of the parents of more than 3,600 children proved that they were basically unprepared to talk with their children about death and terribly uneasy about doing so, but not unwilling to say something once they were prepared by someone or given appropriate information.

The bits of information that I am going to present are not a standard message. They are building materials. The blueprint is individual to each family, so what we do is to take the family's blueprint, which has their particular death circumstance, then take the building materials, and build a message that parents can give to their children. For the families that I serve, I do this on an individual basis.

TALKING TO CHILDREN ABOUT DEATH

Thinking about talking to children about death is upsetting. It makes many parents anxious. It has been helpful for parents to know how many other parents feel. On Memorial Day two years ago, at three in the morning, I received a call that my brother had been killed in an automobile accident. I have five children, and I knew that four hours from then I was going to have to explain

to them about their uncle. I said to my wife, "It's unusual—I've done this with hundreds of families, but I have this thing in the pit of my stomach. I *know* what to say to these kids; I know exactly what I'm going to do. Can you imagine how it must be for somebody who doesn't know what to say?"

What do people say about speaking to children about death? Some are sure that they do have to talk to their children and some say they are not sure that it is necessary. Some parents who believe that something should be said are told by others that they should avoid upsetting their children. Parents naturally tend to build a protective wall around their children. What I say to them is "Let's look at the wall, let's see if it works, and if it does work, who is it working for? Is it working for you, to protect you from your child's grief? If we look over the wall, what do we see on the other side? Do we see a kid who is comfortable or do we see, in fact, a kid who is a solitary mourner?"

When parents plan to speak to their children about death, they have to understand that what they are about to do is not easy, that they are going to be upset and stressed, that they are probably going to lack energy, and that they are going to feel unable to concentrate. They are going to be afraid of their own emotions and the effect that these emotions will have on their children. They are not going to know what their children understand, and basically they have to realize that they want to protect their children from pain. It is important that parents know ahead of time that they are going to feel this way.

What do other people say to them? They say, "Your kids don't know what's going on," "Wait until later," "Tell them a fairy tale," "Don't say anything," "Send them away until the funeral is over," or "Do you really want to put your kids through all this?" implying that no loving parent would. It is almost frightening to talk with one's children on this subject, but I believe that it is dangerous not to.

Almost all parents will agree that children are surprisingly perceptive. They overhear conversations, read emotions and responses around them, and ask questions, directly and indirectly. They *will* receive messages; it is impossible not to communicate. No matter how hard parents try not to, they are going to communicate their grief to their children. Without some explanation, the children will be confused and anxious. What I say to parents is, "Since you're going to be sending a message out anyway, why don't you try to control the message?" A message is controlled by making sure that the information is true, geared for the age of the child, and, if possible, delivered in surroundings that make the child's reception of the message a little easier to handle.

For parents, feeling in control is important at a time when feeling out of control is routine and common, and when helping the child—the most dependent person in the family at that time—is also critical. The discussion between parent and child may be the child's only chance to understand what is happening. Sometimes, however, the pressure and enormity of this task, along with the advice of others, really proves too great for parents. They choose a short-term covering for themselves, without realizing the long-term effect on their children.

Explaining the How and Why of Death

Children have to know from the beginning what sad is. They have to know why their parents are sad and why they themselves are sad. So parents can begin with, "This is a very sad time," or "A very sad thing has happened," or "Mommy and Daddy are sad because...." Children have to know that it is a death that has made the parents sad: with no explanation, they may think that they have caused the sadness. They also have to know that it is appropriate to feel sad.

The next stage involves an explanation of death and what it means. Death basically means that a person's body stops working and will not work any more. It won't do any of the things it used to do. It won't walk, talk, or move; none of its parts work; it does not see and it does not hear. This foundation is what parents feel comfortable referring back to when children ask questions like "Will Grandpa ever move again?" "Why can't they fix him?" "Why isn't he moving?" "Is he sleeping?" "Can he hear me?" "Can he eat after he's buried?" If parents come up with different answers to all of these questions, it becomes confusing, but when they have a foundation, they can come back to it repeatedly. The notion that something has stopped working is a firm foundation for children, and parents feel comfortable in not lying or deceiving in using this type of explanation.

Because death is a form of abandonment, the words "passed away," "gone away," or "left us," that many people use hold out to the child the hope that the deceased will return, which of course causes tremendous frustration while they wait for the person to return. Appropriate explanations to children of why a particular death happened might be, for example, in a case of terminal illness, "Because the disease couldn't be stopped. The person became very, very sick, the body wore out, and the body stopped working"; in a case of suicide, "Some people's bodies get sick and don't work right, and some people's minds don't work right. They can't see things clearly, and they feel that the only way to solve their problems is to take their own life"; in a case of miscarriage, "Sometimes a baby is just starting to grow; something happens and makes it stop. We don't know what it was—it wasn't anything that anyone did."

CHILDREN'S REACTIONS TO DEATH

When people start to take this information and relate it to their own family situations in preparation for confronting their families, they want to know what they need to be concerned about and what to look for. Even newborn infants and toddlers know when things are different. The smaller they are, the less likely it is that they will be able to figure out why. Children respond to changes in behavior; they sense when life patterns change. Infants may alter their nursing patterns; toddlers become cranky, and change their sleeping and eating patterns. Excitement at home, new people around, parents gone at odd times, a significant person missing, a sad atmosphere—children know that something is different and react accordingly. When parents expect these changes in their children, they can respond to them more sensibly.

Piaget says that children between the ages of three and six years see death as reversible. The way this translates for parents (and for children) is that people will come back, that dead is not forever. Parents have said to me, "How could a child think that somebody will return?" From a child's point of view, ET returns, Jesus and Lazarus returned, and Road Runner returns constantly. And children may misinterpret the rise-again eulogies often given by clergy.

Several years ago (1978), "Sesame Street" produced a program dealing with the death of Mr. Hooper. The program was written up in newspapers and other publications as being an advance for the education of children. The problem is that Mr. Hooper has returned in reruns of the show, so that children who experienced his death now find that Mr. Hooper is back again.

People may say, "My child isn't affected by his grandfather's death—he's only four years old." I say, "Why should he be affected? As far as he's concerned, Grandpa's only going to be dead for a little while." Knowing how children perceive death helps parents to understand their children better, so that they will not become upset when a child continues to ask questions. They know that children in that age range can be expected to ask more questions.

Children also tend to connect events that are not connected. Does this death mean that someone else is going to die? "Grandpa died after he had a headache. Mommy has a headache. Does that mean that she is going to die?" "Old people die. Daddy is old [he is thirty]. Is he going to die?" This means that we have to explain the difference between being very, very sick and just sick like Mommy or Daddy might be; the difference between being very, very old and over twenty; and the difference between being very old and very sick and being very old but not very sick.

Children ages six to nine know that death is final, but they still think about return. They need a more detailed explanation of why a person has died than younger children do. With these children, it is much more important to distinguish between a fatal illness and just being sick—to say, "It's not like when you get sick, or when Mommy or Daddy get sick." If a parent tells a child, "Grandpa had a pain in his stomach, went to the hospital, and died," what is the child to think the next time that Mommy has menstrual cramps? What are children to think when a grandparent dies from lung cancer after a tremendous bout of coughing and then find that their father has a cough? It is normal for children in that situation to start to cling to the father and ask, "Are you okay?"

Children of this age may not want to go to a house where a person has died because "it's spooky." They also have to deal with and understand their emotions, to know that crying, feeling bad, and being angry are all acceptable behaviors.

Children ages nine to twelve move much closer to an adult sense of grieving. They are more aware of the details of an illness and more aware of the impact of a death on them. Consequently, they need more emotional support. They need to know that their feelings are acceptable and that someone is supportive of those feelings.

Teenagers also need support with their new feelings. Parents may find it better to share their own feelings with their adolescent children. Teenagers also have to understand why a person has died.

At the funeral of a friend, I met a man I used to know, another funeral director. He said to me, "It's strange. When I grew up in Queens with my grandfather, we lived in a two-family house for ten-and-a-half years. When my parents had enough money, they bought a house on Long Island, and we moved there. That was in the summer. On my birthday, in October, Grandpa didn't send me a card. I was a little concerned about that, but when Grandpa didn't come for Thanksgiving, and then when he didn't come for Christmas, I asked my mother where Grandpa was. She said he couldn't come." My friend went on: "I couldn't think what I could possibly have done to this dear man that I had spent my childhood with that would cause him not to like me any more. Then it went on again. Grandpa never came in the summer, then it was another Thanksgiving and another

Christmas. It wasn't until I was thirteen that they told me that my grandfather had died. I thought that was bizarre until a woman came into my funeral home three weeks ago and when I said to her, as I say to everybody, 'What did you say to your kids about the death of your mother?' she said, 'I haven't told them. I just told them she went on vacation in Vermont.' " So the difference between ten years ago, or fifteen, or twenty years ago and today is not so great for uninformed parents.

Responsibility

People say, "How can a child feel responsible for the death of another person?" Yet, they will say to their children, "You're driving me crazy," "You'll be the death of me yet," or "Don't give me a heart attack!" Adults may say such things as figures of speech, but children do not always see it that way. "If only I had prayed harder," they may say. Children basically see God as a rewarder or punisher; He rewards good behavior and punishes bad. Therefore, if a child does a bad thing that only he or she knows about, God may punish the child by the death of someone in the child's family. If illness or death follows a misdeed, the child can feel really responsible for this. For example, when a parent leaves the home, a child may say, "If I had cleaned my room (done my chores, hadn't wet my pants, done better in school), maybe he (or she) wouldn't have left." This is what happens when no explanation is given to a child about why a person has died. When a grandparent stops visiting, the child again may say, "What did I do?"

Magical Thinking

Some children believe that by wishing that a person will die, they can cause the person's death. They sometimes also believe that if they think about the death of a person who is dying, they themselves may die.

Anger

This is a common response at the time of a death and one that is extremely damaging to families. Understanding it and anticipating its presence helps families deal with anger from both sides, the parent's and the children's. Children can be angry at parents for not telling them that the deceased was sick, for having spent so much time with the deceased and not enough time with them, for not allowing them to attend the funeral, or just because they need someone to be angry at.

I offer two examples of children's anger at parents. When my brother died, two days after the funeral there was a tremendous downpour. There were two inches of water in the back yard, and my ten-year-old son came to me and said, "I want to pitch my tent in the back yard." I said, "David, you can't pitch a tent. There are two inches of water in the yard!" He became angry, threw the tent down, and walked away. I said to him, "Look, I'll tell you why you're angry: you don't have anyone to be angry at. You can't be angry at your uncle because he was in an automobile accident. He wasn't drunk and he wasn't driving fast. It was a wet road, he didn't know it, and the car turned over and he was killed. You can't be angry at the doctors or the hospital because he was dead when he arrived there." I said, "There's nobody else to be angry at, so the next possibility is to be angry at me. As long as you understand that, it's okay." He came back a while later and said, "You know, after thinking about it, I don't know why I ever wanted to pitch my tent in the yard."

The second example came a few days ago when I spoke to a woman about coming to a funeral. She said, "You know, I was seven years old when they took me to my grandfather's funeral. I could go to the funeral, I could sit outside—my parents even bought me a brand new dress—but I was not allowed to go in and say goodbye to Grandpa. So you know what? I never wore the dress again and I never talked about Grandpa again."

Children can also be angry at themselves for wishing that a person would die or for not visiting or helping a dying person. One young boy had seen his grandfather walking down the street carrying some packages and noticed that his grandfather was not doing so well. But Grandfather did not do well a lot of the time, so the boy helped his grandfather take the packages inside, went on home, and did not say anything to his father about his grandfather. The grandfather died of a heart attack in the house. Later, the boy's father came to me and asked, "What am I going to say? My son said, 'If only I'd told you this time that Grandpa didn't look well, maybe we could have done something.'" Two weeks ago a mother came to me and said, "My daughter thinks that my mother may have died because she failed to send her a get-well card. She thought that maybe it would have saved her if she had sent it."

The driver of a car, the doctor at a hospital, the deceased for putting themselves in dangerous situations, even the event that caused a death—these are just a few examples of the legitimate targets of children's anger. When parents know that children are responding with anger or that they may do so, the parents will do best if they address it directly with the children. The important point for parents is that they feel much more in control when they can anticipate this kind of anger. They know the historical background of their old circumstances, their own blueprint, and if they consider these they can help their children through their anger.

Guilt

This is another aspect of grief and grieving. Knowing that a child may feel guilt, or having it pointed out, lets parents know that their children can, on one hand, be angry at the deceased and, on the other, feel guilty about

being angry. Children may express their guilt in statements such as "I didn't do enough," "I should have visited him before he died," and "If only I hadn't gone to the movies last week instead of going to see Grandpa, I would have been able to say goodbye before he died." All of these "shoulds" and "if onlys" can have a tremendous impact on a family if they are not directed, if nobody anticipated them, and if nobody explains them to the children.

CHILDREN AND FUNERALS

People feel the need to know how to explain what is going to happen next: "After I've explained to my children that this person has died, what do I say to them about what's going to happen now?" I have some material in script form that I offer to families, but basically parents have to start from the beginning with a child. They can say, "Grandpa will be taken from where he died to a funeral home; it's a place where they'll keep him for a few days until he's buried. He'll be dressed in clothes he liked and put into a casket—that's a box we use so that no dirt gets on him when he's buried. People will come to the funeral home to visit and say how sorry they are that Grandpa has died. Because his body isn't working any more, it won't move or do any of the things it used to do, but if you want to come and say some prayers, you can."

The basic premise here is that people will ask whether or not they should bring a child to the funeral home. People are surprised when I say, "Never! Don't ever bring children to a funeral home if you're not going to prepare them for it ahead of time." My son had cardiac surgery a year and a half ago. Before his operation, they showed him the operating room, the recovery room, and the intensive care unit. He knew everything that was going to happen to him before he went into the hospital for the surgery. His doctor even drew a diagram of the operation for him and made a model of the surgical repair out of clay for him. But people will still waltz children into a funeral home and say, "We're just going to see Grandma." Then they wonder why the children are upset when they walk in and find out that Grandma is lying down in a casket and not moving.

Children should be treated like people and given the same concern we give anyone else. They should hear an explanation of what will happen and then be given the opportunity to come to the funeral home or not, but they cannot make that decision without information. If children decide to come, they should be prepared further. They should be told the color of the rugs and walls, whether there are plants or paintings, whether there are flowers, what color the casket is, what color clothing the deceased is wearing, and that the deceased is lying down and not moving. The children should be informed so completely that when they walk into the funeral home it is almost as if they have been there before. Does it work? Children have walked into my funeral home and checked off exactly the points that I covered with their parents three hours before—"Oh, there's a green rug, there's the painting on the wall, there are the flowers." When this happens, I know that the parents have used the information I have provided, and I know that the children are comfortable because the place is not strange to them. All of this draws a child into the family support network on the same side of the wall, rather than putting the child alone on the other side of the wall.

We cannot assume that parents speak to their children about death or that they know how to do so. We cannot assume that if a death occurs suddenly in the middle of the night the parents will be prepared to talk to their children about it at seven o'clock in the morning when they get up. We cannot assume that "user-friendly" information is available, that if parents were given a booklet it would apply, or even that they would read it. I used to think that talking to children about death was only the concern of parents, but another funeral director who is using my program told me that a senior citizen came to him and said, "I'm here because I want to make sure that when I die my children will provide my grandchildren with this type of information."

We cannot assume that children are not talking or thinking about a death, that they are not affected when a family pet dies or by the deaths they see every day on television, or by the death of a neighbor or classmate. We cannot assume that children are prepared in any way to come to a funeral. We cannot assume that their parents have answered their questions or that the children have asked questions. For example, I have found that about 85 percent of the children between the ages of four and twelve who come to a funeral home and see a half-closed casket do not realize or believe that the deceased's legs are in the bottom of the casket. How do I know? Because I have said to parents, address that issue with children:

Walk into the funeral home and up to the casket, and say, "You know, some kids think that the whole person isn't there, so if you want us to, we'll show you the rest of the person." Some parents respond by saying "No, I don't want to do that, I don't want to deal with that." But I have found that their children will accept my invitation to have the bottom part of the casket opened so that they can look inside. I have been putting a family into a limousine and heard a child ask, "Why did they cut Grandma up?" and heard the mother say, "What do you mean they cut Grandma up?" So I have said, "She only saw half of Grandma; let's go back inside." We have gone back in, opened the bottom of the casket, and the child has said, "Oh, yes, she is all there."

Children constantly ask for this type of information. A mother said to me, "Why does my child ask if that's a dummy inside the casket? And why does she ask me how they got the dummy to look so much like Grandpa?" And I say, "What did you say to your child? And she says that she told the child that her grandfather had died and gone to heaven. So I say, "If Grandpa died and went to heaven, who's inside the casket?"

A psychiatrist told me that he had one patient, a five-year-old boy who had been very close to his grandmother. When she died, the boy was told that Grandma had gone right up to heaven. His mother later found the boy standing on the windowsill of the apartment, about to jump out. After the boy was safely on the floor again, his mother asked him why he had been going to jump and what he thought would happen if he did. The boy said, "I would go up, just like Grandma."

So many of the points that seem like separate, discrete bits of information are actually the building materials to be fitted into a family blueprint. When I present this information to parents, they ask, "How do you expect us to put all of this together in our grief? How do you expect us to do that?" I say, "I don't expect you to do that; I expect your funeral director to do it."

Children, Death, and Fairy Tales*

Abstract

"Children, Death and Fairy Tales" examines the evolution and transformation of themes relating to death and dying in children's literature, using illuminating parallels from historical demographics of mortality and the development of housing. The classic fairy tale "Little Red Riding Hood" is used to draw these trends together.

Elizabeth P. Lamers, M.A.

Malibu, California

Historical Background

There is a history behind each of the familiar stories that parents read at their children's bedsides. Many of what have now become common fairy tales had their origin in an oral tradition intended as adult entertainment, replete with ribald humor and sensational events. As these tales began to be transcribed and considered more specifically as material intended for children, they began to contain incidents and behavior that reflected the customs of the place and period in which they were written down and that were intended to provide children with a moral education. Especially in the earliest versions, death had a place in children's stories because of its ubiquity and drama. There have been significant transformations to fairy tales, and to the content of children's stories in general, since a literature for children first appeared. Until recently, topics that have come to be considered disturbing to young people, concerning issues that adults would wish to protect them from, have been diluted, softened, and removed from the literature for children. In our modern generations, children have been insulated from an awareness of mortality.

Particularly in the last hundred years, a significant movement away from issues of morality and mortality has taken place. This has reflected the tremendous changes in attitudes concerning children and death over the last century. These changes have coincided with the shifting of the demographics

of death in this time period and with the changing of attitudes toward children and their upbringing.

Up to the end of the nineteenth century, the highest mortality rate was to be found in children under the age of fifteen; today the highest rate is found in adults of far more advanced years. In the past, children were exposed to dying because it occurred almost exclusively at home after a short illness; death now occurs almost exclusively in some sort of health care institution following a prolonged illness. Although in recent years hospice programs have sought to return dying to the home, the majority of elderly persons still die either in a rest home or a hospital. As a result, children and even young adults today are commonly separated from the reality of death.[1] This isolation is reinforced by a paucity of material that would introduce children to the universal experiences of dying and death.

The changing composition and structure of the modern family has also had an isolating effect on the young person's awareness of mortality. At the end of the last century, it was common for children to grow up as a member of an extended family consisting of parents, grandparents, aunts and uncles who all lived in the same rural area. A child today is more likely a member of a "nuclear" or one parent family, living in an urban area, often separated from relatives by hundreds of miles. Children in rural areas once were exposed to dying and death in their families, in their communities, and among farm animals. They had repeated opportunities to be close to death, to ask questions about death, and to participate in healing religious and social bereavement ceremonies and rituals.

While once the loss of a relative was an occasion for ceremonies that emphasized and reinforced family coherence, today the death of a relative, especially an elderly or distant one, may pass with little or no observance. Many parents have come

---

*This article also appeared as a chapter in *Awareness of Mortality,* J. Kauffman (ed.), Baywood, Amityville, New York, 1995.

to believe that children should be shielded from dying and the facts of death, and it is common today for children to not attend funeral services.[2]

Although children may be exposed to literally hundreds of deaths in television programs and cartoons, these are a different kind of death, typically of a "bad" person, who, because of some evil actions, "deserved" to die. Children's cartoons consistently present a distorted view of mortality, even fostering the especially erroneous conclusion that death is somehow "reversible." With little contradiction, beliefs like these can continue to influence and pervade perceptions of death.[3] They come to stand in place of substantial experiences with dying and death, giving rise to difficulties and misunderstandings in later years, when the child, as an adult, has real experiences with mortality. Beliefs like these have been fostered by the isolation of the child from the experience of death as a part of life, an isolation that can be traced in the transformation that has occurred in the stories and fairy tales that have been read to children since such tales first appeared in written form in the early 1700s.

Books about Death for Children

The removal and glossing over of incidents of dying and death from material that children are exposed to has been occurring regularly since about the 1920s. At the same time religion was being removed from school books. It is only in the last twenty years that this tendency has begun to be reversed, and children's books now often contain topics that were previously taboo, including, feelings, divorce, sex and even death. Religion is still taboo in school books.

From the early 1800s until the 1920s, American children were commonly taught to read with a series of textbooks, such as those by Lyman Cobb, Worcester, Town, Russell, Swan or McGuffey. In *McGuffey's Eclectic Readers,*[4] the subject of many of the selections and poems was the death of a mother or child. These deaths were typically presented as a tragic but an inevitable part of life. The manner in which death was portrayed can be found in such representative examples as William Wordsworth's poem "We Are Seven,"[5] in which a little girl describes her family as having seven children, even though two are dead and buried in the churchyard near their house. The experience of the death of an older sister is also described in this poem. Other selections from the Readers in which death is a theme are: *Old Age and Death*[6] by Edmund Waller, *The Death of Little Nell*[7] by Charles Dickens, *Elegy in a County Churchyard*[8] by Thomas Gray, and *He Giveth His Beloved Sleep*[9] by Elizabeth Barrett Browning.

A selection in the Fourth Reader by an anonymous author, entitled "My Mother's Grave,"[10] provides an emotional account of a young girl's experience with her dying mother. The story aims to make children polite and obedient to their parents, by giving the example of a young girl who didn't realize how fleeting life can be. The author of the story recaptures her thoughts while revisiting the grave of her mother, who had died thirteen years previously. She remembers how she had been unkind to her mortally-ill mother after coming home from a trying day at school. Realizing her lapse in manners later in the evening, she returns to her mother's room to ask forgiveness, to find her mother asleep. The little girl vows to awaken early to "tell how sorry I was for my conduct," yet when she rushes to her mother's room in the brightness of morning she finds her mother dead, with a hand so cold "it made me start." The author relates how, even thirteen years later, her remorse and pain are almost overwhelming. This is not the type of subject matter and emotional content that is generally considered appropriate for today's basal readers.[11] The basal readers commonly used today in classrooms rarely contain any references to death or dying. They might contain a chapter from a book such as *Charlotte's Web,* by E. B. White,[12] but the chapter would not be the one in which Charlotte dies.

Insight into the fashion in which scenes of death and dying were typically portrayed in the nineteenth century can be found in the book *Little Women,* written by Louisa May Alcott in 1869, and still widely read by young readers today. Alcott wrote of the death of young Beth in a straightforward manner that was especially uncommon for her day. Recognizing that her depiction was at odds with the melodramatic scenes that were current in more romantic literature, Alcott added in the paragraph following Beth's death: "Seldom, except in books, do the dying utter memorable words, see visions, or depart with beatified countenances. . . ."[13]

The elements that Alcott took exception to were all common in death scenes in the literature of 1830 to 1880, where they reflected the expectations of an audience that was accustomed to being given a romanticized picture of death and its consequent "final reward" in what was known as "consolation literature." A preoccupation with death and a glorification of the afterlife was evident in popular literature from both England and America in this period. Much of this literature was written either by Protestant clergy (especially Congregationalists and Unitarians), their wives, or other pious women of the congregation.[14]

Between 1940 and 1970 only a few children's books contained references to death. Two that have become classics are *The Dead Bird* by Margaret W. Brown[15] and *Charlotte's Web* by E. B. White.[16] White's publisher initially refused to publish *Charlotte's Web* unless the ending was modified to allow Charlotte to live. White refused.[17] The book was criticized by reviewers who said that death was not "an appropriate subject for children." *Charlotte's Web* is still a best-seller, and often is one of the books which second or third grade teachers choose to read to their classes.

The separation of children from death has diminished somewhat in the last twenty years. Elizabeth Kubler-Ross'[18] early work helped make death a subject that could be discussed and studied. Children's books in the late sixties began to discuss subjects that had previously been neglected, such as death and divorce. During the nineteen seventies and eighties over 200 fiction books were written for children with death as a major theme. Unfortunately very few measured up to the standard set by *Charlotte's Web, Little Women, The Yearling* or *The Dead Bird.* During the same period some very good non-fiction books about death were written for children of various ages. (See resource list at end of chapter.)

This cornucopia of books on death has helped to begin to make death a more acceptable topic for discussion. The hospice movement has also helped by reintroducing home care for dying persons to many communities. Even so, many children are still insulated from death and often are discouraged from attending funerals. It is not unusual to find adults in their forties who have never attended a funeral.[19] The diminished awareness of mortality that begins in childhood is often carried on into adulthood.

The Development of Children's Literature

Prior to the development of a literature intended specifically for children in the middle of the seventeenth century, there were two characteristic ways in which children were considered. The first was a holdover from the age of the Greeks and Romans, in which children were perceived as miniature adults. Another manner of perceiving children, as something infra-human, was distinguished by Michel de Montaigne, the French humanist and essayist of the sixteenth century. It is difficult, however, from a modern perspective, to be sympathetic to Montaigne's assertion that children possessed "neither mental activities nor recognizable body shape."[20]

Authors writing children's literature in the eighteenth century were primarily interested in educating children and assisting them to become socially acceptable human beings. Beyond providing just a certain amount of book learning, they also sought to teach the correct ways to behave. For this reason, all the tales of Charles Perrault had an emphatic moral at their end. They were cautionary tales of what could happen to a child if he or she didn't act in a proper fashion. Some of Perrault's titles were: La Belle au Bois Dormant (Sleeping Beauty),[21] Le Petit Chaperon Rouge (Little Red Riding Hood)[22] and Les Fées (Toads and Diamonds).[23] As pointed out by Maria Tartar in Off With Their Heads!:

> From its inception, children's literature had in it an unusually cruel and coercive streak—one which produced books that relied on brutal intimidation to frighten children into complying with parental demands. This intimidation manifested itself in two very different forms, but both made examples of children. First, there were countless cautionary tales that managed to kill off their protagonists or make their lives perpetually miserable for acts of disobedience. Then there were stories about exemplary behavior which, nonetheless, had a strange way of also ending at the deathbeds of their protagonists."[24]

In 1658, John Amos Comenius's Orbis Sensualium Pictus (A World of Things Obvious to the Senses Drawn in Pictures), a Latin school book, was published. This teaching device was the first picture book for children,[25] and it was also the first to respond to the recognition that children needed their own literature because they were not scaled-down adults. It was still almost a century later, however, before children's literature began to come into its own. In 1744, John Newbery wrote A Little Pretty Pocket Book[26] for children. This book is credited as signifying the "real" start of children's literature in England.

Fairy Tales

Fairy tales provide an excellent example of the fashion in which themes that came to be considered distressing to children have been moderated over time, and insulation of children from an awareness of mortality can be traced through the progression of different versions of typical stories. A generalization can be made about fairy tales as they came to be thought of specifically as children's stories: the sexual content was diminished, and the amount of violence tended to be increased. This process can be seen in successive editions of the Brothers Grimm's Fairy Tales. To understand this evolution, it is necessary to have a picture of the environment in which it took place. According to the perception of children's needs current at the time that the Brothers Grimm were writing, children did not need to be protected from portrayals of violence.

William Jordan in Divorce Among the Gulls provides a dramatic context for the state of life that was not untypical for children in London a mere one hundred years after the time that a children's literature came into being:

> "I doubt that any of us can comprehend how brutal the fight for survival has been throughout evolution. We ignore our prehistoric, evolutionary legacy, a world in which most children died in infancy or childhood, where teeth rotted out by the age of twenty, where gangrene took the lives of the injured, where thirty-five was foul old age. Even as recently as 1750 in London, the toll of disease staggers the mind: of 2,239 children born that year, only 168 were still alive five years later."[27]

From its inception, literature for children has been motivated by a belief that children needed written material, not so much for entertainment, but to prepare them for life. The majority of books published and intended for children up through the 1800s can be compared to James Janeway's A Token for Children: Being an Account of the Conversion, Holy and Exemplary Lives, and Joyful Deaths of Several Young Children (1671–72).[28] The London Bills of Mortality for the period shortly following the publication of Janeway's book show that the mortality rate of children age five and under was running as high as 66 percent.[29] Writers of this era commonly concurred with Janeway's position that they held a sacred duty to salvage the souls of those who were "not too little to go to Hell." The exemplary stories in A Token for Children were also designed to provide comfort to children faced with the tragedy of a sibling's death or confronted with their own mortality when visited by some dread disease.[30]

The violence and death in stories written for children takes on a different light when put in the context of such high rates of mortality. The practice of abandoning unwanted children either at the Foundlings' Hospital or on church steps was increasing in the seventeen hundreds. It was not just the poor but all classes who contributed to the ranks of abandoned children. The foundling institution was established to make it possible to dispose of infants without leaving any record. Buffon noted in 1772 that about one-third of all children born in Paris that year were abandoned. Jean-Jacques Rousseau (1712–1778) claimed to have turned his five children over to the state, leaving them at the Foundlings' Hospital at birth.[31]

A high mortality rate for children was reflected in children's literature. As Freud noted in *The Interpretation of Dreams*, half the human race failed to survive the childhood years.[32] The characteristically romanticized depiction of an afterlife, that was superior to the life of this world, was seen as a way to help children cope with the brutal facts of the life they had no choice but to lead. In the seventeenth and eighteenth centuries, children were routinely required—not just encouraged—to attend public executions so that they could see the price of criminal behavior. This says much about the methods of child rearing believed appropriate in this era.[33]

The Brothers Grimm's story "Aschenputtel," or "Cinderella," shows an emphasis on punishment that was lacking in the earliest oral versions, and that increased in intensity in subsequent editions. In the early version, taken by Perrault from the oral tradition, Cinderella forgave her stepsisters for mistreating her and introduced them at court. Grimm's first version has Cinderella's sisters turning pale and being horrified when Cinderella becomes a princess, but in the second edition the sisters are punished by being blinded by pigeons that peck out their eyes.[34]

In the Brothers Grimm's "Hansel and Grethel" there is a description of how horribly the witch howled when Grethel pushed her into her own oven and how "... Grethel ran away, and therefore she was left to burn, just as she had left many poor little children to burn."[35] The use of violence as punishment for bad behavior is typical in fairy stories. And violent occurrences were frequently shown to be the result of even minor misdeeds. This tendency is evident in the collection of stories found in *Struwwelpeter*. In these short tales Little Pauline plays with matches and goes up in flames, and Conrad the Thumbsucker gets his thumbs sliced off. As Tartar observes the interesting point here is that "... the weight is given to the punishment (often fully half the text is devoted to its description) and the disproportionate relationship between the childish offense and the penalty for it make the episode disturbing."[36]

The removal of sexuality from books intended for children was a development that paralleled the evolution of housing in Europe. In the Middle Ages houses were rarely more elaborate than was necessary. Few homes had more than one room. The poor had hovels which were little more than a shelter for sleeping. Family life tended to be compromised. Because there was no room for children, only for infants, the older children were commonly sent away to work as apprentices or servants.

The living quarters of the bourgeoisie would typically be above a store or artisan's shop. It generally consisted of a single, large room in which the household cooked, ate, transacted business, entertained and slept. Households of up to twenty-five people were not uncommon. Privacy was unknown,[37] and children were not sent to bed in their own rooms so that racy stories could be told to adults only. Beds were generally large because they were intended to hold more than one or two people. Children lived and worked alongside adults and listened to the same stories. Since children were in the company of adults who were not their parents, but were employers or other servants, there was not the same concern then about what children were exposed to that parents of today have.

By the seventeenth century, living arrangements had evolved so that there tended to be greater segregation between quarters allocated to working, food preparation and sleeping. There still tended to be a main room used for dining, entertaining and receiving visitors, but servants and children began to be separated into smaller rooms adjacent to the central, common areas.[38] It was at this time that fairy stories began to be transformed into works intended more strictly for children. This transformation of living spaces coincides with other changes that had great impact on children, including attitudes about how children should be taught about proper behavior, and about death and dying.

By looking at the changes in one fairy tale, Little Red Riding Hood, we can observe the changes in attitudes toward death, children and their education. The earliest known oral version of the tale of Little Red Riding Hood, for example, would not generally be considered suitable entertainment for children today. In the version of the story traditionally told in Brittany, Little Red is unwittingly led by the wolf to eat her grandmother's flesh and drink her blood, and she performs a provocative striptease for the disguised wolf before climbing into bed with him. Little Red later escapes from the wolf when she goes outside to relieve herself. As this tale was originally told, its primary purpose was to entertain adults, so it was not as heavily encumbered with the admonitions and advice that later came to distinguish versions of this tale intended for children.

The earliest written version of Little Red Riding Hood was recorded in French by Charles Perrault in 1696–97. The title of the story in French was 'Le Petit Chapeon Rouge.' The 'chapeon' was a hat worn in the Middle Ages, which suggests an even earlier oral tradition.[39] One of the fullest texts faithful to the traditional, oral versions of "Little Red Riding Hood" was also recorded in France at the end of the nineteenth century.[40]

Perrault's first version of the tale was published in *Histoires ou Contes du Temps Passé* (Stories [Tales] of Times Passed), subtitled *Contes de Ma Mère L'Oye* (Tales of My Mother Goose). Perrault included seven other tales along with the tale of Little Red Riding Hood. Each of these tales had a moral in verse at the end. In this version of Little Red's tale, the grandmother and Little Red are both eaten by the wolf, and both perish. Although Perrault did not have Little Red's mother giving her any initial warnings before she departed for her grandmother's house, he did conclude the story with a moral suitable for the intended audience of children: Do not speak to strangers or you, too, may provide a wolf with his dinner. The violence of this story is later moderated in the Brothers Grimm's retelling, by the introduction of an additional character, a hunter or woodcutter, who is able to rescue Little Red and her grandmother by slicing open the wolf and letting them out.

The version of Little Red's tale as told by the Brothers Grimm also gives an expanded role to Little Red's mother, who gives Little Red many warnings and much advice before sending her off through the forest to her grandmother's house. Little Red is admonished to "make haste . . . go straight . . . behave prettily and modestly . . . do not run . . . and do not forget to curtsy and say 'good morning' to everyone who knows you."[41] These initial admonitions served to educate the young audience of the story in the manners that were expected of them, and they provided a framework in which the resulting action of the story would be played out. The Brothers Grimm vividly portrayed the consequences of not heeding mother's advice. Interestingly, in this version, the hunter refers to the wolf as "old sinner,"[42] perhaps as an oblique reference to risqué incidents excised from the children's version but remembered from the oral tradition.

In a popular nineteenth century retelling of Little Red's tale the grandmother still gets eaten by the wolf, but Little Red survives and learns to pay closer attention to her mother's words: "For she saw the dreadful end to which/ A disobedient act may lead."[43] This version of the tale has an interesting emphasis on avoiding any unnecessary suffering of the characters. Here is the depiction of the wolf putting an end to the grandmother:

"He jumped up on the bed, and ate her all up. But he did not hurt her so much as you would think, and as she was a very good old woman it was better for her to die than to live in pain; but still it was very dreadful of the wolf to eat her."[44]

The editor of *Old Favorite Fairy Tales* was apparently undecided about whether the grandmother's fate was good or bad. When the woodcutter arrives on the scene to rescue Little Red, he advises her that one shouldn't "tell one's affairs to strangers, for many a wolf looks like an honest dog,"—an interesting way of warning a young girl that looks can be deceiving!

In later versions, the hunter arrives in time to shoot the wolf before he eats either Little Red or her grandmother, and in still other versions, even the wolf is spared to escape through an open window, or to become Little Red's pet. The moral or message of the story also evolves with the transformation of the events depicted in the tale. In the traditional, oral version of Little Red Riding Hood, Little Red was not forewarned by her mother about the dangers of talking to strangers, therefore Little Red cannot be seen as naughty or disobedient. In Perrault's original written version, the mother does not give Little Red any cautions, either, while in later versions the mother often gives many instructions and admonitions to her daughter. Upon rescuing Little Red from the dire misfortune she brings upon herself, the hunter/woodcutter inevitably gives her a lecture on obedience and points out to her that she now knows what can happen if she disobeys her mother's warnings. The role that mortality plays in the changing tale of Little Red Riding Hood is seen to diminish as the tale evolves. Rather than being the graphic and unmourned event as Perrault depicted it, it becomes unrealistically softened in the later versions, eventually being banished to the periphery of the young audiences' attention.

What Is a Fairy Tale?

To better understand the significance of the place that fairy tales, and other tales told to children, have in determining the formation of attitudes relating to death and dying, it is helpful to become familiar with some of the different definitions that these tales have been given. Fairy tales have been defined in various ways by different people. Rollo May considered fairy tales to be " . . .our myths before we become conscious of ourselves."[45] Bruno Bettelheim wrote,

"The figures and events of fairy tales . . . personify and illustrate inner conflicts, but they suggest ever so subtly how these conflicts may be solved, and what the next steps in the development toward a higher humanity might be . . . presented in a simple homely way. . . . Far from making demands, the fairy tale reassures, gives hope for the future, and holds out the promise of a happy ending."[46]

Madonna Kolbenschlag writes:

"Fairy tales are the bedtime stories of the collective consciousness. They persist in cultural memory because they interpret crises of the human condition that are common to all of us. They are shared wish fulfillments, abstract dreams that resolve conflicts and give meaning to experience."[47]

Edwin Krupp makes a distinction between fairy tales and the rest of children's literature:

"The term 'fairy tale' is sometimes used for all children's stories, but the fairy tale really has its own special character. It involves or takes place in another realm or world, not in the one in which we usually reside. Fairy tales are really stories of the supernatural. Other laws prevail in them, and the creatures that inhabit them do not belong to ordinary reality."[48]

All of these definitions are good and even have merit in their own context, yet they are unsatisfying in their failure to consider the origin of these tales in adult entertainment and the purposeful manner in which they were converted into tales intended for children.

There is an easily confusing overlap between fairy tales, folk tales and myths. Myths are the most easily distinguishable, as they are mainly stories intended to provide explanations for the occurrence of natural phenomenon, generally by personifying a natural effect as an animistic or anthropomorphic deity. The depiction of the sun in its course as Apollo driving his fiery chariot, and winter being caused by Demeter mourning for the six months of Persephone's captivity in Hades, are typical of mythological stories. Even though, in their later elaborations, myths might come to deal with models of behavior and other topics commonly found in fairy tales, their origins can be found in the earliest explanations of natural phenomena. Broad definitions like Rollo May's seem to apply more clearly to myths than to fairy tales.

Folk tales and fairy tales are not as easily distinguished, as indicated by the fact that published collections of folk tales and fairy tales may very well contain some of the same stories.

A characteristic of fairy tales is the flexible way that they have been perceived by authors. Authors in different times and places have recognized that fairy tales are capable of carrying a message that can be tailored to fit their particular needs. Existing as they do in the common domain, fairy tales and their characters provide an easily accessible medium for both writers and their audience. The task of the audience is eased by the familiarity of the characters and situations with which they are presented, and the writer's burden is lightened as he brings stories from an earlier time into conformity with the standards he is trying to represent. The subtle or obvious manner in which a fairy tale departs from its audiences' expectations, while still fulfilling their desires, is a measure of its successful telling. A current example of this phenomenon is the bestseller *Women Who Run With the Wolves,*[49] in which many fairy tales are retold with an emphasis on their pertinence to the modern female experience.

Fairy tales are also significant in the wide range of characters and situations that may be found in them. Children are presented characters that they can identify with in fairy tales—commonly in the guise of a child not unlike him or herself—who is faced with an adverse situation in which he or she is called upon to make new judgments and exhibit mature behaviors. Children can be exposed to a range of novel situations through the fairy tale, and exposed to models for their own behavior to fit a variety of needs. The most popular fairy tales, especially, have always adapted as adult perceptions of children's needs have changed, and adult needs to communicate various lessons to children have changed.[50]

In distinction to fairy tales, folk tales often concern the actions of pseudo-historical or typical personages who are engaged in activities that represent cultural standards that children are expected to aspire to. The unerring accuracy of William Tell is related in a folk tale, as is George Washington's chopping down of the cherry tree and his precocious, unwavering honesty. The adventures of Paul Bunyan and his gigantic blue ox, Babe, are folk tales that recast popular stories from the era of the westward expansion of the United States as "tall tales" with a common, main character.

It cannot be maintained, as Bettelheim's definition suggests, that a fairy tale invariably holds the promise of a happy ending. The Little Mermaid, which is a definite fairy tale, has been subjected to a great of distortion, or "artistic license," to produce a happy ending. At the conclusion of the tale as Hans Christian Andersen originally wrote it, the Little Mermaid chooses death for herself rather than murdering the Prince, which would have enabled her to regain her form as a mermaid. The only consolation for the Little Mermaid, who had already sacrificed her home, family, and voice to pursue her love for the mortal, human Prince, is, that after performing deeds of kindness for three hundred years as a "daughter of the air," she might gain a human soul and join the Prince in heaven. The very morning that the Little Mermaid sacrifices herself and spares the Prince, he marries a princess from another land whom he mistakenly believes had rescued him from drowning, when actually the Little Mermaid had saved him. Only in Disney's version does the Little Mermaid manage to displace the "other woman" and marry the Prince. Disney justifies this alteration by casting the evil sea-witch in disguise as the other princess.

The classic fairy tale "Bluebeard" also presents a problematic ending. In this fairy tale, one of three sisters marries a wealthy but mysterious man, distinguished primarily by a beard of blue color. After the wedding, the wife is given access to all Bluebeard's possessions, but she is forbidden to use one small golden key. When she inevitably opens the door the key unlocks, she discovers the bloody bodies of Bluebeard's previous wives. When Bluebeard discovers his wife's transgression, he prepares to add her to his collection. At the last moment, the wife is saved by the sudden appearance of her brothers, who hack her husband into pieces before her eyes. The happiness of the ending of this tale must be considered more one of degree; although the latest wife did not meet the fate of her predecessors, is it really a happy ending to have your brothers murder your husband? This tale also leaves unresolved the dilemma of the wife's part in the action. Her disobedience is a necessary part of the story, yet there is no clear resolution to this issue. The fast and easy way to conclude a fairy tale is to recite "and they lived happily ever after," yet when one takes a close look at fairy tales there are many which do not have a "perfect" ending.

The Future of Fairy Tales

When folk and fairy tales existed solely in an oral medium, every storyteller was able to tell a version of a story that was personalized by the demands of his or her time, place and audience. When stories came to exist more exclusively in printed form, they began to reflect more enduringly the nature of the time and place in which they were recorded. For this reason, it is especially odd that we continue to read to our children—often without the slightest degree of critical reflection—unrevised versions of stories that are imbued with the values of a different time and place. L. Frank Baum, the originator of the tales of the Land of Oz (1900), recognized this predicament, and recommended that it was time for a new set of 'wonder tales,' and that previous fairy tales should be classed as 'historical.'[51]

There is a growing perception that children are capable of having an understanding of dying and death as natural processes, and that the lifelong relationship a person has to dying and death is based in no small measure on the experiences of childhood. In the last twenty years, there has been a revolution in the practices and perceptions surrounding dying and death, yet little has been effectively done to transmit these changes to children. Adults are beginning to recognize the difficulties they have experienced as a result of being sheltered from an awareness of mortality and the need is felt for a way to transmit a realistic awareness of mortality to children.

Denoting traditional fairy tales as 'historical' would help distinguish the changes in values and behaviors that have occurred in the many years since they were recorded, and would encourage parents and teachers to more critically examine just what they are presenting to children. Modern editions of fairy tales have enormous appeal, demonstrated by the lavishly illustrated editions that have been offered recently by some of the large publishing houses. It is interesting to note that reviews of these books have concentrated on the beauty of the illustrations, the size of the book, the quality of the paper . . . in other words on everything but the content. The assumption seems to be that the buying public already knows what the content is and that no explanation is necessary.

But it is important to consider the implications of fairy tales in our modern world. Perhaps it is time to begin transforming them to reflect the tremendous changes that have occurred in a world increasingly forced to accept the limits of medical technology, where death is being acknowledged again as a necessary and inevitable counterpart to life.

Reading with a child is a wonderful activity; introducing someone to the world of books is to offer them the promise of a greater and better world. Fairy tales can be an important part of this process, because their "real" existence is in the imagination of a child. Through the action of a fairy tale a child can learn that he or she can confront circumstances that are new or frightening and be able to do the right thing. It is important that the tales we tell to our children reflect what we ourselves believe. Rather than continuing to insulate children from the realities of death and dying—especially by providing the unsuitable types of messages that Saturday morning T.V. provides—fairy tales can provide a medium for children to be introduced to the types of situations that they will encounter all their lives.

One of the few activities that haven't changed since the eras of our parents and grandparents is tucking a child into bed with a story, even down to the story we might choose to read. There is a comfort in this nostalgia, and a sense of continuity to this activity that can make all involved believe in the truth of the final " . . . and they lived happily ever after." A cartoon in a recent edition of *the New Yorker* magazine illustrated this, while also showing the capacity fairy tales have to portray facets of the world that are not necessarily easy to explain. The cartoon showed a mother reading a bedtime story to her daughter with the caption, "She married and then divorced, and then she married and divorced, and then she married and lived happily ever after."

Although this cartoon was certainly intended to be ironic, it still points out the purpose of providing moral instruction that fairy tales can fulfill. With the expanding use of hospice programs and the corresponding increase in opportunities for children to be exposed to meaningful death experiences, and the increase of the awareness of the lethalness of AIDS, it is important that even the tales told to children come to reflect current perceptions of dying and death.

Notes

1. De Spelder, Lynne A. & Strickland, Albert L. 1983. *The Last Dance.* Palo Alto, CA: Mayfield Publishing.
2. Lamers, E. P. 1986. The dying child in the classroom. In G. H. Paterson (Ed.), *Children and Death* (pp. 175–186). London: King's College.
3. Lamers, E. P. 1986. The dying child in the classroom. In G. H. Paterson (Ed.), *Children and Death* (pp. 175–186). London: King's College.
4. *McGuffey's Eclectic Readers* (Vols. 2–6) (1920). New York: Van Nostrand.
5. Wordsworth, William. We Are Seven, *McGuffey's Eclectic Readers* (Vols. 2–6) (1920). New York: Van Nostrand, Third Reader, p. 163.
6. Waller, Edmund. Old Age and Death, *McGuffey's Eclectic Readers* (Vols. 2–6) (1920). New York: Van Nostrand. Sixth Reader, p. 95.
7. Dickens, Charles. The Death of Little Nell, *McGuffey's Eclectic Readers* (Vols. 2–6) (1920). New York: Van Nostrand. Sixth Reader, p. 96.
8. Gray, Thomas. Elegy in a County Churchyard, *McGuffey's Eclectic Readers* (Vols. 2–6) (1920). New York: Van Nostrand. Sixth Reader, p. 108.
9. Browning, Elizabeth Barrett. He Giveth His Beloved Sleep, *McGuffey's Eclectic Readers* (Vols. 2–6) (1920). New York: Van Nostrand, Sixth Reader, p. 195.
10. Anonymous, My Mother's Grave. *McGuffey's Eclectic Readers* (Vols. 2–6) (1920). New York: Van Nostrand, Fourth Reader, p. 253.
11. A basal reader is a text with which reading is taught. There are many different series, each usually having one book per grade level.
12. White, E. B. 1952. *Charlotte's Web.* New York: Harper & Row.
13. Alcott, Louisa M. 1947. *Little Women.* New York: Grosset & Dunlop, (originally pub. 1869), p. 464.
14. Douglas, Anne. 1988. *The Feminization of American Culture.* New York: Anchor Press. "The Domestication of Death," p. 200–226.
15. Brown, Margaret W. 1965. *The Dead Bird.* Reading, MA: Addison-Wesley.
16. White, E. B. 1952. *Charlotte's Web.* New York: Harper & Row.
17. Guth, D. L. 1976. *Letters of E. B. White.* New York: Harper & Row, p. 531.
18. Kubler-Ross, E. 1969. *On Death and Dying.* New York: Macmillan.
19. Newton, F. I. 1990. *Children and the Funeral Ritual: Factors that Affect Their Attendance and Participation,* Masters Thesis, California State University, Chico.
20. Encyclopaedia Britannica. 1976. Children's Literature, Macropaedia, Vol. 4, p. 229.
21. Perrault, Charles. *La Belle au Bois Dormant* (Sleeping Beauty). In Mulherin, Jennifer (Ed.). 1982. *Favorite Fairy Tales.* London: Granada Publishing, p. 12.
22. Perrault, Charles. *Le Petit Chapeon Rouge* (Little Red Riding Hood). In Mulherin, Jennifer (Ed.). 1982. *Favorite Fairy Tales.* London: Granada Publishing, p. 22.
23. Perrault, Charles. *Les Fees* (Toads and Diamonds). In Mulherin, Jennifer (Ed.). 1982. *Favorite Fairy Tales.* London: Granada Publishing, p. 52.
24. Tatar, Maria. 1992. *Off With Their Heads! Fairytales and the Culture of Childhood.* Princeton, NJ: Princeton University Press. p. 9.
25. Johnson, Clifton. 1963. *Old-Time Schools and School Books.* New York: Dover (reprint of the Macmillan 1904 edition), p. 16.
26. Newbery, John. 1744. *A Little Pretty Pocket Book.* Encyclopaedia Britannica, (1976), Children's Literature, Macropaedia, Vol. 4, p. 231.
27. Jordan, William. 1991. *Divorce Among the Gulls,* New York: Harper Collins, p. 169.
28. Janeway, James. *A Token for Children: Being an Account of the Conversion, Holy and Exemplary Lives, and Joyful Deaths of Several Young Children.* (1671–72). In Tatar, Maria. 1992. *Off With Their Heads! Fairytales and the Culture of Childhood.* Princeton, NJ: Princeton University Press, p. 14.
29. Tatar, Maria. 1992. *Off With Their Heads! Fairytales and the Culture of Childhood.* Princeton, NJ: Princeton University Press, p. 14–15.
30. Tatar, Maria. 1992. *Off With Their Heads! Fairytales and the Culture of Childhood.* Princeton, NJ: Princeton University Press, p. 87.
31. Boorstin, D. J. 1992. *The Creators.* New York: Random House, p. 573.
32. Freud, S. The Interpretation of Dreams, Vol. 4 of the Standard Edition, trans. James Strachery (London: Hogarth, 1953), p. 254. In Tatar, *Off With Their Heads! Fairytales and the Culture of Childhood.* Princeton, NJ: Princeton University Press, p. 46.
33. Tatar, Maria. 1992. *Off With Their Heads! Fairytales and the Culture of Childhood.* Princeton, NJ: Princeton University Press, p. 46.
34. Tatar, Maria. 1992. *Off With Their Heads! Fairytales and the Culture of Childhood.* Princeton, NJ: Princeton University Press, p. 7.
35. Owens, L. 1981. *The Complete Brothers Grimm Fairy Tales.* New York: Avenel, p. 57.

36. Tatar, Maria. 1992. *Off With Their Heads! Fairytales and the Culture of Childhood.* Princeton, NJ: Princeton University Press, p. 34.

37. Rybcznski, Witold. 1987. *Home: A Short History of an Idea.* New York: Penguin, p. 28.

38. Rybcznski, Witold. 1987. *Home: A Short History of an Idea.* New York: Penguin, p. 38.

39. Mulherin, Jennifer (Ed.). 1982. *Favorite Fairy Tales.* London: Granada Publishing, p. 22.

40. Tatar, Maria. 1992. *Off With Their Heads! Fairytales and the Culture of Childhood.* Princeton, NJ: Princeton University Press, p. 37.

41. Owens, Lily. (Ed.) 1981. *The Complete Brothers Grimm Fairy Tales.* New York: Avenel Books, p. 109.

42. Owens, Lily. (Ed.) 1981. *The Complete Brothers Grimm Fairy Tales.* New York: Avenel Books, p. 112.

43. Tatar, Maria. 1992. *Off With Their Heads! Fairytales and the Culture of Childhood.* Princeton, NJ: Princeton University Press, p. 39.

44. 1933. *Old Favorite Fairy Tales,* National Publishing Co., p. 20.

45. May, Rollo. 1992. *The Cry for Myth.* New York: Delta, p. 196.

46. Bettelheim, Bruno. 1977. *The Uses of Enchantment.* New York: Vintage Books, p. 26.

47. Kolbenschlag, Madonna. 1981. *Kiss Sleeping Beauty Good-Bye.* New York: Bantam, p. 2.

48. Krupp, Edwin C. 1991. *Beyond the Blue Horizon: Myths and Legends of the Sun, Moon, Stars, and Planets.* New York: Harper Collins, p. 11.

49. Estés, Clarissa P. 1992. *Women Who Run With the Wolves.* New York: Ballantine Books.

50. Tucker, Nicholas. 1982. *The Child and the Book.* New York: Cambridge, p. 80.

51. Tatar, Maria. 1992. *Off With Their Heads! Fairytales and the Culture of Childhood.* Princeton, NJ: Princeton University Press, p. 19.

Books about Death for Children and Young Adults

The following list of books is a sample of general books (fiction and non-fiction) about death available for children.

Non-fiction:

Bernstein, Joanne, & Gullo, Stephen J., *When People Die,* New York: Dutton, 1977.

Le Shan, Eda J., *Learning to Say Good-by: When a Parent Dies,* New York: Macmillan, 1976.

Richter, Elizabeth, *Losing Someone You Love. When a Brother or Sister Dies,* New York: Putnam's, 1986.

Rofes, Eric E. & The Unit at Fayerweather Street School, *The Kids' Book About Death and Dying,* Boston: Little, Brown & Co., 1985.

Segerberg, Osborn, Jr., *Living With Death,* New York: Dutton, 1976.

Stein, Sara B., *About Dying,* New York: Walker, 1974.

Zim, Herbert, & Bleeker, Sonia, *Life and Death,* New York: Morrow, 1970.

Fiction:

Alcott, Lousia M., *Little Women,* New York: Grosset & Dunlop, 1947. (originally pub. 1869) (sister—illness)

Alexander, Sue, *Nadia the Willful,* New York: Pantheon, 1983. (brother—accidental)

Aliki, *Two of Them,* New York: Greenwillow, 1979. (grandfather—old age)

Bartoli, Jennifer, *Nonna,* New York: Harvey House, 1975. (grandmother—natural death)

Blume, Judy, *Tiger Eyes,* Scarsdale, NY: Bradbury, 1981. (father—murdered in robbery)

Brown, Margaret W., *The Dead Bird,* Reading, MA: Addison-Wesley, 1965. (wild bird—natural death)

Bunting, Eve, *The Empty Window,* New York: Frederick Warne, 1980. (friend—illness)

Coerr, Eleanor, *Sadako and the Thousand Paper Cranes,* New York: Putnam, 1977. (Hiroshima—leukemia caused by radiation)

Craven, Margaret, I *Heard the Owl Call My Name,* New York: Doubleday, 1973. (young priest—illness)

de Paola, Tomie, *Nana Upstairs and Nana Downstairs,* New York: Putnam, 1973. (great-grandmother and grandmother—natural death)

Douglas, Eileen, *Rachel and the Upside Down Heart,* Los Angeles: Price, Stern, Sloan, 1990. (father—heart attack)

Gerstein, Mordicai, *The Mountains of Tibet,* New York: Harper & Row, 1987. (reincarnation)

Hermes, Patricia, *You Shouldn't Have to Say Good-bye,* New York: Harcourt, 1982. (mother—illness)

Hickman, Martha W., *Last Week My Brother Anthony Died,* Nashville, TN: Abingdon, 1984. (infant brother—congenital heart condition)

Kantrowitz, Mildred, *When Violet Died,* New York: Parent's Magazine Press, 1973. (pet bird—natural death)

Mann, Peggy, *There Are Two Kinds of Terrible,* New York: Doubleday, 1977. (mother—illness)

Miles, Miska, *Annie and the Old One,* Boston: Little, Brown, 1971. (Navajo Indians—grandmother—natural death)

Paterson, Katherine, *Bridge to Terabithia,* New York: Crowell, 1977. (friend—accidental death)

Saint Exupery, Antoine de, *The Little Prince,* New York: Harcourt, 1943. (death—general)

Smith, Doris B., *A Taste of Blackberries,* New York: Crowell, 1973. (friend—bee sting allergy)

Talbert, Marc, *Dead Birds Singing,* Boston: Little, Brown, 1985.(mother, sister—car accident)

Tobias, Tobi, *Petey,* New York: Putman, 1978. (gerbil—illness)

Varley, Susan, *Badger's Parting Gifts,* New York: Lothrop, Lee & Shepard, 1984. (personified animals—remembering someone after death)

Viorst, Judith, *The Tenth Good Thing About Barney,* New York: Atheneum, 1971. (pet cat—natural death)

Warburg, Sandol Stoddard, *Growing Time,* Boston: Houghton Mifflin, 1969. (pet dog—natural death)

White, E. B., *Charlotte's Web,* New York: Harper & Row, 1952. (death as a natural consequence of life)

Wilhelm, Hans, *I'll Always Love You,* New York: Crown, 1985. (pet dog—natural death)

Williams, Margery, *The Velveteen Rabbit,* New York: Holt, Rinehart & Winston, 1983 edition. (life and death—general)

Zolotow, Charlotte, *My Grandson Lew,* New York: Harper & Row, 1974. (grandfather—remembering him)

Failing to Discuss Dying Adds to Pain of Patient and Family

TALKING AROUND DEATH

ESTHER B. FEIN

Joan Siff and her father, Martin Isaacs, were as close, she thought, as parent and child could be. She had always enjoyed the facility of his mind and the generosity of his heart. Though he never went to college, they would have lengthy talks about classical literature and class division in American society. His passion was poetry, and in 1991, Mrs. Siff's sons, Andrew and Michael, published a volume of their grandfather's verse as a family legacy.

But for all the time they spent talking about his life, Mrs. Siff and her father never once talked about his death. When he was young and healthy, working as a social worker for New York City, it never occurred to Mrs. Siff to raise the subject.

As he aged, Mr. Isaacs had no real physical problems until he reached his late 80's, when he suffered a series of strokes that compromised his memory, his balance and eventually his thinking. Yet even then, as the situation grew more urgent, father and daughter never talked about death.

Mrs. Siff and Mr. Isaacs are not unusual. For all the vociferous political debates about how best to allow people to die with dignity, few people discuss with their doctors or their families what kind of treatment they want when they are dying.

Talking in advance about death is clearly no salve for the pain of losing a mother, a child or a friend. But when people avoid the subject, many health care experts say, dying often becomes even more traumatic to patients and those caring for them, compounding the loss that even the most careful planning can never erase.

People die after undergoing lengthy and frequently painful treatments that they never told anyone they did not want. Families are forced to make critical decisions for loved ones who are no longer mentally competent and who never voiced their wishes. And doctors—many of whom do not initiate discussions about care at the end of life even with terminally ill patients—treat the dying not knowing whether their patients would consider their care too aggressive or not aggressive enough.

For Mrs. Siff, the fact that Mr. Isaacs never spoke to her or to his own doctor about the kind of care he wanted at the end of life meant that three times during her father's hospitalization, as he lay in a coma unable to communicate, she was alone in making wrenching decisions about how aggressively doctors should treat him, decisions that she says still haunt her more than a year after his death.

Mr. Isaacs was among 20 people who died at Beth Israel Medical Center in Manhattan during the first 11 days of November 1995, a period chosen at random to consider the overwhelming decisions that patients, health care workers and families confront in an era of medical advances that have enabled bodies to function long after brains have ceased to.

Administrators at Beth Israel, which lies at First Avenue and 16th Street in Stuyvesant Town, agreed to contact the families and doctors of people who had died at the hospital during this period and to provide their charts to the New York Times on the condition that each name be used only with the family's consent.

Twenty deaths in 11 days is about average for Beth Israel. And as in any other 11 days, some people died slowly, others quickly, some in great pain, others more comfortably. Some came from nursing homes. One was a 5-year-old. Some were surrounded by family and private doctors. Others relied on emergency room physicians. A few had thought about death and planned what sort of care they wanted. Most had not.

In addition to the 20 who died in the hospital, 14 people died during that time in Beth Israel's hospice program, most of them at home. Although nearly 400,000 Americans will die this year in such programs, which allow them to die at home with a minimum of intrusive care, most of the 2.3 million people who die each year in this country still die in hospitals, many unprepared for the decisions that they and their families will face.

In the last decade, public debate about death and dying has intensified. The Supreme Court is reviewing two Federal court rulings that have opened the way for doctors to help mentally competent terminally ill patients who choose to end their lives—rulings that are opposed by a broad range of people who fear that the right to die will become the obligation to die.

Medical schools are revamping their curriculums to teach young doctors how to advise dying patients and their families. (Now, only 5 of 126 medical schools in the nation have a separate, required course about dealing with death.) And hospitals and insurers are creating complicated formulas to determine when to use costly life-prolonging treatments.

A growing number of people are choosing friends or relatives to act as proxies should they become unable to make decisions for themselves, and more hospitals have ethics committees to help medical personnel, patients and families sort through the harrowing emotions and choices that dying presents.

But examining the records of the 20 people who died at Beth Israel Medical Center—a pioneer in confronting medical and ethical issues surrounding death—and speaking with surviving relatives, doctors, nurses, social workers and hospital administrators, show that to many people, death remains a subject never broached in private, a taboo.

"If people don't express what they want, or someone doesn't do it for them, it's a matter of pure luck if they get what they want," said Dr. Robert G. Newman, president and chief executive at Beth Israel and an ardent supporter of patients' rights. "There's a spectrum of horror to blessing in the death process. To leave it to luck is foolhardy at best, dangerous at worst."

The Daughter
Not Ready to Speak for
Her Father

Joan Siff said she thought little about death until Oct. 23, 1995, when an ambulance brought her 91-year-old father, Martin Isaacs, to the Beth Israel Medical Center emergency room. He was disoriented, feverish and suffering from bedsores. Senility had robbed him of his ability to speak for himself, and his wife, Mrs. Siff's stepmother, was too emotionally fragile to make decisions for him. Mrs. Siff assumed the role of her father's advocate.

After several difficult days, Mr. Isaacs' bedsores began healing. A social worker was putting together a plan to sent him home.

But then, at 6:30 P.M. on Nov. 1, a nurse on routine rounds found that Mr. Isaacs had stopped breathing. His blood pressure had plummeted so low, she could not get a reading. He was deathly pale.

Doctors raced to his room and performed cardiopulmonary resuscitation. They revived his heart, but Mr. Isaacs fell into a coma. Unable to breathe on his own, he had a stiff tube inserted down his throat and into his lungs, and he was attached to a ventilator. Instead of going home, he was transferred to the intensive care unit.

The next day, Dr. Yoav Borsuk, a second-year resident in internal medicine, and Dr. Paul Mayo, co-director of the medical intensive care unit, sat down with Mrs. Siff and her stepmother to discuss Mr. Isaacs' condition. His brain was functioning only minimally. There was scant chance he would breathe again without the ventilator. Although he had stopped writing poetry years earlier, he would now no longer even appreciate hearing its rhythms.

"Dr. Mayo was so kind," said Mrs. Siff, a teacher of adult education. "The first thing he said was: 'Tell me about Mr. Isaacs. I only see him now, like this, but tell me what he was like when he was young and healthy.' "

Nonetheless, Mrs. Siff said her meeting with Dr. Mayo and Dr. Borsuk was devastating. For the first time, she realized that her father was dying, and she was forced to make what she said was the most difficult decision of her life. Dr. Borsuk, the resident, noted in the chart that Mrs. Siff and her stepmother "expressed their wishes that no aggressive medical treatment or intervention be taken because 'he suffered so much so far.' "

Dr. Mayo's note in the chart, however, indicated that the family was still struggling with what such an approach meant, considering that Mr. Isaacs was attached to a respirator that could keep his hopeless body technically alive for a long time. "The family does not request active disconnect," Dr. Mayo wrote, "but rather a peaceful completely noninterventional approach leading to peaceful death."

To give the family time to absorb the reality of Mr. Isaacs' condition, Dr. Mayo said he waited a day before discussing with them whether they wanted to place in his chart a "do not resuscitate," or D.N.R., order, instructing doctors not to revive him should he suffer the kind of attack he had four days earlier.

Mrs. Siff agonized over the decision.

"I am in general a believer in not keeping people alive if in general they are more dead, but I had a hard time signing something saying that they shouldn't save my father," she said. "If he had told me, if we had talked, it would be different. Maybe he would want those few extra weeks or days no matter what. It's possible.

"I don't think he would, but without ever having spoken directly about it, I'm just guessing."

The Personal Physician
'I'm Still Lazy' in Preparing Patients

Mrs. Siff was not alone in her ignorance about her father's wishes. Mr. Isaacs also never talked about death with his regular doctor, Alan R. Raymond, even as he began to slide from health to infirmity.

Dr. Raymond, 42, said that he never learned about preparing patients for death either in medical school training or on the wards. "It's just not ingrained as part of our history and practice," he said.

Beth Israel has been at the forefront of demystifying the dying process by encouraging patients to name health proxies, which empower someone else to make decisions about health care when a patient no longer can, and urging doctors to have frank conversations with their patients about issues involving the end of life.

It was one of the first hospitals in the state to create an ethics committee to explore these difficult matters. It is one of the few medical centers in the nation that distributes proxy forms and information about choices for the dying to patients who make routine visits to its outpatient offices. And Beth Israel requires residents training there to demonstrate three times their ability to talk with

patients and their families about death.

But even here the reality of how patients and doctors talk about death intrudes daily on decisions about care.

As Dr. Raymond saw Mr. Isaacs began to falter, he never suggested to his patient that he name a health proxy, nor did he talk to him about how aggressively he wanted doctors to prolong his life. Dr. Raymond said he "very rarely" discussed proxies and death with any of his patients—including those in frail health—even though he had, in the past, "been nicely chastised by the ethics committee" because such omission had complicated the care of patients.

In fact, on the day he was interviewed, four of Dr. Raymond's terminally ill patients were in the hospital. Only one, who had severe heart disease, had a proxy. The other three, two with advanced lung cancer and one with pancreatic cancer, had none.

The ethics committee has no power to force private doctors who practice at Beth Israel to raise these issues with their patients, but can only try to educate and persuade them.

"As a practicing physician you'd think I'd have learned," he said. "But I'm still lazy on the subject."

In Mr. Isaacs' case, Dr. Raymond acknowledged that he "absolutely should have" talked to him about proxies and "end of life" care options, but did not. "Even if I couldn't talk with him," Dr. Raymond conceded, "I should have with his wife or daughter."

The Staff
Mixing Directness and Compassion

On Nov. 5, after getting the full support of her family, Mrs. Siff signed the request asking doctors not to revive her father if his heart stopped.

Days passed with no improvement in Mr. Isaacs' condition. He

developed bacterial pneumonia. Dr. Patricia Villamena, an attending physician in pulmonary and critical care medicine, gently suggested to Mrs. Siff that she consider disconnecting her father from the machine that inflated his lungs 10 times a minute, a hissing and whooshing sound accenting each artificial breath.

Mrs. Siff was stunned. Agreeing to the "do not resuscitate" order, not knowing her father's wishes, had been tortuous. This decision seemed unbearable. "The question of whether he lived or died was on my head," she said.

Though it is often a brutal process, it is critical to be direct, even blunt, with families, Dr. Villamena said. Too often, she said, doctors resort to medical jargon or euphemisms, either because they want to preserve a kind of superiority over patients and families or out of sheer discomfort. But that only intimidates and confuses families.

"When it's true, you need to use absolute terms, like 'There's no hope,' " Dr. Villamena said. "That allows families and patients to make appropriate decisions with the least amount of guilt and grief."

As she visited her father and stared for hours at his withered body, tethered to a web of tubes, Mrs. Siff said she became lost trying to fathom what he would want and what she had a right to do. Although a few months earlier, on the advice of an estate lawyer, she had had her father sign a document naming her as his health proxy, Mrs. Siff doubted his capacity to understand what he was signing and why. Even at that point, the two did not talk about "end of life" care and death.

Driven by indecision, Mrs. Siff turned to Navah Harlow, who started as Beth Israel's first patient advocate in 1979 and is now director of its 14-person department of medical ethics. With Mrs. Harlow's help, Mrs. Siff scoured her memory for conversations with her father, searching for a hint of what he might have wanted.

When Mrs. Siff's mother was dying of rheumatoid arthritis, her father fretted about the tormenting stream of testing and probing that would never change the fact that the woman he so adored, a woman just 48 years old, would soon die. She also remembered a discussion about the landmark case of Karen Ann Quinlan, whose parents successfully argued to the New Jersey Supreme Court that they had the right to disconnect their brain-dead daughter from a respirator.

"I remembered he had said, 'It's sad, but it's not a life,' " Mrs. Siff recalled.

Speaking to Mrs. Harlow, Dr. Mayo and Dr. Villamena, Mrs. Siff said she felt comforted by the hospital staff's compassion. But as she struggled deciding what to do, blind to her father's wishes, she said she grew increasingly distressed at what she called the "lack of sensitivity" her father's longtime doctor showed to his dying patient and at what she saw as the doctor's failure to prepare Mr. Isaacs and his family for complicated decisions they would face near his death.

"It's like he saw Dad as a patient, not as a person," she said, "like he was his symptoms, not a whole human being."

The Decision
Suddenly, Room Grows
Quiet

On Nov. 8, Mrs. Siff finally asked that her father be disconnected from the ventilator. In a letter to Dr. Villamena, she wrote that although her father had left no written directions for his death, "he would clearly be opposed to any extraordinary means of life support" and "would wish to carry on in a natural way without mechanical intervention."

Dr. Raymond, as his primary care doctor, concurred. The medical center's ethics committee was brought in. As its rules require, Dr. Mark Rosen, chairman of the ethics committee, and chief of the pulmonology department, evaluated Mr. Isaacs on the morning of Nov. 10 to verify his medical status. He agreed that given the patient's irreversible condition, mechanical ventilation should be withdrawn.

Beth Israel allows families of patients with no proxies or written directions great leeway in showing proof of what a patient would have wanted. Many other hospitals, concerned over possible lawsuits or sanctions by regulatory agencies, demand either written documentation of a patient's wishes or a conversation witnessed by more than one person.

Dr. Newman said that Beth Israel's policy was based on the premise that as long as each decision was made with the best interest of the patient paramount, nobody would challenge its practice. Nobody ever has.

On Nov. 10, two hours after the ethics committee gave its approval and 18 days after Mr. Isaacs was admitted to the hospital, Dr. Deborah Ushkow withdrew the tube that ran from the ventilator down Mr. Isaac's throat to his lungs and shut the machine off.

The room went suddenly quiet. Mr. Isaacs' pulse was a steady 82 beats per minute. His blood pressure was a weak 90/40. He was taking 16 labored breaths a minute on his own. An hour and a half later, at 2:15 P.M., he was pronounced dead.

A year later, Mrs. Siff still revisits her decision. She asks herself whether in some way she betrayed her father: did she allow him to die in a way he might not have wanted? She is haunted by ambiguity.

"It's a good thing for healthy people not to be obsessed by death, but you have to be prepared," she said.

And yet, with all that she has experienced, Joan Siff has not chosen a health proxy for herself; nor has she written out her wishes for when her own end nears.

Judith Treas is professor of sociology at the University of California, Irvine. She holds a Ph.D. in sociology from UCLA and is the author of numerous articles on population, aging, family, and inequality.

The author gratefully acknowledges the research assistance of Quan Nguyen, the editing of Mary Kent, and the helpful comments of reviewer Jacob S. Siegel. She is also grateful for research support from the National Institute on Aging and the California Policy Seminar, and for access to computer resources through the University of California.

Older Americans in the 1990s and Beyond

by Judith Treas

The population age 65 and older quadrupled during the first half of the 20th century.

The growth and change of America's older population rank among the most important demographic developments of the 20th century. Falling fertility and longer lives transformed the elderly from a small component to a significant part of the U.S. population. A sizable segment of all consumers, voters, homeowners, patients, and family members are older adults. In one way or another, every social institution in American society has had to accommodate to older people's needs, court their favor, or mobilize their resources and contributions.

Older people are living a lifestyle that few could have envisioned in their youth. Public programs for the elderly—and the succession of increasingly wealthy cohorts—has brought retirement (and even early retirement) within the reach of most people. In fact, active retirement has emerged as an idealized lifestyle that encompasses social engagements, travel, hobbies, volunteer activities, independent living, Sunbelt migration, and even part-time jobs.

Although many older Americans fully enjoy this active and relatively affluent lifestyle, many others cannot. Poverty is no longer endemic in the older population—as it was 40 years ago—but it is still a reality for 12 percent of all elderly people, 28 percent of older African Americans, and 21 percent of elderly Hispanics.

Disability and the loss of independence is also a concern. Because the same demographic developments that contributed to the growth of the older population have lengthened the number of years people will live in advanced old age, chronic illness, disability, and dependency are a poignant reality for many of today's older Americans.

The future elderly population of the United States can be seen today in the large baby-boom generation and their less numerous younger siblings and children. Some current trends will be accentuated among the elderly of the 21st century—such as increasing educational levels and ethnic diversity. Their economic security, however, hinges on many unknowns, including the future of Social Security and other government programs that have benefited older Americans.

As most 65-year-olds will testify, age 65 is an arbitrary marker for entry into old age. In the 1990s, most people retire well before age 65, and most "young-old," people age 65 to 74, are reasonably healthy and live active and independent lives. It is those age 75 and older, particularly the "oldest-old" (age 85 or older),

From *Population Bulletin,* May 1995, pp. 2-10, 12-19. © 1995 by the Population Reference Bureau, Inc., Washington, DC 20036. Reprinted by permission.

Table 1

U.S. Population and Population Age 65 and Older, 1900-2050

Year	Population in thousands		Percent Age 65+	Percent increase from preceding decade	
	Total	Age 65+		Total	Age 65+
1900	75,994	3,099	4.1	—	—
1910	91,972	3,986	4.3	21.0	28.6
1920	105,711	4,929	4.7	14.9	23.7
1930	122,755	6,705	5.5	16.1	36.0
1940	131,669	9,031	6.9	7.3	34.7
1950	152,271	12,397	8.1	15.6	37.3
1960	180,671	16,675	9.2	18.7	34.5
1970	205,502	20,107	9.8	13.5	20.6
1980	227,225	25,707	11.3	10.6	27.9
1990	249,415	31,224	12.5	9.8	21.5
Projections					
1995	263,434	33,649	12.8	—	—
2000	276,241	35,322	12.8	10.8	13.1
2010	300,431	40,104	13.3	8.8	13.5
2020	325,942	53,348	16.4	8.5	33.0
2030	349,993	70,175	20.1	7.4	31.5
2040	371,505	77,014	20.7	6.1	9.7
2050	392,031	80,109	20.4	5.5	4.0

Source: U.S. Bureau of the Census, *Historical Statistics of the United States: Colonial Times to 1970* (Washington, DC: GPO, 1975); and *Current Population Reports* P25-1104 (Washington, DC: GPO, 1993), Table 2.

Growing Numbers

In 1995, almost 34 million Americans had lived past their 65th birthday, accounting for one in eight Americans. By virtue of its size, this older population has made itself felt throughout U.S. society—in national politics, in the health care system, at the corner market, and in the multigenerational family.

In 1900, there were only 3 million older adults in the United States, and they made up 1 in 25 Americans (see Table 1). The growth of the older population can be traced to the surer survival of the increasingly large generations of Americans born during the first quarter of this century when birth rates were higher than they are today. The aging of the 19 million immigrants who entered the United States in the first three decades of this century also contributed to this growth. While most of today's foreign-born elderly entered the United States long ago as children or young adults, others arrived fairly recently to join family members already here. These recent arrivals have added further to the size of America's older population.

Although the population age 65 and older quadrupled during the first half of the 20th century, the pace of growth is slowing as the relatively small cohort born during the Great

who are most vulnerable to the problems we associate with old age—widowhood, declining health, and the difficulty of going about daily life without assistance.

This *Population Bulletin* focuses on the demographic trends and economic well-being of the U.S. population age 65 and older, and looks at how this group will change. The elderly population of the first half

of the 21st century is already here. They are the young and middle-age adults of today. But how long and how well these future elderly will live depends upon medical advances, lifestyle changes, economic trends, political developments, and many other uncertainties. For now, today's older Americans provide the best yardstick for gauging what tomorrow's elderly will be like.

Figure 1

U.S. Population by Age and Sex, 1900, 1970, 1995, and 2030

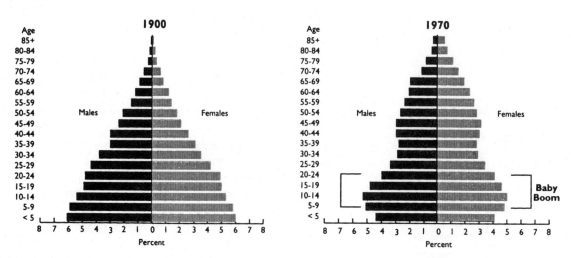

Source: U.S. Bureau of the Census, *Historical Statistics of the United States: Colonial Times to 1970* (Washington, DC: GPO, 1975); and *Current Population Reports* P25-1104 (Washington, DC: GPO, 1993), Table 2.

Figure 2

Dependency Ratios for Child and Older Populations, United States, 1900-2050

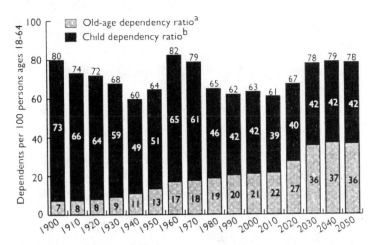

a Old-age dependency ratio is the number of persons age 65 and older per 100 persons of working age (ages 18-64).
b Child dependency ratio is the number of children under age 18 per 100 persons of working age (ages 18-64).

Source: U.S. Bureau of the Census, *Historical Statistics of the United States: Colonial Times to 1970* (Washington, DC: GPO, 1975); and *Current Population Reports* P25-1104 (Washington, DC: GPO, 1993), Table 2.

share of the total U.S. population owes much to trends in fertility. Except during the baby boom (1946 to 1964), U.S. birth rates have moved downward throughout this century. In the last quarter of the century, American women have averaged 2.1 or fewer births each. Such long-run fertility declines enlarge the share of the population in older ages because fewer children are born to fill out the lower end of the age spectrum.

The demographic trends of the 20th century are reflected in the population pyramids appearing in Figure 1. In 1900, high fertility assured that each new generation was larger than the one that preceded it. The United States had a young population with relatively few older persons. As fertility fell and more people survived to old age, the elderly's share of total population climbed. By 1970, this growing elderly population crowned a population pyramid that had been pinched in the middle by the small cohorts born during the 1930s Depression. The bottom of the pyramid bulged with the baby boomers, who were between 6 and 24 years of age in 1970. The baby boomers temporarily "younged" the U.S. population, but the falling fertility rates during the 1970s produced the smaller "baby bust" cohort and population aging resumed. By 1995, the baby boomers

Depression of the 1930s moves into old age. After the first baby boomers turn 65 in 2011, however, the ranks of the older population will begin to swell again. After 2030, the older population's rate of increase will fall sharply as the smaller baby-bust generation begins to turn age 65. By the middle of the 21st century, there will be 80 million people age 65 or older, roughly one in five Americans.

Because the number of older persons grew faster than the overall population, the older population's share of total population almost doubled— from 4 to 8 percent—between 1900 and 1950. By 1995, the percent age 65 and older reached nearly 13 percent of the U.S. population. Although declining mortality and the aging of increasingly larger generations account for the numbers of elderly, their

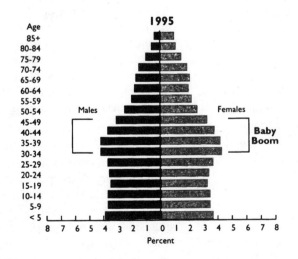

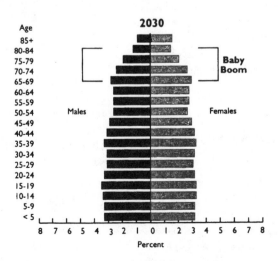

had moved to the middle of the population pyramid, raising the median age of Americans to 34 years from 28 in 1970.[1] By the third decade of the 21st century, however, this entire generation will have joined the ranks of the older population, and the median age of the U.S. population is projected to be 38.6 years.

The aging of the U.S. population has prompted concern and even alarm about society's capacity to pay for pensions, finance health care for chronically ill elders, and offer the personal assistance that disabled older adults need in their daily lives. This capacity will depend largely on the long-run performance of the economy, a trend that is more difficult to forecast than the inevitable aging of generations already born. From a purely demographic perspective, however, a society's ability to support its oldest members depends not only on the number of elderly in relation to the number of "working age breadwinners, taxpayers, and caretakers, but also on the number of dependent children. The number of persons age 65 and older per 100 adults ages 18 to 64 nearly tripled between 1900 and 1990—from 7 to 20—while the relative number of children declined (see Figure 2). Overall dependency is lower now than it was in the early decades of the 20th century when fertility was higher, and substantially lower than in the 1960s and 1970s when the baby boom was young. Today, both young and old can look to nearly 60 million middle-age baby boomers for support. The societal burden will become much heavier in the 21st century when the relative number of old-age dependents begins to climb sharply.

Aging of the Elderly Population

The older population is growing older. In part, because of gains in life expectancy at advanced ages, the population age 85 and older makes up the fastest growing age group in the U.S. population. The number of

American centenarians, which more than tripled to 52,000 between 1980 and 1995, may reach 1 million by the middle of the 21st century. Because advanced old age is associated with

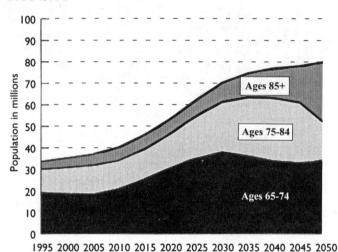

Figure 3

Projection of the U.S. Elderly Population by Age, 1995-2050

Source: U.S. Bureau of the Census, *Current Population Reports* P25-1104 (Washington, DC: GPO, 1993). Table 2.

chronic illness and functional impairments, the aging of the older population portends a substantial increase in the need for health care and supportive social services.

The relatively vigorous "young-old" (ages 65 to 74) will continue to make up the majority of older Americans until about 2030. After that time, people age 75 or older will account for more than half of all elderly. By the middle of the 21st century, most of the projected growth of older Americans will occur because of increases in the population age 85 and older (see Figure 3). This surge in the number of oldest old can be explained both by the aging of the baby-boom generation into extreme old age and by the continuing mortality declines at the advanced ages that many scientists expect.

Unbalanced Sex Ratio

Older women outnumber older men in almost all societies. Among Americans age 65 and older in 1995, there

were 60 men for every 100 women. The disparity becomes even more marked for those age 85 and older—39 men per 100 women. This shortfall of men reflects higher male mortality at all ages. Male babies have higher infant mortality rates; men have higher death rates in the teen and young adult years (primarily from injuries and, more recently, AIDS); and middle-age and older men have higher death rates from heart disease and other chronic illnesses. Although about 105 boys are born for every 100 girls, women outnumber men by age 30 because of the higher male mortality rates. At age 64, the sex ratio, or the number of men per 100 women, is 88. At age 65 and older, the sex ratio is highly skewed, especially for some population groups. It is 69 for older whites, for example, 63 among elderly African Americans, and 76 among older Asians.

Women benefited more than men from improvements in life expectancy in this century. Consequently, the gender differentials in mortality widened and the sex ratio of men to women decreased. The lopsided sex ratio that resulted from the greater life expectancy gains for women has some nega-

Figure 4
U.S. Elderly and Non-Elderly Population by Race/Ethnicity, 1995 and 2050

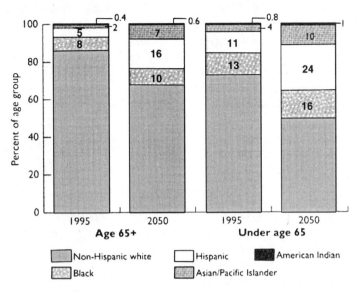

Source: U.S. Bureau of the Census. *Current Population Reports* P25-1104 (Washington, DC: GPO, 1993). Table 2.

tive side effects: The brunt of widowhood, solitary living, and late-life poverty has fallen on women.

The long downward slide in the sex ratio for older adults came to a surprising halt during the 1980s, probably because deaths from heart disease declined significantly for men but not for women.[2] If the sex differential in mortality continues to narrow, it may help equalize the number of men and women in the older population and ease some of the loneliness, poverty, and other ill effects of an extremely low sex ratio.

Ethnic Diversity

The older population is becoming more ethnically and racially diverse—although at a slower pace than the overall population of the United States. Because of higher birth rates and immigration rates of ethnic and racial minority groups, African-American, Hispanic, and Asian populations are increasing more rapidly than is the non-Hispanic white population. Non-Hispanic whites made up about 80 percent of the U.S. population in 1980, but this share slipped to 74 per-

cent by 1995. Similarly, the ranks of the minority elderly are growing more rapidly than those of the non-Hispanic whites. Non-Hispanic whites' share of the elderly population declined from 88 percent in 1980 to 85 percent in 1995. This trend will accelerate in coming decades. By 2050, the non-Hispanic white share of the elderly population is projected to fall to 67 percent (see Figure 4).

The ethnic composition of the elderly minority population will change dramatically in coming decades. Although blacks and Native Americans will slowly gain population shares, the most remarkable growth is projected for Hispanics and for Asians and Pacific Islanders. Blacks are the largest minority in 1995, with 8 percent of the 65-and-older population, but they may be surpassed in number by Hispanic elderly before 2020. By the middle of the 21st century, one in six Americans age 65 and older is expected to be Hispanic. Asians and Pacific Islanders are expected to grow from 2 percent of older Americans in 1995 to 7 percent in 2050.

Some senior centers already offer *tai chi* exercise classes or serve

tamales for lunch, a reflection of greater ethnic diversity. As the ranks of elderly minorities grow, however, their needs, values, and preferences may call for fundamental changes in programs and services for the elderly. In general, minorities come to old age with fewer economic resources than do non-Hispanic whites. They tend to be less educated, have lower incomes and fewer assets, and are less likely to own their own homes. Many elderly immigrants speak little English, and some follow the diets and health practices of their cultures. Minority seniors also have distinctive health needs: African Americans, for example, are more likely than whites to have hypertension (high blood pressure), which requires medical screening to identify people who would benefit from diet and lifestyle changes or medication. In dealing with the frailties of old age, minority seniors have relied more on family members and less on formal services and nursing home care than have other older Americans.

Although the elderly are becoming more ethnically diverse, they still look very different from the under-65 population that helps to support them because the racial and ethnic composition of the younger population is changing even faster. In 1995, 72 per-

Table 2
Countries of Birth for Elderly Immigrants Admitted in 1993

Country	Immigrants (in 1000s)	Percent
All countries	39.8	100.0
Former Soviet Union	7.0	17.5
Philippines	4.7	11.9
China	4.3	10.7
India	2.2	5.6
Mexico	2.2	5.6
Vietnam	2.1	5.4
Iran	1.9	4.7
Cuba	1.5	3.9
Dominican Republic	1.0	2.6
South Korea	0.8	2.1
Other	12.1	30.0

Source: Immigration and Naturalization Service, *1993 Statistical Yearbook of the Immigration and Naturalization Service* (Washington, DC: GPO, 1994). Table 13.

cent of the population under age 65 was non-Hispanic white. By 2050, however, the under-65 population will be only 49 percent non-Hispanic white; nearly one-fourth will be Hispanic, 16 percent African American, and 10 percent Asian. The plurality of ethnic groups will eventually be reflected in the older population as these younger generations age.

International Immigration

Immigration has been one of the major engines of ethnic change among the elderly. It adds to their numbers and diversity both through the aging of immigrants who arrived as youngsters or working-age adults, and through the more recent entry of elderly immigrants. One-tenth of the U.S. population age 65 and older is foreign born. The share is much greater in states that have been important destinations for immigrants. The foreign born make up about one-fifth of the older populations of California, New York, and Hawaii.

Because people who immigrate are typically young, immigration bolsters the middle of the population age structure and slows the aging of the U.S. population. This "younging" effect is dampened by emigration from the United States, which probably ranges between 150,000 and 200,000 annually.[3] Unless immigration continues, the younging effect is short lived. Immigrants who stay on eventually grow old and ultimately add to the ranks of the elderly. Most foreign-born elderly Americans immigrated when they were young; more than half entered the United States before 1950. In 1990, however, 10 percent of foreign-born persons age 65 and older were recent immigrants who arrived during the 1980s. Many of these newcomers are among the more than 1 million older people who say they are unable to speak English very well.

Why do older people move to the United States? Nearly one-fourth (23 percent) of legal immigrants age 65 or older admitted in 1993 were refugees, but most older people who immigrated came to be closer to family members already living in the United States. More than two-thirds of older people lawfully admitted to permanent U.S. residence in 1991 gained entry as the parents of U.S. citizens, an admission category that is not subject to direct numerical limitation under U.S. immigration law.

Elderly newcomers differ markedly from the foreign-born individuals who have lived in the United States for many decades. They are younger, less likely to speak English, and more likely to trace their origins to Asia and Latin America than to Europe. More than half of the 40,000 persons age 65 and older who were granted permanent residency in 1993 were born in Asia or the Pacific region. The Soviet Union was the only European birthplace reported by significant numbers of older immigrants in 1993 (see Table 2). The former Soviet Union unleashed a flow of refugees in the early 1990s when it relaxed immigration restrictions in the face of economic hardship and the demise of communism, but this is likely to taper off over the next few years.

When immigrants enter the United States after retirement age, they seldom have pensions or other regular income. They must either depend on their kin or seek public assistance. More than one-quarter of the elderly immigrants who entered the United States since 1980 received welfare in 1989, compared with about 7 percent

of U.S.-born elderly.[4] In 1992, over 400,000 legal aliens age 65 and older received Supplemental Security Income (SSI), the federal assistance program for the aged, blind, and disabled. More than half had been U.S. residents for at least five years.[5]

Most adults remain in their own homes or communities after retirement.

Although most noncitizens are already barred from collecting public assistance for five years after entering the United States, the rapid increase in immigrant SSI recipients has prompted proposals in Congress to limit SSI to citizens, refugees, and legal immigrants age 75 and older. Because most elderly aliens have no other income and very poor employment prospects, the consequence of eliminating federal benefits is likely to shift more responsibility for the support of destitute elderly newcomers to state and local agencies. The impact of greater local responsibility for older immigrants will weigh most heavily on the

Table 3

Life Expectancy at Birth and at Age 65 by Sex, 1900-1993

| | Life expectancy in years | | | | | |
| | At birth | | | At age 65 | | |
Year	Total	Male	Female	Total	Male	Female
1900[a]	47.3	46.3	48.3	11.9	11.5	12.2
1950	68.2	65.6	71.1	13.9	12.8	15.0
1960	69.7	66.6	73.1	14.3	12.8	15.8
1970	70.8	67.1	74.7	15.2	13.1	17.0
1980	73.7	70.0	77.4	16.4	14.1	18.3
1990	75.4	71.8	78.8	17.2	15.1	18.9
1993[b]	75.5	72.1	78.9	17.3	15.3	18.9

[a] Based on 10 states and the District of Columbia (Death Registration Area); age 65 data from 1900-1902 period.
[b] Provisional data.
Source: National Center for Health Statistics, *Vital Statistics of the United States, 1989: Volume II, Mortality, Part A* (Washington, DC: GPO, 1993), Table 6-4; and unpublished data.

states with the most elderly immigrants, such as California and Hawaii. . . .

Living Longer

The life expectancy of Americans made extraordinary gains in this century. In 1900, a newborn could expect to live only 47.3 years. By 1993, U.S. life expectancy was 75.5 years—a gain of 28.2 years (see Table 3).

Before improved sanitation, better nutrition, and medical advances curbed many acute and infectious diseases, high levels of infant and child mortality depressed overall life expectancy; thus, initial increases in overall life expectancy owed more to the improved odds of infants reaching adulthood than to a greater likelihood of adults surviving to old age. While infant mortality remains higher than the national average in some localities and among some minority groups, the U.S. rate is low by world standards—8.3 deaths to infants under age one per 1,000 births in 1993. Children's crude death rates are now so low—an estimated 30 deaths annually per 100,000 children age 1 to 14 in 1993—that only small improvements can be expected in the average mortality of U.S. children.

Deaths are concentrated among the old. In 1993, 73 percent of all deaths occurred to persons age 65 and older; 23 percent occurred to persons age 85 and older. Although deaths averted among the old contribute fewer years of remaining life than can infant lives saved, declining death rates among the 65-and-older population have become an important force for gains in overall life expectancy.

The effect of these recent gains at older ages may be offset by recent increases in mortality for young adults. Provisional data for 1993 show life expectancy at birth down slightly from 1992 as a consequence of HIV, now the third leading cause of death among young adults age 25 to 44.[11]

Long-run declines in mortality contributed to the growth of the older population by permitting Americans to survive to older and older ages. Contin-

Table 4

Leading Causes of Death for Persons 65 and Older, 1992

Cause	Number of deaths	Percent
All causes	1,575,214	100.0
Diseases of the heart	595,314	37.8
Malignant neoplasms (cancer)	362,060	23.0
Cerebrovascular diseases (stroke)	125,392	8.0
Chronic lung diseases	78,182	5.0
Pneumonia and influenza	67,489	4.3
Diabetes mellitus	37,328	2.4
Unintentional injuries	26,633	1.7
Kidney diseases	18,711	1.2
Artherosclerosis	15,995	1.0
Septicemia	15,884	1.0

Source: National Center for Health Statistics, *Monthly Vital Statistics Reports* 43, no. 6, Supplement (Dec. 1994), Table 6.

ued improvements in mortality permit the old to live even longer. In 1900, a 65-year-old could expect to live another 11.9 years. By 1993, life expectancy at age 65 had risen to 17.3 years. With a life expectancy of 10.9 years, a 75-year-old in 1993 had almost as many remaining years of life as the average 65-year-old at the beginning of the 20th century. Even at age 85 and older, Americans averaged 6.0 years of remaining life in 1993.

Longer lives for older people are a fairly recent phenomenon. Although half of the 20th century's gains in life expectancy at birth were accomplished before the 1940s, most of this reflected lower death rates among younger people. Half of this century's gains in life expectancy after age 65 occurred since 1960. In fact, the population age 65 and older gained an additional year of life just between 1980 and 1991.

Women generally live longer than men and have made greater gains in life expectancy during this century. Over the past decade, however, this gender gap has begun to narrow. In 1900, women's life expectancy at birth was 48.3 and exceeded men's by 2 years. Because women's life expectancy rose more quickly than men's, this gender gap widened. The gulf was widest in 1979, when women lived 7.8 years longer than

men, on average. Life expectancy for men began to catch up to that of women in the 1980s. In 1993, female life expectancy at birth was 78.9 years while that for males was 72.1. Although the sex differential was dramatically higher in 1993 than it was at the beginning of the century, the gender gap in life expectancy—6.8 years in 1993—has narrowed by a full year since 1979.

Racial gaps in life expectancy, however, show little sign of closing. The average life expectancy for African Americans has remained six to eight years lower than for whites since the 1970s.[12] In 1993, provisional figures for life expectancy at birth were 73.0 for white men, compared with 64.7 for black men. Among women, the figures were 79.5 years for whites versus 73.7 years for blacks. Although life expectancy has improved for both racial groups, African Americans still have a striking and persistent mortality disadvantage to whites. African-American men live 8.3 fewer years than white men, on average, while African-American women can expect to live 5.8 fewer years than white women. This racial gap is just as wide as it was several decades ago, and could increase because of racial differences in AIDS and homicide deaths.

Much of the racial difference in life expectancy stems from higher mortality in younger ages. Black infants die at more than twice the rate of white and Hispanic babies, and young black males are more than twice as likely to die as young white males. By age 65, white Americans' advantage has dwindled to about two years. In 1993, black men age 65 could expect to live another 13.4 years, compared with 15.4 years for white men this age. Sixty-five-year-old black and white women had an estimated 17.0 and 19.0 remaining years of life, respectively.[13] At very advanced ages, African Americans register lower mortality rates than do whites—a surprising reversal that some demographers call the "black-white crossover" in mortality. Because African Americans are exposed to many threats to health, one might conclude that those who survive into their 80s must be especially fit. Other evidence, however, suggests that age misreporting for elderly African Americans may account for the crossover.[14] Some researchers report that older black adults—many of whom lack birth certificates and had little schooling—appear to exaggerate their age more than their better-educated white counterparts.

Causes of Death

As life expectancy increased, the causes of death shifted from acute and infectious diseases of infancy and childhood to the chronic, degenerative illnesses of old age. Higher standards of living, improved public health, and medical advances such as immunizations reduced the threat posed by infectious disease. Tuberculosis was the leading cause of death in the 1800s. In the 1990s, heart disease, cancer, and strokes are the major killers of Americans and account for more than two-thirds of deaths among persons age 65 and older (see Table 4). About three-quarters of all deaths can be attributed to more than one cause. Because people often have numerous health problems by the end of life, the aging of the population contributes to an increase in the percent of deaths linked to multiple causes.[15]

Heart disease is the most frequent cause of death for older Americans. It killed almost 600,000 older Americans in 1992. More than one-third (38 percent) of all deaths to persons age 65 and older are attributed to heart disease. Death rates from heart disease have fallen steadily since 1968, however, probably because of widespread reductions in smoking and improved control of high blood pressure. Progress against this disease is the major reason total mortality declined and life expectancy improved so much over the past two decades.

Malignant neoplasms (cancers) are second only to heart disease as a

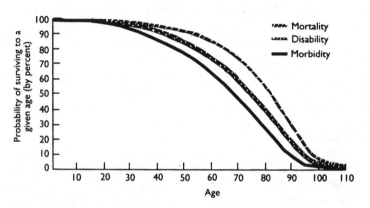

Figure 5

Mortality, Disability, and Morbidity Survival Curves for U.S. Females, 1980

Note: Mortality rates are observed; morbidity and disability rates are hypothetical.
Source: Adapted from Kenneth G. Manton and Beth J. Soldo, *Milbank Memorial Fund Quarterly* 63, No. 2 (Spring 1985): 210.

cause of death. They accounted for 23 percent of deaths to persons age 65 and older in 1992. Cancer deaths have actually increased among the elderly in recent decades, possibly because progress against heart disease has permitted more people to live long enough to succumb to cancer. This overall increase in cancer deaths masks declines in deaths from some specific cancers—declines that can be traced to healthier lifestyles, earlier detection, and better treatment. Deaths from stomach cancer have fallen since the 1930s, for example, because Americans eat less smoked and salted food than they once did. Uterine cancer deaths have declined, in part because routine medical screening

detects cervical cancer earlier, which allows women to receive effective treatment.[16] Male deaths from lung cancer have begun to fall, too, as a consequence of declines in smoking that began three decades ago. Lung cancer deaths continue to climb, however, because recent cohorts of elderly women are more likely to have smoked than the generation that preceded them.

Although the United States long ago experienced the epidemiological transition that shifted major causes of death from infectious disease to chronic illness, both new and old infectious diseases are a health threat for older Americans. The emergence of new infectious diseases (such as AIDS and Lyme disease), newly virulent forms of known bacteria (such as Legionnaire's disease and toxic shock syndrome), and newly drug-resistant strains of tuberculosis, pneumonia, and other diseases pose substantial risks, particularly for those whose immune systems are compromised by aging, chronic health problems, chemotherapy, organ transplants, or other factors. The poor health and close quarters of nursing home residents, for example, place them at a high risk for tuberculosis.[17] Even today, pneumonia and influenza (as well as septicemia, a blood poisoning from bacterial infection) are acute infectious diseases that rank among the top 10 causes of death for older Americans.

Continued Improvements Expected

Although advances in overall life expectancy have been slowed by the AIDS epidemic, there are several reasons to expect continued increases in life expectancy, especially at the older ages.

First, several countries have achieved life expectancies that surpass those of the United States. In 1990, the United States tied for 23rd in the world in life expectancy at birth for men and ranked 15th for women.[18] The United States ranked 10th for both men and women at age 65.

Japan—with the highest life expectancy at birth and at age 65—represents a level of mortality that other developed nations might reasonably hope to attain. In 1990, the life expectancy at birth of Japanese women was 82.5 years, which exceeded that of American women by 3.7 years. Japanese men, with a life expectancy at birth of 76.2 years, outlived their American counterparts by 4.4 years.

Second, even if Americans were unable to match the Japanese, life expectancy would rise if all Americans enjoyed the higher life expectancies achieved by advantaged groups in U.S. society. Life expectancy would rise if blacks had the same mortality rates as whites, for example.

Third, many risk factors for life-threatening chronic disease (such as smoking, obesity, high blood pressure, and high cholesterol) are known and amenable to control. Reductions in these risks through healthier lifestyles and medical interventions translate into later onset of disease and added years of life, particularly at older ages. Smoking is an example of a declining risk factor: 42 percent of Americans 18 and older smoked in 1965, but only 27 percent were smokers in 1992.[19]

Does a longer life expectancy imply more healthy years of life, or simply more years of coping with increasingly severe disabilities? The answer to this question has important implications for public policy and future health costs. Scientists, however, disagree about whether the proportion of elderly with disabilities will increase as life expectancy lengthens. The possible course of morbidity and mortality over a lifetime can be illustrated by the survival curves shown in Figure 5. The lines represent the percentage of individuals at given ages who have not yet developed a chronic illness, become disabled, or died. The percentage of individuals surviving each of these three contingencies declines with age.

There are several reasons to expect continued increases in life expectancy, especially at the older ages.

Longer lives do not necessarily imply better health or less disability if the mortality curve shifts toward the upper ages, but the disease onset and disability curves remain the same. Under this scenario, the percentage of people who are ill or disabled would increase. This creates a so-called "failure of success," in which medical advances permit the survival of chronically ill older people whose lives would have been cut short in the era before there was effective diagnosis and treatment of their conditions.[20] Insulin injections, for example, prolong the lives of diabetics, but these individuals may eventually live to experience disabling complications of diabetes, such as blindness. Thus, longer life expectancies could result in a sicker older population simply by changing the mix of healthy and unhealthy people.

In surveys taken in the 1970s and early 1980s, older Americans reported declines in their health, consistent with the failures of success model.[21]

Several factors other than worsening health might have produced increased reporting of health problems, however. For, example, improvements in survey design may have elicited more complete reporting of poor health, and survey respondents may be more aware of their health problems because of better diagnostic tools and more physician contact. Older adults today may be more willing or better able to adapt their lives to accommodate their illnesses, which may also account for increases in reported health-related activity limitation.

Since the late 1980s, however, the health status of the elderly appears to have improved.[22] Expanded knowledge of the causes and treatment of many diseases delayed their onset or slowed their progress. Earlier detection and treatment of hypertension, for example, reduces the likelihood of a disabling stroke. If disease and disability can be delayed, the morbidity and mortality curves in Figure 5 shift to the right, challenging the failures of success thesis.[23]

The evidence that morbidity and disability are being delayed among the elderly appears to support the "compression of morbidity" argument put forth by physician James Fries.[24] In this scenario, the onset of chronic illness will be delayed longer and longer. Fries believes that life expectancy is already close to the biological maximum for the human species and will increase little if any. If so, the years of life spent with a chronic health condition would be squeezed between the increasing age for the onset of illness and the age of death. Illness would be confined to a brief period before death.

The likelihood that morbidity will be compressed to a brief period before death depends on the validity of Fries' assumption that the human life span is about 85 years. Although empirical support for this thesis is mixed at best, the argument merits attention because it raises important issues about how old humans can live to be. Is there a fixed limit that will eventually stop the advance of the mortality survival curve?

Health deteriorates in advancing years because of age-related diseases and because of the process of aging itself. Although progress against age-related disease has extended life expectancy, death is a certainty even in the absence of chronic disease, because organ function, immunity, and the body's adaptive capacity eventually decline to a point where life cannot be sustained.

But what is the maximum number of years humans can live, and what is the likely upper limit for average life expectancy in a population? Continuing gains in life expectancy have called into question the maximum life span of 85 years assumed by Fries. Some gerontologists think that the human life span is 110 years or even 120 years. There have been documented cases of individuals living as long as 120 years, although such individuals may have extraordinary and unique genetic endowments. The Census Bureau estimates there are 52,000 people 100 years or older in the United States in 1995. If the life span of the human species is 110 or 120 years, there is little danger of life expectancy bumping up against a biological limit to life any time soon. One intriguing question, however, is whether the process of aging itself can be slowed. Scientific developments that suggest the potential malleability of the "maximum" life span include the selective breeding of long-lived fruit flies, the prolongation of life in mice by limiting calorie intake, and the cumulating evidence

about the mechanisms of aging at the systemic and cellular level. If scientific advances result in a more complete understanding of complex aging processes, the middle of the 21st century may witness markedly higher life expectancies.[25]

References

1. U.S. Bureau of the Census, "Population Projections of the United States, by Age, Sex, Race, and Hispanic Origin: 1993 to 2050," *Current Population Reports* P25–1104, by Jennifer Cheeseman Day (Washington, DC: GPO, Nov. 1993): Table 2; and *Statistical Abstract of the United States, 1994* 114th Ed. (Washington, DC: GPO, 1994): 13.
2. U.S. Bureau of the Census, "Population Trends in the 1980s," *Current Population Reports* P23–175 (Washington, DC: GPO, 1992): 4.
3. Philip Martin and Elizabeth Midgley, "Immigration to the United States: Journey to an Uncertain Destination," *Population Bulletin* 49, no. 2 (Washington, DC: Population Reference Bureau, Sept. 1994): 4–5.
4. Michael Fix and Jeffery S. Passel, *Immigration and Immigrants: Setting the Record Straight* (Washington, DC: Urban Institute, 1994), 63.
5. Charles Scott, "SSI Payments to Lawfully Resident Aliens," (Office of Supplemental Security Income, May 1993)....
11. Stanley Kranczer, "Changes in U.S. Life Expectancy, *Metropolitan Life Statistical Bulletin* 75, no. 3 (1994): 11–17.
12. National Center for Health Statistics, *Vital Statistics of the United States 1988*, vol. 2, Life Tables (Table 6-5).
13. National Center for Health Statistics, unpublished data.
14. Irma T. Elo and Samuel M. Preston, "Estimating African-American Mortality from Inaccurate Data," *Demography* 31, no. 3 (Oct. 1994): 427–58.
15. National Center for Health Statistics, "Aging in the Eighties: The Prevalence of Comorbidity and Its Association with Disability," *Advance Data*, no. 170, pre-

pared by Jack M. Guralnik, Andrea Z. LaCroix, Donald F. Everett, and Mary Grace Kovar (May 26, 1989).
16. Gary Williams, "Causes and Prevention of Cancer," *Metropolitan Life Statistical Bulletin* 72, no. 2 (1991).
17. "Tuberculosis Increases in the United States," *Metropolitan Life Statistical Bulletin* 71, no. 4 (1991): 18.
18. National Center for Health Statistics, *Health, United States, 1993* (Hyattsville, MD: Public Health Service, 1994), 89–92.
19. Ibid., 156.
20. Ernest M. Gruenberg, "The Failures of Success," *The Milbank Quarterly* 55, no. 1 (Winter 1977): 3–24.
21. Lois M. Verbrugge, "Recent, Present, and Future Health of American Adults," *Annual Review of Public Health,* vol. 10 (1989): 333–51; and Eileen M. Crimmins, Yasuhiko Saito, and Dominique Ingegneri, "Changes in Life Expectancy and Disability-Free Life Expectancy in the United States," *Population and Development Review* 15, no. 2 (June 1989): 235–67.
22. Kenneth G. Manton, Larry S. Corder and Eric Stallard, "Estimates of Change in Chronic Disability and Institutional Incidence and Prevalence Rates in the U.S. Elderly Population from the 1982, 1984, and 1986 National Long Term Care Surveys," *The Journals of Gerontology* 48, no. 4 (July 1993): S153–66; and Eileen M. Crimmins and Dominique G. Ingegneri, "Health Trends in the American Population," in *Demography and Retirement: The 21st Century,* eds. Anna M. Rappaport and Sylvester J. Schieber (Westport, CT: Greenwood, 1992), 259–78.
23. Eileen M. Crimmins, Mark D. Hayward and Yasuhiko Saito, "Changing Mortality and Morbidity Rates and the Health Status and Life Expectancy of the Older Population," *Demography* 31, no. 1 (Feb. 1994): 168–69.
24. James F. Fries, "Aging, Natural Death and the Compression of Morbidity," *New England Journal of Medicine* 303, no. 11 (1980): 130.
25. Ricki L. Rusting, "Why Do We Age?" *Scientific American* 267, no.6 (Dec. 1992): 130–41.

Schools Struggle to Teach Lessons in Life and Death

■ **Many take on the sensitive subject of suicide prevention. But critics fear classes can do more harm than good.**

By SONIA NAZARIO

TIMES URBAN AFFAIRS WRITER

It seems, on the surface, a reasonable response to the nation's teenage suicide problem: teach schoolchildren that life is better than death.

But this deceptively simple concept has touched off an emotionally raw debate over whether suicide prevention lessons taught in thousands of classrooms—often without parental knowledge—help students or introduce the idea of self-destruction to susceptible young minds.

California's children spend more class time talking about suicide than in any other state, experts say, and could be the guinea pigs who ultimately determine which side is right.

SUICIDAL TENDENCIES
When Kids See Death as an Answer
■ Second of two parts

Proponents of prevention courses contend that they have saved countless children. They say suicide has become a fact of life and must be confronted, whether parents agree or not.

In 1995, according to a survey by the Centers for Disease Control and Prevention, one in 12 high school students attempted suicide. An even larger number—24%—seriously thought about taking their lives. Although fatalities have dropped among high school students in Los Angeles, the CDC survey showed that the city still ranks well above the national average in suicide attempts requiring medical intervention.

During the last school year, teachers and counselors in the Los Angeles district identified as many as 2,000 suicidal children.

Karen Owens, an eighth-grade teacher at Magruder Middle School in Torrance, says she needn't look beyond her own classroom to see the importance of prevention courses. In a survey of her students, 10% said they were considering ending their lives.

On a recent day, as Owens launches into her lesson, it becomes obvious the students are versed in the topic. When she asks what might prompt someone to take his or her life, several hands shoot into the air.

Matthew St. John says a 13-year-old friend tried to kill himself because "his parents were getting divorced." Kristen Crofut, 13, sitting in the back, says she became suicidal after watching her father die slowly of lung cancer. At the age of 10, she says, she locked herself in a neighbor's bathroom and began slicing her left arm with a knife. "I was alone and scared. I thought if I died I'd be with my dad. It'd be better."

Critics of suicide prevention lessons say such an approach is dangerously broad. A wiser alternative, they say, would be to identify troubled children and get them individual help.

"If one kid has a headache, you don't give the whole class an aspirin," says Phyllis Schlafly, president of the Eagle Forum.

Her conservative lobbying group and others say teachers can't be trusted with the fragile psyches of children. Some teachers, they say, have gone so far as to have students write their own suicide note, eulogy or obituary and to take them on field trips to the local mortuary—all to emphasize the finality of death. Such an immensely personal and sensitive topic as suicide, opponents say, should be handled at home.

That was Pamela and Dennis Angelo's deeply held belief. Last year, they successfully sued the Antioch Unified School District, which had refused to let their 15-year-old son, Mikel, out of a class that taught suicide prevention. A state court ruled that the family had the right to pull Mikel from the required course. Since then, the district has allowed parents to voluntarily withdraw their children.

"I'm not advocating to stick your head in the sand and pretend this doesn't exist," says Dennis Angelo. "But I don't want teachers who aren't trained in this to open up a Pandora's box."

The opposition's poster child is a boy from Canton Township, Mich., named Stephen Nalepa.

In 1990, the 8-year-old was shown the film "Nobody's Useless" in the second grade at Gallimore Elementary. In it, a disabled boy is teased. The boy overhears his father call him "useless." He tries to hang himself but ultimately is saved. Stephen saw the film on a Friday. On Saturday, he hanged himself with a belt from his loft bed, even though his mother says her gifted son was not depressed.

"You put something like this in front of children," says Deborah Nalepa, "and they are going to recreate it."

The Nalepas sued the local school district but lost when the Michigan courts ruled that government employees are immune from most negligence claims, including those filed by the dead boy's parents.

California in the Forefront

Suicide prevention classes began sweeping the country in the mid-1980s after several clusters of students killed themselves and a federal court ruled that school districts could be held liable if inadequate prevention measures contributed to a death.

In the vanguard was California, where suicides were soaring above the national average, prompting educators and mental health experts to begin instituting pilot classes. Today, 41% of the state's public school districts have suicide prevention programs. Nationwide, the number is an estimated 15%.

During the typical lesson, which lasts about a week, junior and senior high school teachers tick off suicide statistics, train children to recognize warning signs and urge them to tell an adult if they or a friend are in peril. It's better to have a mad friend, they're taught, than a dead one.

The Los Angeles Unified School District, which has seen a sharp decline in suicide deaths, requires between two and eight prevention lessons in seventh and 10th grades during health classes. Elementary schools typically focus on enhancing self-esteem, impulse control and communication skills instead of explicitly talking about suicide.

Many other districts throughout South California also have embraced anti-suicide instruction. The Los Angeles County Office of Education is in the process of retooling and expanding its suicide prevention program to five weeks.

In Room 101 of Lincoln Middle School in the Santa Monica-Malibu Unified School District, 29 students get ready to hear life-skills teacher Al Trundle's passionate pitch. Now in seventh grade, their first anti-suicide instruction came last year with a film about a girl who slit her wrists. Some students say their teachers raised the topic in fifth grade.

On this day, Trundle begins by asking the children to write a letter to an imaginary suicidal friend. "Why do you want to commit suicide?" a thin girl reads aloud from her letter. "Why not wait until you are 100 years old?" Another girl, her blond hair pulled back with a flowered headband, says: "Think about the impact this would have on others."

When asked what might lead a teen to want to die, students mention depression, a feeling no one cares, losing a family member, divorce. "Sometimes," one boy with thick glasses says, "there's just so much pressure."

The teacher then holds up a magazine cover showing grunge rocker Kurt Cobain and the headline: "Suicide."

"This," says Trundle slowly, deliberately, "is a permanent solution to a temporary problem."

He tells the class about a 10-year-old who shot himself in the head at a Los Angeles school—"a kid two years younger than you." The boys and girls stir in their plastic molded seats. Some let out a little gasp.

"My concern for this class," he continues, "is that none of you say suicide makes sense. I consider it a personal victory when I open the paper and don't see your name in there."

Next, he tells them what to look for in friends.

"If they say, 'I want to blow my head off,' that's a red flag!" The teacher points a finger at his temple, as though ready to fire. "If they know where a gun is," he adds, "big red flag!"

Trundle tells them that if a classmate is considering suicide, they should get adult help. "If you are considering it, call one of these people," he says, unfurling a list of school officials and hotlines. "Talk about what's going on."

As the bell rings, Angela Melo, 12, straps on a backpack that nearly overwhelms her and says she thinks the day's message will stick with Trundle's students.

"If someone in class was thinking about doing it, I think this probably made them change their mind."

She wishes she could have had the course three years ago when a friend turned suicidal after her grandfather's death. "She thought if she died she would join him in heaven."

Angela, who says she felt helpless back then, vows she'll summon a counselor if another friend begins talking about death. Scampering to her next class, she says she can't see the harm in prevention classes. "If they show why you shouldn't do it, I don't think it will make someone do it."

Advocates of suicide education point to data showing that in California, self-inflicted deaths for older teens dropped 39% between 1970 and 1994. At the same time, the U.S. rate nearly doubled. In Los Angeles, one of two cities where the courses were piloted, the teenage suicide rate dropped from nearly triple the national average to 28% below it between 1970 and 1994.

And although suicide attempts requiring medical treatment in Los Angeles remain twice the national average, advocates say the dropping death rate proves that prevention courses are ensuring that students get help before repeated attempts turn lethal.

Says Los Angeles Unified suicide counselor Rosemary Rubin: "We know we are saving kids."

Different Studies, Different Results

The forces for and against suicide prevention courses draw ammunition from two conflicting studies, both examining what has happened in New Jersey schools.

One was authored by Rutgers University's John Kalafat, an assistant professor of applied and professional psychology. He found that in Bergen County, which launched intensive anti-suicide lessons in most of its schools in 1987, suicides have been halved during the past decade.

"This disproves that talking to kids about suicide will make them do it," Kalafat says.

He has also found that the percentage of children willing to seek help for a suicidal friend jumped from 20% to 40% after courses.

The other study was authored in 1990 by Columbia University's David Shaffer, a professor of psychiatry and pediatrics. He concluded that prevention courses erroneously present suicide attempts as a fairly common reaction to intense stresses, not as a deviant act by the mentally ill. The effect of this, he says, is that a child may come to believe that suicide is normal, even acceptable.

Shaffer's study of prevention classes in six New Jersey high schools found that the attitudes of students who believed suicide was a reasonable solution remained unchanged. His study, unlike others, also showed that students who took the classes were no more likely to seek help for a suicidal friend.

Shaffer says his research shows that the best way to help suicidal students is to identify those at risk so they can be individually counseled—with parental consent and a qualified instructor. "You need a lot of training to do these things in a skilled way," says Shaffer, who notes that some teachers begin suicide prevention instruction after a single training session.

Although some researchers argue that Shaffer's sample of students was too small to be meaningful, his findings have been seized upon by conservative groups long critical of the time schools spend on nonacademic topics such as sex, drugs and multiculturalism.

Many schools, particularly along the East Coast, where Shaffer's studies carry more influence, stopped suicide prevention classes.

"We ought to use our schools to learn to read and write. Children get their self-esteem from doing that," says Sara Divito Hardman, California chairwoman of the Christian Coalition. "If schools were doing what they are designed to do, there wouldn't be as much suicide."

Some school districts say there's just not enough time—nor always the inclination—to expand beyond academics.

"Our philosophy is to spend most of our time on the basic skills," says Margaret Herron, assistant superintendent of curriculum for the Lowell Joint School District in Whittier. Suicide prevention, she says, "hasn't been a priority."

Opponents of the courses question whether California's decline in teen suicide is linked more to the state's rising minority population than to anything the schools are doing. Minorities, according to most experts, are less likely to commit suicide because their anger more often is directed toward a society they see as discriminatory—instead of inward at their own perceived failings.

Critics contend, moreover, that asking children to take on the nerve-racking responsibility of spotting signs of potential suicides among peers is too much pressure for them.

Teacher A'lyce Baldazelli thinks much of what passes as suicide prevention in the classroom borders on risky group therapy.

In a study skill class she taught until recently at Chino High School, she says, she refused to do certain exercises. One was called "hot seat." It required that one student be bombarded with personal questions by classmates. "I didn't feel I was qualified," she says, "or that it was good to have the bell ring and say: 'OK, we'll pick this up tomorrow.' "

She says one boy, whose problems were raised to the surface, began waving a gun over his head on campus and yelling, "I'm not going to make it!"

Particularly under attack by critics of prevention courses are lessons that, to them, seem to cross the line between education and glorification.

During the 1993–94 school year, students at Palm Desert Middle School in the Desert Sands Unified School District were shown the video "Carl."

Carl is teased and called "pimplehead" and "dirtball" by classmates. The boy, whose mother is dead, is shoved around by the school bullies. Depressed and friendless, Carl listens to graduation speeches. In one, a student says that "from this day on, your life will get better." Carl ends up as a janitor working for the classmates who abused him. One day, he drops to the ground with his broom, sobbing and pleading, "Help me, God!" Then Carl is shown in silhouette, dangling from a noose as music plays: "Amazing grace, how sweet the sound, that saved a wretch like me. . . ."

A speaker eulogizes Carl: "From this day on he will find a better life." The narrator tells viewers that the tape isn't intended to promote suicide: "The message is simple: stop teasing."

Julie Sullivan demanded to see the video after her sixth-grade son, Michael, came home announcing he was going to see a movie about a hanging the next day. What Sullivan saw, she says, made her go ballistic.

She and local members of the Eagle Forum challenged the video's use, prompting its discontinuation.

In Calistoga, Cindi Frediani says her daughter, Stephanie, returned in tears one day from her fifth-grade class. "Mom," she said, "they made me draw my own headstone with my own death date!"

Stephanie told her mother she had refused to follow her teacher's instructions but relented after being told she could not go to lunch until the assignment was done. She wrote that she would die in 2,000 years.

Furious, Frediani pulled her daughter out of Calistoga Elementary School permanently.

Drama Looks at Self-Esteem Issue

Despite naysayers, schools in many areas such as Long Beach are expanding the amount of time spent on suicide prevention.

At Woodrow Wilson High, there is a mental health trailer near the football field where students can stop in and share suicidal thoughts with counselors. Health classes drill lessons on how to raise self-esteem and cope with stress, bad impulses and anger.

In the center of campus, at the Rainbow Playhouse, an evening performance by the school's drama students is about to debut. The house is full for "The Girl in the Mirror: A Play about Teenage Suicide." At the theater entrance, dozens of news stories are displayed about teens who have taken their lives.

Onstage, a 17-year-old girl lies in a hospital bed with an IV drip in her arm. She has taken a bottle of sleeping pills and is in a coma. An angel clad in a black robe takes the girl through her life. Her parents fight, then divorce. Her father moves to London with a second wife and starts a new family. Her mother drinks too much. She loses her best friend over a boy. She is rejected by a London school to which she has applied so she could be close to her father. The angel shows the teenager how her hopelessness is, in part, a matter of interpretation, that she can go on.

"Admit it was a mistake. Have the strength to go back!" the angel tells the girl, who is still in a coma. "The choice is yours. It always has been yours."

"Nurse! Get the crash cart!" the doctor yells as the girl's heart stops. The stage goes black as the medical crew works feverishly to revive her. The audience is left not knowing if the girl lives or dies.

Misconceptions

MYTH: Most suicides are caused by one traumatic event.
REALITY: Such an event may precipitate a decision to kill yourself, but it is unlikely to be the single cause.
MYTH: Most suicides occur with little or no warning.
REALITY: Four in five people give some warning signs.
MYTH: You shouldn't talk about suicide with someone who you think might be at risk, because you could give them the idea.
REALITY: Suicide isn't passed along like a contagious disease; it is best to directly ask someone if they are thinking of killing themselves and get them help.
MYTH: People who make non-fatal attempts are just trying to get attention and are not serious about committing suicide.
REALITY: Attempters who don't get help with their problems may conclude help will never come and make a lethal attempt.
MYTH: A suicidal person clearly wants to die. There is no way to stop them.
REALITY: Most suicidal people are quite ambivalent about their intention right up to the point of dying. They are usually open to a helpful intervention, even a forced one.
MYTH: Once a person attempts suicide, they won't do it again.
REALITY: The suicide rate for those who have attempted before is 45 to 50 times higher than for the general population.
MYTH: If a person has been depressed and suddenly seems to feel better, the danger of suicide has passed.
REALITY: People who are severely depressed may not have the energy to kill themselves; a lifting depression may provide the needed energy or give clarity to the perceived hopelessness of continuing with life. Someone who is very depressed and then is suddenly chipper may be happy because they have made definite plans to take their life.

Los Angeles Times

Afterward, outside the theater, cast members kiss each other and accept bouquets from well-wishers.

Sean Brady, 16, who portrays the girl's boyfriend, says the play has helped him put his own troubles in perspective and weather the ordeal of having a friend who recently slashed her wrists.

Suicide, he says, "is all over the place. You can't hide it."

Unit Selections

Key Points to Consider

❖ In an environment of advanced technology that has altered the ways in which we die, how are we to change our understanding of the dying process, enrich our engagement with those who are dying, and find a basis for our own growth toward death?

❖ How do we address the profound challenges raised by the questions of how and when we die and who decides?

❖ With the impressive experiences of the hospice movement to guide us, how can we improve our community witness to good care so that we can be present to the dying in ways that enrich their journey?

 **Links**   **www.dushkin.com/online/**

13. **American Academy of Hospice and Palliative Medicine**
    http://www.aahpm.org

14. **As Death Draws Near**
    http://www.emanon.net/~kcabell/signs.html

15. **Death in America, Project on: Death, Dying, Bereavement**
    http://www.soros.org/death.html

16. **Hospice Foundation of America**
    http://www.hospicefoundation.org

17. **Hospice Hands**
    http://hospice-cares.com

18. **National Prison Hospice Association**
    http://www.npha.org

19. **The Zen Hospice Project**
    http://www.zenhospice.org

These sites are annotated on pages 4 and 5.

Death is the final stage of life. While death comes at varied ages and in differing circumstances, for most of us there will be some time to reflect on our lives, our work, our relationships, and what our expectations are for the ending of that life. This is called the process of dying. In the past two decades, a broad range of concerns has arisen about that process and how aging, dying, and death can be confronted in ways that are enlightening, enriching, and supportive of those who are coming to the close of their lives. Efforts have been made to delineate and define various stages in the process of dying so that comfort and acceptance of our inevitable death will be eased. Awareness of approaching death allows us to come to grips with the profound emotional upheaval that will be experienced. Fears of the experience of dying are often more in the imagination than in reality, as the articles in this unit will demonstrate.

There are many and varied social, religious, and psychological responses that constitute and inform the process of dying, and the supports sought can be studied and used to the benefit of all. Spiritual questions and dilemmas are significant issues as life comes to a close and must be focused on as we learn to care for others. Key players in the drama that will unfold are physicians and nurses who attend the dying. Their personal attitudes and their professional roles are being examined by their professions, by the courts and legislatures, and by the public as increasingly serious attention is paid to the dying process. How do we decide on the care of the incompetent person who is dying? How do we delegate authority for end-of-life decisions and provide the comfort and assurance so needed as the end of life comes? The process of dying can be profoundly influenced by the compassion and the support of those trained to be with—and for—the dying. It is important for professional caregivers to learn the ways of comfort and compassion; it is also a challenge for family and friends to learn to be attentive to the demanding needs of those who are dying. Sensitivity to the needs we all have for love and consolation, awareness of the exquisitely personal nature of death, and willingness to attend to the difficult tasks at hand will greatly enhance and enrich the experience for all. There is also the rich reward we receive when the dying teach us about the richness of living for others.

The care of dying persons has always been difficult and demanding. The relatively recent use of the hospital as the place of death raises concerns about its appropriateness. Many persons are seeking to regain control of the process of dying: how, where, and with whom are valid questions to be considered. The high technology of the hospital and the lack of sensitivity of some caregivers to the personal aspects of dying have fanned the demands of many to die at home within their own defined environment. In former times, persons died at home with family and friends in attendance. Many fear the abandonment

of being left to die in an isolated room down a long corridor in a large hospital. For many, death is accepted for what it is: a time of transition or of ending. The thought of dying alone can be terrifying.

Neglected aspects of the care of the dying are the spiritual, the psychological, and the quality-of-life dimensions. The intensely personal aspects of spiritual issues, and commonly observed ignorance of them, can produce uneasiness in caregivers, both professionals and friends. It is important to be informed and alert to this profound support for those who suffer, are in pain, and coming to the end of life. Treatment—psychological and pharmacological—and attention to daily living needs can modify and often relieve the depression and sadness that so often darken the closing days of a life. Another aspect that is often ignored is the effect of ethnic and cultural factors on our care and on our understanding of the significance of death on persons from widely disparate traditions.

The development of the Hospice movement in the United States over the past 20 years offers an alternative to the impersonal aspects of hospital-ization. Hospice offers both home care and institutional care for the dying in a quiet environment with personal attention to the extremely intimate process of dying and assurance of the relief of pain. Though Hospice had its conceptual origin in the Middle Ages, the present-day model is St. Christopher's Hospice in London, developed in the late 1960s by Dame Cecily Saunders. The essay "Hospice Care for the 1990s: A Concept Coming of Age" brings the reader current information on this important movement.

The Dying Process

Planning to Die

Jeanne Guillemin

Jeanne Guillemin is professor of sociology at Boston College. She has published widely on questions of medical technology and is co-author (with Lynda L. Holmstrom) of Mixed Blessings. Intensive Care for Newborns.

Thirty years ago, in *The American Way of Dying,* Jessica Mitford roundly criticized Americans for their obsessive denial of death and their equally obsessive fixation on immortality. To the puritanical American sensibility, a miasma of shame surrounds the event of death. The quicker one died and the less the family and community were troubled, the better. Funeral directors, a uniquely American profession, assumed all responsibility for the corpse, including its embalmed, cosmetic display and its rapid dispatch to the cemetery or to the crematorium. Denial of death was also the theme of Philippe Ariès' work *Western Attitudes Toward Death* (1974). He credits early twentieth-century America with the invention of the modern attitude toward mortality. Death, once so banal a presence that Renaissance markets were held in graveyards and so communal that relatives and friends crowded the bedchambers of the dying, lost its tame aspect. Under the influence of urban industrialization, it became detached from domestic traditions, not the least of which was a religious understanding of the appropriateness and even the banality of the self's demise. In our times, Ariès argues, death became wild and obscene because we cherish an individualism that cannot be relinquished without extreme anguish. As with sex, death was not to be talked about in front of children or in polite company.

Today the American public is confronting mortality in ways that were unthinkable when Mitford was writing and improbable even to Ariès. The emphasis now is on rational planning for one's death that goes far beyond buying a burial plot. Topics such as traversing the emotional stages of dying, how to compose a living will to instruct final medical decisions, and the merits of rational suicide are ordinary fare on television and radio talk shows and in popular magazines. The head of the Hemlock Society, Derek Humphry, has a bestseller in *Final Exit,* a how-to book on "happy death." Jack Kevorkian, another book author, has gained notoriety for his "mercitron" devices, recently used by three women to end their lives. Despite his subsequent indictment for homicide, the public is far from outraged by the idea of physician-assisted suicide. In 1991, the state of Washington gained national attention with a popular referendum on the issue. The voting public there ultimately balked at granting it legal status, but polls had already revealed widespread support for the option of medically supervised suicide. In 1992, the state of New Hampshire initiated the nation's first legislation that would authorize physicians to write prescriptions to hasten the death of terminally ill patients.

This new frankness concerning death is due in part to changing demographics. The population of the United States has aged, with more people than ever living out a seventy-two year life span. Many are surviving decades beyond it. Perhaps aging alone would shift any society's focus to the end of life. Yet death itself has become unexpectedly familiar because of the AIDS epidemic, which has brought grief to hundreds of thousands of young victims, their families, and friends. Add to this the fact that the United States has the highest homicide rate of any industrialized country, with a disproportionate number of casualties among young minority males, and the difficulties of denying death and its repercussions become clear. Old or young, one thinks, "This could be me."

Still, death is far from tamed; it is now newly wild and familiar. The current discussion of how to die gives evidence of terrible fears that those final circumstances are beyond one's control. In a culture that prizes individual autonomy, there is a no more degrading scenario than the gradual diminution of physical and mental powers, the prolonged and painful helplessness, with mental lapses preceding and even obscuring the experience of dying. American anxiety about dying centers on how the individual can avoid dependence. Unfortunately, the two environments where death is likely to happen are poorly prepared to reduce this anxiety and are, in fact, increasing it. Neither the hospital, where 80 percent of Americans die, nor the home, where growing numbers of patients are being cared for, can be counted on to alleviate fears about death as a scenario of degradation.

Hospital Care and Uncare

In pondering the phenomenon of shameful death ("la mort inversée"), Ariès sees the modern hospital as the environment where depersonalized efficiency and order quell the fears of the dying. As a cultural instrument of

 From *Society,* July/August 1992, pp. 29-33.

repression, the hospital guarantees that the graceless, physically repulsive facts of expiration are hidden from view and that the emotional climate at the bedside is restrained. The sheets are clean, the meals regular, and the staff professional. Replacing family and friends is the hospital team, led by the physician. "They are," wrote Ariès, "the masters of death—of the moment as well as of the circumstances. . . ."

In the last two decades, hospital-based medicine has undergone radical changes and Americans have largely lost confidence in its protective guarantees, as chill and repressive as they have been. Hospital organization, once able to guarantee benign order for both birth and death, has been altered not with reference to the social or spiritual needs of patients, but in reaction to market incentives that favor large hospitals selling progressive medicine. The hospitals that survived the fierce competition of the 1980s did so by heavy investment in new and experimental technologies and by the build-up of centralized facilities offering a profitable mixture of specialized and acute care services. Small community hospitals closed by the hundreds. Public hospitals, burdened with welfare patients, are foundering. Private mega-hospital chains, like Humana, thrive because they serve only privately insured patients.

Far from being beneficent institutions, most hospitals today are businesses that serve clients. Linked to proliferating technological options and required to support high-priced professionals, their main incentive is to maximize returns on their investments. They are only unlucky if they do not. Cost control measures to cap procedure charges, such as Diagnostic Related Groups (D.R.G.'s), have merely succeeded in moving patients more quickly out of their hospital beds to make room for more. Costs for hospital medicine and services continue to rise and inflate health insurance coverage, which growing numbers of Americans cannot afford.

The progressive technologies being marketed through American hospitals fall into two categories. Both affect how we die. One kind addresses the diseases of the growing numbers of patients fortunate enough to survive past youth, at which point they become vulnerable to cardiac disease, cancer, stroke, kidney and liver failure. When Aaron Wildavsky coined the phrase, "doing better and feeling worse," in reference to modern American health care, he aptly summarized its major problem. The important determinants of health and illness—life style, genetics, and the environment—are outside the scope of medicine. Its principal technologies, geared toward an aging clientele, must be of the patch-and-mend variety, lacking the "magic bullet" efficiency of penicillin and sulfa drugs. Success with these "half-way technologies," as Lewis Thomas called them, is difficult and uncertain. Very sick patients do much more than lose faith in medicine. They take it on, they wrestle with it, and often they feel defeated by it. They are not just disappointed consumers. They engage their bodies and souls in a battle for life.

Hospitals were organized, not for the patients' social and spiritual needs, but in reaction to market conditions.

The role of the physician in treating the very sick patient is problematic, in part because doctors are only apparently disinterested in advising about medical treatment options. Many patients fail to understand that physicians like car dealers, will promote their products, if asked. Not that physicians are necessarily driven by profit motives, but they are integrated into the hospital reward system, now heavily invested in high-technology resources—machines, laboratories, consultants—that must be used to get a return. Perhaps unwittingly, physicians often inform seriously ill patients about therapy in ways that encourage it. The use of statistical odds, for example, is a commonplace, as when a doctor refers to scientific studies to inform a patient about survival rates for cancer, using surgery or drugs or some combination of both. When cancer or any other disease is in an advanced stage, this tactic is little better than offering a lottery ticket to someone who is destitute. What even educated patients often do not know is that many clinical studies are poorly executed—without controls and on small samples—and yield only the most tentative results. Or, if they are well conceived and implemented, the patients researched may share none or few of the characteristics—age, gender, medical history, and so on—of the patient being informed. There is little or nothing in their training that prepares physicians to develop a posture of integrity and more genuine disinterest or new words of counsel for the seriously ill who should perhaps not venture any therapeutic course.

For a very sick patient, surgery, chemotherapy, or organ transplant might work. Then again, it might not. It will certainly be a physical and emotional ordeal, causing pain that is especially alienating because it is impossible to know whether it is part of recuperation or a sign of further degeneration. The patient cannot know, nor can the therapist, until test results come back. Even then, many therapies require years of monitoring, especially in the case of cancer, during which one simply does not know if a true cure has been effected. Starting with Susan Sontag's *Illness As Metaphor* to the essay on resisting chemotherapy by the anthropologist Susan DiGiacomo, the patient-as-survivor literature constitutes a searing criticism of how physicians mishandle patients confronting death.

The really bad news is that medical technology can offer multiple sequential therapeutic options for the same fatal disease. This creates uncertainty and uncertainty in medicine, as Wildavsky and others have noted,

Subjection to experimental medicine is the pathway of everyone's last cure.

is often resolved by doing more. If drugs and surgery fail, other drugs or more surgery are substituted. The more advanced the disease, the more the desperate patient will value inclusion in an experimental trial of some new therapy, whereby she or he is diminished to a statistic and risks more physical devastation. This way of progressing toward death—by hopes raised and dashed, by technological assaults on the body, followed by periods of incomplete and uncertain recuperation—is, of course, not the road traversed by people who are cured. Many people overcome blocked arteries, for example, or cancer because the therapy works. But subjection to experimental medicine is the pathway of everyone's last cure. No matter what the patient's age or how advanced the disease, or even if it is considered incurable, the options for more tests and treatment exist, in refined or experimental form, appropriate or inappropriate, as the physician advises.

The intensive care unit is the other important kind of technology that hospitals market. It has revolutionized the way Americans die, but not for the better. The concept of high-technology life support took hold in the early 1970s in response to a perceived need, public and professional, for emergency medical services. The argument for emergency medical units was and is based on the reduction of waste in human lives. Immediate aggressive intervention, not unlike that of a M.A.S.H. unit, would save victims of accidents, of heart attack and stroke, as well as premature infants, and post-operative patients. The key was vigorously sustained intervention with the maximum resources of a large central hospital. Emergency and intensive care facilities, costing billions of dollars, became part of the expansion of central hospitals throughout the 1970s and 1980s. Patients *in extremis* are always in good supply and treating them quickly in high-use beds has often helped hospitals underwrite less profitable services. Such heavy investment in acute care emphatically denied a preventive and more cost-efficient approach to health problems and to the general social problem of death by violence. Nor did emergency care enthusiasts predict that many whose lives were saved would not be able to resume normal lives or even a conscious existence, and would be passed off to chronic care facilities or to their families.

Even less concern is being expressed for the I.C.U. patient's experience of having to live attached to machines or dying that way. From the perspective of the conscious patient, experiencing what it means to be "worked on" by teams of strangers, to be coded for resuscitation (or

not), to lie among others near death or already dead, to be dependent on and surrounded by wires and machines, intensive care imposes the most feared scenario: prolonged helplessness, often in pain. For years, hospital staff have known about "I.C.U. psychosis," the severe and not uncommon disorientation of patients reacting to the windowless, mechanical environment. For years, the only remedy has been to set a clock where the patient could see it.

The impact of the intensive care unit on the American way of dying has been profound, for it is there that contemporary medicine routinely eliminates the primary actor, the patient, from the ritual of dying. This is done by first selecting uncommonly passive patients in crisis. Medicine then perfected the way of artificially sustaining the clinically (if not legally) dead patient and replacing the old rituals of professional-patient interaction with emergency medical intervention, that is, professional team management of machines and bodies. Dying in this context is not something the individual patient, potentially a living corpse, really does, since it is a matter of the staff's withdrawing life supports. It has also become increasingly unclear what responsibility the once "masters of death" assume in hospital death scenarios. With few exceptions, modern physicians are revolted by death, leaving to nurses the "dirty work" of interacting with grieving families, the actual release of the patient from support machines, and ministering to the dead body.

Dying at Home

Recalling a time, long gone, when people died at home, Michel Foucault describes the family's gaze fixed on the sick person as full of "the vital force of benevolence and the discretion of hope." The contemporary alternative of dying at home guarantees no such comfort. Yet many households, prepared or not, must accept the prospect of such caretaking, even though the patient's death at the last minute takes place in the hospital.

Since the introduction of D.R.G.'s in 1983, the allowable length of hospital stay for Medicare patients has been sharply decreased. Growing numbers of chronically ill and elderly people are being cared for by relatives. But the family context has its problems: emotional ambivalence, instability, isolation from the larger community, and even violence. Hospice care, once hailed as the humane alternative to dying in the hospital, provides only minor support in terms of supplies and service.

The choice to refuse medication or food may be rational if one truly believes it is time to die.

Family members, especially women, are left with the daily responsibility for patient care, which now often includes complex regimens of infusion drugs, intravenous feeding, oxygen support, and physical therapy. For most of the elderly, long-term nursing home care is economically not feasible. Hospitals have no room for those who are dying slowly—but then who does?

The toll of rejection may be seen in the increasing rate of suicide among the elderly. Between 1981 and 1986, suicides among people over sixty-five rose sharply, from 12.6 per 100,000 to 21.8. Starvation, refusal of medication, and guns were the principal means. How such private decisions are reached or even if they can count as rational, we do not know, although fear of being a burden is frequently reported in anecdotes. Such a fear itself is not irrational. Government and professional support for home care is minimal. Home-care providers receive scant training for the technical tasks they perform, no provision for relief, and no credit for the round-the-clock time they give. Having little or no reimbursement incentives, physicians generally ignore patients cared for at home. Cost coverage for home care varies with the insurance carrier. Even under private insurance plans, many items must be paid for out-of-pocket. In the last ten years, unregulated commercial agencies have taken over the growing, multi-billion dollar home-care industry and have inflated the retail cost of everything—needles, gauze, plastic tubing, rubber sheets, bed rentals, and drugs—in ways that parallel hospital charges for aspirin and the price of Pentagon coffee pots.

As death re-enters the American household, it is tamed only by the resources a family or perhaps only a single relative or friend can muster. Maybe the community has a free slot in the hospice program, maybe the physician will do more than telephone, maybe a member of the clergy will visit. But there are no guarantees. If the scenario of hospital death is daunting, so too is the vision of a drawn-out, painful expiration, resented and uncomforted by those intimates or the intimate to whom one is a burden. The choice to refuse medication or even food may be rational, if one truly believes it is time to die. But the rationale "I am only a burden" threatens all of us, for we are all at some time in our lives completely dependent on others.

Confronting Death

The present controversy surrounding physician-assisted suicide and rational suicide in general may be all to the good, if it promotes change in our institutions. How many people would be interested in a quick (six minutes), painless death in a parked van (the scenario for Janet Adkins, the first user of Kevorkian's mercitron machine), if hospitals and homes provided a more humane context for dying? Or is it that Americans, Puritans still, ask for nothing more than clean sheets and a morphine drip? This may be true. The rational suicides reported in the media all have a tidy, pain-free aura about them.

Critics, such as Mitford and Ariès, accurately identified our cultural denial of death as a serious aberration. We want death to never happen, to be a non-experience, or an event that cannot threaten our dignity. Yet, as the philosopher Paul Ramsey used to say, there is nothing at all dignified about dying—one might add, nor happy either. Death must be seen for what it is—cruelly inevitable, a painful rendering, our finitude—if we are to understand the human condition and even begin to ask about the meaning of life. Death is momentous, in the general and in the specific. For the dying person, spirit and body are inescapably involved in a final reckoning. No witness can be untouched, except by a distortion of the most fundamental truth, that we are mortal. The distance between us and the dying person is only an accident of time.

It is this sense of mortality we try to hide from and the reason we have created institutions of denial. Oddly enough, we even deny the extent to which these institutions contribute to our problems. In the innumerable debates and discussions about death, the focus remains on individual strategies, as if, for example, one person's choice of suicide over protracted terminal illness constituted a justification in itself, prompted by psychology, legitimated by one's will, and with no social consequences or meaning. Yet our hospitals are strange and alienating environments to the extent that they obfuscate this truth of mortality by therapeutic experimentalism, intensive care, and also the "harvesting" of organs from living corpses. Our homes are threatening to the extent that people are left in isolation to deal with life as a burden and death as an obscenity. The quick-fix suicide machine or the plastic bag method described in *Final Exit* might relieve the individual of woe and suffering, but what about the rest of us, who will dutifully attend to our living wills and then await the worst? We know that death is not obscene; it cannot by itself deprave us. But it is frightening in its familiarity and cannot be simply planned away. Rather, we should envision institutional reforms. We need physicians educated to say more to the dying patient than "Have a nice trip" (Kevorkian's farewell to Janet Adkins). We need hospitals with staff motivated to give humane attention, not overtreatment, to the dying. We need compensation for families that give home care so that they can afford to be kind and old people can die in relative peace. Death is indeed a wild beast of sorts. These are ways to tame it.

READINGS SUGGESTED BY THE AUTHOR:

Philippe Ariès. *Western Attitudes Toward Death.* Baltimore, Md.: Johns Hopkins University Press, 1974.
Susan DiGiacomo. "Biomedicine in the Cultural System: An Anthropologist in the Kingdom of the Sick," in *Encounters with Biomedicine: Case Studies in Medical Anthropology,* Hans Baer (ed.). New York: Gordon and Breach Science Publishers, 1987.
Susan Sontag. *Illness as Metaphor.* New York: Farrar, Straus, and Giroux, 1988.

Attitudes to death and bereavement among cultural minority groups

Caroline Walker, SRN, SCM, DipN (Lond.)

Ms Walker wrote this study as part of her JBCNS course. She is a student health visitor at Oxford Polytechnic.

A s members of a caring team both in community and hospital nursing, it is helpful to know something of the cultural background of the patients we are to care for. This is especially important when caring for the terminally ill patient and in supporting his family and friends.

In times of great stress a person will lean towards his own culturally acquired ways of coping which may seem strange to people of a different culture. We should try to ensure that the patient is allowed to die his own death[1], not one imposed upon him by someone else. In hospital there can be conflict between the routine of ward work and an individual's expectations which can lead to fear as well as loss of dignity and identity.

Culture and religion

Culture can be described as a way of living of people of a particular

---

The extended family is the centre of all Asian cultures and has a very strong influence on behaviour and outlook

---

group[2]. Therefore, to understand a person's attitude to death and bereavement one must have an idea of his philosophy of life. In this respect it is difficult to separate cultural influences from religious beliefs; described in *The Concise Oxford Dictionary* as the recognition of a superhuman controlling power of a personal God entitled to obedience, and the effect of such recognition on personal conduct and mental attitude.

It is interesting to note that for the majority of our population, in death more than any other event, religious tradition holds a monopoly. Many infants are not christened, many marriages take place in register offices, but it is very rare for funeral ceremonies not to be accompanied by religious rites. However, under 20% of people appear regularly to practise religious devotions. Orthodox Christianity teaches that the soul continues to exist after death but 25% of the population firmly state that they do not believe in a future life of any kind, 25% are uncertain and only 15% are sure of a future existence[3]. This appears to be a contradiction between what is normal funeral ceremonial practice, usually based on the belief of some form of afterlife and what the majority of people would state and practice as their normal religious beliefs. In effect, the majority of people turn, at times of great stress, towards the religion of their culture despite their usual apathy towards it.

Cultural traditions change far more slowly in respect of social structure and personal relationships than in any other aspect. This is important to remember in health care as failure to allow the individual to exercise traditional and religious responsibilities, perhaps in the form of ritual ceremonies at important family events (such as birth and death), can result in feelings of guilt and failure[2]. Of immigrant residents only 3% form a cultural minority. It is also very significant to note that: the majority of these people are in the under 40 age group[4]. As the average life expectancy is 'three score years and ten' in generations to come those involved in health care will undoubtedly have more contact with death among cultural minority groups than they do at present.

Experience of death

Among the minority groups from third world countries (the Asian and African continents in particular, but also the West Indies) natural death has been a much more common experience, particularly for the older generation. The majority of people would not have reached adulthood without experiencing the death of a close relative. Death did not hold the mystery or taboo that it does to many people today and this seems to enable them to cope with it more easily. There is an expected pattern of behaviour for the bereaved. Rites performed for the dead have important effects for the living[3] resulting in less fear of death for an individual and easier adjustment for the bereaved. This is something that I witnessed many times when working with the Shona people in Zimbabwe where death was more common among all age groups but particularly so in young children and babies than in western societies.

Asian culture

There are 4–5000 Asians living in Oxford, mostly from Pakistan and Bangladesh with a smaller group originating from East Africa. It is important to remember that they have come from very different social, educational and economic backgrounds. While sharing many basic values and attitudes, they have certain differences—a Sikh from the Punjab and a Moslem from Bangladesh may have as little in common as a Protestant from Sweden and a Catholic from Spain but are grouped together as Asian[5].

Most Asians originating from the Indian sub-continent come from rural areas while those from East Africa come from towns and cities, mostly from commercial backgrounds but with great variation in wealth[5].

Extended family system

The extended family is the centre of all Asian cultures and has a very strong influence on behaviour and outlook. Each member considers himself as a part of the extended family group rather than as an independent individual; important decisions cannot be made without consultation with the whole family. This can create problems when the head of the family group is still resident in India. Illness is traditionally the responsibility of the whole family and the obligation to take part in appropriate celebrations of family events is binding on all members of the group, not just the closest relatives, as in British society. As a result hospital admission in illness may appear as rejection of the patient by the family leaving the individual to the mercy of strangers in a strange and often forbidding environment[2].

The attitude to old people is also different. Factors which a British family may find difficult to accept and cope with, such as confusion, incontinence and overcrowded accommodation, are happily contained within the extended Asian family. The elderly are respected, their dependence accepted and rarely would the family consider not caring for them at home. However, it is important to remember that at present there are relatively few old people in the Asian community.

Attitudes to medical care

Many Asians have a fear of hospitals because of the differences in medical care experienced in their country of origin. On the whole, only the very seriously ill are admitted to hospital and the practical care is very different. The idea of bed rest is a good example. Most Asians feel that the sick (including postoperative patients and after childbirth) should stay in bed as long as possible with minimum activity. Therefore they become very distressed when encouraged to mobilise. There is also a great fear of catching a chill when ill, so they do not usually take cold drinks, they wrap up well and do not like to bathe too much.

A sick person is expected to express anxiety and suffering openly, he is not expected to be cheerful or active, so that the idea of active rehabilitation and physiotherapy in illness is considered very odd. In our culture, a very ill person, particularly in the terminal stages, will only expect immediate family or very close friends to intrude on what is often considered a very private situation. However, in the Asian community the opposite situation prevails, the whole family feeling bound to visit as often as possible.

The family expect to play a major part in supporting the sick person, usually day and night and like to undertake much of the bedside nursing care[5]. If this is not allowed, the family can be made to feel neglectful and very guilty and it may well make it more difficult later to come to terms with the death of the patient. A sick person should never be left alone.

Many Asian women fear being examined by a male; they should be attended by females whenever possible. Male doctors should always be chaperoned and unnecessary removal of undergarments avoided. In the home, Asian women would prefer examinations to be made in complete privacy and any interpreters should be of the same sex as the patient. A mixed hospital ward would be very distressing for an Asian patient. In some cultures, especially among Moslems, nurses are held in low esteem, because their job involves physical contact with the opposite sex, and this can sometimes account for the attitude of Asian patients towards nursing staff[5].

If we are to care adequately and compassionately for the terminally ill patient all these feelings must be taken into consideration both on a practical and emotional level. Tact and flexibility will be necessary while taking into consideration the feelings of other patients.

To most Asians, religion is a natural part of life. Most traditions have a religious significance by which people will judge themselves and others[5]. These traditions will become particularly important in stressful times such as serious illness, death and bereavement.

The Moslem community

The majority of the Asians in Oxford belong to the Moslem community whose faith is Islam, founded in the seventh century by the prophet Mohammed. Their philosophy is based on the 'Five Pillars of Islam' with Friday as the holy day when prayer is particularly important. Prayer is always preceded by a ritual cleansing and the head must face towards Mecca (south-east). Everyone is accountable to God for what he does on earth, and when he dies he will be judged and rewarded or punished in the life hereafter. Therefore if a patient is unable to adhere to his religious duties great distress may result, particularly to a person who feels that he is soon to be judged.

It may be necessary to rearrange the furniture so that the patient can face Mecca. Personal hygiene is very important to Moslem people as it is linked with spiritual purity. They prefer to wash in running water, women usually do not undress completely but wear a special petticoat and the left hand is always used for washing after toilet purposes and considered 'unclean'.

A patient's bed-table and food should always be placed in reach of the right hand. Food regulations are strict—all pork and alcohol are prohibited. Moslems are vegetarian outside the home, as meat should be ritually prepared.

When a Moslem is dying, a relative or another person of the same faith recites appropriate verses from the Koran so that these are the last words heard by the person

---

When a Moslem is dying, a relative or another person of the same faith recites appropriate verses from the Koran so that these are the last words heard by the person. The custom of undertakers is foreign to most Asian people and it may be difficult to enable the family to attend to their duties while conforming to the legal regulations.

It is usual for the family to wash and prepare the body, so other attendants should, wearing gloves, straighten the body and remove any drainage tubes; the head of the deceased being turned towards the left shoulder, so that the person can be buried facing Mecca[6].

A member of the family of the same sex will wash the body, preferably at home, reciting special passages from the Koran. The body is then clothed in white and buried without a coffin within 24 hours of death. The men take the body to the mosque or graveside for further prayers before burial, the body facing towards Mecca and the grave unmarked.

Moslems are opposed to cremation and also to post-mortem examinations. In Islam a person is not the owner of his body so no part of it should be cut out or harmed, so organ donation is not allowed. It is very difficult to comply with all these customs and consequently very devout Moslems may go to the expense of taking their dead home to be buried[5].

The grave is visited every Friday for 40 days and alms are given to the poor. The whole family comes together to show grief, a period of unconcealed sorrow is considered necessary to allow the grief to heal. A widow is not expected to be brave or to be in control of her feelings and there is an obligation for the family to visit her and share in the mourning.

The Hindu community

There is a small Hindu group in Oxford and a temple at the home of one of the leaders. The Hindu faith is centred on the transmigration of the soul with indefinite reincarnation. When a person dies, that person is born again as another child in another place on earth. The new body a person gets depends upon what sort of life he has led. If they are good they will have whole bodies in the next life, but if not they will have some defect such as being deaf, dumb or blind. As the soul moves from body to body it hopes to become purer and purer until in the end it reaches God[7].

Again prayer is important, with ritual cleansing, and the left hand is considered 'unclean'. The feelings of loss of dignity and fear of affecting the quality of one's next life can be very great if religious customs cannot be adhered to. There are strict dietary regulations, both beef and pork are banned and many Hindus are vegetarians.

Hindu women wear a nuptial thread around the neck and sometimes a red mark on the forehead—these should not be removed. A male may have a sacred thread around the arm indicating attainment of adult religious status—it will cause great distress if this is removed. In the case of a dying patient the Hindu priest will tie a thread round the neck or wrist to indicate that a blessing has been given—again this should not be removed. Readings from the *Bhagavad Gita* give great comfort to the dying person. A Hindu person would usually prefer to die at home and may wish to be on the floor, near to mother earth[7].

The eldest son is responsible for the funeral arrangements (in India he sets fire to the funeral pyre) so it is very important to a Hindu to have a surviving son to perform these rites.

There is no ritual washing of the body so this can be performed by nursing staff. Cremation is usual and the ashes are traditionally scattered on water. The Ganges is the Hindu holy river and some devout people may wish the ashes to be sent home to the holy city of Benares for the ashes to be scattered in the Ganges[8].

There is a set pattern of mourning, relatives and friends visiting regularly to comfort the close family and to offer gifts of money, food and clothes. A final service is held on the 11th day called the kriya—the priest recites: 'Death is certain for the born, rebirth is certain for the dead: you should not grieve for what is unavoidable'[8].

Sikh community

There is a small group of Sikhs in Oxford, mostly from the Punjab area of India. Their faith is a combination of elements of both Hindu and Moslem beliefs but tends to be more flexible. It was founded in 1469. They share the Hindu belief in transmigration of the soul and favour cremation for disposal of the dead with the ashes being thrown into water.

There is no objection to hospital staff handling the body.

There are five traditional symbolic marks which all practising Sikhs should wear:

1. Kesh—Long, uncut hair and unshaven head.

2. Kanga—a comb to keep the hair in place and symbolise discipline.

3. Kara—A steel bangle worn on the right wrist to symbolise strength and unity.

4. Kirpan—A sword, the symbol of authority and justice, often worn as a brooch.

5. Kachj—A pair of shorts initially to allow freedom of movement in battle, now a symbol of spiritual freedom.

It could cause distress for any of these symbols to be removed from a dying person. Following death, relatives and friends take part in a series of services, either in the deceased's home or in the temple, for a period of 10 days with a final service to mark the end of the official mourning period[8].

Buddhists

Buddhism began in the sixth century BC against a background of Hinduism, Buddha being a former Hindu prince. It has spread to many parts of the world and there is a lot of variation between different geographical areas. However, the underlying principle of all Buddhism is belief in reincarnation of the soul. There is great emphasis on meditation to relax the mind and body in order to see life in its true perspective. Many people believe in meditating on one's death while still in health.

It is important for a patient to be allowed quietness and privacy for meditation. Great importance is also attributed to the state of the mind at death which should be calm and hopeful and as clear as possible. To this end some patients may be reluctant to take drugs, which must be respected. There are no special rituals

regarding the body and cremation is common[7].

The Jewish community

For the Orthodox Jew there is a very specific structure with regard to death and a specific pattern of mourning for the bereaved. Comfort is drawn from a confession which acts as a *rite de passage* to another phase of existence and also from readings from the Psalms. The family may wish to be present at death and a Rabbi should visit if one is available.

It is not acceptable for a non-Jewish person to handle the dead body, so gloves should be worn so that there is no direct contact. The family may express a wish to prepare the body themselves or send a member of their community to do so. Burial should take place within 24 hours of death, unless it involves the Sabbath (Saturday) in which case it may be slightly longer. Strict Orthodox Jews may want someone to stay with the body until burial, which can create difficulties in a hospital mortuary.

The chief mourner, usually the spouse, is expected to take full responsibility for the funeral arrangements and during the service is expected and encouraged openly to express grief. The mourners do not leave the graveside until it has been completely filled. There is a period of intense mourning for seven days, during which the mourners do no work, are visited frequently, brought their food and encouraged to talk of the deceased. The tearing of clothes is accepted as a visible symbol of being inwardly torn by grief. There follows a period of 30 days of gradual readjustment and then, at the end of a year, a gravestone is erected and the official period of mourning is completed[3].

Conclusion

It must be remembered that members of any cultural group vary considerably in their observance of that culture. It is important to treat each person as an individual and to consult with the patient and his family as to their specific needs. Every effort must be made to find an interpreter when there is a language problem.

It is interesting to note that in the various groups considered there are many similarities. All appear to have very specific guidelines of behaviour associated with dying, death and bereavement. This is different from the majority of the population who do not have particularly strong religious beliefs and, as a result, no specific guidelines to help them cope with the stress.

On the whole, people are expected to keep their grief under control, carry on as normal and not discuss it as this tends to embarrass others. As a result they tend to become very isolated in their grief. In the long term this will make it more difficult to cope with. Perhaps we have much to learn from the minority groups in our society whose ways may seem strange.

References

1. Speck, Rev. P. *The chaplain and other cultures*. Extracts from a talk at the Royal Free Hospital, London. Hospital Chaplain, 1981, **75**.
2. Read, M. *Culture, Health and Disease*. London, Tavistock Publications, 1966.
3. Gorer, G. *Death, Grief and Mourning*. London. The Cressett Press, 1965.
4. Rathwell, T. Health planning sensitive to the needs of ethnic minorities. *Radical Community Medicine*, 1981, **6**: 3–7.
5. Henley, A. *Asian patients in hospital and at home*. London. King Edward Hospital Fund, 1979.
6. Speck, Rev. P. *Loss and Grief in Medicine*. London. Bailliare Tindall, 1978.
7. Bridger, P. *A Hindu family in Britain*. Religious Education Press, 1979.
8. Owen-Cole, W. *A Sikh family in Britain*. Religious Education Press, 1973.

I would like to thank Canon John Barton, chaplain, John Radcliffe Hospital, for his help and introduction to useful literature and to Mrs Anornita Goswami, health liaison officer, Oxfordshire Council for Community Relations.

The Spiritual Needs of the Dying*

Kenneth J. Doka

It has become a truism to describe contemporary American culture as secular. To Becker it is that very secularization that has led to the denial of death [1]. Yet the term "secularization" often has very ambiguous, different, and even conflicting meanings [2]. To many, secularization is essentially a social process whereby religious symbols and doctrines lack social significance and societal decisions are made on a rational and pragmatic rather than on a theological or spiritual basis. Such definition does not deny the potency of both religion and spirituality on an individual level. Gallup polls affirm that vast majorities of Americans both believe in God and consider religion and spirituality important in their lives. This is clearly evident when one faces the crisis of dying, a crisis when scientific explanations are largely silent.

Individuals, of course, differ in the extent that religion plays a part in their lives. These differences continue even throughout the dying process. As Pattison noted, dying persons will use belief systems as they have used throughout life—constructively, destructively, or not at all [3]. To some individuals, belief systems can be a source of comfort and support; to others, it will be a cause for anxiety. Pattison even notes that individuals who seem to find religion in terminal illness often show a basic continuity, for these "foxhole" religionists are likely to be individuals who seek out and grasp each new treatment, diet, or drug.

Counselors are increasingly recognizing the value in exploring religious and spiritual themes with the dying; for dying is not only a medical and personal crisis, it is a spiritual one as well. Though individuals may adhere to different religious beliefs and explanations, or even then lack them, dying focuses one on questions such as the meaning of life, the purpose of one's own existence, and the reason for death, that have an inherently spiritual quality. Thus as individuals struggle with dying, spiritual and religious themes are likely to emerge. In fact, often these spiritual interpretations are, to paraphrase Freud "a royal road into the unconscious."

While this chapter will emphasize religious and spiritual themes in the terminal phase of disease, it is important to recognize the presence of these themes throughout the illness. Even at the point of diagnosis, persons may interpret the disease in a spiritual or religious sense. For example, one person may define AIDS as a punishment from God. That interpretation is likely to have very different reverberations throughout the illness than those from someone who sees the disease as a result from an unfortunate exposure to a virus.

It is not unusual for a person's interpretation of the disease to have religious and spiritual dimensions. Every disease has a component of mystery. Why does one smoker get lung cancer and another not? Why does a disease manifest itself at any given time? Why, in fact, do we die? None of these questions yield to totally satisfactory scientific and rational explanations.

Hence in exploring someone's interpretation of disease, it is essential to be sensitive to these religious or spiritual dimensions. Often because religious or spiritual explanations are not socially validated, individuals may be reluctant to share them or even be fully aware of them. There is a need then for counselors to probe for such issues in a permissive and nonjudgmental atmosphere.

---

*A section of this chapter has been previously published by the author in the *Newsletter of the Forum for Death Education and Counseling*, 6, pp. 2–3.

Religions of spiritual themes may also be intertwined with affective responses evident in the living-dying interval. Numerous observers have noted that persons with a life-threatening or terminal disease often exhibit emotions such as anger, guilt, bargaining, resignation, hope and anxiety [4, 5]. All of these responses may be tied to spiritual concerns. Anger may not only be directed against significant others but also cosmically—against nature, the universe, fate, or God. And such anger can be combined with both guilt and fear that anger toward the deity or other transcendental power is both wrong and dangerous. One person, for example, was both angry at God for her disease, but also was fearful that God would continue to punish her for that anger. In counseling, the woman has been able to reinterpret her anger as a form of prayer, and with that a reaffirmation of both her relationship to God (e.g., she had the freedom to communicate such anger) and his power. A comment by Easson helped [6]. In describing the anger of a thirteen-year-old boy with leukemia, he noted the child's comment that "if God is God, He will understand my anger, if He does not understand my anger, He is not God" [6, p. 91]. This allowed the woman to see her anger as an aspect of faith.

Similarly bargaining may be directed toward God leading to a sense of hope or resignation if the bargain is perceived as accepted and a sense of anger, guilt and fear is perceived as denied. One man with leukemia gave up hope at the time of his first relapse. In his mind he had made a "bargain" with God at the time of his first hospitalization. At that time he had hoped for the health to participate in a family event. When a relapse soon followed, he now believed that God had fulfilled his part of the deal—the man was now resigned to dying. Such bargains do not have to be theistic in nature. One woman once had made a deal with "the universe" to give something back if she achieved a desired success. In her own intensely spiritual frame of reference, her illness was a manifestation of her selfishness and unwillingness to part with her time or possessions. She had not fulfilled her promise, her illness was the result.

It is important then for counselors to recognize that *any* response to life-threatening illness can be intertwined with religious themes. Throughout the illness, these religious or spiritual interpretations should be explored as they can facilitate or complicate a person's response to illness.

Religious and spiritual values may also influence treatment decisions. Extreme examples of this may be found when adherence to particular beliefs precludes certain medical procedures such as blood transfusions or even causes patients to reject any conventional medical therapies. But even in other cases, religious and philosophical perspectives may certainly be part of treatment decisions. For example, persons may decline treatments because of personal perspectives on quality of life or because they perceive a value to life or an obligation to God or fellow humans. Perspectives in euthanasia may be profoundly influenced by religious and spiritual values.

While religious and spiritual themes are often found throughout the struggle with life-threatening illness, they are often especially critical in the terminal phase. For beyond the medical, social, and psychological needs of dying individuals,

there are spiritual needs as well. The terminally ill patient recognizes Becker's paradox that humans are aware of finitude yet have a sense of transcendence [1]. It is this paradox that underlies the three spiritual needs of dying persons: 1) the search for meaning of life, 2) to die appropriately, and 3) to find hope that extends beyond the grave.

1. THE SEARCH FOR MEANING OF LIFE

One major crisis precipitated by dying is a search for the meaning of one's life. Theoreticians of various disciplines have long recognized that we are creatures who create and share meaning. This purposiveness extends to self as well. In the prologue of the play *Ross,* a biography of Lawrence of Arabia, various characters posthumously assess Lawrence's life. As the spotlight descends on one Arab chieftain, he defiantly exclaims "that history will sigh and say 'this was a man!'" It is a statement that in one way or another we wish to make that our life had purpose, significance, and meaning. Developmental psychologists and sociologists, such as Erikson, Butler, and Marshall, assert that the knowledge of impending death creates a crisis in which one reviews life in order to integrate one's goals, values and experience [7–9]. This awareness of finitude can be a consequence of either old age or serious illness. Even very young children, and their families, will review the child's life to find that sense of purpose.

The failure to find meaning can create a deep sense of spiritual pain. Individuals may feel that their lives changed or meant nothing. This has implications for caregivers. One of the most important things that caregivers can do for dying persons is to provide time for that personal reflection. While the caregiver can help dying persons find significance in their lives, things they have done, events they have witnessed, history that they have experienced all provide fruitful areas for exploration. Counselors may use varied techniques to facilitate this process. Reviewing life and family histories, viewing family or period photographs and mementos or sharing family humor and stories can facilitate this process. Films, music, books, or art that evoke earlier periods or phases of life can encourage reminiscence and life review.

Religious beliefs or philosophical and spiritual systems can be very important here. They can give one's life a sense of cosmic significance. And, they can provide a sense of forgiveness—to oneself and to others—for acts of commission and omission and for dreams not accomplished.

2. TO DIE APPROPRIATELY

People not only need assurance that they have lived meaningfully, they must die meaningfully as well. First, people want to die in ways consistent with their own self-identity. For example, a group of elderly women have established a call system to each other. Each woman has a set of multiple keys to each other's apartment. "This," one woman assured, "was so we don't die stinking up the apartment and nobody has to break down any doors." To these old-world women, cleanliness and orderliness are key virtues. The thought of leaving dirt and disorder even at the moment of demise is painful. They wish to die congruent with the ways in which they lived.

Dying appropriately also means dying comprehendingly. It means being able to understand and interpret one's death. If one suffers, it means having a framework to explain suffering. Pope John Paul noted that our secular and comfort-oriented society lacks a theology of pain. This suggests that caregivers need to explore with patients their beliefs about pain and death.

To die appropriately is difficult in a technological world. The fantasy of a quick death surrounded by loving relatives contrasts starkly with the reality of dying by chronic disease, alone, and institutionalized. It is little wonder that people fear not so much the fact of death as the process of dying. Caregivers can be helpful here in a number of ways. First, by empathetic listening, they allow the dying space to interpret their deaths. Second, whatever control can be left to the dying aids in their construction of their deaths. The opportunity to discuss one's death with relatives, either near the time of death or earlier, permits occasion to prepare to die as one lived. This allows specifying modes of treatment, ritual requests, special bequests, or simply educating families in the details that accompany death.

3. TO FIND HOPE THAT EXTENDS BEYOND THE GRAVE

Another spiritual need is transcendental. We seek assurance in some way that our life, or what we left, will continue. Perhaps the popularity of Moody's *Life After Life* [10] is that it recasts traditional images of the afterlife in a quasiscientific framework.

But there are many ways that we can look toward continued existence. Lifton and Olson spoke of five modes of symbolic immortality in our progeny [11]. A second mode is the creative mode in which we see continuance in our creations. This can include the singular accomplishments of the great or the more mundane contributions of the average. The last three modes, theological, eternal nature, and transcendental, relate to conceptualizations of immortality preferred in various belief systems. We might add a sixth—a communal mode where we see our life as part of a larger group. The continued survival of the group gives each life significance and each person lives in the community's memory. Such a theme is often evident in Jewish thought.

Religion and other belief systems are one way to provide critical reassurance of immortality. Religious rituals may affirm a sense of continuity even beyond death. Yet Lifton and Olson's typology remind that there are other things that help as well. Actions of caregivers are important too. The presence of personal artifacts and dignified treatment of the terminally ill reaffirm personhood and suggest significance. Institutional policies that encourage intergenerational visiting provide subtle reminders of one's biological legacy.

SUMMARY

Yet while there seems some recognition of these spiritual needs, it remains unclear as to how well these needs are being met. Observers have recognized a variety of obstacles to religious or spiritual wholeness [12]. Some of these obstacles may be structural. Lack of access to clergy, a lack of privacy, or a reluctance of caregivers to explore religious and spiritual issues can inhibit any attempt to address their spiritual concerns.

The lack of structure may also be an inhibitor. Within the Christian tradition, there is an absence of recognized ritual that mandates the presence of clergy and focuses on spiritual issues such as reconciliation and closure. Such a ritual has never been particularly significant in Protestant liturgy or theology. In the Roman Catholic tradition, the sacrament of extreme unction, or popularly "last rites," has changed its meaning significantly since 1974. Retitled (or restored to the title of) "anointing of the sick," it now emphasizes a holistic notion of healing that is rooted in a context of prayer and counseling. While much is gained by this change, it ends the notion of a sacramental rite of passage into death. Death becomes simply a medical event where clergy have no defined role. There then is an absence of any structure of ritual that focuses on addressing these spiritual needs.

Other failures may be failures of personnel. Clergy or clinicians may be unable to facilitate this process. There may be a number of reasons for this. Clergy may be intolerant of other beliefs or seek to proselytize. They may fail to be understanding. They may hide behind prayer or ritual. Intellectually or emotionally they may have little to offer dying persons. Other caregivers may not be religious, may not have explored their own spiritual beliefs, or are hesitant to explore beliefs of others.

Finally, dying persons may be unable to meet their own spiritual needs. They may lack conviction in their own beliefs, fail to appreciate or explore their own spiritual needs, or be consumed by dysfunctional elements of their own belief system [12].

Clergy and clinicians can facilitate spiritual wholeness in a number of ways. First, in their own conversations with dying persons, they can provide individuals with opportunities to explore these concerns in a nonthreatening and nonjudgmental atmosphere. These are times to listen and explore the individual's perspective. Should some of these beliefs have dysfunctional elements, counselors can explore the ways that these issues can be addressed within the belief structure. For example, in one case, a man was consumed with religious guilt. Exploration of his own beliefs allowed him to address how that guilt could be expiated.

Varied rituals may facilitate this process. Rituals such as confession or communion can provide a visible sign of forgiveness. As DeArment notes, prayer can be a powerful way to express emotion or approach intimate reflection without the patient feeling exposed or vulnerable [13]. It can also be useful to explore faith stories or "paricopes" with individuals. By asking persons to relate faith stories that they believe speak to their situations, one can assess significant issues and themes in their own spiritual journeys. Sometimes one can help individuals reframe these faith stories to derive additional support. For example, many individuals in the Judaic-Christian tradition interpret Job as fatalistically responding to loss. "The Lord giveth and taketh." Another way to view that story, though, is as a long intense struggle of Job as he experiences loss. The latter is often more helpful to people in struggle and is quite faithful to text. In those cases in which the counselor cannot utilize such rituals or beliefs, they are still able to assist in locating empathic clergy or layperson of the person's own faith. This also reminds one that faith communities—the churches, congregations, and temples—that individuals may belong to can be helpful resources.

In recent years, there has been increasing recognition that dying persons not only have medical needs but psychological and social needs as well. Recognition of spiritual needs, too, will allow individuals to approach death as they have approached life—wholly.

REFERENCES

1. E. Becker, *The Denial of Death,* Free Press, New York, 1973.
2. J. A. Winter, *Continuities in the Sociology of Religion,* Harper and Row, New York, 1977.
3. G. M. Pattison, *Religion, Faith, and Healing, The Experience of Dying,* Prentice Hall, New Jersey, 1977.
4. E. Kubler-Ross, *On Death and Dying,* Macmillan, New York, 1969.
5. T. Rando, *Grief, Dying and Death: Clinical Interventions for Caregivers,* Research Press, Champaign, Illinois, 1984.
6. W. Easson, *The Dying Child: The Management of the Child or Adolescent Who is Dying,* Charles C. Thomas, Springfield, Illinois, 1970.
7. E. Erickson, *Childhood and Society,* Macmillan, New York, 1963.
8. R. Butler, The Life Review: An Interpretation of Reminiscence in the Aged, *Psychiatry,* 26, p. 1, 1963.
9. V. Marshall, *Last Chapters: A Sociology of Aging and Dying,* Brooks/Cole, Monterey, California, 1980.
10. R. Moody, *Life After Life,* Bantam Books, New York, 1975.
11. R. Lifton and E. Olson, *Living and Dying,* Bantam Books, New York, 1974.
12. T. Attig, Respecting the Dying and Bereaved as Believers, *Newsletter of the Forum for Death Education and Counseling,* 6, pp. 10–11, 1983.
13. D. DeArment, Prayer and the Dying Patient: Intimacy Without Exposure, in *Death and Ministry,* J. Bane, Kutcher, Neale and Reeves, Jr. (eds.), Seabury Press, New York, 1975.

The Patient-Physician Relationship

The Request to Die

Role for a Psychodynamic Perspective on Physician-Assisted Suicide

Philip R. Muskin, MD

Published reports indicate that 2.5% of deaths in the Netherlands are the result of euthanasia or physician-assisted suicide. It is not known how many patients make these requests in the United States, but the issue has gained considerable attention, including that of the Supreme Court. The focus of the writing and discussion regarding the request to die has been on a patient's capacity. There has not been an adequate focus on the possible meanings contained within the request to die. A patient's request to die is a situation that requires the physician to engage in a dialogue to understand what the request means, including whether the request arises from a clinically significant depression or inadequately treated pain. This article outlines some of the thoughts and emotions that could underlie the patient's request to die. Recommendations are made regarding the role of the primary care physician and the role of the psychiatric consultant in the exploration of the meaning of the request.

J.A.M.A. 1998;279:323–328

T HE ISSUE to be addressed in this article is not one of ethics or law. The focus is on the variety of potential psychodynamic meanings contained within a patient's request for assistance in bringing about his or her death, and the important role a psychodynamic understanding can play in the physician's response to the patient. Some treatment refusals will result in the death of the patient and, thus, should also be carefully assessed.[1] The principle that every request to die should be subjected to careful scrutiny of its multiple potential meanings has not been part of the standard response to such requests.

Data from a 1995 survey of death certificates in the Netherlands reveals that 2.5% of all deaths result from euthanasia.[2] This is an increase from the 1.7% rate found in the 1990 survey.[2] Whether this increase indicates a "slippery slope" is a matter of controversy.[3] It is not known how many patients in the United States request help in dying. As noted by Hendin, "Strikingly, the overwhelming majority of those who are terminally ill fight for life to the end."[4] Chochinov et al[5] reported that 44% (89 of 200) of terminally ill patients report occasional wishes that death would come soon. Only 9% report a "serious and pervasive wish to die."[5] As in other studies, the desire for death correlates with both physical pain and with poor social support.[5] The most significant correlation is with depression, as 59% of patients who wish to die have a depressive syndrome.[5] Breitbart et al[6] found that 63% of patients infected with the human immunodeficiency virus (HIV) supported policies favoring physician-assisted suicide, and 55% considered physician-assisted suicide as a personal option. This study demonstrated a strong correlation with depression and low social support (patients' rating of fewer visits by family and friends, patients' experiencing less support from family and friends), but not with patients' rating of physical pain.[6] It is possible that the stigma, prejudice, and discrimination that patients with HIV infection experience increases their risk for depression and the wish to die. Some studies demonstrate that uncontrolled pain correlates strongly with suicide in cancer patients[7,8]; others show a negative correlation between patients with pain and a positive attitude toward euthanasia and physician-assisted suicide.[9] The survey of oncology patients by Emanuel et al[9] found that 25% thought about asking their physician for euthanasia or physician-assisted suicide. This study

From the Department of Psychiatry, Columbia-Presbyterian Medical Center, Columbia University, College of Physicians and Surgeons, and Columbia University Psychoanalytic Center for Training and Research, New York, NY.

Presented at the American Academy of Psychoanalysis, New York, NY, May 3, 1996.

Reprints: Philip R. Muskin, MD, Columbia-Presbyterian Medical Center, 622 W 168th St, Mailbox 427, New York, NY 10032-3784.

The Patient-Physician Relationship section editor: Richard M. Glass, MD, Deputy Editor, *JAMA*.

confirmed the association between depression and patients' consideration of death. The patients who were "depressed and psychologically distressed were significantly more likely to seriously discuss euthanasia, hoard drugs, or bought or read *Final Exit*."[9]

Surveys report a wide range in physicians' reports of requests from patients for assisted death and in physicians' willingness to give a lethal dose of a drug or perform assisted death.[9–18] Seventeen percent of critical care nurses reported receiving requests for death from patients or from the patient's family; 16% reported they aided in a patient's death, and 4% reported that they hastened a patient's death by pretending to provide life-sustaining treatment ordered by the physician.[19] Fifteen percent of nurses who work with patients with the acquired immunodeficiency syndrome in San Francisco, Calif, have assisted in a patient's suicide.[20] Physicians and other clinicians thus find themselves continuing to struggle with patients' requests to die.

A psychodynamic approach to a patient's communication attempts to understand both the manifest content and also to explore unconscious meanings. Critics of this approach label the search for meaning reductionist, indicating that it entails seeking a different origin or a "true" meaning hidden from that apparent on the surface, without acknowledging the importance of the manifest content. A modern view of psychodynamics is expansionist, ie, seeking to find other important hidden meanings within emotion, thought, and behavior rather than searching for a singularity, a core unity, or a "truth." The premise that follows from this conceptual framework is that every case of a patient requesting to die should be explored in depth by the physician primarily responsible for the care of the patient, mindful of the complex psychodynamics that might be involved. No action should be taken prior to such close scrutiny. Discussions of the psychiatric evaluation of a patient's request to die often focus on whether the patient is "competent," which is too simplistic an approach for so complex a matter. This article is designed to explore some of that complexity using general categories of thoughts and emotion present in patients who express suicidal ideation. This may shed light on the significance to the patient and to the physician of conscious and unconscious meanings in a medically ill patient's request to die.

THE REQUEST TO DIE AS A COMMUNICATION

When a person commits suicide, the note left behind communicates (overtly and symbolically) the reasons for the choice of death. Of greatest importance is the fact that his communication follows the death. There must be a difference between patients who commit suicide, with no communication save the note left behind, and patients who say to their physicians "Would you assist me in my death?" or "Would you kill me?" The very fact that there is a communication while the person is alive suggests the expectation of an interaction with the physician. What could such a request mean to the patient and what does the request signify as a communication to the physician? There are many possibilities, but one that should be considered is that the request to die is an attempt to be given a reason to live[21]; ie, the patient is asking, "Does anyone care enough to talk me out of this request, to want me to be alive, to be willing to share my suffering?" Acting on a patient's wish because he or she is judged to be rational and competent ignores the unspoken or unconscious meaning(s) of the request. Acknowledging this dynamic without stating it overtly, a physician might respond to the patient, "I want to try to do everything I can to work with you and provide you with the best care I can offer. If you die, you will be greatly missed; how can we understand together why you want to die right now?"

CONTROL

"It is always consoling to think of suicide: in that way one gets through many a bad night."[22] Nietzsche's comment suggests that one possibility contained within a patient's request to die may be an effort to take control over life, even if this control is illusory and paradoxical. When a patient has lost control over every aspect of life, the only place control may be established is by asking for death. Many patients find great solace in knowing they can kill themselves at any time by hoarding a lethal dose of medication, even though the medication is never used. Is the person actually seeking death or a magical protection in the form of the pills, a talisman against the agonizing helplessness of having no control? A discussion with the physician could provide the patient with the reassurance that the ability to control his or her destiny is maintained without requesting to die.

A patient awaiting a heart for transplant informed the physician that patients had the "right" to request physician-assisted suicide. A psychiatric consultation was requested to evaluate the patient's "suicidality," and there was great concern on the ward that the patient might remove the battery from the left ventricular assist device (LVAD). When interviewed, the patient was lively and engaging, clearly enjoying the back-and-forth discussion of a patient's right to end his or her life. There were no symptoms of depression, and the patient was hopeful about obtaining a new heart. The patient came from a tradition of argument as a way of interaction with others, and physician-assisted suicide was a topic of personal importance. The discussion made clear the patient's need to feel in control of every aspect of life, control that the idiopathic cardiomyopathy had taken away. In talking about the "right to die," the question of the LVAD arose, especially the fact that this individual could end life at any moment by removing the batteries. The patient responded instantly and passionately that a major concern was that there would not be an adequate supply of batteries to guarantee a charged battery be available every moment of the day, at work, at home, or while traveling. The patient looked directly at the interviewer and said, "Do you think I am crazy, if I did that I would die! We're not talking about death here, we're talking about my rights."

SPLIT IN THE EXPERIENCE OF THE SELF

A cognition found in suicide and in some medically ill patients' request to die is the wish that the bad, ie, medically sick, part of the self be killed, leaving the healthy self to survive. This fantasized split may be unconscious; however, some patients may have a conscious experience of another, "sick self," who feels like an alien within the patient. Such patients make comments such as "I don't know the person I've become" or "This isn't how I usually act." Patients may complain that they feel "taken over" by their physical, medical, or emotional needs to the exclusion of their "normal" personality. Conscious or not, the wish to kill off a part of the self in order to survive or to be willing to die along with the sick self with the fantasy that the healthy self will be reborn may be a motivation contained within the request to die. In such a situation a psychological intervention could enable the individual to resolve this split so that there is no longer a healthy and sick self but one self who is suffering and ill. The physician might make a comment such as "It may feel at times as if you don't recognize yourself, particularly when you have many complaints or when you have a great deal of physical discomfort. But the 'real' you still comes through. It's okay to complain and okay to have needs." Such patients, after an initial discussion with their physician, should be referred for psychological treatment if the split in self-experience persists.

RAGE AND REVENGE

Patients who are desperately ill may feel some degree of rage: rage at themselves, rage at their doctors, rage at the world, rage at God for their illness and for their suffering. Rage, caused by physical suffering, psychological suffering, or both, may induce wishes to kill. The impact of hopelessness, the experience of being helpless, the agony of experiencing oneself as out of control, the terror of the unknown, and the physical suffering from inadequately treated pain may cause the patient to seek revenge by demanding death. To kill whom? Along with the emotion of rage comes the wish for revenge. A psychodynamic understanding of some suicidal patients indicates they are seeking revenge by murdering what is an unconscious image of an important person who is simultaneously loved and hated. Atonement for the murder is achieved by the person's death via suicide. This mental mechanism is presumed to be unconscious, though patients with severe character disorder are often aware of the wish to seek revenge on others via their own death. These are patients for whom a psychiatric consultation is necessary. Patients can have fantasies of harming the doctor or of harming significant others by dying. A successful psychotherapeutic intervention could lead to the realization on the part of the patient that there is no actual revenge that will accrue from his or her death. The patient arrives at an understanding that the focus of this love and hatred is a psychological creation. Suicide will end his or her life and potentially have an emotional impact on people who care about the person, but not the impact the patient desires.

HOPELESSNESS AND SUFFERING

Beck et al[23] note that the seriousness of suicidal intent correlates better with the degree of hopelessness about the future than with any other indicator of depressive severity. When a patient is hopeless, the physician should investigate whether the patient is depressed. Hopelessness, desperation, and despair are also emotions that accompany suffering. Suffering poses a great challenge to patient and physician. Is it the prospect of death some days, weeks, months, or years in the future that causes the patient to feel despair, hopelessness, and desperation and request death now? Or is it the patient's prospect of suffering unremitting physical pain that prompts the request for death (see below)? Patients' experience of hopelessness or hopefulness is associated with what they have been told by their physician. Informing patients about their illness and treatment necessitates that the physician strike a balance between giving too little or too much information. Inadequate information fosters a situation of hopelessness because patients have no facts with which they can make decisions. Patients can usually sense when information is withheld or is slanted. This creates distrust of the physician and seriously damages the potential effectiveness of the patient-physician relationship. At the other end of the communication spectrum is "truth dumping," which takes away all hope by telling patients morbid statistical "facts" without balancing the seriousness of the illness with a basis for hope. The physician's evaluation of the patient's hopelessness relies on his or her understanding of what information has been provided to the patient, and how that information has been communicated. The physician of a patient with diabetes, hypertension, and renal disease received a call when the patient regained consciousness after an unsuccessful suicide attempt. The patient requested that the physician assist in suicide because the diabetes and renal dysfunction were experienced as intolerable. The physician arranged for the patient to be taken to an emergency room of another hospital, where the patient was admitted in mild diabetic ketoacidosis and uncontrolled hypertension. The patient described a state of despair and felt physician-assisted suicide was a reasonable plan given the hopelessness of the renal disease. The ketoacidosis and hypertension were quickly stabilized. The family was contacted, and the patient's mother flew from out of state to bring her adult child home. History from a friend and the mother and some from the patient revealed the onset of juvenile onset diabetes 20 years previously. The patient had recently sent all personal effects to the parents' home, simultaneously refusing to talk with them or with friends. This occurred after the physician had informed the patient of the need for dialysis (and likelihood of a kidney transplant) within the next year at the rate the renal function was declining. It was also revealed that the physician had presented the "facts" that there was little long-term hope for a successful transplant 2 days before the suicide attempt and the request for physician-assisted suicide. The patient's mother, having contacted a group investigating renal and pancreatic transplants, came ready to take the patient home for such an evaluation. The despair disappeared when this news was received. The patient spoke about the "important things left to do with life" and was "glad" that the suicide attempt had been unsuccessful.

PAIN

Pain is a physical experience that also creates emotional suffering. Inadequate pain control may cause rage, sadness, and hopelessness or contribute to the development of an affective illness. Some patients suffer from ineffective treatment of physical pain as a result of insufficient analgesia, the product of inadequate physician education and moralistic views regarding narcotics.[24,25] The situation has not been remedied by journal articles, textbooks, newspaper articles, or guidelines.[26–29] In the Netherlands the request for "hastened death" is withdrawn in 85% of patients when their symptoms are better controlled.[30] The availability of reliable and effective palliative care may reduce dramatically the requests for physician-assisted suicide.[31] Without optimal treatment, we cannot be sure that the request for death does not derive from an attempt to escape from physical pain. No more powerful statement can be made to a patient who is in pain than that of the physician who says, "I will do everything that can be done to alleviate your pain, and I guarantee that nothing will be withheld from you unless you tell me to do otherwise."

SADNESS AND DEPRESSION

Distinction must be made between depression, a treatable medical illness, and the experience of sadness. "Periods of sadness are inherent aspects of the human experience. These periods should not be diagnosed as a Major Depressive Disorder."[32] Arriving at a diagnosis of depression in physically ill patients may be complicated by the somatic symptoms that accompany illness and medical or surgical therapies.[33–35] Nonpsychiatric physicians frequently miss the diagnosis of depression,[36–38] particularly where "depression" is presumed to be a normal response to the situation. This "pseudoempathy" prevents physicians from distinguishing sadness from depression.[1] Physicians are not convinced that they could recognize depression in terminally ill patients.[10] As the patient's request for death may arise from a depression, the evaluation should be performed by physicians skilled in making the diagnosis. The judge who ruled that the Oregon physician-assisted suicide law was unconstitutional commented, "The very lives of terminally ill persons depend on their own rational assessment of the value of their existence, and yet there is no requirement that they be evaluated by a mental health specialist."[39] The physician should ask for a psychiatric consultation in every case where he or she is unsure whether the patient's request for death arises from a depression.

That does not mean that every patient who is depressed is suicidal or that the depression is the source of every patient's request to die. Ganzini et al[40] note, "When depression influences decision making, this influence is evident to a trained observer on clinical interview." While it may be difficult for physicians always to be sure of the diagnosis of depression, Chochinov et al[41] recently demonstrated that the easiest and best method for quickly assessing depression in terminally ill patients is to ask the question, "Are you depressed?" A 90-year-old woman was admitted to the hospital after a fall. Though she did not sustain a fracture, she was found to be in congestive heart failure, with pitting edema of her legs. She was anemic and had heme-positive stools. She had been widowed several years and complained that all of her friends had

passed away. All of her family lived out of state except for a grandchild attending a local college. It was expected that she would fully recover with medical treatment. From the beginning of her admission she asked if she could die, and she was uncooperative with the medical evaluation. Ambulation had become increasingly difficult for her, and she stated strongly that she was "old and had lived long enough." A piece of history casually revealed during the psychiatric consultation was that she was once a professional dancer with a famous dance troupe. The many losses in her life, including the recent loss of the use of her legs, suggested a clinically significant depression, and a psychostimulant was prescribed. She was disappointed in the doctor's decision not to end her life but reluctantly complied with the continuation of the medical evaluation and with taking medication. After a week of treatment, realizing that she would regain the ability to walk, she began to press for more aggressive physical therapy. When a nursing home placement was obtained, she refused the transfer because she believed the physical therapy offered in the hospital was superior to the nursing home, and she was anxious to regain full use of her legs and return home.

GUILT, SELF-PUNISHMENT, AND ATONEMENT

Guilt is a potentially destructive emotion that may occur in both patient and physician. Patients may attribute their cancer to unacceptable emotions and bad deeds.[42] Some patients may conclude, "If I was not bad, I would not have gotten this terrible illness. I don't love people who are bad; thus, nobody could love me. Now I have been a bad patient because I have not recovered from my illness. My failure has made my doctor fail and my doctor must hate me. If I die, it will make amends for being a bad person." Self-punishment and the desire to atone can thus become a motivation for the request to die. In patients for whom illness is equated with a personal failure, death is equated with deserved punishment. Such thoughts may seem logical to patients influenced by the regressive pull of physical illness, by pain, by the threat of loss of body parts or functions, by the chaos of the hospital, and by the intrusive nature of being a patient.[43]

Patients' feelings of guilt may be stimulated or exacerbated by interactions within the patient-physician relationship. Physicians are imbued with omnipotent powers by patients, derived from the child's experience of the parent as omnipotent.[44,45] One has only to witness or participate in the "kissing of a boo-boo" to perceive the power of the child's belief in the parent's omnipotence to heal. Powerful fantasies about the physician, deriving from the patient's childhood experiences, often remain unknown. The patient may perceive that his or her physical and emotional suffering causes the physician to suffer, accompanied by the patient's perception of the physician's wish to end his or her own emotional suffering. This wish may be interpreted by the patient as the physician's wish that the patient be dead. The patient's request to die can therefore be an attempt to accede to what the patient believes is the "doctor's wish."

When the physician cannot accept that some patients do not respond to treatment, he or she may experience guilt for having failed. Some physicians blame the patient for having the illness or for the poor treatment response. The patient's guilt influences the physician's response to the patient's request to die.[46] The patient's experience of the physician's guilt and the physician's unchallenged acquiescence to the patient's request to die confirm the patient's guilty experience of being bad and unworthy of the physician's healing power. Where there is no avenue for a discussion that will uncover these complex dynamics, action may replace affects and words. The patient's death thus replaces the opportunity for understanding and life. Miles[47] has stated, "Openness to my distress at a patient's suffering improves therapeutic insight into a patient's pain, demoralization, and depression." There are times that the physician might benefit from a discussion with a psychiatric colleague about thoughts and feelings encountered in the relationship with a particular patient.

THE LIVING DEAD

Some patients who request to die seem to experience themselves as already dead. This may occur more readily in individuals rendered vulnerable by a childhood devoid of a warm, nurturing parent. This self-experience may also occur as the result of physical suffering, emotional suffering, or both, the fear of unremitting agony, the loss of social support that accompanies catastrophic illness for some patients, and the impact of significant depressive and/or anxiety disorders. While not a diagnosis in the *Diagnostic and Statistical Manual of Mental Disorders, Fourth Edition,* this self-experience takes the form of a condition that might be called "the living dead," and it robs the person of all hope for recovery or for a more comfortable existence. The person "knows" that he or she is going to die, which leads to the decision to attempt to get it over with quickly. It is extremely challenging for the physician to work with such a patient, as the physician too may have the experience that the person, though alive, feels already deceased. The physician's confrontation of the patient's self-experience requires skill, tact, and the belief that there remains life worth living for this patient. Therapeutics for pain, insomnia, anxiety, and depression, as well as recommending and instituting psychological treatments, can effectively treat this condition. The patient is restored to the living, able to acknowledge the seriousness of the illness, without feeling overwhelmed. An emergency consultation was requested for a woman in her mid-40s who decided she was unable to continue with chemotherapy. She complained of severe pain, nausea, and fear of the pain associated with each treatment. Aware that she had a rare cancer that carried a poor prognosis, she questioned continuation of the treatment that had just begun. During the consultation, which lasted 3 hours, she cried continuously, referring frequently to the fact she would never see her garden bloom again, though spring was only a few months away. "I have no reason to go on with this," she stated, simultaneously listing all of the things and people that were important to her, especially her impending graduation from professional school, while repeatedly emphasizing the pain of not seeing her garden again. The comment was made to her

that she acted as if she were already dead, in spite of the fact that the indications were that she had many months to live, and live comfortably, even if the therapy was ultimately unsuccessful. Her response was dramatic and instantaneous, her tears dried up, she looked at the consultant and took his hand, "You mean I have something to live for?" she asked; "I will see my garden bloom again, won't I." This was not asked as a question. She never again, through her difficult course and her death a year later, stopped being alive, often reminding the consultant and herself of the importance of "not being dead until your time comes."

THE ROLE OF THE PSYCHIATRIST

Psychiatrists bring the potential for expert exploration and understanding of the issues involved in a patient's request to die. In the evaluation of the patient's request, psychiatrists help identify both the psychodynamic issues and psychiatric disorders, particularly depression, that would benefit from treatment.[1] These evaluations should not be limited to the determination of a patient's capacity to make decisions.[48] Nor should the evaluation be a single diagnostic visit. Only a small number of psychiatrists surveyed in the Oregon study felt confident that they could determine whether a psychiatric disorder impairs a patient's judgment in a single visit.[49] There is an additional significant role for the psychiatrist, who, through the psychotherapeutic process, can offer relief from psychological suffering in a terminally ill patient.[50,51] This is not the tendering of foolish optimism or naive hope, but offers an expectation of self-understanding that can lead to a reduction of the individual's suffering. It is a coming to terms with oneself and with the significant people in one's life, both those who are living and those who are dead but with whom the patient continues an active relationship. In concert with the physician responsible for the person's medical care, psychiatrists can assist in assuring the patient that his or her suffering will be reduced to a minimum with appropriate treatment. This includes a frank discussion of the possibility that the person's consciousness might be compromised by maximal analgesic treatment.

There may be times that the psychiatrist's role in the process requires that he or she tell a colleague "You are overinvolved, it is time to let this patient die" or "You are not adequately treating this patient's pain" or "You have given the patient information in such a way as to rob him or her of hope." In each of these and other communications, the psychiatrist must make it clear that these observations do not reflect on the colleague's competence or ideals, but rather that the psychiatrist's focus is on different needs of the patient that may have gone unrecognized.

In speaking with patients, I (and psychiatrists who have described their experiences to me) have encountered the criticism from patients and families that, under the guise of investigating the meaning of a patient's communication, we are violating the patient's basic human rights, ie, "the right to die." I contend that not discussing a patient's motivation is the real violation of his or her rights, as there exists the possibility that the role of psychological factors has been underestimated.[52] Some of the skills in communication required for this exploration are those that every physician should possess[53–55]; however, some of the skills required for the in-depth exploration are not those of the primary care physician, the oncologist, or the surgeon. These are the skills of the psychiatrist who has the training and skills in both psychodynamic exploration and interaction with medically ill patients. Not all psychiatrists are comfortable in this arena, nor do all psychiatrists have clinical experience with medically ill and dying patients. The psychiatrist in these cases should have the training and experience to provide patient and physician with a meaningful consultation. There are some psychologists and social workers who have clinical expertise from their work with patients who have medical illness. Such consultants would also be appropriate to conduct this type of psychological exploration.

POLICY, PHYSICIAN-ASSISTED SUICIDE, AND THE ROLE OF THE PHYSICIAN

In every situation where a patient makes the request for his or her physician to end the person's life, the physician's answer should not be a simple yes or no. Answering yes without exploring the meaning of the request, while seemingly giving the patient what he or she asks for, in actuality may abolish the opportunity for patient and physician to more fully understand and know one another. Answering no leaves the patient in a situation of helplessness to control his or her destiny and closes off further communication. Inquiring about the patients' emotional state, validating the patient's experience, and helping the patient identify the motivations for the request to die allow the physician to engage in a truly meaningful communication at a crucial time in the patient's life. An initial response might be, "That is a serious request. Before we can know what would be the best way to proceed, let's talk about why you are asking me to help you die now." Not every request for physician-assisted suicide indicates complex unspoken psychodynamics, but that cannot be known until the physician and the patient talk. A psychiatric consultation is necessary in cases where there is complexity regarding the psychological motivations, cases where the physician feels there is a psychiatric disorder, cases where there is a suggestion that the patient is clinically depressed, and cases where the physician has intense emotions regarding the patient (particularly feelings of guilt, anger, or inadequacy). The request for suicide may be found to be "rational" but not until there has been an adequate exploration of its meaning.[56] The willingness of a physician to enter into such a dialogue with patients is not without an emotional impact on the physician, but it is what is required if physicians are to appropriately respond to such requests.[47]

The US Supreme Court decision on physician-assisted suicide has not ended the debate. Decriminalizing physician-assisted suicide is insufficient as there is no requirement to explore the patient's request. It is our professional responsibility to make provision for an exploration of the motivation in patients who make such a request. Regardless of the outcome of the societal and legal debate regarding physician-assisted suicide, physicians should recognize that patients who make a request to die deserve a compassionate and comprehensive evaluation.

I am indebted to Donald Kornfeld, MD, and Karen Antman, MD, for their encouragement and invaluable assistance in the preparation of this article.

References

1. Sullivan MD, Youngner SJ. Depression, competence and the right to refuse lifesaving medical treatment. *Am J Psychiatry.* 1993;151:971–978.
2. van der Maas PJ, van der Wal G, Haverkate I, et al. Euthanasia, physician-assisted suicide, and other medical practices involving the end of life in the Netherlands, 1990–1995. *N Engl J Med.* 1996;335:1699–1705.
3. Hendin H, Rutenfrans C, Zyliez Z: Physician-assisted suicide and euthanasia in the Netherlands: lessons from the Dutch. *JAMA.* 1997;277:1720–1722.
4. Hendin H. *Seduced by Death: Doctors, Patients and the Dutch Cure.* New York, NY: WW Norton & Co; 1997.
5. Chochinov HM, Wilson KG, Enns M, et al. Desire for death in the terminally ill. *Am J Psychiatry.* 1995;152:1185–1191.
6. Breitbart W, Rosenfeld BD, Passik SD. Interest in physician-assisted suicide among ambulatory HIV-infected patients. *Am J Psychiatry.* 1996;153:238–242.
7. Breitbart W. Cancer pain and suicide. *Adv Pain Res Ther.* 1990;16:399–412.
8. Helig S. The San Francisco Medical Society euthanasia survey: results and analysis. *San Francisco Med.* 1988;61:24–34.
9. Emanuel EJ, Fairclough DL, Daniels ER, Clarridge BR. Euthanasia and physician-assisted suicide: attitudes and experiences among oncology patients, oncologists, and the general public. *Lancet.* 1996;347:1805–1810.
10. Lee MA, Nelson HD, Tilden VP, et al. Legalizing assisted suicide: views of physicians in Oregon. *N Engl J Med.* 1996;334:310–315.
11. Kuhse H, Singer P. Doctors practices and attitudes regarding voluntary euthanasia. *Med J Aust.* 1998;148:623–627.
12. Caralis PV, Hammond JS. Attitudes of medical students, housestaff, and faculty physicians toward euthanasia and termination of life-sustaining treatment. *Crit Care Med.* 1992;20:683–690.
13. Shapiro RS, Derse AR, Gootlieb M, et al. Willingness to perform euthanasia: a survey of physician attitudes. *Arch Intern Med.* 1994;154:575–584.
14. Back AL, Wallace JI, Starks HE, Pearlman RA. Physician-assisted suicide and euthanasia in Washington State: patient requests and physician responses. *JAMA.* 1996;275:919–925.
15. Bachman JG, Alcser KH, Doukas DJ, et al. Attitudes of Michigan physicians and the public toward legalizing physician-assisted suicide and voluntary euthanasia. *N Engl J Med.* 1996;334:303–309.
16. Cohen JS, Fihn SD, Boyko EJ, Jonsen AR, Wood RW. Attitudes toward assisted suicide and euthanasia among physicians in Washington State. *N Engl J Med.* 1994;331:89–94.
17. Ward BJ, Tate PA. Attitudes among NHS doctors to requests for euthanasia. *BMJ* 1994;308:1332–1335.
18. Roberts LW, Muskin PR, Warner TD, et al. Attitudes of consultation-liaison psychiatrists toward physician-assisted death practices. *Psychosomatics.* 1997;38:459–471.
19. Asch DA. The role of critical care nurses in euthanasia and assisted suicide. *N Engl J Med.* 1996;334:1374–1379.
20. Leiser RJ, Mitchell TF, Hahn JA, Abrams DI. The role of critical care nurses in euthanasia and assisted suicide. *N Engl J Med.* 1996;335:972–973.
21. Block SD, Billings JA. Patient requests for euthanasia and assisted suicide in terminal illness: the role of the psychiatrist. *Psychosomatics.* 1995;36:445–457.
22. Nietzsche F. *Beyond Good and Evil* (1886). Quoted in: *The Columbia Dictionary of Quotations.* New York: NY: Columbia University Press; 1993.
23. Beck AT, Steer RA, Kovacs M, Garrison G. Hopelessness and eventual suicide: a 10-year prospective study of patients hospitalized with suicidal ideation. *Am J Psychiatry.* 1985;142:559–563.
24. Marks RM, Sachar ES. Undertreatment of medical inpatients with narcotic analgesics. *Ann Intern Med.* 1973;78:173–181.
25. Foley KM. The relationship of pain and symptom management to patient requests for physician-assisted suicide. *J Pain Symptom Manage.* 1991;6:289–297.
26. Cleeland C. Barriers to the management of cancer pain. *Oncology.* 1987;1(April suppl):19–26.
27. Massie MJ, Holland JC. The cancer patient with pain: psychiatric complications and their management. *Med Clin North Am.* 1987;71:243–258.

28. Max MB. Improving outcomes of analgesic treatment: is education enough? *Ann Intern Med.* 1990;113:885–889.
29. Jacox A, Carr DB, Payne R, et al. *Management of Cancer Pain: Clinical Practice Guideline No. 9.* Rockville, Md: Agency for Health Care Policy Research, US Dept of Health and Human Services; March 1994. AHCPR publication 94-0592.
30. Admiraal p. Personal communication. Cited in: Lo B. Euthanasia: the continuing debate. *West J Med.* 1988;49:211–212.
31. McKeogh M. Physician-assisted suicide and patients with HIV disease. *N Engl J Med.* 1997;337:56.
32. American Psychiatric Association. *Diagnostic and Statistical Manual of Mental Disorders, Fourth Edition.* Washington, DC: American Psychiatric Association; 1994:326.
33. Cavanaugh S. The diagnosis and treatment of depression in the medically ill. In: Guggenheim F, Weiner MF, eds. *Manual of Psychiatric Consultation and Emergency Care.* New York, NY: Jason Aronson; 1984:211–222.
34. Ormel J, Van Den Brink W, Koeter MWJ, et al. Recognition, management and outcome of psychological disorders in primary care: a naturalistic follow-up study. *Psychol Med.* 1990;20:909–923.
35. Sherbourne CD, Wells KB, Hays RD, et al. Subthreshold depression and depressive disorder: clinical characteristics of general medical and mental health specialty outpatients. *Am J Psychiatry.* 1994;151:1777–1784.
36. Schulberg HC, Saul M, McCelland M, et al. Assessing depression in primary medical and psychiatric practices. *Arch Gen Psychiatry.* 1985;42:1164–1170.
37. Eisenberg L. Treating depression and anxiety in primary care: closing the gap between knowledge and practice. *N Engl J Med.* 1992;326:1080–1084.
38. Badger LW, deGruy FV, Hartman J, et al. Patient presentation, interview content, and the detection of depression by primary care physicians. *Psychosomat Med.* 1994;56:128–135.
39. *Lee v State of Oregon,* 891 F Supp 1429, WL 471792 (D Or 1995).
40. Ganzini L, Lee MA, Heintz RT, et al. The effect of depression treatment on elderly patients' preferences for life-sustaining medical therapy. *Am J Psychiatry.* 1994;151:1631–1636.
41. Chochinov HM, Wilson KG, Enns M, Lander S. 'Are you depressed?' screening for depression in the terminally ill. *Am J Psychiatry.* 1997;154:674–676.
42. Sontag S. *Illness as Metaphor.* New York, NY: Farrar Straus & Giroux: 1978.
43. Muskin PR. The medical hospital. In: Schwartz HJ, Bleiberg E, Weissman SH, eds. *Psychodynamic Concepts in General Psychiatry.* Washington, DC: American Psychiatric Press; 1995:69–88.
44. Kohut H. *The Analysis of the Self.* New York, NY: International Universities Press; 1971.
45. Kohut H. *The Restoration of the Self.* New York, NY: International Universities Press; 1977.
46. Goldstein WN. Clarification of projective identification. *Am J Psychiatry.* 1991;148:153–161.
47. Miles SH. Physicians and their patients' suicides. *JAMA.* 1994;271:1786–1788.
48. Huyse FJ, van Tilburg W. Euthanasia policy in the Netherlands: the role of consultation-liaison psychiatrists. *Hosp Community Psychiatry.* 1993;44:733–738.
49. Ganzini L, Fenn DS, Lee MA, Heintz RT, Bloom JD. Attitudes of Oregon psychiatrists toward physician-assisted suicide. *Am J Psychiatry.* 1996;153:1469–1475.
50. Eissler KR. *The Psychiatrist and the Dying Patient.* New York, NY: International Universities Press; 1955.
51. Druss RG. *The Psychology of Illness.* Washington, DC: American Psychiatric Press; 1995.
52. Ganzini L, Lee MA. Psychiatry and assisted suicide in the United States. *N Engl J Med.* 1997;336:1824–1826.
53. Cohen-Cole SA. *The Medical Interview: The Three-Function Approach.* St Louis, Mo: Mosby-Year Book Inc; 1991.
54. Roter DL, Hall JA. *Doctors Talking With Patients/Patients Talking With Doctors.* Westport, Conn: Auburn House; 1992.
55. Roter DL, Hall JA. Strategies for enhancing patient adherence to medical recommendations. *JAMA.* 1994;271:80.
56. Battin MP. Rational suicide: how can we respond to a request for help? *Crisis.* 1991;12:73–80.

Quality End-of-Life Care

Patients' Perspectives

Peter A. Singer, MD, MPH, FRCPC
Douglas K. Martin, PhD
Merrijoy Kelner, PhD

BECAUSE EVERYONE DIES, END-of-life care is among the most prevalent issues in health care. Both health care professionals and patients see room for improvement.[1] Encouragingly, major initiatives, such as the American Medical Association's Education for Physicians on End-of-Life Care project, Open Society Institute's Project on Death in America, and Robert Wood Johnson Foundation's Last Rites Campaign, are under way to improve the quality of end-of-life care.

A necessary scientific step to focus these efforts is the development of a taxonomy or conceptual framework for quality end-of-life care.[2] However, what end-of-life care means and how to measure it is still a matter of debate and ongoing research. Three expert groups have recently published frameworks for quality end-of-life care (TABLE 1).[3-5] These taxonomies derive from the medical expert perspective rather than the perspective of patients and families.[6] We are unaware of any descriptions of quality end-of-life care from the patient perspective, from which quality end-of-life care is arguably most appropriately viewed. This is the perspective that clinicians and health care organizations will need to understand to improve the quality of care they deliver to dying patients. Therefore, the purpose of this study was to identify and describe elements of quality end-of-life care as identified by those most affected: patients.

METHODS

Design

This study used a qualitative research method called *content analysis*, in which "standardized measurements are applied to metrically defined units [of text] and these are used to characterise and compare documents."[7]

Context Quality end-of-life care is increasingly recognized as an ethical obligation of health care providers, both clinicians and organizations. However, this concept has not been examined from the perspective of patients.

Objective To identify and describe elements of quality end-of-life care from the patient's perspective.

Design Qualitative study using in-depth, open-ended, face-to-face interviews and content analysis.

Setting Toronto, Ontario.

Participants A total of 126 participants from 3 patient groups: dialysis patients (n = 48), people with human immunodeficiency virus infection (n = 40), and residents of a long-term care facility (n = 38).

Outcome Measures Participants' views on end-of-life issues.

Results Participants identified 5 domains of quality end-of-life care: receiving adequate pain and symptom management, avoiding inappropriate prolongation of dying, achieving a sense of control, relieving burden, and strengthening relationships with loved ones.

Conclusion These domains, which characterize patients' perspectives on end-of-life care, can serve as focal points for improving the quality of end-of-life care.

JAMA. 1999;281:163–168   www.jama.com

Participants

We analyzed data from interviews with patients who participated in 3 recent studies.[8-10] Participants from the 3 studies were dialysis patients, persons infected with the human immunodeficiency virus (HIV), and residents of a long-term care facility. In this study, we examined all participant interviews from the dialysis (n = 48) and long-term care (n = 38) studies, and a random selection of 40 participant interviews (from a total of 140 participants) from the HIV study.

Dialysis patients were a sample of individuals receiving hemodialysis at all 6 units serving adults in metropolitan Toronto, Ontario. They were originally enrolled in a study examining the acceptability of generic vs. dialysis-specific advance directive (AD) forms[11] and interviewed 6 months later.[8] Participants were excluded if they were younger than 18 years, were unable to understand written English, were incapable of completing an AD form, would experience undue emotional distress from completing an AD form, had received di-

Author Affiliations: *Toronto Hospital and the Department of Medicine (Dr Singer), Joint Centre for Bioethics (Drs Singer and Martin), and the Institute of Human Development, Life Course, and Aging (Dr Kelner), University of Toronto, Toronto, Ontario.*
Corresponding Author and Reprints: *Peter A. Singer, MD, MPH, FRCPC, University of Toronto Joint Centre for Bioethics, 88 College St, Toronto, Ontario, Canada M5G 1L4 (e-mail: peter.singer@utoronto.ca).*

alysis for less than 3 months, or refused to participate in the research. Of 532 patients receiving hemodialysis, 310 were excluded, 81 refused, 43 withdrew, 7 died, 43 were not approached, and 48 completed the study.

Participants with HIV were a sample of persons who responded to the study advertisements or posters distributed by the AIDS Committee of Toronto and placed in the waiting rooms of the Toronto Hospital Immunodeficiency Clinic. They were originally enrolled in a previous study that examined the preference for either an HIV-specific or generic AD form[12] and interviewed 6 months later.[9] Participants were excluded if they were younger than 16 years, were not fluent in English, could not read, were incapable of completing an AD form (as measured by a Standardized Mini-Mental State Examination test score <23), would experience undue emotional distress from completing an AD form, resided outside metropolitan Toronto, or refused to participate in the research. Of 587 possible participants, 200 were not approached for the study, 85 were excluded, 52 refused, 93 withdrew, 17 died, and 140 were interviewed (of whom 40 were randomly selected for this analysis).

Long-term care residents were a sample of persons from a 398-bed hospital in Toronto that provides both rehabilitative and long-term care for adults who are chronically ill and disabled by neurological problems, respiratory conditions, amputations, and age-related disorders.[10] The purpose of the original study was to examine residents' views about control at the end of life. Three criteria were established for selecting participants: patients had to be 65 years or older, capable of understanding

and answering questions in English, and healthy enough, both physically and mentally, to take part in a short interview. Nurse managers recruited participants in each unit of the hospital in which appropriate patients could be identified. No patients refused. The 38 participants represent the total population of eligible patients during the data collection period.

Data Collection

Data were gathered by in-depth, open-ended, face-to-face interviews. The interviewer asked open-ended questions, followed up participants' responses, pursued themes as they arose, and sought clarification or elaboration as required. In the dialysis and HIV studies, the interviews were audiotaped and transcribed; in the long-term care study, the interviewer wrote down the participants' comments. Opportunities were consistently made available for participants to express unsolicited opinions and recount their clinical experiences and life histories. As the interviews proceeded and ideas were suggested by patients' reflections and clarifications, new questions were added and others were refined. The interview guide was modified to follow up issues emerging from the data as the interviews and analysis progressed.

The initial interview guide for dialysis patients covered 3 themes: (1) had the participant completed an AD form? (2) if not, why not? and (3) if so, what was the process and was it acceptable?

In the HIV study, participants were asked about their reasons for engaging in advance care planning (ACP), the process and content of their ACP discussions, their perspective on the importance of ACP, and their evaluation of the ACP process.

Long-term care residents were asked the following questions about patient control at the end of life: (1) had they previously thought about it? (2) what were their general views on control over decision making at the end of life? (3) what would be their personal preference "when the time comes"? (4) did they see any potential obstacles to having their wishes honored? and (5) what were their personal views about withdrawal or termination of treatment, as well as euthanasia and physician-assisted suicide?

Data Analysis

The data were read and participants' views regarding quality end-of-life care were identified. These units of text were underlined and descriptive notes were written in the margins of the transcripts, a process referred to as *coding*. Coded units were then labeled as specific end-of-life care issues. Many issues were not mutually exclusive, but issues that were conceptually different were given different descriptive labels. Labeled issues were then compared within and between interviews. Similar issues were grouped together under 1 overarching domain label and the data were recoded by domain. The prevalence of each domain was recorded and descriptive statements about each were developed using the patients' words. Quotes that were selected for presentation in the article were good illustrations of the domain and provide data from the various patient populations. This process was conducted by 1 analyst (D.K.M.), who frequently consulted with a second analyst (P.A.S.) regarding excerpts of the primary transcript data and the clustering of the data into domains.

Several steps were taken to verify the results, a concept in qualitative research analogous to reliability and validity in quantitative research.[13,14] These included (1) use of 3 separate data sets to verify the conceptual domains, (2) general familiarity with the data sets by investigators (P.A.S. and M.K.) other than the primary analyst, (3) systematic checking of the developing conceptual domains against supporting quotations by a second analyst (P.A.S.), (4) review of the manuscript by an independent scholar studying quality end-of-life care (James Tulsky, MD), and (5) explicit comparison of our taxonomy with 3 other taxonomies derived from a different methodological perspective.[3–5]

Sample Size

Sample size was not formally calculated. Instead, participants were enrolled until no new concepts arose during analysis of the successive interviews, a concept called *saturation* by qualitative researchers.

Table 1. Domains of Quality End-of-Life Care

Journal of the American Geriatrics Society Statement[3]	Institute of Medicine Committee[4]	Emanuel and Emanuel[5]*	Patient Perspectives†
• Physical and emotional symptoms	• Overall quality of life	• Physical symptoms	• Receiving adequate pain and symptom management
• Support of function and autonomy	• Physical well-being and functioning	• Psychological and cognitive symptoms	• Avoiding inappropriate prolongation of dying
• Advance care planning	• Psychosocial well-being and functioning	• Social relationships and support	• Achieving a sense of control
• Aggressive care near death	• Spiritual well-being	• Economic demands and caregiving needs	• Relieving burden
• Patient and family satisfaction	• Patient perception of care	• Hopes and expectations	• Strengthening relationships
• Global quality of life	• Family well-being and perceptions	• Spiritual and existential beliefs	
• Family burden			
• Survival time			
• Provider continuity and skill			
• Bereavement			

*"Modifiable dimensions of patient's experience" from Emanuel and Emanuel.[5]
†Patient perspectives are from the current study.

Research Ethics

All 3 studies were approved by the University of Toronto Committee on Research With Human Subjects, and written informed consent was obtained from all subjects.

RESULTS

Demographic characteristics of the 126 patients from the 3 data sets are shown in TABLE 2. As shown in TABLE 3, the analysis identified 5 domains of quality end-of-life care: receiving adequate pain and symptom management, avoiding inappropriate prolongation of dying, achieving a sense of control, relieving burden, and strengthening of relationships with loved ones. The next most prevalent theme was mentioned by less than 5% of participants. We present a description of these domains with verbatim quotes from participants.

Receiving Adequate Pain and Symptom Management

Pain was a concern for many respondents. A few participants mentioned other symptoms such as vomiting, breathlessness, and diarrhea.

I've been adamant that I wanted treatment in sort of end stage to be minimal—pain reduction, but not life sustaining. I don't—if anyone could say they did—like being in pain and I don't find the idea of being incontinent or bowel-dysfunctional, not to mention mentally incompetent, remotely interesting.

I wouldn't want a lot of pain; it's one of the worst ways to go.

If I'm in pain, severe pain, and the doctors can do nothing, the pain persists and there's nothing to take the pain away, I don't think it's fair to let me suffer like that, or anybody. We don't let the animals suffer; why should we?

Avoiding Inappropriate Prolongation of Dying

Participants were afraid of "lingering" and "being kept alive" after they no longer could enjoy their lives. Quality-of-life concerns seemed to fuel this fear; many were terrified of becoming a "vegetable" or living in a coma. These participants adamantly denounced "being kept alive by a machine." They wanted to be "allowed to die naturally" or "in peace."

I didn't want to be kept alive artificially forever just to die later on and suffer, you know, without need for an extra year. Let me go anyways. Get it done with the first time.

I wouldn't want life supports if I'm going to die anyway. There's no dignity in it. It's just a guinea pig thing.

I've always told my mother . . . if it ever comes down to being put on a life-support system, I wouldn't go for it unless there's a chance that I would come around and be normal again. But if there is chance of me being put on a life-support system and becoming a vegetable, I said forget it.

Achieving a Sense of Control

Participants were adamant that they wanted to retain control of their end-of-life care decisions while they were capable of doing so, and that they wanted the proxy of their choice to retain control if they became incapable.

I have very definite ideas of what I would want done and what I wouldn't want done, especially after watching various friends go through their deaths.

I want control, but it shouldn't be disruptive. It can be productive if it's thoughtful and if others are consulted.

That's my life. Nobody has any right to tell me that. I can't let a stranger talk me out of anything. That's what I want. They don't know how I live. It's very, very important to me now that I can make choices for myself.

Table 2. Participant Characteristics

Characteristics	Participants		
	Dialysis (n = 48)	HIV* (n = 40)	Long-term Care (n = 38)
Sex, No.			
Male	30	35	13
Female	18	5	25
Race/ethnicity, No.			
White	30	37	35
African American	8	0	0
Hispanic	2	1	0
Asian	3	0	0
Other	5	2	3
Education, No.			
No high school	2	0	6
Some high school	4	3	12
High school graduate	13	3	9
Some college	7	17	3
College graduate	22	17	8
Age, mean (range), y	48.3 (20-80)	39.6 (25-54)	76.3 (65-≥85)†

*HIV indicates human immunodeficiency virus.
†In long-term care study, data were gathered by strata. Therefore, mean age was derived using an estimated and weighted calculation.

Table 3. Domains of End-of-Life Care From Patients' Perspectives*

	Participants			
	Dialysis (n = 48)	HIV/AIDS (n = 40)	Long-term Care (n = 38)	Total (N = 126)
Receiving adequate pain and symptom management	3 (6.2)	10 (25.0)	15 (39.5)	28 (22.2)
Avoiding inappropriate prolongation of dying	23 (47.9)	29 (72.5)	25 (65.8)	77 (61.1)
Achieving a sense of control	9 (18.8)	21 (52.5)	18 (47.4)	48 (38.1)
Relieving burden	14 (29.2)	21 (52.5)	13 (34.2)	48 (38.1)
Strengthening relationships with loved ones	16 (33.3)	21 (52.5)	12 (31.6)	49 (38.9)

*Data are number (percentage). HIV indicates human immunodeficiency virus; AIDS, acquired immunodeficiency syndrome.

Relieving Burden

The participants were greatly concerned about the burden that their dying would impose on loved ones. They identified 3 specific burdens: provision of physical care, witnessing their death, and substitute decision making for life-sustaining treatment.

> I don't want them making the decisions for me without knowing how I would decide the same thing. It just makes life easier for everybody. They don't have to say, 'Well, what would he do in this situation?' if it's already written down. I know if I was incapacitated, it would be a stressful time for the people I've chosen as my proxy. It would be tough in some situations to make those decisions. So by doing it in advance I save them the bother. . . . I chose not to designate my parents as proxies. I felt that would probably be a little bit hard on them. I mean, I'm sure they'd be willing to do so, but I think from the standpoint of just saving their feelings as much as possible, I'd rather not have them make those decisions, if the time came that it was necessary.

> I'd want to die here, not at home. I wouldn't want to put that burden on my family.

> I hope to stop myself from becoming a burden to them [children]. Looking after somebody either takes a lot of money, in which case you may get somebody to baby-sit for you, or you have to do it yourself, and I do not wish my children to be in the position of having to do that. Therefore, I would rather die faster than later.

Strengthening Relationships With Loved Ones

A majority of participants felt that considerations with respect to loved ones were integral to their dying experience. For the dying experience to be meaningful, participants desired the full involvement of loved ones in communication about their dying. At times, this meant overcoming resistance, their own and others', to engage with uncomfortable subject matter. But even so, participants felt that the need for communication with loved ones was of overwhelming importance. When this intimacy was achieved, participants found their relationships strengthened.

> I've never told anyone in my family that I was HIV-positive. And so, in order to complete my living will, I had to tell him [brother] I was HIV-positive, which was really quite a challenge for me. And I did tell him, and everything has just worked out fine. He's a hundred percent supportive and it couldn't be better. Our relationship is even closer now; we were close before—we've always been a close family. But now we're really close.

> It was one of the decisions we discussed and she [wife] says when I am in this situation she is capable to make decisions for me. She didn't want to leave it to me because I cannot make decisions when I, you know. It was nice because she was showing me this kind of love and this kind of sympathy; when I am in that situation, she will be able to continue assisting me. So I was very happy about that, really. She always tells me she is going to be there for me when I cannot make a decision.

> It helped me get closer to my family, to get an idea how they feel about me. There were so many times I wanted to get their opinion on certain things, and when I discussed that with them they showed me that they are going to be there for me every time.

COMMENT

From these patients' perspectives, quality end-of-life care includes 5 domains: receiving adequate pain and symptom management, avoiding inappropriate prolongation of dying, achieving a sense of control, relieving burden on loved ones, and strengthening relationships with loved ones.

Comparison With Expert Models

Table 1 compares the patients' perspectives on quality end-of-life care with 3 models derived from an expert perspective. The similarities among the models support the validity of the conceptual domains with respect to all the models.

There are also important differences between patient- and expert-derived models. First, compared with taxonomies from an expert perspective, the patient-derived description of quality end-of-life care is simpler and more straightforward. For instance, it has the fewest domains of the 4 models. Second, the patient-derived taxonomy is more specific. For example, rather than using general labels such as "psychological," the patient perspective speaks of "achieving a sense of control"; rather than "social," it speaks of "relieving burden" and "strengthening relationships." Third, the patient-derived taxonomy is less bound by established concepts for which measurement scales are available (such as quality of life). This raises the question of whether the measurable has been driving out the important in the development of expert-derived taxonomies of quality end-of-life care. Fourth, the patient-derived model omits general and possibly vague concepts such as "global quality of life," "overall quality of life," and "patient perception of care." Fifth, the patient-derived taxonomy is more homogeneously focused on outcomes rather than processes of care (such as ACP or "provider continuity and skill") or periods of care (such as "bereavement"). Finally, the description is derived from the perspective of patients, giving it inherent authenticity. The patient's (and family's) concerns rightfully belong in the center of our focus because they are at the center of the dying experience. The following comments explore the individual domains from the patient's perspective with reference to existing knowledge.

Receiving Adequate Pain and Symptom Management

Although the issue of treating pain and other symptoms has been championed by the palliative care movement, it is still a problem for many dying patients. For instance, Lynn et al[15] found that 4 in 10 dying patients had severe pain most of the time. Greater attention to the attitudes and skills of health care workers with respect to pain and symptom control may be warranted. Clearer guidelines separating appropriate pain control from euthanasia may also help alleviate clinicians' fears with respect to pain management.

Avoiding Inappropriate Prolongation of Dying

Ahronheim et al[16] found that 47% of incurably ill patients with advanced dementia and metastatic cancer received nonpalliative treatments. Solomon et al[17] found that 78% of health care professionals surveyed reported that they sometimes felt the treatments they offered patients were overly burdensome. Hanson et al[18] found that a frequent recommendation of bereaved family members was to improve end-of-life care, emphasizing better communication. Based on their own observations and data from Tulsky et al,[19] which highlighted inadequacies in end-of-life communication, Hanson et al speculated that "discussions that focus on specific treatment decisions may not satisfy the real needs of dying patients and their families."[18] This is also the sense that one gets when reading the data from our study. The current approach of asking for consent to specific treatments may not meet the needs of dying patients and their families. Dying patients sometimes overestimate their survival probabilities, and these estimates may influence their treatment choices.[20] Specific treatment discussions may not adequately support the patient's hope and discourage false hope. Indeed, emphasizing consent for specific procedures may often be a way to avoid confronting the larger issue of death and discussing the patient's dying. Physicians may use informed consent discussions as a proxy for the more important communications about values and dying. Although such consent is legally required and, therefore, necessary, it is not sufficient. The primary focus of discussions about the use of life-sustaining treatment should be on the realistic and achievable goals of care.[21,22]

Achieving a Sense of Control

When participants said they wanted to achieve a sense of control, they seemed to have in mind a psychosocial outcome rather than a precise specification of what treatments would be received. Although the SUPPORT study[23] showed that incorporating patients' wishes into care may not affect the rate of use of life-sustaining treatments, this may not be the outcome patients have in mind, based on our data. Patients want a voice in their end-of-life care rather than specific control over each life-sustaining treatment decision. This finding further supports the notion discussed herein that our current approach to end-of-life communication, which focuses on the use of individual treatments, may be too specific to address patients' psychosocial needs in the face of death.

Relieving Burden and Strengthening Relationships With Loved Ones

Participants emphasized their desire to relieve burdens and strengthen relationships with their loved ones. These psychosocial outcomes were achieved through involving loved ones in decisions about end-of-life treatments. When dying patients had discussions with their loved ones, they seemed to feel less isolated in the face of death. The discussions also relieved their loved ones of the burden of having to make treatment decisions alone. These social and family considerations are not well captured in the current approach to end-of-life decision making in bioethics, which focuses on the patient's rights individually and not in his or her social and family context. Traditional approaches to bioethics may underestimate the importance of social and family ties.[24-27] As noted by Byock,[28] dying offers important opportunities for growth, intimacy, reconciliation, and closure in relationships. Although most commentators focus on end-of-life communication between physicians and patients,[29,30] these results suggest that communication between dying people and their loved ones is crucial.

Implications for Research and Practice

This taxonomy has implications for research and practice. Researchers are beginning to improve end-of-life care in "breakthrough" collaboratives of health care organizations. If the focus of these initiatives is primarily (or exclusively) on medical expert-derived domains of quality end-of-life care, it is likely that they will miss issues of concern to patients and families. This study underscores the importance of a patient perspective in these important quality improvement initiatives.

The domains of quality end-of-life care described here can be easily used by clinicians at the bedside to review the quality of care of dying patients, and to teach students principles of quality end-of-life care.[31] One of us (P.A.S.) has used this framework at the bedside of dying patients and found that it can clarify the goals of treatment for the health care team and provide a helpful conceptual framework for teaching the care of dying patients to medical students and residents. The domains we have identified from the patient perspective can be used by clinicians as a checklist for the adequacy of the end-of-life care they provide. Some questions clinicians can ask themselves are: Am I adequately treating pain and other symptoms? Am I appropriately prolonging dying? Am I helping patients achieve a sense of control, relieve burdens on their families, and strengthen relationships with loved ones?

Strengths and Limitations

Generalizability is both a strength and a limitation of this study. The patient perspective on quality end-of-life care was derived from 3 diverse populations: dialysis, HIV, and long-term care. Moreover, this study includes patients not traditionally studied; most of what we know about palliative care comes from studies of patients with cancer. However, the data should be generalized with caution beyond the specific patient populations studied. Also, our participants were predominantly white; culture and ethnicity influence perceptions of end-of-life care.

The main limitation of this study is that it represents a secondary analysis of data. The original purpose of the studies was to examine ACP (for the dialysis and HIV studies) and control at the end of life (for the long-term care studies). Thus, the data may overemphasize issues related to ACP and underemphasize other issues in end-of-life care. Three of the issues identified in this study (achieving a sense of control, relieving burden, and strengthening relationships with loved ones) were identified in the previous studies on ACP.[8,9] However, 2 other issues (avoiding inappropri-

ate prolongation of dying and receiving adequate pain and symptom control) were identified in this study alone. There may be other domains, such as spirituality or economic issues (identified in some of the expert taxonomies), that were overlooked. Moreover, this limitation may also have distorted the relative importance of the issues we identified to patients; we make no claim that the frequency with which these issues were mentioned indicates their priority to patients.

CONCLUSIONS

From a patient's perspective, quality end-of-life care includes 5 domains: receiving adequate pain and symptom management, avoiding inappropriate prolongation of dying, achieving a sense of control, relieving burden, and strengthening relationships with loved ones. These domains could form the conceptual foundation for research and practice with respect to quality end-of-life care.

Funding/Support: Dr Singer was supported by the National Health Research and Development Program, Ottawa, Ontario, through a National Health Research Scholar Award and is currently supported by a Scientist Award from the Medical Research Council of Canada, Ottawa. Dr Singer is Sun Life Chair in Bioethics at the University of Toronto, Toronto, Ontario. The work was also supported by the Physicians' Services Incorporated Foundation of Ontario.
Disclaimer: The views expressed herein are those of the authors and do not necessarily reflect those of the supporting groups.
Acknowledgment: We thank Edward E. Etchells, MD, Laura Purdy, PhD, James Tulsky, MD, Leigh Turner, PhD, and James G. Wright, MD, for reviewing an early version of the manuscript; Elaine C. Thiel, for serving as research coordinator of the dialysis and HIV studies; and reviewers for helpful comments.

References

1. Council on Scientific Affairs, American Medical Association. Good care of the dying. JAMA. 1996;275:474–478.

2. Feinstein AR. Clinical Judgment. Baltimore, Md: Williams & Wilkins; 1967.

3. Measuring quality of care at the end of life: a statement of principles. J Am Geriatr Soc. 1997;45:526–527.

4. Field MJ, Cassel CK, eds, for the Institute of Medicine. Approaching Death: Improving Care at the End of Life. Washington, DC: National Academy Press; 1997.

5. Emanuel EJ, Emanuel LL. The promise of a good death. Lancet. 1998;351(suppl 2):21–29.

6. Cleary PD, Edgeman-Levitan S. Health care quality: incorporating consumer perspectives. JAMA. 1997;278:608–612.

7. Manning PK, Cullum-Swan B. Narrative, content, and semiotic analysis. In: Denzin NK, Lincoln YS, eds. *Handbook of Qualitative Research.* Thousand Oaks, Calif: Sage Publications Inc; 1994:463–477.

8. Singer PA, Martin DK, Lavery JV, Thiel EC, Kelner M. Mendelssohn DC. Reconceptualizing advance care planning from the patient's perspective. *Arch Intern Med.* 1998;158:879–884.

9. Martin DK, Thiel EC, Singer PA. A new model of advance care planning: observations from people with HIV. *Arch Intern Med.* In press.

10. Kelner MJ. Activists and delegates: elderly patients' preferences about control at the end of life. *Soc Sci Med.* 1995;4:537–545.

11. Singer PA, Thiel EC, Naylor CD et al. Treatment preferences of dialysis patients: implications for advance directives. *J Am Soc Nephrol.* 1995;6:1410–1417.

12. Singer PA, Thiel EC, Salit I, Flanagan W, Naylor CD. The HIV-specific advance directive. *J Gen Intern Med.* 1997;12:729–735.

13. Strauss A, Corbin J. Grounded theory methodology: an overview. In: Denzin NK, Lincoln YS, eds. *Handbook of Qualitative Research.* Thousand Oaks, Calif: Sage Publications Inc; 1994:273–285.

14. Strauss A, Corbin J. *Basics of Qualitative Research: Grounded Theory Procedures and Techniques.* Thousand Oaks, Calif: Sage Publications Inc; 1990.

15. Lynn J, Teno JM, Phillips RS, et al. Perceptions by family members of the dying experience of older and seriously ill patients. *Ann Intern Med.* 1997;126:97–106.

16. Ahronheim JC, Morrison S, Baskin SA, Morris J, Meier DE. Treatment of the dying in the acute care hospital. *Arch Intern Med.* 1996;156:2094–2100.

17. Solomon MZ, O'Donnell L, Jennings B, et al. Decisions near the end of life: professional views on life-sustaining treatments. *Am J Public Health.* 1993;83:14–23.

18. Hanson LC, Danis M, Garrett J. What is wrong with end-of-life care? opinions of bereaved family members. *J Am Geriatr Soc.* 1997;45:1339–1344.

19. Tulsky JA, Chesney MA, Lo B. How do medical residents discuss resuscitation with patients? *J Gen Intern Med.* 1995;10:436–442.

20. Weeks JC, Cook F, O'Day SJ, et al. Relationship between cancer patients' predictions of prognosis and their treatment preferences. *JAMA.* 1998;279:1709–1714.

21. Fischer GS, Alpert HR, Stoeckle JD, Emanuel LL. Can goals of care be used to predict intervention preferences in an advance directive? *Arch Intern Med.* 1997;157:801–807.

22. Pearlman RA, Cain KC, Patrick DL, et al. Insights pertaining to patient assessments of states worse than death: *J Clin Ethics.* 1993;4:33–41.

23. The SUPPORT Principal Investigators. A controlled trial to improve care for seriously ill hospitalized patients: the Study to Understand Prognoses and Preferences for Outcomes and Risks of Treatments (SUPPORT). *JAMA.* 1995:274:1591–1598.

24. Lindemann Nelson H, Lindemann Nelson J. *The Patient in the Family.* New York, NY: Routledge; 1995.

25. Hardwig J. What about the family? *Hastings Cent Rep.* March/April 1990:5–10.

26. Blustein J. The family in medical decision making. *Hastings Cent Rep.* May/June 1993:6–13.

27. High DM. Families' roles in advance directives. *Hastings Cent Rep.* November/December 1994 (suppl):S16–S18.

28. Byock I. *Dying Well: Peace and Possibilities at the End of Life.* New York, NY: Riverhead Books; 1997.

29. Emanuel LL, Danis M, Pearlman RA, Singer PA. Advance care planning as a process: structuring the discussions in practice. *J Am Geriatr Soc.* 1995;43:440–446.

30. Virmani J, Schneiderman LJ, Kaplan RM. Relationship of advance directives to physician-patient communication. *Arch Intern Med.* 1994; 154:909–913.

31. Singer PA, MacDonald N. Bioethics for clinicians, 15: quality end of life care. *CMAJ.* 1998;159:159–162.

A Piece of My Mind

Maumee: My Walden Pond

For the second time in my life, I face the prospect of premature death. In 1969, I was in Vietnam and part of a team that removed a live 40-mm grenade from a soldier's abdomen. I survived—as did the patient and the other members of my team—and also won a Medal of Valor. Now, nearly 30 years later, I am faced with metastatic renal cancer. Barring a miracle, I have few doubts about the outcome. I know only months remain. But I am not afraid.

In Vietnam I was a 28-year-old captain in the Army Medical Corps, just starting a new part of my life as a husband, father, and fledgling physician. Now I am a 55-year-old professor of medicine, pretty much at the top of my field of pulmonary and critical care medicine. I am a professional caretaker with three decades of experience in attending the deaths of others, who is now about to experience death personally.

It would be untruthful to say I look forward to dying. I would rather live another 20 or 30 years, grow old with my wife, watch my two daughters mature, play with my grandchildren, and continue to deepen my appreciation for good literature, for great music, and, above all else, for nature. This is not, on balance, a great deal to ask for, and yet it is everything.

Before my illness was diagnosed, I was working on a new hypothesis of sepsis and septic shock—one of the areas of medicine in which I believe I have made my most important contributions. If I were granted 20 more years, I would certainly continue my research, but with one difference: It would not be the controlling factor in my life. One of the things I have learned from the process of my dying is that the most important things in the process of my living were not what I—and most others—usually think are important. They are

rather in the category of things we usually take for granted—health, family, friends, and a relationship with our Creator.

My appreciation of life is continually being enhanced by a deepening appreciation of literature and music. Artists and thinkers plumb depths and attain heights that are beyond my reach, but I can share the insights they offer in the bodies of their works. By taking the time to really listen to what they have to say, I continue to learn at the feet of Beethoven, Grieg, Vivaldi, Tolstoy, Emerson, and Thoreau.

Emerson and Thoreau are my teachers of nature as metaphor. I have loved nature all my life, from boyhood in rural Arkansas to this very moment, watching the Maumee River roll past my home. In nature, my wife Rosemary and I find metaphors for our lives and beliefs. Thoreau and Emerson taught us that nature invites contemplation about ourselves and our place in the scheme of things. Watching the passage of the seasons on the Maumee becomes a way of summing up our life together.

My last months will probably be spent during the spring and summer. I'm happy about that. Rosemary and I can sit on our terrace in the evening, watch the sunset over the Maumee, and sip a glass of wine while we listen to Vivaldi's *Four Seasons*. The blue heron will come, just as he does every evening, to perch on the old gnarled tree at the riverbank. Soaring buzzard hawks will keep their ages-old aerial patrol over the river. An occasional fisherman will putt-putt down the river in search of walleyes. Day will shade into evening, and we will sit holding hands until the night envelops us.

I write this to record my last months of life. I write it for myself, for my family, and, I hope, for those many people in the future who might find comfort in it as they also face death. Three years ago, this could not have been written—at least

Edited by Roxanne K. Young, Associate Editor

not the way it is now. The reason is simple: Three years ago, I was not dying. But even more than that, I had no idea what dying is all about, although I thought I had a fair understanding of death. I saw death more times than I can count. I always thought that death caused a collapse of the dying person inward upon himself. The dying person appeared to be little more than a shrunken shell lying in a hospital bed. Physical collapse meant that there was a collapse of mental and spiritual being as well.

I know now I could not have been more wrong.

Death has opened my eyes to life—literally. Since learning that I have a terminal illness, I believe my mind has expanded and its appetite has become insatiable. I want to know and experience everything. I feel at times what Thomas Wolfe described when he first walked into the New York Public Library: I want to grasp everything, read every book, listen to every piece of music. I believe that I will walk toward death with that same quest to know.

My evenings now have not one but three remarkable sunsets, each changing as my perspective of the sun changes. As I step on the first rung and begin the ascent of the stairs that lead to our house, the sun goes down over the opposite shore, disappearing among the trees and over the rooftops of the little village of Maumee, Ohio. As I climb the 11 steps to the first platform—slowly, of course, with my constant companion, my chemotherapy infusion pack—the scene is repeated with small variations. At the next platform, 11 steps higher, it is sunset again, but now the shadows from the opposite shore have edged out further into the river. When I climb the final 11 steps and stand on the lawn, the river is no longer visible, but its voice can be heard—hissing, gurgling. The river is black, but the western horizon is lit by the flash of a red sun.

It has taken me a while to climb the stairway. On the way up, I watched the buzzard hawks and a pair of ducks. A woodpecker hammers away at a tree on the other side of the river, taking advantage of the last light to pick a last juicy grub out of the bark. A fish flops somewhere in the black water—probably one of the large carp that school in the shallows. Rosemary is waiting in the house. She didn't come to the river today; she was preparing food that she hoped would tempt my appetite.

No life is without gift, even when it may seem giftless to others. Contemplation and introspection in the context of nature have brought me to a point of enlightenment I would probably not have had under other circumstances. Cancer has allowed me a measure of insight.

On one shelf in the library, Rosemary has displayed my Vietnam medals—a reminder of death as an unwelcome visitor.

However, who knows? After winter, there is spring.

Roger C. Bone, MD
Toledo, Ohio

Hospice care for the 1990s:

A concept coming of age

In this article the authors present an overview of the history, development, and design of the typical American hospice. Focus is placed on the interdisciplinary team which is the primary implement for the delivery of hospice care. Common clinical and management issues are discussed.

Marian Gentile, RN
Hospice Manager Forbes Hospice

Maryanne Fello, RN MEd
Director, Cancer Services
Forbes Health System
Pittsburgh, Pennsylvania

THE ROOTS OF HOSPICE

Even though its roots can be traced to the Middle Ages, the modern hospice program did not take shape until the mid-1960s. At that time, the work of two remarkable physicians, Elisabeth Kubler-Ross, and Dame Cicely Saunders, converged to bring the emotional and physical needs of the dying to the forefront.

In 1970, Kubler-Ross' landmark book, *On Death and Dying,*[1] revolutionized the psychologic approaches to patients with terminal illness. After several years of observation and actual interviews with the dying, Kubler-Ross created a theoretic framework describing the psychologic stages of dying and pointed out to health care workers a sobering fact: as dying patients needed *more* attention and support, they were actually receiving *less*. Indeed, Kubler-Ross brought death and dying "out of the closet," making health care providers and society in general more aware that death is a part of life and a legitimate part of clinical care, and that with sensitivity and understanding it can be faced openly and honestly.

In 1967, while Kubler-Ross was working at the University of Chicago Hospital, a British physician, Cicely Saunders, MD, opened the doors of St Christopher's Hospice in London. Trained as a nurse and social worker, she received her medical degree and set about her life's work to improve the care of the dying—and what better background? Some have called Saunders "a whole hospice team wrapped up in one person"!

Saunders' approach to the dying was first and foremost geared to achieving and maintaining comfort. Her approach to pain management has shaped the development of a pain control philosophy that has become a benchmark of hospice care.

Her model, prescribing an interdisciplinary team, communicating effectively, treating symptoms of terminal disease, including the patient *and* family,[2] has been replicated in concept over 1,400 times in the United States today.

HOSPICE IN THE UNITED STATES

In the early 1970s, as the work of Kubler-Ross and Saunders became known, individuals in the United States became eager to put their concepts into action. The United States programs, however similar in concept to the British world, were very different in design. The first US hospice, Hospice of Connecticut (New Haven) began to deliver care to the dying at home, since funding problems forced delays in the construction of a free-standing facility. After 6 years of delays an inpatient unit was christened in 1980 "but its early years as a home care program left an indelible impression on the purposes and practices of the hospice staff and administrators. It provided the country with a new and different model of care for the dying, care focused primarily on patients at home."[2(p11)]

As the hospice movement spread across the United States, programs took on various shapes and sizes. In most instances the shape of each hospice was determined by its genesis. For example, if a hospital felt that its commitment included the provision of terminal care, its hospice program would probably be a hospital-based hospice; if a group of ac-

From *The Journal of Home Health Care Practice*, November 1990, pp. 1–15. © 1990 by Aspen Publishers, Inc. Reprinted by permission.

tive lay volunteers began a program, it might be a consortium model hospice. In all, there are at least six common program designs for hospice.

In an effort to more exactly define this concept, the National Hospice Organization (NHO) and the then Joint Commission on Accreditation of Hospitals (JCAH) developed standards of care to which hospice should adhere. Standards were developed in seven areas: (1) the patient and family as the unit of care, (2) interdisciplinary team services, (3) continuity of care, (4) home care services, (5) symptom control, (6) bereavement, and (7) quality assurance.

Most significant in the creation of uniformity of hospice programming was the addition of hospice to the Federal Medicare Program in 1982. Maintenance of a certification to deliver hospice care calls for rigid adherence to the standards developed. As we look toward the 1990s, many uncertainties still exist, many questions remain unanswered, such as

• What is the best model for delivery of hospice care?
• Will hospice in the United States face a dilemma as larger programs force out small, community programs?
• Will hospice care be assimilated into mainstream health care, or can it only stand alone?
• Will patients be *forced* to participate in hospice?
• What will be the impact of high technology on the dying process?

CRITERIA FOR ADMISSION

Probably the most crucial in the management of a hospice in today's society is the development of the program's admission criteria. Surely the kinds of support the hospice offers might be well received by any patient and family facing a major illness, but just when during that illness does a patient become eligible?

After years of developing a careful decision-making process, the authors' hospice has developed a fairly rigid set of three criteria for admission:

1. completion of all active, curative treatment

Fig. 1. Behind the scenes discussions during an interdisciplinary team meeting.

2. patient's awareness of diagnosis and prognosis
3. patient and family's clear understanding of the goals of hospice care.

Clearly these criteria bring to mind grey areas for questioning such as, "What if a patient is receiving palliative chemotherapy?" "What if a patient knows the diagnosis but not the prognosis?" "What if the family is divided about how the patient's illness should be treated?" And more recently, "What if the patient wants no life supports, but does want artificial hydration and nutrition?" These so-called grey areas demand that each patient's application for hospice care is reviewed in depth with the *most* important question: "Are the patient and family choosing supportive care for a terminal disease with the care delivered primarily in the home setting?"

WHO WORKS IN A HOSPICE PROGRAM?

In this age of nursing shortages across the country, the opportunity to work in a hospice setting still draws nurses. Why?

Two reasons come to mind. The first is the satisfaction of the work itself. To assist the patient and family during the dying process carries many rewards. Becoming involved after a family has been told "there is nothing more to be done"

can restore the family's faith that it will not be abandoned even though curative medical treatment has been exhausted. Helping a family know what to expect, putting effective symptom management skills into practice, and supporting with effective counseling skills makes a hero of many nurses in the eyes of grateful families.

The second draw is the role of the nurse within the hospice team itself. Medical intervention takes a back seat to nursing intervention in terminal care. This fact thrusts the nurse into a primary role for both direct care and the coordination of the care provided by other members of the team. More will be said about that role later in the discussion of the interdisciplinary team.

An early study done by Amenta[3] has proven itself true many times: nurses (and others) who are drawn to hospice tend to be religious, realistic revolutionaries and they find in a hospice program a setting that is just short of an ideal medium for fundamental, holistic, independent nursing practice.

THE INTERDISCIPLINARY TEAM

The essence of hospice care is derived from the multifaceted and comprehensive approach of the hospice interdisciplinary team, whose members look for solutions to a patient's medical, psychosocial, and spiritual problems. The diversity of talent, cultural and eth-

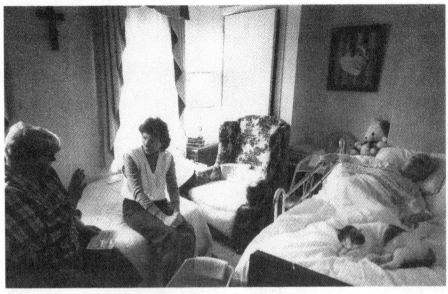

Fig.2. Hospice nurse spending time with the family.

nic backgrounds, life style, and educational background creates a blend that can sort out various problems to find the approach most suitable for that individual patient and family. A well-coordi-

The essence of hospice care is derived from the multifaceted and comprehensive approach of the hospice interdisciplinary team, whose members look for solutions to a patient's medical, psychosocial, and spiritual problems.

nated, confident group of hospice professionals can work together with everyone having equal say in most matters only if each team member is comfortable offering information from his or her experience and knowledge as well as listening to and accepting the differing contributions of others (see Fig 1).

"Role blurring" (overlapping of duties of various professional disciplines) is acceptable and actually encouraged to some extent within hospice programs. Every team member has an area of expertise accompanied by some primary responsibilities but each also must have some knowledge of other disciplines

and be sensitive to problems and needs not directly related to the particular area of expertise. A common example of role blurring is when a hospice nurse spends time with family members advising them on how to approach the children about an impending death. There is no need (and often, no time) to wait until the counselor can be called to talk or meet with the family. A well-trained, experienced, and sensitive hospice nurse can give meaningful and accurate information in this situation. However, the lines must be drawn when the problems require more specific expertise and that team member must defer to another member of the team. Furthermore, sharp distinctions must be made in some areas because of primary responsibility and liabilities (ie, the patient's physician has the final decision in the ordering of medications, treatments, etc). Hospice personnel need to be cognizant of and comfortable with role blurring and to know their boundaries.

THE COMPOSITION OF THE INTERDISCIPLINARY TEAM AND THE MEMBERS' ROLES

The composition of the hospice team may vary from program to program depending on the model and whether the program is Medicare certified to provide hospice care. Typical members are discussed below.

Hospice nurse

Often the nucleus of a hospice team, the nurse may find herself or himself in the role of coordinating the care of most patients. Because the majority of hospice patients need some assistance with symptom management along with accompanying problems related to their physical care, the discipline of nursing is drawn on heavily by hospice care. It is the hospice nurse who is available 24 hours a day as needed by patients and families; it is usually the nurse who has the most day-by-day contact with the families, who visits regularly and calls frequently to give added reassurance and guidance (see Fig 2). Regardless of the setting, the nurses are the principal support to patients and their families.

Clinical competence coupled with sensitivity and kindness seem to be key ingredients in the practice of hospice nursing. Hospice nurses generally have a great deal of autonomy on the job which, in itself, means that they must have good decision-making skills in addition to better than average communication abilities. The ability to communicate is demonstrated most keenly when a patient and family have chosen an avenue of treatment (or more often, nontreatment) that is contrary to the physician's plan. On the other hand, the hospice nurse may need to help a patient understand why no further treatment is advocated by the patient's physicians; the nurse must then employ gentle methods of reinforcing bad news. By staying open to communication from many directions, the hospice nurse can open up meaningful and useful dialogue not only for that patient and family but also for the community at large.

Hospice aide

Working closely with the hospice nurses, the home health aide is one of the most valuable members of the hospice team. Formally the home health aide's role is to help provide personal care and light housekeeping duties in the home. The home health aide is encouraged to provide the care in the way that is most satisfying to the family—either by working with the family member to help provide the care or by doing the care alone to allow the family a much needed rest. (It is important for some families to feel like they have "done it all" even when it drives them to the point of exhaustion.) By working *with* the family they give the family members some assistance and help lighten the load and still allow them to feel that they really have done it all (see Fig 3).

Light housekeeping duties can be of great importance in some households. At times the primary caregiver is somewhat incapacitated or just plain tired. Having someone clean up last night's supper dishes or vacuum the carpets or launder a few loads of clothes can be supportive to a caregiver and an emotional boost as well.

Without question, however, the home health aide plays an important informal role. The aide's visits are generally longer than those of other members of the team (except the volunteer) and are geared to giving the caregiver a break. This may be the time the family relaxes just a bit more than usual and starts talking. Relationships between families and home health aides often become very intimate. Caregivers may derive their greatest support from the chance to talk over coffee with their friend, the home health aide. There is less professional distance obvious in these relationships. And, even though the relationships are encouraged, the aide must attempt to remain objective and not become enmeshed in family problems.

Counselor

The person looking most closely at families and family dynamics is the hospice counselor. The counselor's educational background is generally in the areas of psychology or social work. This specialized training is brought into practice in the usual ways of seeking out community resources, and finding help with financial, legal, and insurance issues. With hospice patients these problems take on exaggerated proportions because so much is happening at once in their lives. Sorting through these issues can bring about some peace of mind for the patient and caregivers but also permits insight into the more critical areas of the family system. Developing a relationship while working on the more tangible problems is a natural link into the more private (and thus guarded) family relationships. The crux of many of the difficulties for hospice families can be found within the family system. The counselor must employ special skills and sensitivity to help the families work through their issues. Most impor-

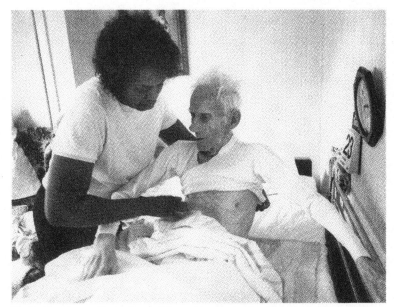

Fig. 3. Hospice staff member helping with a patient's personal care at home.

tant, the counselor must sort through the details of the particular difficulty and offer options but allow the family to make the actual decision. This is a formidable task at times because many families have great difficulty making decisions or may be asking the counselor to rescue them. Developing skills that help people adapt to the crisis of terminal illness and all of its ramifications requires much emotional fortitude and keen perceptive talents on the part of the counselor.

Therapists

Physical therapists, occupational therapists, and speech therapists contribute in their own way to the enhancement of each day of life for a hospice patient. Physical therapists usually teach families transfer techniques, proper positioning, and maintenance exercises for the patients. Because rehabilitation is generally not feasible for the terminally ill patient, the emphasis is on maintaining strength and mobility as long as possible. In conjunction with this maintenance plan the occupational therapist evaluates the patient and the home setting for ways to continue a semblance of the patient's former activities of daily living. In both cases the emphasis is on maintaining function as long as possible and conserving energy so that remaining energy can be channeled into the patient's most important activities. Speech therapists emphasize communication and swallowing problems, both of which might be seen in the same patient (such

as patients with brain tumor or amyotrophic lateral sclerosis [ALS]). Some hospice programs also include music and art therapists as part of the interdisciplinary team. Each of these therapists, using individual expertise, tries to enable patients to maximize their diminishing physical and communication abilities.

Nutritionist

Specializing in the nutritional aspects of terminal illness, the nutritionist counsels families on the special needs of these patients. The nutritionist focuses on understanding the meaning of food in each individual family system. Recognizing different ethnic and cultural views relating to food, the nutritionist attempts to help families look at these nutritional problems from their own perspective. Families for whom food was the center of life and pleasure need to continue to work on feeding and nourishing their dying family member. For them the emphasis is on getting as much nourishment as possible into every bite while knowing that the patient's food intake will probably continue to decline. At the same time the nutritionist emphasizes that what is most important at this stage of life is to eat and *enjoy*—not just to eat for the sake of eating. Families need to be told that nutritional problems are commonplace and that it is not their failing if the patient continues to lose weight and has a poor appetite. No one

Table 1. Equianalgesic comparison of common narcotic analgesics

Drug	Onset (min)	Peak (h)	Duration* (h)	Plasma half life (h)	Equianalgesic dosest (mg) IM	PO
Morphine	15–60	.5–1	3–7	2–4	10	60
Levorphanol	30–90	.5–1	4–8	12–16	2	4
Hydromorphone	15–30	.5–1	4–5	2–3	1.5	7.5
Oxymorphone	5–10	.5–1	3–6	nd	1	6
Methadone	30–60	.5–1	4–6‡	15–30	10	20
Meperidine	10–45	.5–1	2–4	3–4	75	300
Fentanyl	7–8	nd	1–2	1.5–6	0.1	nd
Codeine	15–30	.5–1	4–6	3	130	200
Oxycodone (PO)	15–30	1	4–6	nd	nd	30
Propoxyphene (PO)	30–60	2–2.5	4–6	6–12	nd	130
Hydrocodone	nd	nd	4–8	3.3–4.5	nd	nd

IM = intramuscular, PO = oral, nd = No data available.
*After IV administration, peak effects may be more pronounced but duration is shorter. Duration of action may be longer with the oral route.
†Based on acute, short-term use. Chronic administration may alter pharmacokinetics and decrease the oral–parenteral dose ratio.
The morphine oral–parenteral ratio decreases to 1.5–2.5:1 on chronic dosing.
‡Duration and half life increase with repeated use due to cumulative effects.
Adapted with permission from *Drug Facts and Comparisons*. Philadelphia; Pa: J.B. Lippincott; 1990:949.

says that more convincingly than the hospice nutritionist.

Medical director

A major force within the interdisciplinary team is the medical director. The medical director presents the physician's view within the hospice framework and then represents the hospice approach to

The hospice medical director can most fully see the patient in the context of prior medical history and will be instrumental in helping the team plan for the patient's medical care in the days ahead.

the medical community whose members often are struggling with decisions related to terminal illness in other settings such as acute care. The medical director must possess expertise in clinical aspects of symptom management in order to help implement effective palliative care. The medical director plays a variety of parts. On one hand, the medical director may actually manage the care of some hospice patients or act as a con-

sultant to the care in other cases. Acting as a teacher, the medical director works with the rest of the hospice staff and interdisciplinary team to understand the various disease processes and their clinical implications. It is the hospice medical director who can most fully see the patient in the context of prior medical history and who, because of the physician's knowledge of the natural history of the disease process, will be instrumental in helping the team plan for the patient's medical care in the days ahead. The hospice medical director must display compassion and patience to the other team members while often acting as a stabilizing force within the group framework.

Chaplain

Spiritual care is an integral component of the hospice concept. Clergy serving as hospice chaplains form the most formal aspect of a hospice pastoral care program. All members of a hospice team must be able to attend to the spiritual needs of patients and families as questions and fears arise when death becomes more imminent. But the chaplain is a resource to both the staff, as staff persons address the spiritual concerns of patients and families, and the terminally ill patients and their families who are grappling with those life and death issues.

Chaplains represent faith and a link to God and eternity. They must be careful to help patients explore spiritual dimensions in a broad sense, not within one particular denomination or religious affiliation unless requested by the patient. Many of the patients to which hospice chaplains minister have been alienated from formal religion and now are feeling a need to reestablish themselves with their spiritual roots. Caution and sensitivity, along with a caring and loving nature, enable the chaplain to explore areas sometimes unreachable by anyone else.

The hospice chaplain represents the religious community within the context of the interdisciplinary team and, in turn, represents the hospice program in the community. Chaplains not only work directly with patients and families but also may participate in staff and volunteer training and continuing education. Hospice chaplains participate regularly in interdisciplinary team meetings where each patient's medical, social, and spiritual picture is reviewed. And the chaplain's involvement continues into the bereavement period when spiritual care may be the most important ingredient in grief support.

Volunteers

Embracing the spirit of hospice care, the volunteers donate their time to hospice programs and the terminally ill patients the programs serve. It is doubtful that any other area of health care involves volunteers to the extent that hospices do. Many hospice programs could not continue to operate without their volunteer constituency and no program could be considered a full-service hospice without a strong volunteer component.

Volunteers are in a position to provide a tremendous contribution to the hospice program and to individual patients and families. Because expectations of the volunteers are naturally high it is vital that they are carefully selected and trained. Hospice programs gear their selection and training programs to their own needs with training usually comprised of 20 to 40 hours of lectures, group discussion, outside reading, and instruction on physical care including hands-on nursing care. Then the volunteers begin assisting the hospice staff, all the while becoming entrenched in the care of terminally ill patients and their

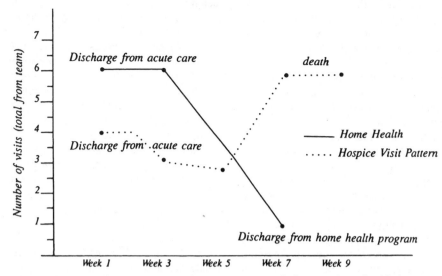

Fig 4. Comparison of visit patterns in a hospice program with those in a home health program.

families. At the same time it is important for staff to supervise volunteers and provide them with outlets for emotional support.

Every component of a hospice program might include volunteers from inpatient care to home care and bereavement care, but they also help with office duties, speaker's bureau work, and fundraising. Some serve on hospice boards and help formulate and enact policy changes. Each area has its own needs and calls upon many different kinds of talents.

The most common area of hospice volunteering is the home care setting. Volunteers in the home act in the capacity of a friend—one who knows how to care for a sick person. Most commonly the volunteer provides respite for the caregivers by affording them an opportunity to get out of the home during the volunteer's visit. Even if the caregivers do not choose to leave the home, they have a chance to rest or do other chores without having to be concerned with the patient's care. Other home care volunteer duties include light housekeeping, laundry, grocery shopping, meal preparation, errands, even babysitting to give caregivers more time with the patient.

Volunteers give an added dimension to the families and the programs they serve. Their perspective is one of kindness and caring, along with a belief in maintaining human dignity in the dying process. They give much of themselves and reap only the gratification that comes from helping people in their darkest hour.

THE ROLE OF THE FAMILY IN HOSPICE CARE

In the early days of the hospice programming, many held the view that hospice staff was essential to do *for* the family, to be a substitute for the family in the care of the patient. Hospice, by its very nature, seemed to attract those helpers caught up with the notion of the "rescue fantasy." This, combined with an underestimation of what families are capable of doing, made for much overfunctioning and early warning signs of staff burnout.

As staff members learned together about the nature of family systems and how best to be helpful, they realized that the primary role of the hospice nurse was to be an enabler. When staff members share their competence in caring with families, rather than taking over, families are able to feel as if *they* did everything they could until their loved one died. One of the highest compliments to hospice staff is the thank-you note that says, "You gave us what it took to be able to do it ourselves. . . ."

PAIN MANAGEMENT

Probably the most valuable contribution to the health care system at large has been the development of the body of knowledge by hospice professionals regarding pain management. Even though only approximately 50% of hospice patients have moderate to severe pain problems, pain is often what pa-

tients and families fear most. Some of the most important pain management concepts follow.

- Chronic pain management requires regularly scheduled (not prn) delivery of appropriate analgesia *in advance of* the return of pain.
- Patients do *not* exhibit signs of drug addiction (ie, drug-seeking behavior, ever-escalating dosages) when placed on appropriate pain management program.
- Various routes of administration (ie, sublingual, rectal, oral) can be equally effective to the IV route when used in equianalgesic ratios (see Table 1).
- Morphine and its derivatives are by far the most useful drugs in the management of intractable pain.
- Knowledge of combinations of drugs such as narcotics with nonsteroidal antiinflammatory drugs can be very effective for bone pain.
- Careful assessment of pain and all of its components is essential to developing an effective intervention.

Before dealing with some of the more complex psychosocial problems such as loss and grief, the hospice nurse must make a thorough evaluation of all symptoms, particularly pain. As Maslow[4] suggested in his theory of human motivation, basic physiologic needs must be addressed and satisfied before higher order needs can be considered.

NUTRITIONAL PROBLEMS IN THE TERMINALLY ILL

Even more common than pain management, nutritional problems call for much expertise from hospice staff. The fundamental piece of information for staff to gather is the meaning of food during the patient's illness and in the life of that patient and family. It is important for the hospice staff to deal with this issue sensitively because of strong individual and cultural beliefs about the importance of food.

Nutritional deficiencies usually result from nausea, with or without subsequent vomiting; mouth soreness, which may be caused by treatment or vitamin deficiencies; or anorexia. Nausea can generally be at least partially controlled by antiemetics. As with pain management, regular and prophylactic administration of antiemetics is important. Mouth soreness can usually be remedied by healing mouthwashes, topical anesthetics, and vitamin supplements. Anorexia is more complex. Quite commonly, terminally ill cancer patients simply have no appetite. Food is unappealing and may taste different from what they recall, and early satiety is the norm. "Two bites and they can't eat another thing" is an often heard lament from many a family. Anorexia as a symptom in this situation is not easily remedied. Families should learn not to make nutrition a battleground; they should encourage the patient to eat but not force feed. The nutritional content of food is far less important at this stage in life than being able to eat and to enjoy the experience of eating. Beer and pizza may be just the thing to get a little nourishment into the disease-ravaged body. No amount of nutrition will stop the progress of the disease but attempting to maintain protein stores can help skin integrity and the patient may not weaken quite so quickly.

More critical is the issue of hydration. A person can live quite a while without food (as evidenced by hunger strikers who do not eat but ingest fluids) but a human being cannot live for any length of time without fluids. IV therapy questions are often raised by families and hospice nurses must be prepared to discuss this sensitive issue. An assessment must be made of the patient's performance status, the rapidity of dehydration, level of consciousness with accompanying thirst, and patient and family views

---

The nutritional content of food is far less important at this stage in life than being able to eat and to enjoy the experience of eating.

---

concerning hydration and other invasive procedures.

If a patient has been ambulatory but is weakening and is dehydrated, a liter or two of fluid can certainly enhance quality of life temporarily. If, however, the patient is in an extremely debilitated state, is bedridden and is barely conscious, starting IVs could be considered invasive and will probably not add an iota of quality. In the authors' experi-

ence, slow dehydration caused by ingestion of less and less fluids and finally no fluid does not usually create much discomfort. The usual symptoms created by this slow dehydration process are slight elevation of body temperature, which can be counteracted by acetaminophen suppositories, and drying of the mucous membranes like the nose and mouth, which should be kept moistened. Rapid dehydration, on the other hand, which is usually caused by prolonged vomiting, severe diarrhea, or mechanical evacuation of stomach contents, can be significantly more uncomfortable. Without replacement IVs a person will weaken and die quickly. Some patients choose to forego IV therapy knowing full well the eventual outcome.

VISIT PATTERNS

Most hospice referrals (75%) are made at the point of a patient's discharge from an acute care facility. Many times, families are asked by the facility to give home care one more try. Often during the hospital stay the patient has been evaluated and "tuned up," providing for a stable medical condition, at least initially. The visit pattern for hospice patients starts moderately at the time of admission to the program with an increase in the frequency of visits as the patient's condition begins to change. This can be contrasted (see Fig 4) with a referral of a nonterminal patient to a home health agency where the patient's needs are the greatest initially and diminish over a period of weeks (eg, a patient with a new colostomy). Generally, the hospice visits increase in number and duration as death approaches. It is vital to be able to increase the number of visits as the patient deteriorates, thus allowing the family to feel the ever-increasing support from the hospice staff.

PREPARATION FOR A HOME DEATH

A person dying at home surrounded by family and the familiar smells, sounds, and sights can be an exceedingly beautiful experience. Almost nothing can make family members feel any better about themselves than caring for someone they love and being able to keep the loved one at home for the duration of the illness. For some a home

death is the ultimate gift. For others the very thought of someone dying at home is repugnant. A hospice nurse's greatest challenge may be discerning the choice relating to home death for each patient and family. Some families feel a home death would be wonderful but unmanageable for them, while others may see a home death in much simpler terms than are accurate and are inadequately prepared physically and emotionally. The hospice nurse needs to convey to these families the sense that (1) a home death is manageable for nearly every patient and family if they have proper support; (2) it is important to address needs as they arise, so that a crisis does not occur because of unrealistic or inadequate preparation; (3) not every patient can die at home no matter how much he or she is loved and supported. It is not an indication of failure if an institutional death is necessary or is chosen by the family.

Preparing for a home death is really not too difficult if the professional people supporting the family believe home death is acceptable and are willing to help the family through it. Most patients and families say that they fear not the death but rather the dying. They are concerned about suffering.

First and foremost it must be explained that the physical symptoms will be kept to a minimum, and that the hospice staff and the patient's physician will see to it that enough of the needed medication will be supplied to keep the symptoms at bay. Some families worry about emotional suffering, but most people worry about physical suffering.

The hospice staff must be aware that many families crumble temporarily and need extra visits, telephone calls, and pats on the back to get through that time when they believe they cannot get through it. One of these crises is generally all that is seen, and the sailing is usually much smoother after that. Families may be more intent than ever to achieve a home death because now they know they can.

It is useful to alert the patient's physician and funeral home that a home death is expected. When a patient dies at home, the physician may not always be required to come and pronounce the patient dead. In some states a nurse may do the pronouncement and in other states the family may simply notify the physician and their funeral home. The words "expected home death" can be magic if the funeral home is called and its staff decides to call the local coroner. Regulations differ from state to state and accepted practices differ from municipality to municipality, but notification of the physician and the funeral home can allay many problems and their accompanying heartache. Somehow being forced to have your loved one's body taken to a local emergency department if no physician (or nurse in some locales) is available lacks the dignity that we strive for when people die at home.

ON-CALL SYSTEM

Essential to the success of a hospice program is the development of a nurse on-call system. Terminal care problems have no respect for the usual 9-to-5 Monday through Friday work week. Families need to be assured that they are only a telephone call away from expert advice or a home visit. It is extremely comforting to a family to know that someone who understands the problems can be reached regardless of the time or the day of the week. Problems always seem worse in the middle of the night and it is important to be able to reach someone and discuss them. That, coupled with the option of a home visit if needed, is often a major reason why hospice patients can remain at home until they die.

Staffing an on-call schedule is done many different ways. Most hospices use their own staff on a rotating basis, others hire extra nurses to work on call, and some use their own staff during the week with the extra staff being on call for weekends and holidays. When hospices are using their own nurses for on call they may change the person on call every day, every few days or even weekly. Whatever works best for each individual program is the right way to

manage an on-call system because being on call is, perhaps, one of the most stressful parts of hospice nursing. It is difficult to work all day or all week and then be on call that night or for the weekend. On the other hand, each nurse has a slightly different way of doing things and sometimes the nurse prefers to be the person on call for better continuity of care and follow through with his or her patients. Opinions on this aspect of hospice nursing are as diverse as the many models of hospice care.

STAFF BURNOUT

One of the common concerns of outsiders viewing a hospice team in action is the expectation of "burnout" of team members. With the experience of successive losses, there is pervasive fear that the staff will not be able to survive in this working environment for long.

With this in mind, the early hospice team developers created support systems, both formal and informal, to prevent burnout from happening. Much to the surprise of hospice managers, the issue of burnout has not been a problem. Staff members come to hospice with an expectation that they will lose every patient they meet, and so for the most part they gear their involvement accordingly. It is wonderful to watch a well-integrated team taking turns with families; moving toward and away from intimacy with patients, knowing that the hospice team as a whole provides even more than the sum of its parts.

What is apparent about burnout, however, is that staff is susceptible to common work setting problems such as patient workload demands, shrinking continuing education monies, and staff personality differences. Hospice staff members have needs similar to those of any workers in a health care setting:

They need to feel support from their managers, to see that their good work is valued by the agency, and to be treated fairly with scheduling, work space, patient load, time-off requests, and compensation.

Staff members leave the hospice setting for all the normal reasons: to pursue education, to change location, to spend more time with children. And, yes, it is sometimes a healthy decision to leave hospice to seek a more varied or diverse health care experience. With each person's coping abilities differing so greatly, there is no standard 2-year or 3-year stint prescribed for hospice. More important, each individual must continually evaluate job satisfaction, self-esteem, and overall personal and career goals.

REFERENCES

1. Kubler-Ross E. *On Death and Dying.* New York, NY: Macmillan; 1970.
2. Torrens PR. *Hospice Programs and Public Policy.* Chicago, Ill: American Hospital Publishing, Inc.; 1985.
3. Amenta MO., Bohnet NL. *Nursing Care of the Terminally Ill.* Boston, Mass: Little, Brown, 1986.
4. Maslow AH. *Motivation and Personality.* New York, NY: Harper & Row; 1954.

SUGGESTED READINGS

Lack SA., Buckingham RW III. *First American Hospice Three Years of Home Care.* New Haven, Conn: Hospice, Inc.; 1978.
Mor V., Greer DS., Kastenbaum R. *The Hospice Experiment.* Baltimore, Md: The Johns Hopkins University Press; 1988.
Stoddard S. *The Hospice Movement A Better Way of Caring for the Dying.* New York, NY: Random House; 1978.
Zimmerman J. *Hospice Complete Care for the Terminally Ill.* Baltimore, Md: Urban and Schwartzenberg; 1986.

Unit 4

Key Points to Consider

❖ The question, "What is a good death?" has been asked for centuries. What would constitute a good death in this time of high-tech medical care? Does the concept of a good death include the taking of a life? Defend your answer.

❖ Does the role of the health care provider include taking life or providing the means for others to do so? Why or why not?

❖ Are constraints required to prevent the killing of persons we do not consider worthwhile contributors to our society? Explain.

❖ Should limits be placed on the length of life as we consider the expenses involved in the care of the elderly and the infirm?

❖ For some individuals, suicide may seem to be the best solution to their situation. How might our society help such individuals "solve" their problems? Is the concept of "rational suicide" rational? Why or why not?

❖ Do you believe that high-risk-taking persons—such as heavy smokers, race car drivers, overeating or undereating individuals, or persons mixing alcohol and drugs—are suicidal? Explain.

 **Links**   **www.dushkin.com/online/**

These sites are annotated on pages 4 and 5.

One of the concerns about dying and death pressing hard upon our consciences is the question of helping the dying to die sooner with the assistance of the physician. Public awareness of the horrors that can be visited upon us by artificial means of ventilation and other support measures in a high-tech hospital setting has produced a literature that debates the issue of euthanasia—a "good death." As individuals think through their plans for care when dying, there is a steady increase in the demand for control of that care.

Another controversial issue is physician-assisted suicide. Is it the function of the doctor to assist patients in their dying—to actually kill them at their request? The highly publicized suicides in Michigan with the earlier jury decisions that found Dr. Kevorkian innocent of murder, as well as the popularity of the book *Final Exit,* make these issues prominent national and international concerns. Legislative action has been taken in some states to permit this, and the issue is pending in a number of others. We are in a time of intense consideration by the courts, by the legislatures, and by the medical and nursing professions of the legality and the morality of providing the means by which a person can be given the means to die. Is this the role of health care providers? The pro and con positions are presented in several of the unit's articles. Although the issue is difficult and personally challenging, as a nation we are in the position of being required to make difficult choices. There are no "right" answers; the questions pose dilemmas that require choice based upon moral, spiritual, and legal foundations.

The word *suicide,* meaning "self" and "to kill," was first used in English in 1651. Early societies sometimes forced certain members into committing suicide for ritual purposes and occasionally expected such of widows and slaves. There is also a strong inheritance from Hellenic and Roman times of rational suicide when disease, dishonor, or failure were considered unbearable. Attitudes toward suicide changed when St. Augustine laid down rules against it that became basic Christian doctrine for centuries.

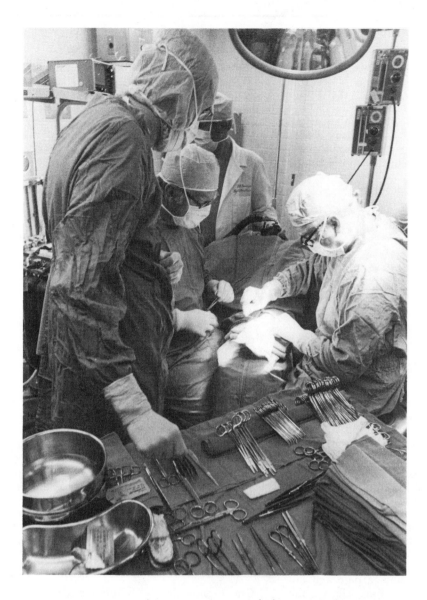

In recent years, suicide has attracted increasing interest and scrutiny by sociologists, psychologists, and others in efforts to reduce its incidence. Suicide is a major concern in the United States today, and understanding suicide is important so that warning signs in others can be recognized. Various suicide types, cross-cultural rates, and a history of suicide are presented in the article "Attitudes toward Suicide Behavior: A Review of the Literature."

Just what constitutes suicide is not clear today. Risky behavior that leads to death may or may not be classified as suicide. We have differing attitudes toward suicide. Suicide rates are high in adolescents, the elderly, and males. A person with high vulnerability is an alcoholic, depressed male between the ages of 75 and 84. Suicidal persons often talk about the attempt prior to the act and display observable signs of potential suicide. Males are more likely to complete suicide than females because they use more lethal weapons. For suicidal persons, the act is an easy solution to their problems—a permanent answer to an often temporary set of problems.

Ethical Issues of Dying, Death, and Suicide

Doctor, I Want to Die. Will You Help Me?

Timothy E. Quill, MD

IT HAD been 18 months since a 67-year-old retired man whose main joy in life was his two grandchildren was diagnosed with inoperable lung cancer. An arduous course of chemotherapy helped him experience a relatively good year where he was able to remain independent, babysitting regularly for his grandchildren.

Recent tests revealed multiple new bony metastases. An additional round of chemotherapy and radiation provided little relief. By summer, pain and fatigue became unrelenting. He was no longer able to tolerate, much less care for, his grandchildren. His wife of 45 years devoted herself to his care and support. Nonetheless, his days felt empty and his nights were dominated by despair about the future. Though he was treated with modern pain control methods, his severe bone pain required daily choices between pain and sedation. Death was becoming less frightening than life itself.

From the Program for Biopsychosocial Studies, School of Medicine, University of Rochester, and the Department of Medicine, The Genesee Hospital, Rochester, NY.

The views expressed in this article are those of the author and do not necessarily represent those of the University of Rochester or the Department of Medicine.

Reprint requests to the Department of Medicine, The Genesee Hospital, Rochester, NY 14607 (Dr Quill).

A particularly severe thigh pain led to the roentgenogram that showed circumferential destruction of his femur. Attempting to preserve his ability to walk, he consented to the placement of a metal plate. Unfortunately, the bone was too brittle to support the plate. He would never walk again.

See also Box "Compassion Needs Reason Too"

One evening in the hospital after his wife had just left, his physician sat down to talk. The pain was "about the same," and the new sleep medication "helped a little." He seemed quiet and distracted. When asked what was on his mind, he looked directly at his doctor and said, "Doctor, I want to die. Will you help me?"

Such requests are dreaded by physicians. There is a desperate directness that makes sidestepping the question very difficult, if not impossible. Often, we successfully avoid hearing about the inner turmoil faced by our terminally ill patients—what is happening to the person who has the disease. Yet, sometimes requests for help in dying still surface from patients with strong wills, or out of desperation when there is nowhere else to turn. Though comfort care (ie, medical care using a hospice philosophy) provides a humane alternative to traditional medical care of the dying,[1–7] it does not always provide guidance for how to approach those rare patients who continue to suffer terribly in spite of our best efforts.

This article explores what dying patients might be experiencing when they make such requests and offers potential physician responses. Such discussions are by no means easy for clinicians, for they may become exposed to forms and depths of suffering with which they are unfamiliar and to which they do not know how to respond. They may also fear being asked to violate their own moral standards or having to turn down someone in desperate need. Open exploration of requests for physician-assisted death can be fundamental to the humane care of a dying person, because no matter how terrifying and unresolvable their suffering appears, at least they are no longer alone with it. It also frequently opens avenues of "help" that were not anticipated and that do not involve active assistance in dying.

"Doctor, I want to die" and "Will you help me?" constitute both a statement and a query that must each be independently understood and explored. The initial response, rather than a yes or no based on assumptions about the patient's intent and meaning, might be something like: "Of course, I will try to help you, but first I need to understand your wish and your suffering, and then we can explore how I can help." Rather than shying away from the depths of suffering, follow-up ques-

From *Journal of the American Medical Association*, Vol. 270, August 18, 1993, pp. 870–875. © 1993 by the American Medical Association. Reprinted by permission.

tions might include, "What is the worst part?" or "What is your biggest fear?"

THE WISH TO DIE

Transient yearnings for death as an escape from suffering are extremely common among patients with incurable, relentlessly progressive medical illnesses.[8-10] They are not necessarily signs of a major psychiatric disorder, nor are they likely to be fully considered requests for a physician-assisted death. Let us explore some of their potential meanings through a series of case vignettes.

Tired of Acute Medical Treatment

A 55-year-old woman with very aggressive breast cancer found her tumor to be repeatedly recurring over the last 6 months. The latest instance signaled another failure of chemotherapy. When her doctor was proposing a new round of experimental therapy, she said, "I wish I were dead." By exploring her statement, the physician learned that the patient felt strongly she was not going to get better and that she could not fathom the prospect of more chemotherapy with its attendant side effects. She wanted to spend what time she had left at home. He also learned that she did not want to die at that moment. A discussion about changing the goals of treatment from cure to comfort ensued, and a treatment plan was developed that exchanged chemotherapy for symptom-relieving treatments. The patient was relieved by this change in focus, and she was able to spend her last month at home with her family on a hospice program.

Comfort care can guide a caring and humane approach to the last phase of life by directing its energy to relieving the patients' suffering with the same intensity and creativity that traditional medical care usually devotes to treating the underlying disease.[1-7] When comprehensively applied, in either a hospice program or any other setting, comfort care can help ensure a dignified, individualized death for most patients.

Unrecognized or Undertreated Physical Symptoms

A stoical 85-year-old farmer with widely metastatic prostate cancer was cared for in his home with the help of a hospice program. Everyone marveled at his dry wit and engaging nature as he courageously faced death. He was taking very little medication and always said he was "fine." Everyone loved to visit with him, and his stories about life on the farm were legendary. As he became more withdrawn and caustic, people became concerned, but when he said he wished he were dead, there was a panic. All the guns on the farm were hidden and plans for a psychiatric hospitalization were entertained. When his "wish for death" was fully explored, it turned out that he was living with excruciating pain, but not telling anyone because he feared becoming "addicted" to narcotics. After a long discussion about pain-relieving principles, the patient agreed to try a regular, around-the-clock dosage of a long-acting narcotic with "as needed" doses as requested. In a short time, his pain was under better control, he again began to engage his family and visitors, and he no longer wanted to die. For the remainder of his life, the physical symptoms that developed were addressed in a timely way, and he died a relatively peaceful death surrounded by his family.

Though not all physical symptoms can be relieved by the creative application of comfort care, most can be improved or at least made tolerable. New palliative techniques have been developed that can ameliorate most types of physical pain, provided they are applied without unnecessary restraint. One must be sure that unrelieved symptoms are not the result of ignorance about or inadequate trials of available medical treatments, or the result of exaggerated patient or physician fears about addiction or about indirectly hastening death. Experts who can provide formal or informal consultation in pain control and in palliative care are available in most major cities and extensive literature is available.[11-14]

Emergent Psychosocial Problems

A 70-year-old retired woman with chronic leukemia that had become acute and had not responded to treatment was sent home on a home hospice program. She was prepared to die, and all of her physicians felt that she would "not last more than a few weeks." She had lived alone in the past, but her daughter took a leave of absence from work to care for her mother for her last few days or weeks. Ironically (though not necessarily surprisingly), the mother stabilized at home. Two months later, outwardly comfortable and symptom-free under the supportive watch of her daughter, she began to focus on wanting to die. When asked to elaborate, she initially discussed her fatigue and her lack of a meaningful future. She then confided that she hated being a burden on her daughter—that her daughter had children who needed her and a job that was beginning to cause serious strain. The daughter had done her best to protect her mother from these problems, but she became aware of them anyway. A family meeting where the problems were openly discussed resulted in a compromise where the mother was admitted to a nursing facility where comfort care was offered, and the daughter visited every other weekend. Though the mother ideally would have liked to stay at home, she accepted this solution and was transferred to an inpatient unit where she lived for 2 more months before dying with her daughter at her side.

Requests for help in dying can emanate from unrecognized or evolving psychosocial problems.[15] Sometimes these problems can be alleviated by having a family meeting, by arranging a temporary "respite" admission to a health care facility, or by consulting a social worker for some advice about finances and available services. Other psychosocial problems may be more intractable, for example, in a family that was not functioning well prior to the patient's illness or when a dominating family member tries to influence care in a direction that appears contrary to the patient's wishes or best interest. Many patients have no family and no financial resources. The current paucity of inpatient hospices and nursing facilities capable of providing comfort care and the inadequate access to health care in general in the United States often mean that dying patients who need the most help and support are forced to fend for themselves and often die by themselves. The health care reimbursement system is primarily geared toward acute medical care, but not terminal care, so the physician may be the only potential advocate and support that some dying patients have.

Spiritual Crisis

A 42-year-old woman who was living at home with advanced acquired immunodeficiency syndrome (AIDS) began saying that she wished she were dead. She was a fundamentalist Christian who at the time of her diagnosis wondered, "Why would God do this to me?" She eventually found meaning in the possibility that God was testing her strength, and that this was her "cross to bear." Though she continued to regularly participate in church activities over the 5 years after her initial diagnosis, she never confided in her minister or church friends about her diagnosis. Her statements about wishing she were dead frightened her family, and they forced her to visit her doctor. When asked to elaborate on her wish, she raged against her church, her preacher, and her God, stating she found her disease humiliating and did not want to be seen in the end stages of AIDS where everyone would know. She had felt more and more alone with these feelings, until they burst open. Once the feelings were acknowledged and understood, it was clear that they defied simple solution. She was clearly and legitimately angry, but not depressed. She had no real interest in taking her own life. She was eventually able to find a fundamentalist minister from a different church with an open mind about AIDS who helped her find some spiritual consolation.

The importance of the physician's role as witness and support cannot be overemphasized. Sharing feelings of spiritual betrayal and uncertainty with an empathetic listener can be the first step toward healing. At least isolation is taken out of the doubt and despair. The physician must listen and try to fully understand the problem before making any attempt to help the patient achieve spiritual resolution. Medically experienced clergy are available in many communities who can explore spiritual issues with dying patients of many faiths so that isolation can be further lessened and potential for reconnection with one's religious roots enhanced.

Clinical Depression

A 60-year-old man with a recently diagnosed recurrence of his non-Hodgkin's lymphoma became preoccupied with wanting to die. Though he had a long remission after his first course of chemotherapy, he had recently gone through a divorce and felt he could not face more treatment. In exploring his wishes, it was evident he was preoccupied with the death of his father, who experienced an agonizing death filled with severe pain and agitation. He had a strong premonition that the same thing would happen to him, and he was not sleeping because of this preoccupation. He appeared withdrawn and was not able to fully understand and integrate his options and the odds of treatment directed at his lymphoma, the likelihood that comfort care would prevent a death like his father's, or his doctor's promise to

work with him to find acceptable solutions. Though he was thinking seriously of suicide, he did not have a plan and therefore was treated intensively as an outpatient by his internist and a psychotherapist. He accepted the idea that he was depressed, but also wanted assurances that all possibilities could be explored after a legitimate trial of treatment for depression. He responded well to a combination of psychotherapy and medication. He eventually underwent acute treatment directed at his lymphoma that unfortunately did not work. He then requested hospice care and seemed comfortable and engaged in his last months. As death was imminent, his symptoms remained relatively well controlled, and he was not overtly depressed. He died alone while his family was out of the house. Since his recently filled prescription bottles were all empty, it may have been a drug overdose (presumably to avoid an end like his father's), though no note or discussion accompanied the act.

Whenever a severely ill person begins to talk about wanting to die and begins to seriously consider taking his or her own life, the question of clinical depression appropriately arises.[16] This can be a complex and delicate determination because most patients who are near death with unrelenting suffering are very sad, if not clinically depressed. The epidemiologic literature associating terminal illness and suicide assumes that all such acts arise from unrecognized and/or untreated psychiatric disorders,[17–19] yet there is a growing clinical literature suggesting that some of these suicides may be rational.[2,16,20–25]

Two fundamental questions must be answered before suicide can be considered rational in such settings: (1) Is the patient able to fully understand his or her disease, prognosis, and treatment alternatives (ie, is the decision rational), and (2) is the patient's depression reversible, given the limitations imposed by his illness, in a way that would substantially alter the circumstances? It is vital not to overnormalize (eg, "anyone would be depressed under such circumstances") or to reflexively define the request as a sign of psychopathology. Each patient's dilemma must be fully explored. Consultation with an experienced psychiatrist can be helpful when there is doubt, as can a trial of grief counseling, crisis intervention, or antidepressant medications if a potentially reversible depression is present and the patient has time and strength to participate.

Unrelenting, Intolerable Suffering

The man with widely metastatic lung cancer described in the introduction felt that his life had become a living hell with no acceptable options. His doctors agreed that all effective medical options to treat his cancer had been exhausted. Physical activity and pride in his body had always been a central part of who he was. Now, with a pathologic fracture in his femur that could not be repaired, he would not even be able to walk independently. He also had to make daily trade-offs between pain, sedation, and other side effects. At the insistence of his doctor, he had several visits with a psychiatrist who found his judgment to be fully rational. Death did not appear imminent, and his condition could only get worse. Even on a hospice program, with experts doing their best to help address his medical, social, personal, and spiritual concerns, he felt trapped, yearning for death. He saw his life savings from 45 years of work rapidly depleting. His family offered additional personal and financial resources. They wanted him to live, but having witnessed the last months of progressive disability, loss, and pain, with no relief in sight other than death, they respected his wishes and slowly began to advocate on his behalf. "We appreciate your efforts to keep him comfortable, but for him this is not comfortable and it is not living. Will you help him?"

Physicians who have made a commitment to shepherd their patients through the dying process find themselves in a predicament. They can acknowledge that comfort care is sometimes far less than ideal, but it is the best that they can offer, or they can consider making an exception to the prohibition against physician-assisted death, with its inherent personal and professional risks. Compassionate physicians differ widely on their approach to this dilemma,[20–24, 26–29] though most would likely agree with an open discussion with a patient who raises the issue and an extensive search for alternatives.

Clinical criteria have been proposed to guide physicians who find assisted suicide a morally acceptable avenue of last resort[25]: (1) the patient must, of his or her own free will and at his or her own initiative, clearly and repeatedly request to die rather than continue suffering; (2) the patient's judgment must not be distorted; (3) the patient must have a condition that is incurable and associated with severe, unrelenting, intolerable suffering; (4) the physician must ensure that the patient's suffering and the request are not the result of inadequate comfort care; (5) physician-assisted suicide should only be carried out in the context of a meaningful doctor-patient relationship[22]; (6) consultation with another physician who is experienced in comfort care is required; and (7) clear documentation to support each condition above should be required (if and when such a process becomes openly sanctioned). It is not the purpose of this article to review the policy implications of formally accepting these criteria or of maintaining current prohibitions.[20–29] Instead, it is to encourage and guide clinicians on both sides of the issue to openly explore the potential meanings of a patient's request for help in dying and to search as broadly as possible for acceptable responses that are tailored to the individual patient.

THE REQUEST FOR HELP IN DYING

Dying patients need more than prescriptions for narcotics or referrals to hospice programs from their physicians. They need a personal guide and counselor through the dying process—someone who will unflinchingly help them face both the medical and the personal aspects of dying, whether it goes smoothly or it takes the physician into unfamiliar, untested ground. Dying patients do not have the luxury of choosing not to undertake the journey, or of separating their person from their disease. Physicians' commitment not to abandon their patients is of paramount importance.

Requests for assistance in dying only rarely evolve into fully considered requests for physician-assisted suicide or euthanasia. As illustrated in the case vignettes, a thorough exploration and understanding of the patient's experience and the reason the request is occurring at a given moment in time often yield avenues of "help" that are acceptable to almost all physicians and ethicists. These clinical summaries have been oversimplified to illustrate distinct levels of meaning. More often, multiple levels exist simultaneously, yielding several avenues for potential intervention. Rather than making any assumptions about what kind of help is being requested, the physician may ask the patient to help clarify by asking, "How were you hoping I could help?" Exploring a patient's request or wish does not imply an obligation to accede, but rather to seriously listen and to consider with an open mind.

Even if the physician cannot directly respond to a rational request for a physician-assisted death because of personal, moral, or legal constraints, exploring, understanding, and expressing empathy can often be therapeutic.[30,31] In addition, the physician and the patient may be able to find some creative middle ground that is acceptable to both.[32,33] Finding common ground that can enhance the patient's comfort, dignity, and personal choice at death without compromising the physician's personal and professional values can be creative, challenging, and satisfying work for physicians.

WHAT DO DYING PERSONS WANT MOST FROM THEIR PHYSICIANS?

Most patients clearly do not want to die, but if they must, they would like to do so while maintaining their physical and personal integrity.[34] When faced with a patient expressing a wish for death, and a request for help, physicians (and others) should consider the following.

Listen and Learn From the Patient Before Responding

Learning as much as possible about the patient's unique suffering and about exactly what is being requested is a vital first step. Physicians tend to be action oriented, yet these problems only infrequently yield simple resolutions. This is not to say they are insoluble, but the patient is the initial guide to defining the problem and the range of acceptable interventions.

Be Compassionate, Caring, and Creative

Comfort care is a far cry from "not doing anything." It is completely analogous to intensive medical care, only in this circumstance the care is directed toward the person and his or her suffering, not the disease. Dying patients need our commitment to creatively problem-solve and support them no matter where their illness may go. The rules and methods are not simple when applied to real persons, but the satisfaction and meaning of helping someone find his or her own path to a dignified death can be immeasurable.

Promise to Be There Until the End

Many people have personally witnessed or in some way encountered "bad deaths," though what this might mean to a specific patient is varied and unpredictable. Patients need our assurance that, if things get horrible, undignified, or intolerable, we will not abandon them, and we will continue to work with them to find acceptable solutions. Usually those solutions do not involve directly assisting death, but they may often involve the aggressive use of symptom-relieving measures that might indirectly hasten death.[3,35] We should be able to reassure all our patients that they will not die racked by physical pain, for it is now accepted practice to give increasing amounts of analgesic medicine until the pain is relieved even if it inadvertently shortens life. Many patients find this promise reassuring, for it both alleviates the fear of pain, and also makes concrete the physician's willingness to find creative, aggressive solutions.

If Asked, Be Honest About Your Openness to the Possibility of Assisted Suicide

Patients who want to explore the physician's willingness to provide a potentially lethal prescription often fear being out of control, physically dependent, or mentally incapacitated, rather than simply fearing physical pain.[36] For many, the possibility of a controlled death if things become intolerable is often more important than the reality. Those who secretly hold lethal prescriptions or who have a physician who will entertain the possibility of such treatment feel a sense of control and possibility that, if things became intolerable, there will be a potential escape. Other patients will be adequately reassured to know that we can acknowledge the problem, talk about death, and actively search for acceptable alternatives, even if we cannot directly assist them.

Try to Approach Intolerable End-of-Life Suffering With an Open Heart and an Open Mind

Though acceptable solutions can almost always be found through the aggressive application of comfort care principles, this is not a time for denial of the problem or for superficial solutions. If there are no good alternatives, what should the patient do? There is

Commentary

COMPASSION NEEDS REASON TOO

A growing number of physicians today believe that it is morally permissible, perhaps even required, to assist certain of their patients in the act of suicide.[1-4] They take their inspiration from Quill's account of the way he assisted his young patient, Diane, to kill herself.[5] They are impressed by Quill's compassion and respect for his patient. Like him, they would limit the physician's participation in suicide to extreme cases in which suffering is unrelenting, unrelievable, and unbearable. Like him, they follow a flawed line of moral reasoning in which a compassionate response to a request for assisted suicide is deemed sufficient in itself to justify an ethically indefensible act.

In his article[6] in this issue of THE JOURNAL, Quill provides a more formal and systematic outline of what he believes the appropriate response of physicians should be to a request for suicide. He emphasizes that the reasons for the request must be identified and ameliorated (ie, pain and depression should be properly treated and psychosocial and spiritual crises resolved). To do these things properly, physicians themselves must listen and learn; accept their own mortality; be compassionate, honest, and "present" to their patients; and remain "open" to assisted suicide. If this approach fails to relieve suffering, Quill deems the case extreme enough to justify transgressing the ethical proscription against assisted suicide.

Most of Quill's recommendations are consistent with a physician's responsibility to provide comprehensive palliative care.[7] They would be equally binding on those opposed to assisted suicide. What is not acceptable is the faulty line of reasoning that underlies Quill's seemingly reasonable and moderate approach. That reasoning is marred by three ethical assumptions: (1) that compassion in decision making confers moral validity on the act of assisted suicide; (2) that Quill's decision-making process is, itself, morally sound; and (3) that, by itself, close analysis of cases is sufficient to establish the right and good thing to do in "extreme" cases.

To begin with, Quill begs the most important ethical question, namely, whether in certain cases assisted suicide can be ethically justified. This is the heart of a debate that is far from settled.[8] It cannot be settled here. Elsewhere,[9] I have tried to show that, like active euthanasia, assisted suicide is never morally permissible: both are acts of intentional killing; they are violent remedies in the name of beneficence; they seriously distort the healing purposes of medicine; they are based on erroneous notions of compassion, beneficence, and autonomy; and they divert attention from comprehensive palliative care.[10-12] Moreover, euthanasia and assisted suicide are socially disastrous. They are not containable by placing legal limits on their practice. Arguments to the contrary, the "slippery slope" is an inescapable logical, psychological, historical and empirical reality.

Quill's first implicit assumption is that assisted suicide can sometimes be justified, ie, a morally wrong act can be made morally right if the process used in deciding to perform it and the way it is performed are compassionate and beneficently motivated. The moral psychology of an act has a certain weight in assessing an agent's guilt, but not in changing the nature of the act itself.[10] Even a person's consent is insufficient to make suicide morally right. Nor is it justified by a gentle or genteel "approach" to the act. This, for example, is the stance of those who reject Jack Kevorkian's unseemly and preemptory use of his death machine, but commend Quill's modulated approach.[3] To be sure, Kevorkian shows a shocking disregard for the most elementary responsibilities of a physician to a patient who becomes desperate enough to ask for assisted death.[18] But regardless of whether patients use Kevorkian's machine or Quill's compassionate prescription for sedatives, they are dead by premeditated intention. In either case, physicians, who are the necessary instruments of the patient's death, are as much a moral accomplice as if they had administered the dose themselves.

Even if we grant Quill's first assumption, we are left questioning the moral validity of Quill's recommended decision-making process. On the surface, Quill seems to place the initiative in the patient's hands and suggests that the physician merely be "open" to assisted suicide under the right circumstances. But, ultimately, the determination of the right circumstances is in the physician's hands. The physician controls the availability and timing of the means whereby the patient kills himself. Physicians also judge whether the patients are clinically depressed, their suffering really unbearable, and their psychological and spiritual crises resolvable. Finally, the physician's assessment determines whether the patient is in the "extreme" category that, per se, justifies suicide assistance.

The opportunities for conscious or unconscious abuse of this power are easy to obscure, even for the best-intentioned physician. Physicians' valuation of life and its meaning, the value or nonvalue of suffering, the kind of life they would find bearable, and the point at which life becomes unbearable cannot fail to influence their decisions. These values will vary widely even among those who take assisted suicide to be morally licit. The physician might follow all of Quill's recommendations (eg, be honest and compassionate and listen to the patient), but find it virtually impossible to separate personal values from interaction with the patient.

From the Georgetown University Medical Center, Washington, DC. Reprints not available.

Moreover, physicians must face their own frustrations, fatigue, and secret hopes for a way out of the burdens of caring for a suffering, terminally ill patient. The kind of intense emotional involvement Quill describes in Diane's case can induce emotional burnout in which the physician moves imperceptibly from awaiting the patient's decision and readiness, to subtle elicitation of a request for death. "Getting it over with" may not be only the patient's desire, but that of the physician, other health professionals, and family and friends.[14] Each will have his or her own reason for being open to assisting in suicide. Each reason is capable of being imputed to a vulnerable, exhausted, guilty, and alienated patient. When assisted suicide is legitimated, it places the patient at immense risk from the "compassion" of others. Misdirected compassion in the face of human suffering can be as dangerous as indifference.

Wesley's[15] astute analysis of Quill's treatment of his patient Diane[5] suggests that Quill himself was not totally immune to some of these psychodynamic dangers. The decision to respond to a request for assistance in suicide can be as much a danger to, as a safeguard of, the patient's right to self-determination. If it is known to be a viable option at the outset, it cannot fail to influence the patient, the physician, and everyone else involved in the patient's care. If it is not known at the outset, the patient is deprived of the clues needed to interpret her physician's actions. No matter how we examine it, Quill's "approach" is as morally dubious as the act to which it leads.

Finally, Quill's article implies that with an ever greater knowledge of the patient's circumstances, thoughts, and values and a sincere effort to understand them, we can reliably arrive at a point at which we move from the morally unacceptable to the morally acceptable. This is the "line of cases" approach that relies for its moral validity on the recently revived method of casuistry.[15] Casuistry is a useful method of case analysis rooted in legal procedure, but it is a dubious way to establish a moral norm.

Brody[1] recently used the casuistic method in a logically fallacious attempt to wipe out the distinction between killing and letting die. The problem with relying solely on the casuistic method of paradigm cases is that there must be something beyond the case by which to judge the case. This would be true even if we could encompass all the details of any case. We must still explicate why this case is a paradigm case that can be used in locating other cases along a moral spectrum. When we do, we discover that a normative principle has been at work. Behind every paradigm case, there is a moral system. Different moral systems judge paradigm cases differently. In the end, we must decide among moral systems, not cases.

It is important, therefore, to read through Quill's metaphorically elegant and compassionate story of Diane's death to the reasons underlying his actions. Clearly for Quill, the undeniably important affect of compassion takes on the status of an overriding moral principle. But compassion is a virtue, not a principle. Morally weighty as it is, compassion can become maleficent unless it is constrained by principle. In the world's history, too many injustices have been committed in the name of someone's judgment about what was compassionate for his neighbor. Compassion, too, must be subject to moral analysis, must have its reasons, and those reasons must also be cogent.

Edmund D. Pellegrino, MD

1. Brody H. Causing, intending and assisting death, *J Clin Ethics.* 1993; 4: 112–113.
2. Wanzer SH, Dyders DD, Edelstein SJ, et al. The physician's responsibility toward hopelessly ill patients, *N Engl J Med.* 1989; 320: 844–849.
3. Cassel CK, Meir DE. Morals and moralism in the debate over euthanasia and assisted suicide. *N Engl J Med.* 1990; 923: 750–752.
4. Ubel PA. Assisted suicide and the case of Dr Quill and Diane. *Issues Law Med.* 1993; 8: 487–502.
5. Quill TE. Death and dignity: a case of individualized decision making. *N Engl J Med.* 1991; 324: 691–694.
6. Quill TE. Doctor, I want to die, will you help me? *J.A.M.A.* 1993; 270: 870–873.
7. Lynn J. The health care professional's role when active euthanasia is sought. *J Palliat Care.* 1988; 4: 100–102.
8. Kass L. Neither for love nor money; why doctors must not kill. *Public Interest.* 1989; 94: 25–46.
9. Pellegrino ED. Doctors must not kill. *J Clin Ethics.* 1992; 8: 95–102.
10. Kamisar Y. Are laws against assisted suicide unconstitutional? *Hastings Cent Rep.* 1993; 23: 32–41.
11. Arkes H, Berke M, Doctor M, et al. Always to care, never to kill; a declaration on euthanasia. *First Things.* 1992; 20: 46.
12. Council on Ethical and Judicial Affairs, American Medical Association. Decisions near the end of life. *J.A.M.A.* 1991; 267: 2229–2233.
13. Kevorkian J. *Prescription Medicine; The Goodness of Planned Death.* Buffalo, NY: Prometheus Books; 1991.
14. It's over, Debbie. *J.A.M.A.* 1986; 259: 272. A Piece of My Mind.
15. Wesley P. Dying safety issues. *J Law Med.* 1993; 8: 467–485.
16. Jonsen AR. Casuistry as a methodology in clinical ethics. *Thsor Med.* 1991; 12: 295–307.

often a moment of truth for health care providers and families faced with a patient whom they care about who has no acceptable options. Physicians must not turn their backs, but continue to problem-solve, to be present, to help their patients find dignity in death.

Do Not Forget Your Own Support

Working intensively with dying patients can be both enriching and draining. It forces us to face our own mortality, our abilities, and our limitations. It is vital to have a place where we can openly share our own grief, doubts, and uncertainties, as well as take joy in our small victories.[37] For us to deepen our understanding of the human condition and to help humanize the dying process for our patients and ourselves, we must learn to give voice to and share our own private experience of working closely with dying patients.

The patients with whom we engage at this level often become indelibly imprinted on our identities as professionals. Much like the death of a family member, the process that they go through and our willingness and ability to be there and to be helpful are often replayed and rethought. The intensity of these relationships and our ability to make a difference are often without parallel. Because the road is traveled by us all, but the map is poorly described, it is often an adventure with extraordinary richness and unclear boundaries.

In memory of Arthur Schmale, MD, who taught me how to listen, learn, and take direction from the personal stories of dying patients.

References

1. Wanzer SH, Adelstein SJ, Cranford RE, et al. The physician's responsibility toward hopelessly ill patients. *N Engl J Med.* 1984; 310: 955–959.

2. Wanzer, SH, Federman, DO, Adelstein SJ, et al. The physician's responsibility toward hopelessly ill patients: a second look. *N Engl J Med.* 1989; 320: 844–849.

3. Council on Ethical and Judicial Affairs, American Medical Association. Decisions near the end of life. *JAMA.* 1992; 267: 2229–2233.

4. Rhymes J. Hospice care in America. *JAMA.* 1990; 264: 369–372.

5. Hastings Center Report. *Guidelines on the Termination of Life-Sustaining Treatment and the Care of the Dying.* New York, NY: The Hastings Center; 1987.

6. Zimmerman JM. *Hospice: Complete Care for the Terminally Ill.* Baltimore, Md: Urban & Schwarzenberg; 1981.

7. Quill T. *Death and Dignity: Making Choices and Taking Charge.* New York, NY: WW Norton & Co; 1993.

8. Aries P. *The Hour of Our Death.* New York, NY: Vintage Books; 1982.

9. Kubler-Ross E. *On Death and Dying.* New York, NY: Macmillan Publishing Co Inc; 1969.

10. Richman J. A rational approach to rational suicide. *Suicide Life Threat Behav.* 1992; 22: 130–141.

11. Foley KM. The treatment of cancer pain. *N Engl J Med.* 1989; 313: 84–95.

12. Kane RL, Bernstein L, Wales J, Rothenberg R. Hospice effectiveness in controlling pain. *JAMA.* 1985; 253: 2683–2686.

13. Twyeross RG, Lack SA. *Symptom Control in Far Advanced Cancer: Pain Relief.* London, England; Pitman Books Ltd; 1984.

14. Kerr IG, Some M, DeAngelis C, et al. Continuous narcotic infusion with patient-controlled analgesia for chronic cancer outpatients. *Ann Intern Med.* 1988; 108: 554–557.

15. Garfield C. *Psychosocial Care of the Dying Patient.* New York, NY: McGraw-Hill International Book Co; 1978.

16. Conwell Y, Caine ED. Rational suicide and the right to die: reality and myth. *N Engl J Med.* 1991; 325: 1100–1103.

17. Allenbeck P, Bolund C, Ringback G. Increased suicide rate in cancer patients. *J Clin Epidemiol.* 1989; 42: 611–616.

18. Breitbart W. Suicide in cancer patients. *Oncology.* 1989; 49–55.

19. MacKenzie TB, Popkin MK. Suicide in the medical patient. *Int J Psychiatry Med.* 1987; 17: 3–22.

20. Cassel CK, Meier DE. Morals and moralism in the debates on euthanasia and assisted suicide. *N Engl J Med.* 1990; 323: 750–752.

21. Quill TE. Death and dignity: a case of individualized decision making. *N Engl J Med.* 1991; 324: 691–694.

22. Jecker NS. Giving death a hand: when the dying and the doctor stand in a special relationship. *J Am Geriatr Soc.* 1991; 39: 831–835.

23. Angell M. Euthanasia. *N Engl J Med.* 1988; 319: 1348–1350.

24. Brody H. Assisted death: a compassionate response to a medical failure. *N Engl J Med.* 1992; 327: 1384–1388.

25. Quill TE, Cassel CK, Meier DE. Care of the hopelessly ill: potential clinical criteria for physician-assisted suicide. *N Engl J Med.* 1992; 327: 1380–1384.

26. Singer PA, Siegler, M. Euthanasia: a critique. *N Engl J Med.* 1990; 322: 1881–1883.

27. Orentlicher D. Physician participation in assisted suicide. *JAMA.* 1989; 262: 1844–1845.

28. Gaylin WL, Kass R, Pellegrino ED, Siegler M. Doctors must not kill. *JAMA.* 1988; 259: 2139–2140.

29. Gomez CF. *Regulating Death: Euthanasia and the Case of the Netherlands.* New York, NY: Free Press; 1991.

30. Novack DH. Therapeutic aspects of the clinical encounter. *J Gen Intern Med.* 1987; 2: 346–355.

31. Suchman AL, Matthews DA. What makes the doctor-patient relationship therapeutic: exploring the connexional dimension of medical care. *Ann Intern Med.* 1988; 108: 125–130.

32. Quill TE. Partnerships in patient care: a contractual approach. *Ann Intern Med.* 1983; 98: 228–234.

33. Fisher R, Ury W. *Getting to Yes: Negotiating Agreement Without Giving In.* Boston, Mass: Houghton Mifflin Co; 1981.

34. Cassel EJ. The nature of suffering and the goals of medicine. *N Engl J Med.* 1982; 306: 639–645.

35. Meier DE, Cassel CK. Euthanasia in old age: a case study and ethical analysis. *J Am Geriatr Soc.* 1983; 31: 294–298.

36. van der Maas PJ, van Delden JJM, Pijnenborg L, Looman CWN. Euthanasia and other medical decisions concerning the end of life. *Lancet.* 1991; 338: 669–674.

37. Quill TE, Williams PR. Healthy approaches to physician stress. *Arch Intern Med.* 1990; 150: 1857–1861.

The Supreme Court and Physician-Assisted Suicide —The Ultimate Right

Editorials

The important and contentious issue of physician-assisted suicide, now being argued before the U.S. Supreme Court, is the subject of the following two editorials. Writing in favor of permitting assisted suicide under certain circumstances is the Journal's *executive editor, Dr. Marcia Angell. Arguing against it is Dr. Kathleen Foley [see next article] co-chief of the Pain and Palliative Care Service of Memorial Sloan-Kettering Cancer Center in New York. We hope these two editorials, which have in common the authors' view that care of the dying is too often inadequate, will help our readers in making their own judgments.*

Jerome P. Kassirer, M.D.

THE U.S. Supreme Court will decide later this year whether to let stand decisions by two appeals courts permitting doctors to help terminally ill patients commit suicide.[1] The Ninth and Second Circuit Courts of Appeals last spring held that state laws in Washington and New York that ban assistance in suicide were unconstitutional as applied to doctors and their dying patients.[2,3] If the Supreme Court lets the decisions stand, physicians in 12 states, which include about half the population of the United States, would be allowed to provide the means for terminally ill patients to take their own lives, and the remaining states would rapidly follow suit. Not since *Roe v. Wade* has a Supreme Court decision been so fateful.

The decision will culminate several years of intense national debate, fueled by a number of highly publicized events. Perhaps most important among them is Dr. Jack Kevorkian's defiant assistance in some 44 suicides since 1990, to the dismay of many in the medical and legal establishments, but with substantial public support, as evidenced by the fact that three juries refused to convict him even in the face of a Michigan statute enacted for that purpose. Also since 1990, voters in three states have considered ballot initiatives that would legalize some form of physician-assisted dying, and in 1994 Oregon became the first state to approve such a measure.[4] (The Oregon law was stayed pending a court challenge.) Several surveys indicate that roughly two thirds of the American public now support physician-assisted suicide,[5,6] as do more than half the doctors in the United States,[6,7] despite the fact that influential physicians' organizations are opposed. It seems clear that many Americans are now so concerned about the possibility of a lingering, high-technology death that they are receptive to the idea of doctors' being allowed to help them die.

In this editorial I will explain why I believe the appeals courts were right and why I hope the Supreme Court will uphold their decisions. I am aware that this is a highly contentious issue, with good people and strong arguments on both sides. The American Medical Association (AMA) filed an amicus brief opposing the legalization of physician-assisted suicide,[8] and the Massachusetts Medical Society, which owns the *Journal*, was a signatory to it. But here I speak for myself, not the *Journal* or the Massachusetts Medical Society. The legal aspects of the case have been well discussed elsewhere, to me most compellingly in Ronald Dworkin's essay in the *New York Review of Books*.[9] I will focus primarily on the medical and ethical aspects.

I begin with the generally accepted premise that one of the most important ethical principles in medicine is respect for each patient's autonomy, and that when this principle conflicts with others, it should almost always take precedence. This premise is incorporated into our laws governing medical practice and research, including the requirement of informed consent to any treatment. In medicine, patients exercise their self-determination most dramatically when they ask that life-sustaining treatment be withdrawn. Although others may sometimes consider the request ill-founded, we are bound to honor it if the patient is mentally competent—that is, if the patient can understand the nature of the decision and its consequences.

A second starting point is the recognition that death is not fair and is often cruel. Some people die quickly, and others die slowly but peacefully. Some find personal or religious meaning in the process, as well as an opportunity for a final reconciliation with loved ones. But others, especially those with cancer, AIDS, or progressive neurologic disorders, may die by inches and in great anguish, despite every effort of their doctors and nurses. Although nearly all pain can be relieved, some cannot, and other symptoms, such as dyspnea, nausea, and weakness, are even more difficult to control. In addition, dying sometimes holds great indignities and existential suffering. Patients who happen to require some treatment to sustain their lives, such as assisted ventilation or dialysis, can hasten death by having the life-sustaining treatment withdrawn, but those who are not receiving life-sustaining treatment may desperately need help they cannot now get.

If the decisions of the appeals courts are upheld, states will not be able to prohibit doctors from helping such patients to die by prescribing a lethal dose of a drug and advising them on its use for suicide. State laws barring euthanasia (the administration of a lethal drug by a doctor) and assisted suicide for patients who are not terminally ill would not be affected. Furthermore, doctors would not be *required* to assist in suicide; they would simply have that option. Both appeals courts based their decisions on constitutional questions. This is important, because it shifted the focus of the debate from what the majority would approve through the political process, as exemplified by the Oregon initiative, to a matter of fundamental rights, which are largely immune from the political process. Indeed, the Ninth Circuit Court drew an explicit analogy between suicide and abortion, saying that both were personal choices protected by the Constitution and that forbidding doctors to assist would in effect nullify these rights. Although states could regulate assisted suicide, as they do abortion, they would not be permitted to regulate it out of existence.

It is hard to quarrel with the desire of a greatly suffering, dying patient for a quicker, more humane death or to disagree that it may be merciful to help bring that about. In those circumstances, loved ones are often relieved when death finally comes, as are the attending doctors and nurses. As the Second Circuit Court said, the state has no interest in prolonging such a life. Why, then, do so many people oppose legalizing physician-assisted suicide in these cases? There are a number of arguments against it, some stronger than others, but I believe none of them can offset the overriding duties of doctors to relieve suffering and to respect their patients' autonomy. Below I list several of the more important arguments against physician-assisted suicide and discuss why I believe they are in the last analysis unpersuasive.

Assisted suicide is a form of killing, which is always wrong. In contrast, withdrawing life-sustaining treatment simply allows the disease to take its course. There are three methods of hastening the death of a dying patient: withdrawing life-sustaining treatment, assisting suicide, and euthanasia. The right to stop treatment has been recognized repeatedly since the 1976 case of Karen Ann Quinlan[10] and was affirmed by the U.S. Supreme Court in the 1990 *Cruzan* decision[11] and the U.S. Congress in its 1990 Patient Self-Determination Act.[12] Although the legal underpinning is the right to be free of unwanted bodily invasion, the purpose of hastening death was explicitly acknowledged. In contrast, assisted suicide and euthanasia have not been accepted; euthanasia is illegal in all states, and assisted suicide is illegal in most of them.

Why the distinctions? Most would say they turn on the doctor's role: whether it is passive or active. When life-sustaining treatment is withdrawn, the doctor's role is considered passive and the cause of death is the underlying disease, despite the fact that switching off the ventilator of a patient dependent on it looks anything but passive and would be considered homicide if done without the consent of the patient or a proxy. In contrast, euthanasia by the injection of a lethal drug is active and directly causes the patient's death. Assisting suicide by supplying the necessary drugs is considered somewhere in between, more active than switching off a ventilator but less active than injecting drugs, hence morally and legally more ambiguous.

I believe, however, that these distinctions are too doctor-centered and not sufficiently patient-centered. We should ask ourselves not so much whether the doctor's role is passive or active but whether the *patient's* role is passive or active. From that perspective, the three methods of hastening death line up quite differently. When life-sustaining treatment is withdrawn from an incompetent patient at the request of a proxy or when euthanasia is performed, the patient may be utterly passive. Indeed, either act can be performed even if the patient is unaware of the decision. In sharp contrast, assisted suicide, by definition, cannot occur without the patient's knowledge and participation. Therefore, it must be active—that is to say, voluntary. That is a crucial distinction, because it provides an inherent safeguard against abuse that is not present with the other two methods of hastening death. If the loaded term "kill" is to be used, it is not the doctor who kills, but the patient. Primarily because euthanasia can be performed without the patient's participation, I oppose its legalization in this country.

Assisted suicide is not necessary. All suffering can be relieved if care givers are sufficiently skillful and compassionate, as illustrated by the hospice movement. I have no doubt that if expert palliative care were available to everyone who needed it, there would be few requests for assisted suicide. Even under the best of circumstances, however, there will always be a few patients whose suffering simply cannot be adequately alleviated. And there will be some who would prefer suicide to any other measures available, including the withdrawal of life-sustaining treatment or the use of heavy sedation. Surely, every effort should be made to improve palliative care, as I argued 15 years ago,[13] but when those efforts are unavailing and suffering patients desperately long to end their lives, physician-assisted suicide should be allowed. The argument that permitting it would divert us from redoubling our commitment to comfort care asks these patients to pay the penalty for our failings. It is also illogical. Good comfort care and the availability of physician-assisted suicide are no more mutually exclusive than good cardiologic care and the availability of heart transplantation.

Permitting assisted suicide would put us on a moral "slippery slope." Although in itself assisted suicide might be acceptable, it would lead inexorably to involuntary euthanasia. It is impossible to avoid slippery slopes in medicine (or in any aspect of life). The issue is how and where to find a purchase. For example, we accept the right of proxies to terminate life-sustaining treatment, despite the obvious potential for abuse, because the reasons for doing so outweigh the risks. We hope our procedures will safeguard patients. In the case of assisted suicide, its voluntary nature is the best protection against sliding down a slippery slope, but we also need to ensure that the request is thoughtful and freely made. Although it is possible that we may someday decide to legalize voluntary euthanasia under certain circumstances or assisted suicide for patients who are not terminally ill, legalizing assisted suicide for the dying does not in itself make these other decisions inevitable. Interestingly, recent reports from the Netherlands, where both euthanasia and physician-assisted suicide are permitted, indicate that fears about a slippery slope there have not been borne out.[14-16]

Assisted suicide would be a threat to the economically and socially vulnerable. The poor, disabled, and elderly might be coerced to request it. Admittedly, overburdened families or cost-conscious doctors might pressure vulnerable patients to request suicide, but similar wrongdoing is at least as likely in the case of withdrawing life-sustaining treatment, since that decision can be made by proxy. Yet, there is no evidence of widespread abuse. The Ninth Circuit Court recalled that it was feared *Roe v. Wade* would lead to coercion of poor and uneducated women to request abortions, but that did not happen. The concern that coercion is more likely in this era of managed care, although understandable, would hold suffering patients hostage to the deficiencies of our health care system. Unfortunately, no human endeavor is immune to abuses. The question is not whether a perfect system can be devised, but whether abuses are likely to be sufficiently rare to be offset by the benefits to patients who otherwise would be condemned to face the end of their lives in protracted agony.

Depressed patients would seek physician-assisted suicide rather than help for their depression. Even in the terminally ill, a request for assisted suicide might signify treatable depression, not irreversible suffering. Patients suffering greatly at the end of life may also be depressed, but the depression does not necessarily explain their decision to commit suicide or make it irrational. Nor is it simple to diagnose depression in terminally ill patients. Sadness is to be expected, and some of the vegetative symptoms of depression are similar to the symptoms of terminal illness. The success of antidepressant treatment in these circumstances is also not ensured. Although there are anecdotes about patients who changed their minds about suicide after treatment,[17] we do not have good studies of how often that happens or the relation to antidepressant treatment. Dying patients who request assisted suicide and seem depressed should certainly be strongly encouraged to accept psychiatric treatment, but I do not believe that competent patients should be *required* to accept it as a condition of receiving assistance with suicide. On the other hand, doctors would not be required to comply with all requests; they would be expected to use their judgment, just as they do in so many other types of life-and-death decisions in medical practice.

Doctors should never participate in taking life. If there is to be assisted suicide, doctors must not be involved. Although most doctors favor permitting assisted suicide under certain circumstances, many who favor it believe that doctors should not provide the assistance.[6,7] To them, doctors should be unambiguously committed to life (although most doctors who hold this view would readily honor a patient's decision to have life-sustaining treatment withdrawn). The AMA, too, seems to object to physician-assisted suicide primarily because it violates the profession's mission. Like others, I find that position too abstract.[18] The highest ethical imperative of doctors should be to provide care in whatever way best serves patients' interests, in accord with each patient's wishes, not with a theoretical commitment to preserve life no matter what the cost in suffering.[19] If a patient requests help with suicide and the doctor believes the request is appropriate, requiring someone else to provide the assistance would be a form of abandonment. Doctors who are opposed in principle need not assist, but they should make their patients aware of their position early in the relationship so that a patient who chooses to select another doctor can do so. The greatest harm we can do is to consign a desperate patient to unbearable suffering—or force the patient to seek out a stranger like Dr. Kevorkian. Contrary to the frequent assertion that permitting physician-assisted suicide would lead patients to distrust their doctors, I believe distrust is more likely to arise from uncertainty about whether a doctor will honor a patient's wishes.

Physician-assisted suicide may occasionally be warranted, but it should remain illegal. If doctors risk prosecution, they will think twice before assisting with suicide. This argument wrongly shifts the focus from the patient to the doctor. Instead of reflecting the condition and wishes of patients, assisted suicide would reflect the courage and compassion of their doctors. Thus, patients with doctors like Timothy Quill, who described in a 1991 *Journal* article how he helped a patient take her life,[20] would get the help they need and want, but similar patients with less steadfast doctors would not. That makes no sense.

People do not need assistance to commit suicide. With enough determination, they can do it themselves. This is perhaps the cruelest of the arguments against physician-assisted suicide. Many patients at the end of life are, in fact, physically unable to commit suicide on their own. Others lack the resources to do so. It has sometimes been suggested that they can simply stop eating and drinking and kill themselves that way. Although this method has been described as peaceful under certain conditions,[21] no one should count on that. The fact is that this argument leaves most patients to their suffering. Some, usually men, manage to commit suicide using violent methods. Percy Bridgman, a Nobel laureate in physics who in 1961 shot himself rather than die of metastatic cancer, said in his suicide note, "It is not decent for Society to make a man do this to himself."[22]

My father, who knew nothing of Percy Bridgman, committed suicide under similar circumstances. He was 81 and had metastatic prostate cancer. The night before he was scheduled to be admitted to the hospital, he shot himself. Like Bridgman, he thought it might be his last chance. At the time, he was not in extreme pain, nor was he close to death (his life expectancy was probably longer than six months). But he was suffering nonetheless—from nausea and the side effects of antiemetic agents, weakness, incontinence, and hopelessness. Was he depressed? He would probably have freely admitted that he was, but he would have thought it beside the point. In any case, he was an intensely private man who would have refused psychiatric care. Was he overly concerned with maintaining control of the circumstances of his life and death? Many people would say so, but that was the way he was. It is the job of medicine to deal with patients as they are, not as we would like them to be.

I tell my father's story here because it makes an abstract issue very concrete. If physician-assisted suicide had been available, I have no doubt my father would have chosen it. He was protective of his family, and if he had felt he had the choice, he would have spared my mother the shock of finding his body. He did not tell her what he planned to do, because he knew she would stop him. I also believe my father would have waited if physician-assisted suicide had been available. If patients have access to drugs they can take when they choose, they will not feel they must commit suicide early, while they are still able to do it on their own. They would probably live longer and certainly more peacefully, and they might not even use the drugs.

Long before my father's death, I believed that physician-assisted suicide ought to be permissible under some circumstances, but his death strengthened my conviction that it is simply a part of good medical care—something to be done reluctantly and sadly, as a last resort, but done nonetheless. There should be safeguards to ensure that the decision is well considered and consistent, but they should not be so daunting or violative of privacy that they become obstacles instead of protections. In particular, they should be directed not toward reviewing the reasons for an autonomous decision, but only toward ensuring that the decision is indeed autonomous. If the Supreme Court upholds the decisions of the appeals courts, assisted suicide will not be forced on either patients or doctors, but it will be a choice for those patients who need it and those doctors willing to help. If, on the other hand, the Supreme Court overturns the lower courts' decisions, the issue will continue to be grappled with state by state, through the political process. But sooner or later, given the need and the widespread public support, physician-assisted suicide will be demanded of a compassionate profession.

MARCIA ANGELL, M.D.

REFERENCES

1. Greenhouse L. High court to say if the dying have a right to suicide help. New York Times. October 2, 1996:A1.

2. Compassion in Dying v. Washington, 79 F.3d 790 (9th Cir. 1996).

3. Quill v. Vacco, 80 F.3d 716 (2d Cir. 1996).

4. Annas GJ. Death by prescription—the Oregon initiative. N Engl J Med 1994;331:1240–3.

5. Blendon RJ, Szalay US, Knox RA. Should physicians aid their patients in dying? The public perspective. JAMA 1992;267:2658–62.

6. Bachman JG, Alcser KH, Doukas DJ, Lichtenstein RL, Corning AD, Brody H. Attitudes of Michigan physicians and the public toward legalizing physician-assisted suicide and voluntary euthanasia. N Engl J Med 1996;334:303–9.

7. Lee MA, Nelson ND, Tilden VP, Ganzini L, Schmidt TA, Tolle SW. Legalizing assisted suicide—views of physicians in Oregon. N Engl J Med 1996;334:310–5.

8. Gianelli DM. AMA to court: no suicide aid. American Medical News. November 25, 1996:1, 27, 28.

9. Dworkin R. Sex, death, and the courts. New York Review of Books. August 8, 1996.

10. In re: Quinlan, 70 N.J. 10, 355 A.2d 647 (1976).

11. Cruzan v. Director Missouri Department of Health, 497 U.S. 261, 110 S.Ct. 2841 (1990).

12. Omnibus Budget Reconciliation Act of 1990, P.L. 101-508, sec. 4206 and 4751, 104 Stat. 1388, 1388-115, and 1388-204 (classified respectively at 42 U.S.C. 1395cc(f) (Medicare) and 1396a(w) (Medicaid) (1994)).

13. Angell M. The quality of mercy. N Engl J Med 1982;306:98–9.

14. van der Maas PJ, van der Wal G, Haverkate I, et al. Euthanasia, physician-assisted suicide, and other medical practices involving the end of life in the Netherlands, 1990–1995. N Engl J Med 1996;335:1699–705.

15. van der Wal G, van der Maas PJ, Bosma JM, et al. Evaluation of the notification procedure for physician-assisted death in the Netherlands. N Engl J Med 1996;335:1706–11.

16. Angell M. Euthanasia in the Netherlands—good news or bad? N Engl J Med 1996;335:1676–8.

17. Chochinov UM, Wilson KG, Enns M, et al. Desire for death in the terminally ill. Am J Psychiatry 1995;152:1185–91.

18. Cassel CK, Meier DE. Morals and moralism in the debate over euthanasia and assisted suicide. N Engl J Med 1990;323:750–2.

19. Angell M. Doctors and assisted suicide. Ann R Coll Physicians Surg Can 1991;24:493–4.

20. Quill TE. Death and dignity—a case of individualized decision making. N Engl J Med 1991;324:691–4.

21. Lynn J, Childress JF. Must patients always be given food and water? Hastings Cent Rep 1983;13(5):17–21.

22. Nuland SB. How we die. New York: Alfred A. Knopf, 1994:152.

COMPETENT CARE FOR THE DYING INSTEAD OF PHYSICIAN-ASSISTED SUICIDE

Editorials

The important and contentious issue of physician-assisted suicide, now being argued before the U.S. Supreme Court, is the subject of . . . two editorials. Writing in favor of permitting assisted suicide under certain circumstances is the Journal *'s executive editor, Dr. Marcia Angell [see previous article]. Arguing against it is Dr. Kathleen Foley, co-chief of the Pain and Palliative Care Service of Memorial Sloan-Kettering Cancer Center in New York. We hope these two editorials, which have in common the authors' view that care of the dying is often too inadequate, will help our readers in making their own judgments.*

JEROME P. KASSIRER, M.D.

WHILE the Supreme Court is reviewing the decisions by the Second and Ninth Circuit Courts of Appeals to reverse state bans on assisted suicide, there is a unique opportunity to engage the public, health care professionals, and the government in a national discussion of how American medicine and society should address the needs of dying patients and their families. Such a discussion is critical if we are to understand the process of dying from the point of view of patients and their families and to identify existing barriers to appropriate, humane, compassionate care at the end of life. Rational discourse must replace the polarized debate over physician-assisted suicide and euthanasia. Facts, not anecdotes, are necessary to establish a common ground and frame a system of health care for the terminally ill that provides the best possible quality of living while dying.

The biased language of the appeals courts evinces little respect for the vulnerability and dependency of the dying. Judge Stephen Reinhardt, writing for the Ninth Circuit Court, applied the liberty-interest clause of the Fourteenth Amendment, advocating a constitutional right to assisted suicide. He stated, "The competent terminally ill adult, having lived nearly the full measure of his life, has a strong interest in choosing a dignified and humane death, rather than being reduced to a state of helplessness, diapered, sedated, incompetent."[1] Judge Roger J. Miner, writing for the Second Circuit Court of Appeals, applied the equal-rights clause of the Fourteenth Amendment and went on to emphasize that the state "has no interest in prolonging a life that is ending."[2] This statement is more than legal jargon. It serves as a chilling reminder of the low priority given to the dying when it comes to state resources and protection.

The appeals courts' assertion of a constitutional right to assisted suicide is narrowly restricted to the terminally ill. The courts have decided that it is the patient's condition that justifies killing and that the terminally ill are special—so special that they deserve assistance in dying. This group alone can receive such assistance. The courts' response to the New York and Washington cases they reviewed is the dangerous form of affirmative action in the name of compassion. It runs the risk of further devaluing the lives of terminally ill patients and may provide the excuse for society to abrogate its responsibility for their care.

Both circuit courts went even further in asserting that physicians are already assisting in patients' deaths when they withdraw life-sustaining treatments such as respirators or administer high doses of pain medication that hasten death. The appeals courts argued that providing a lethal prescription to allow a terminally ill patient to commit suicide is essentially the same as withdrawing life-sustaining treatment or aggressively treating pain. Judicial reasoning that eliminates the distinction between letting a person die and killing runs counter to physicians' standards of palliative care.[3] The courts' purported goal in blurring these distinctions was to bring society's legal rules more closely in line with the moral value it places on the relief of suffering.[4]

In the real world in which physicians care for dying patients, withdrawing treatment and aggressively treating pain are acts that respect patients' autonomous decisions not to be battered by medical technology and to be relieved of their suffering. The physician's intent is to provide care, not death. Physicians do struggle with doubts about their own intentions.[5] The courts' arguments fuel their ambivalence about withdrawing life-sustaining treatments or using opioid or sedative infusions to treat intractable symptoms in dying patients. Physicians are trained and socialized to preserve life. Yet saying that physicians struggle with doubts about their intentions in performing these acts is not the same as saying that their intention is to kill. In palliative care, the goal is to relieve suffering, and the quality of life, not the quantity, is of utmost importance.

Whatever the courts say, specialists in palliative care do not think that they practice physician-assisted suicide or euthanasia.[6] Palliative medicine has developed guidelines for aggressive pharmacologic management of intractable symptoms in dying patients, including sedation for those near death.[3,7,8] The World Health Organization has endorsed palliative care as an integral component of a national health care policy and has strongly recommended to its member countries that they not consider legalizing physician-assisted suicide and euthanasia until they have addressed the needs of their citizens for pain relief and palliative care.[9] The courts have disregarded this formidable recommendation and, in fact, are indirectly suggesting that the World Health Organization supports assisted suicide.

Yet the courts' support of assisted suicide reflects the requests of the physicians who initiated the suits and parallels the numerous surveys demonstrating that a large proportion of physicians support the legalization of physician-assisted suicide.[10–15] A smaller proportion of physicians are willing to provide such assistance, and an even smaller proportion are willing to inject a lethal dose of medication with the intent of killing a patient (active voluntary euthanasia). These survey data reveal a gap between the attitudes and behavior of physicians; 20 to 70 percent of physicians favor the legalization of physician-assisted suicide, but only 2 to 4 percent favor active voluntary euthanasia, and only approximately 2 to 13 percent have actually aided patients in dying, by either providing a prescription or administering a lethal injection. The limitations of these surveys, which are legion, include inconsistent definitions of physician-assisted suicide and euthanasia, lack of information about nonrespondents, and provisions for maintaining confidentiality that have led to inaccurate reporting.[13,16] Since physicians' attitudes toward alternatives to assisted suicide have not been studied, there is a void in our knowledge about the priority that physicians place on physician-assisted suicide.

The willingness of physicians to assist patients in dying appears to be determined by numerous complex factors, including religious beliefs, personal values, medical specialty, age, practice setting, and perspective on the use of financial resources.[13,16–19] Studies of patients' preferences for care at the end of life demonstrate that physicians' preferences strongly influence those of their patients.[13] Making physician-assisted suicide a medical treatment when it is so strongly dependent on these physician-related variables would result in a regulatory impossibility.[19] Physicians would have to disclose their values and attitudes to patients to avoid potential conflict.[13] A survey by Ganzini et al. demonstrated that psychiatrists' responses to requests to evaluate patients were highly determined by their attitudes.[13] In a study by Emanuel et al., depressed patients with cancer said they would view positively those physicians who acknowledged their willingness to assist in suicide. In contrast, patients with cancer who were suffering from pain would be suspicious of such physicians.[11]

In this controversy, physicians fall into one of three groups. Those who support physician-assisted suicide see it as a compassionate response to a medical need, a symbol of nonabandonment, and a means to reestablish patients' trust in doctors who have used technology excessively.[20] They argue that regulation of physician-assisted suicide is possible and, in fact, necessary to control the actions of physicians who are currently providing assistance surreptitiously.[21] The two remaining groups of physicians oppose legalization.[19,22-24] One group is morally opposed to physician-assisted suicide and emphasizes the need to preserve the professionalism of medicine and the commitment to "do no harm." These physicians view aiding a patient in dying as a form of abandonment, because a physician needs to walk the last mile with the patient, as a witness, not as an executioner. Legalization would endorse justified killing, according to these physicians, and guidelines would not be followed, even if they could be developed. Furthermore, these physicians are concerned that the conflation of assisted suicide with the withdrawal of life support or adequate treatment of pain would make it even harder for dying patients, because there would be a backlash against existing policies. The other group is not ethically opposed to physician-assisted suicide and, in fact, sees it as acceptable in exceptional cases, but these physicians believe that one cannot regulate the unregulatable.[19] On this basis, the New York State Task Force on Life and the Law, a 24-member committee with broad public and professional representation, voted unanimously against the legalization of physician-assisted suicide.[24] All three groups of physicians agree that a national effort is needed to improve the care of the dying. Yet it does seem that those in favor of legalizing physician-assisted suicide are disingenuous in their use of this issue as a wedge. If this form of assistance with dying is legalized, the courts will be forced to broaden the assistance to include active voluntary euthanasia and, eventually, assistance in response to requests from proxies.

One cannot easily categorize the patients who request physician-assisted suicide or euthanasia. Some surveys of physicians have attempted to determine retrospectively the prevalence and nature of these requests.[10] Pain, AIDS, and neurodegenerative disorders are the most common conditions in patients requesting assistance in dying. There is a wide range in the age of such patients, but many are younger persons with AIDS.[10] From the limited data available, the factors most commonly involved in requests for assistance are concern about future loss of control, being or becoming a burden to others, or being unable to care for oneself and fear of severe pain.[10] A small number of recent studies have directly asked terminally ill patients with cancer or AIDS about their desire for death.[25-27] All these studies show that the desire for death is closely associated with depression and that pain and lack of social support are contributing factors.

Do we know enough, on the basis of several legal cases, to develop a public policy that will profoundly change medicine's role in society?[1,2] Approximately 2.4 million Americans die each year. We have almost no information on how they die and only general information on where they die. Sixty-one percent die in hospitals, 17 percent in nursing homes, and the remainder at home, with approximately 10 to 14 percent of those at home receiving hospice care.

The available data suggest that physicians are inadequately trained to assess and manage the multifactorial symptoms commonly associated with patients' requests for physician-assisted suicide. According to the American Medical Association's report on medical education, only 5 of 126 medical schools in the United States require a separate course in the care of the dying.[28] Of 7048 residency programs, only 26 percent offer a course on the medical and legal aspects of care at the end of life as a regular part of the curriculum. According to a survey of 1068 accredited residency programs in family medicine, internal medicine, and pediatrics and fellowship programs in geriatrics, each resident or fellow coordinates the care of 10 or fewer dying patients annually.[28] Almost 15 percent of the programs offer no formal training in terminal care. Despite the availability of hospice programs, only 17 percent of the training programs offer a hospice rotation, and the rotation is required in only half of those programs; 9 percent of the programs have residents or fellows serving as members of hospice teams. In a recent survey of 55 residency programs and over 1400 residents, conducted by the American Board of Internal Medicine, the residents were asked to rate their perception of adequate training in care at the end of life. Seventy-two percent reported that they had received adequate training in managing pain and other symptoms; 62 percent, that they had received adequate training in telling patients that they are dying; 38 percent, in describing what the process will be like; and 32 percent, in talking to patients who request assistance in dying or a hastened death (Blank L: personal communication).

The lack of training in the care of the dying is evident in practice. Several studies have concluded that poor communication between physicians and patients, physicians' lack of knowledge about national guidelines for such care, and their lack of knowledge about the control of symptoms are barriers to the provision of good care at the end of life.[23,29,30]

Yet there is now a large body of data on the components of suffering in patients with advanced terminal disease, and these data provide the basis for treatment algorithms.[3] There are three major factors in suffering: pain and other physical symptoms, psychological distress, and existential distress (described as the experience of life without meaning). It is not only the patients who suffer but also their families and the health care professionals attending them. These experiences of suffering are often closely and inextricably related. Perceived distress in any one of the three groups amplifies distress in the others.[31,32]

Pain is the most common symptom in dying patients, and according to recent data from U.S. studies, 56 percent of outpatients with cancer, 82 percent of outpatients with AIDS, 50 percent of hospitalized patients with various diagnoses, and 36 percent of nursing home residents have inadequate management of pain during the course of their terminal illness.[33-36] Members of minority groups and women, both those with cancer and those with AIDS, as well as the elderly, receive less pain treatment than other groups of patients. In a survey of 1177 physicians who had treated a total of more than 70,000 patients with cancer in the previous six months, 76 percent of the respondents cited lack of knowledge as a barrier to their ability to control pain.[37] Severe pain that is not adequately controlled interferes with the quality of life, including the activities of daily living, sleep, and social interactions.[36,38]

Other physical symptoms are also prevalent among the dying. Studies of patients with advanced cancer and of the elderly in the year before death show that they have numerous symptoms that worsen the quality of life, such as fatigue, dyspnea, delirium, nausea, and vomiting.[36,38]

Along with these physical symptoms, dying patients have a variety of well-described psychological symptoms, with a high prevalence of anxiety and depression in patients with cancer or AIDS and the elderly.[27,39] For example, more than 60 percent of patients with advanced cancer have psychiatric problems, with adjustment disorders, depression, anxiety, and delirium reported most fre-

quently. Various factors that contribute to the prevalence and severity of psychological distress in the terminally ill have been identified.[39] The diagnosis of depression is difficult to make in medically ill patients[3,26,40]; 94 percent of the Oregon psychiatrists surveyed by Ganzini et al. were not confident that they could determine, in a single evaluation, whether a psychiatric disorder was impairing the judgment of a patient who requested assistance with suicide.[13]

Attention has recently been focused on the interaction between uncontrolled symptoms and vulnerability to suicide in patients with cancer or AIDS.[41] Data from studies of both groups of patients suggest that uncontrolled pain contributes to depression and that persistent pain interferes with patients' ability to receive support from their families and others. Patients with AIDS have a high risk of suicide that is independent of physical symptoms. Among New York City residents with AIDS, the relative risk of suicide in men between the ages of 20 and 59 years was 36 times higher than the risk among men without AIDS in the same age group and 66 times higher than the risk in the general population.[41] Patients with AIDS who committed suicide generally did so within nine months after receiving the diagnosis; 25 percent had made a previous suicide attempt, 50 percent had reported severe depression, and 40 percent had seen a psychiatrist within four days before committing suicide. As previously noted, the desire to die is most closely associated with the diagnosis of depression.[26,27] Suicide is the eighth leading cause of death in the United States, and the incidence of suicide is higher in patients with cancer or AIDS and in elderly men than in the general population. Conwell and Caine reported that depression was under-diagnosed by primary care physicians in a cohort of elderly patients who subsequently committed suicide; 75 percent of the patients had seen a primary care physician during the last month of life but had not received a diagnosis of depression.[22]

The relation between depression and the desire to hasten death may vary among subgroups of dying patients. We have no data, except for studies of a small number of patients with cancer or AIDS. The effect of treatment for depression on the desire to hasten death and on requests for assistance in doing so has not been examined in the medically ill population, except for a small study in which four of six patients who initially wished to hasten death changed their minds within two weeks.[26]

There is also the concern that certain patients, particularly members of minority groups that are estranged from the health care system, may be reluctant to receive treatment for their physical or psychological symptoms because of the fear that their physicians will, in fact, hasten death. There is now some evidence that the legalization of assisted suicide in the Northern Territory of Australia has undermined the Aborigines' trust in the medical care system[42]; this experience may serve as an example for the United States, with its multicultural population.

The multiple physical and psychological symptoms in the terminally ill and elderly are compounded by a substantial degree of existential distress. Reporting on their interviews with Washington State physicians whose patients had requested assistance in dying, Back et al. noted the physicians' lack of sophistication in assessing such nonphysical suffering.[10]

In summary, there are fundamental physician-related barriers to appropriate, humane, and compassionate care for the dying. These range from attitudinal and behavioral barriers to educational and economic barriers. Physicians do not know enough about their patients, themselves, or suffering to provide assistance with dying as a medical treatment for the relief of suffering. Physicians need to explore their own perspectives on the meaning of suffering in order to develop their own approaches to the care of the dying. They need insight into how the nature of the doctor-patient relationship influences their own decision making. If legalized, physician-assisted suicide will be a substitute for rational therapeutic, psychological, and social interventions that might otherwise enhance the quality of life for patients who are dying. The medical profession needs to take the lead in developing guidelines for good care of dying patients. Identifying the factors related to physicians, patients, and the health care system that pose barriers to appropriate care at the end of life should be the first step in a national dialogue to educate health care professionals and the public on the topic of death and dying. Death is an issue that society as a whole faces, and it requires a compassionate response. But we should not confuse compassion with competence in the care of terminally ill patients.

KATHLEEN M. FOLEY, M.D.
Memorial Sloan-Kettering Cancer Center
New York, NY 10021

REFERENCES

1. Reinhardt, Compassion in Dying v. State of Washington, 79 F. 3d 790 9th Cir. 1996.
2. Miner, Quill v. Vacco 80 F. 3d 716 2nd Cir. 1996.
3. Doyle D, Hanks, GWC, MacDonald N. The Oxford textbook of palliative medicine. New York: Oxford University Press, 1993.
4. Orentlicher D. The legalization of physician-assisted suicide. N Engl J Med 1996; 335: 663–7.
5. Wilson WC, Smedira NG, Fink C, McDowell JA, Luce JM. Ordering and administration of sedatives and analgesics during the withholding and withdrawal of life support from critically ill patients. JAMA 1992; 267: 949–53.
6. Foley KM. The relationship of pain and symptom management to patient requests for physician-assisted suicide. J Pain Symptom Manage 1991; 6: 289–97.
7. Cherny NI, Coyle N, Foley KM. Guidelines in the care of the dying patient. Hematol Oncol Clin North Am 1996; 10: 261–86.
8. Cherny NI, Portenoy RK. Sedation in the management of refractory symptoms: guidelines for evaluation and treatment. J Palliat Care 1994; 10(2): 31–8.
9. Cancer pain relief and palliative care. Geneva: World Health Organization, 1989.
10. Back AL, Wallace JI, Starks HE, Pearlman RA. Physician-assisted suicide and euthanasia in Washington State: patient requests and physician responses. JAMA 1996; 275: 919–25.
11. Emanuel EJ, Fairclough DL, Daniels ER, Clarridge BR. Euthanasia and physician-assisted suicide: attitudes and experiences of oncology patients, oncologists, and the public. Lancet 1996; 347: 1805–10.
12. Lee MA, Nelson HD, Tilden VP, Ganzini L, Schmidt TA, Tolle SW. Legalizing assisted suicide—views of physicians in Oregon. N Engl J Med 1996; 334: 310–15.
13. Ganzini L, Fenn DS, Lee MA, Heintz RT, Bloom JD. Attitudes of Oregon psychiatrists toward physician-assisted suicide. Am J Psychiatry 1996; 153: 1469–75.
14. Cohen JS, Fihn SD, Boyko EJ, Jonsen AR, Wood RW. Attitudes toward assisted suicide and euthanasia among physicians in Washington State. N Engl J Med 1994; 331: 89–94.
15. Doukas DJ, Waterhouse D, Gorenflo DW, Seid J. Attitudes and behaviors on physician-assisted death: a study of Michigan oncologists. J Clin Oncol 1995; 13: 1055–61.
16. Morrison S, Meier D. Physician-assisted dying: fashioning public policy with an absence of data. Generations. Winter 1994: 48–53.
17. Portenoy RK, Coyle N, Kash K, et al. Determinants of the willingness to endorse assisted suicide: a survey of physicians, nurses, and social workers. Psychosomatics (in press).
18. Fins J. Physician-assisted suicide and the right to care. Cancer Control 1996; 3: 272–8.
19. Callahan D, White M. The legalization of physician-assisted suicide: creating a regulatory Potemkin Village. U Richmond Law Rev 1996; 30: 1–83.
20. Quill TE. Death and dignity—a case of individualized decision making. N Engl J Med 1991; 324: 691–4.
21. Quill TE, Cassel CK, Meier DE. Care of the hopelessly ill—proposed clinical criteria for physician-assisted suicide. N Engl J Med 1992; 327: 1380–4.
22. Conwell Y, Caine ED. Rational suicide and the right to die—reality and myth. N Engl J Med 1991; 325: 1100–3.
23. Foley KM. Pain, physician assisted suicide and euthanasia. Pain Forum 1995; 4: 163–78.
24. When death is sought: assisted suicide and euthanasia in the medical context. New York: New York State Task Force on Life and the Law, May 1994.
25. Brown JH, Henteleff P, Barakat S, Rowe CJ. Is it normal for terminally ill patients to desire death? Am J Psychiatry 1986; 143: 208–11.

26. Chochinov HM, Wilson KG, Enns M, et al. Desire for death in the terminally ill. Am J Psychiatry 1995; 152: 1185–91.

27. Breitbart W, Rosenfeld BD, Passik SD. Interest in physician-assisted suicide among ambulatory HIV-infected patients. Am J Psychiatry 1996; 153: 238–42.

28. Hill TP. Treating the dying patient: the challenge for medical education. Arch Intern Med 1995; 155: 1265–9.

29. Callahan D. Once again reality: now where do we go. Hastings Cent Rep 1995; 25 (6): Suppl: S33–S36.

30. Solomon MZ, O'Donnell L, Jennings B, et al. Decisions near the end of life: professional views on life-sustaining treatments. Am J Public Health 1993; 83: 14–23.

31. Cherny NI, Coyle N, Foley KM. Suffering in the advanced cancer patient: definition and taxonomy. J. Palliat Care 1994; 10 (2): 57–70.

32. Cassel EJ. The nature of suffering and the goals of medicine. N Engl J Med 1982; 306: 639–45.

33. Cleeland CS, Gonin R, Hatfield AK, et al. Pain and its treatment in outpatients with metastatic cancer. N Engl J Med 1994; 330: 592–6.

34. Breitbart W, Rosenfeld BD, Passik SD, McDonald MV, Thaler H, Portenoy RK. The undertreatment of pain in ambulatory AIDS patients. Pain 1996; 65: 243–9.

35. The SUPPORT Principal Investigators. A controlled trial to improve care for seriously ill hospitalized patients. JAMA 1995; 274: 1591–8.

36. Seale C, Cartwright A. The year before death. Hants, England: Avebury, 1994.

37. Von Roenn JH, Cleeland CS, Gonin R, Hatfield AK, Pandya KJ. Physician attitudes and practice in cancer pain management: a survey from the Eastern Cooperative Oncology Group. Ann Intern Med 1993; 119: 121–6.

38. Portenoy RK. Pain and quality of life: clinical issues and implications for research. Oncology 1990; 4: 172–8.

39. Breitbart W. Suicide risk and pain in cancer and AIDS patients. In: Chapman CR, Foley KM, eds. Current and emerging issues in cancer pain. New York: Raven Press, 1993.

40. Chochinov H, Wilson KG, Enns M, Lander S. Prevalence of depression in the terminally ill: effects of diagnostic criteria and symptom threshold judgments. Am J Psychiatry 1994; 151: 537–40.

41. Passik S, McDonald M, Rosenfeld B, Breitbart W. End of life issues in patients with AIDS: clinical and research considerations. J Pharm Care Pain Symptom Control 1995; 3: 91–111.

42. NT "success" in easing rural fear of euthanasia. The Age. August 31, 1996: A7.

A Piece of My Mind

A Conversation With My Mother

You have already met my father.[1] Now meet my mother. She died a few weeks ago. She wanted me to tell you how.

Her name was Virginia. Up until about 6 months ago, at age 84, she was the proverbial "little old lady in sneakers." After my father died of colon cancer several years ago, she lived by herself in one of those grand old Greek revival houses you see on postcards of small New England towns. Hers was in Middlebury, Vermont.

My mother was very independent, very self-sufficient, and very content. My brother and his family lived next door. Although she was quite close to them, she tried hard not to interfere in their lives. She spent most of her time reading large-print books, working word puzzles, and watching the news and professional sports on TV. She liked the house kept full of light. Every day she would take two outings, one in the morning to the small country store across the street to pick up the *Boston Globe,* and one in the afternoon to the Grand Union across town, to pick up some item she purposefully omitted from the previous day's shopping list. She did this in all but the worst weather. On icy days, she would wear golf shoes to keep from slipping and attach spikes to the tip of her cane. I think she was about 5 feet 2 and 120 pounds, but I am not certain. I know she started out at about 5 feet 4, but she seemed to shrink a little bit each year, getting cuter with time as many old people do. Her wrinkles matched her age, emphasizing a permanent thin-lipped smile that extended all the way to her little Kris Kringle eyes. The only thing that embarrassed her was her thinning gray hair, but she covered that up with a rather dashing tweed fedora that matched her Talbots outfits. She loved to tease people by wearing outrageous necklaces. The one made from the front teeth of camels was her favorite.

To be sure, she had had her share of problems in the past: diverticulitis and endometriosis when she was younger, more recently a broken hip, a bout with depression, some hearing loss, and cataracts. But she was a walking tribute to the best things in American medicine. Coming from a family of four generations of physicians, she was fond of bragging that, but for lens implants, hearing aids, hip surgery, and Elavil, she would be blind, deaf, bedridden, and depressed. At age 84, her only problems were a slight rectal prolapse, which she could reduce fairly easily, some urinary incontinence, and a fear that if her eyesight got much worse she would lose her main pleasures. But those things were easy to deal with and she was, to use her New England expression, "happy as a clam."

"David, I can't tell you how content I am. Except for missing your father, these are the best years of my life."

Yes, all was well with my mother, until about six months ago. That was when she developed acute cholelithiasis. From that point on, her health began to unravel with amazing speed. She recovered from the cholecystectomy on schedule and within a few weeks of leaving the hospital was resuming her walks downtown. But about six weeks after the surgery she was suddenly hit with a case of severe diarrhea, so severe that it extended her rectal prolapse to about 8 inches and dehydrated her to the point that she had to be readmitted. As soon as her physician got her rehydrated, other complications quickly set in. She developed oral thrush, apparently due to the antibiotic treatment for her diarrhea, and her antidepressants got out of balance. For some reason that was never fully determined, she also became anemic, which was treated with iron, which made her nauseated. She could not eat, she got weak, her skin itched, and her body ached. Oh yes, they also found a lump in her breast, the diagnosis of which was postponed, and atrial fibrillation. Needless to say, she was quite depressed.

Her depression was accentuated by the need to deal with her rectal prolapse. On the one hand, she really disliked the thought of more surgery. She especially hated the nasogastric tube and the intense postoperative fatigue. On the other hand, the prolapse was very painful. The least cough or strain would send it out to rub against the sheets, and she could not push it back the way she used to. She knew that she could not possibly walk to the Grand Union again unless it was fixed.

It was at that time that she first began to talk to me about how she could end her life gracefully. As a physician's wife, she was used to thinking about life and death and prided herself on being able to deal maturely with the idea of death. She had signed every living will and advance directive she could find, and carried a card that donated her organs. Even though she knew they would not do anyone much good (*"Can they recycle my artificial hip and lenses?"*), she liked the way the

Edited by Roxanne K. Young, Associate Editor.

card announced her acceptance of the fact that all things must someday end. She dreaded the thought of being in a nursing home, unable to take care of herself, her body, mind, and interests progressively declining until she was little more than a blank stare, waiting for death to mercifully take her away.

"I know they can keep me alive a long time, but what's the point? If the pleasure is gone and the direction is steadily down, why should I have to draw it out until I'm 'rescued' by cancer, a heart attack, or a stroke? That could take years. I understand that some people want to hang on until all the possible treatments have been tried to squeeze out the last drops of life. That's fine for them. But not for me."

My own philosophy, undoubtedly influenced heavily by my parents, is that choosing the best way to end your life should be the ultimate individual right—a right to be exercised between oneself and one's beliefs, without intrusions from governments or the beliefs of others. On the other hand, I also believe that such decisions should be made only with an accurate understanding of one's prognosis and should never be made in the middle of a correctable depression or a temporary trough. So my brother, sister, and I coaxed her to see a rectal surgeon about having her prolapse repaired and to put off thoughts of suicide until her health problems were stabilized and her antidepressants were back in balance.

With the surgeon's help, we explored the possible outcomes of the available procedures for her prolapse. My mother did not mind the higher mortality rates of the more extensive operations—in fact, she wanted them. Her main concern was to avoid rectal incontinence, which she knew would dampen any hopes of returning to her former lifestyle.

Unfortunately, that was the outcome she got. By the time she had recovered from the rectal surgery, she was totally incontinent "at both ends," to use her words. She was bedridden, anemic, exhausted, nauseated, achy, and itchy. Furthermore, over the period of this illness her eyesight had begun to fail to the point she could no longer read. Because she was too sick to live at home, even with my brother's help, but not sick enough to be hospitalized, we had to move her to an intermediate care facility.

On the positive side, her antidepressants were working again and she had regained her clarity of mind, her spirit, and her humor. But she was very unhappy. She knew instinctively, and her physician confirmed, that after all the insults of the past few months it was very unlikely she would ever be able to take care of herself alone or walk to the Grand Union. That was when she began to press me harder about suicide.

"Let me put this in terms you should understand, David. My 'quality of life'—isn't that what you call it?—has dropped below zero. I know there is nothing fatally wrong with me and that I could live on for many more years. With a colostomy and some luck I might even be able to recover a bit of my former lifestyle, for a while. But do we have to do that just because it's possible? Is the meaning of life defined by its duration? Or does life have a purpose so large that it doesn't have to be prolonged at any cost to preserve its meaning?

"I've lived a wonderful life, but it has to end sometime and this is the right time for me. My decision is not about whether I'm going to die—we will all die sooner or later. My decision is about when and how. I don't want to spoil the wonder of my life by dragging it out in years of decay. I want to go now, while the good memories are still fresh. I have always known that eventually the right time would come, and now I know that this is it. Help me find a way."

I discussed her request with my brother and sister and with her nurses and physician. Although we all had different feelings about her request, we agreed that she satisfied our criteria of being well-informed, stable, and not depressed. For selfish reasons we wanted her to live as long as possible, but we realized that it was not our desires that mattered. What mattered to us were her wishes. She was totally rational about her conviction that this was "her time." Now she was asking for our help, and it struck us as the height of paternalism (or filialism?) to impose our desires over hers.

I bought *Final Exit*[2] for her, and we read it together. If she were to end her life, she would obviously have to do it with pills. But as anyone who has thought about this knows, accomplishing that is not easy. Patients can rarely get the pills themselves, especially in a controlled setting like a hospital or nursing home. Anyone who provides the pills knowing they will be used for suicide could be arrested. Even if those problems are solved and the pills are available, they can be difficult to take, especially by the frail. Most likely, my mother would fall asleep before she could swallow the full dose. A way around this would be for her to put a bag over her head with a rubber band at her neck to ensure that she would suffocate if she fell asleep before taking all the pills. But my mother did not like that idea because of the depressing picture it would present to those who found her body. She contemplated drawing a happy smile on the bag, but did not think that would give the correct impression either. The picture my mother wanted to leave to the world was that her death was a happy moment, like the end of a wonderful movie, a time for good memories and a peaceful acceptance of whatever the future might hold. She did not like the image of being a quasi-criminal sneaking illegal medicines. The way she really wanted to die was to be given a morphine drip that she could control, to have her family around her holding her hands, and for her to turn up the drip.

As wonderful as that might sound, it is illegal. One problem was that my mother did not have a terminal condition or agonizing pain that might justify a morphine drip. Far from it. Her heart was strong enough to keep her alive for 10 more years, albeit as a frail, bedridden, partially blind, partially deaf, incontinent, and possibly stroked-out woman. But beyond that, no physician would dare give a patient access to a lethal medicine in a way that could be accused of assisting suicide. Legally, physicians can provide lots of comfort care, even if it might hasten a patient's death, but the primary purpose of the medicine must be to relieve suffering, not to cause death. Every now and then my mother would vent her frustration with the law and the arrogance of others who insist that everyone must accept their philosophy of death, but she knew that railing at what she considered to be misguided laws would not undo them. She needed to focus on finding a solution to her problem. She decided that the only realistic way out was for me to get her some drugs and for her to do her best to swallow them. Although I was very nervous at the thought of being turned in by someone who discovered our plan and felt it was their duty to stop it, I was willing to do my part. I respected her decision, and I knew she would do the same for me.

I had no difficulty finding a friend who could write a prescription for restricted drugs and who was willing to help us from a distance. In fact, I have yet to find anybody who agrees with the current laws. (*"So why do they exist?"*) But before I actually had to resolve any lingering conflicts and obtain the drugs, my mother's course took an unexpected and strangely welcomed twist. I received a call that she had developed pneumonia and had to be readmitted to the hospital. By the time I made contact with her, she had already reminded her attendants that she did not want to be resuscitated if she should have a heart attack or stroke.

"Is there anything more I can do?"

Pneumonia, the old folks' friend, I thought to myself. I told her that although advance directives usually apply to refusing treatments for emergencies such as heart attacks, it was always legal for her to refuse any treatment. In particular, she could refuse the antibiotics for the pneumonia. Her physician and nurses would undoubtedly advise her against it, but if she signed enough papers they would have to honor her request.

"What's it like to die of pneumonia? Will they keep me comfortable?"

I knew that without any medicine for comfort, pneumonia was not a pleasant way to die. But I was also confident that her physician was compassionate and would keep her comfortable. So she asked that the antibiotics be stopped. Given the deep gurgling in her throat every time she breathed, we all expected the infection to spread rapidly. She took a perverse pleasure in that week's cover story of *Newsweek*, which described the spread of resistant strains.

"Bring all the resistant strains in this hospital to me. That will be my present to the other patients."

But that did not happen. Against the odds, her pneumonia regressed. This discouraged her greatly—to see the solution so close, just to watch it slip away.

"What else can I do? Can I stop eating?"

I told her she could, but that that approach could take a long time. I then told her that if she was really intent on dying, she could stop drinking. Without water, no one, even the healthiest, can live more than a few days.

"Can they keep me comfortable?"

I talked with her physician. Although it ran against his instincts, he respected the clarity and firmness of my mother's decision and agreed that her quality of life had sunk below what she was willing to bear. He also knew that what she was asking from him was legal. He took out the IV and wrote orders that she should receive adequate medications to control discomfort.

My mother was elated. The next day happened to be her 85th birthday, which we celebrated with a party, balloons and all. She was beaming from ear to ear. She had done it. She had found the way. She relished her last piece of chocolate, and then stopped eating and drinking.

Over the next four days, my mother greeted her visitors with the first smiles she had shown for months. She energetically reminisced about the great times she had had and about things she was proud of. (She especially hoped I would tell you about her traveling alone across Africa at the age of 70, and surviving a capsized raft on Wyoming's Snake River at 82.) She also found a calming self-acceptance in describing things of which she was not proud. She slept between visits but woke up brightly whenever we touched her to share more memories and say a few more things she wanted us to know. On the fifth day it was more difficult to wake her. When we would take her hand she would open her eyes and smile, but she was too drowsy and weak to talk very much. On the sixth day, we could not wake her. Her face was relaxed in her natural smile, she was breathing unevenly, but peacefully. We held her hands for another two hours, until she died.

I had always imagined that when I finally stood in the middle of my parents' empty house, surrounded by the old smells, by hundreds of objects that represent a time forever lost, and by the terminal silence, I would be overwhelmingly saddened. But I wasn't. This death was not a sad death; it was a happy death. It did not come after years of decline, lost vitality, and loneliness; it came at the right time. My mother was not clinging desperately to what no one can have. She knew that death was not a tragedy to be postponed at any cost, but that death is a part of life, to be embraced at the proper time. She had done just what she wanted to do, just the way she wanted to do it. Without hoarding pills, without making me a criminal, without putting a bag over her head, and without huddling in a van with a carbon monoxide machine, she had found a way to bring her life gracefully to a close. Of course we cried. But although we will miss her greatly, her ability to achieve her death at her "right time" and in her "right way" transformed for us what could have been a desolate and crushing loss into a time for joy. Because she was happy, we were happy.

"Write about this, David. Tell others how well this worked for me. I'd like this to be my gift. Whether they are terminally ill, in intractable pain, or, like me, just know that the right time has come for them, more people might want to know that this way exists. And maybe more physicians will help them find it."

Maybe they will. Rest in peace, Mom.

David M. Eddy, MD, PhD
Jackson, Wyo

My mother wants to thank Dr Timothy Cope of Middlebury, Vermont, for his present on her 85th birthday.

1. Eddy DM. Cost-effectiveness analysis: a conversation with my father. *JAMA.* 1992;267:1669–1672, 1674–1675.

2. Humphry D. *Final Exit.* Secaucus, NJ: Carol Publishing Group; 1991.

EUTHANASIA

To cease upon the midnight

The putative right of an individual to determine the manner of his own death conflicts with the supreme value that most societies place on the preservation of life. Recently, the individual has been gaining ground

CRIPPLED in a swimming accident in 1968, Ramon Sanpedro can move only his head. He wants someone to help him commit suicide. So far, two Spanish courts have refused their consent.

Tony Bland, a British football fan, suffered terrible brain injuries in a crowd pileup at a sports stadium in April 1989, and was left in a persistent vegetative state with no hope of recovery. In March 1993 the House of Lords, Britain's highest judicial authority, gave permission for Bland's feeding tubes to be disconnected. He died 20 days later.

Sue Rodriguez, a Canadian, was suffering from amyotrophic lateral sclerosis, an incurable disease which attacks the brain and spinal cord and impairs functions such as walking, speaking and breathing, when she asked in 1992 for someone to be allowed, legally, to help her die. Canada's Supreme Court found against her by five votes to four. She died in February 1994 with the help of an anonymous doctor.

Jack Kevorkian—"Dr Death"—is an American former pathologist whose eccentricities include creating ghoulish paintings using his own blood. He has "assisted" 20 suicides in the state of Michigan; juries have refused to convict him.

Such are the cases that are driving forward a public and legal debate in the West about the right to die and the right to medical assistance in doing so—a debate mainly for the rich West because in poor countries the artificial prolongation of life is at best a rare luxury; in Japan patients are often not told when they are terminally ill. The

debate has been intensifying with the development of medical technologies capable of supporting life, in a narrowly defined form, almost indefinitely; and it has been influenced by a growing sense in many western societies that more responsibility for, and control over, medical treatment should be transferred from doctors to patients. Last year, the Dutch parliament voted to permit doctors to kill severely ill patients under certain conditions (see box, The Dutch Way of Dying). This week, Germany's constitutional court ruled that doctors could allow a terminally ill patient to die. Previously, German doctors had been allowed only to withdraw life-support from patients who were actually dying.

In America, many of the terms of the euthanasia debate in its present form were defined in 1976 by the tragedy of a young woman called Karen Ann Quinlan, who was being kept alive by machines while in a coma that doctors judged to be irreversible. When her parents asked that the machines be disconnected, the hospital refused; the Quinlans won a court judgment establishing the right of a patient or his surrogate to refuse treatment. The right to pull the plug, sometimes referred to as "passive euthanasia", is now well established.

Doctors in most countries now honour the wish of a terminally ill or very old patient not to be revived should he suffer cardiac or respiratory arrest in hospital. The policy of the American Medical Association is that a doctor "has an ethical obligation to honour the resuscitation preferences expressed by the patient." In Britain, the Royal College of Nursing, and the doc-

tors' professional body, the British Medical Association (BMA), have come to a similar conclusion. They recommend that hospitals try to determine the wishes of such patients.

More recently, ethicists and the medical establishment have reached a consensus on the treatment of pain in the terminally ill. The principle used to be that pain-relievers should not be administered in such a way as to expose a patient to risk of addiction. The absurdity of worrying about addiction in someone with a short time left to live is now acknowledged. Pain relief is recognised as an overriding priority; and it is considered ethical to provide as much pain relief as necessary even if a doctor believes that doing so may hasten death. Even so, according to Mildred Solomon, co-founder of a Massachusetts organisation called Decisions Near the End of Life, which provides training to carers for the terminally ill, four out of five doctors surveyed in 1993 said that under-treatment of pain among the dying was a more serious problem than over-treatment.

Agreement is more elusive on the issue of what constitutes "appropriate care" of the terminally ill and dying. Some ethicists, for example, see significance in the means needed to nourish a patient, arguing that the surgical insertion of feeding tubes may amount to over-treatment. Other authorities, such as the Royal College of Nursing, see feeding a patient as a basic duty just like keeping him clean, and as difficult to disregard. When the House of Lords agreed that Tony Bland's feeding tubes could be disconnected, it said the decision should not be taken as a

The Dutch way of dying

HOLLAND has the most liberal regime for voluntary euthanasia of any western country. As a case study, its lessons are much disputed. Admirers cite the care with which the Dutch debated the issue until consensus was reached, and the safeguards that they built into their system. Critics say the safeguards are ineffective and that Holland is skidding down a slippery slope towards licensed killing.

The Dutch parliament decided last year to authorise euthanasia under certain conditions—thus recognising officially a practice common there for at least 20 years. No legal right to euthanasia was created, and doctors could still face prosecution if they failed to follow strict guidelines. These were that a patient must be in a state of unbearable suffering; the desire to die must be "lasting"; the decision to die must be given freely; and the patient must have a clear understanding of his condition.

Few would quarrel with such propositions taken in isolation. But there is a worrying drift in the Dutch experience. An official report found that, in addition to 2,300 reported cases of euthanasia in Holland in 1990, a further 1,040 people had had their deaths hastened without making a formal request for intervention. That figure gives pause for thought; so does the case of a physically healthy but severely depressed Dutch woman who in 1991 asked her psychiatrist to help her die. After consulting with seven colleagues the psychiatrist agreed to the request and gave the patient sleeping pills and a toxic potion; she took them and died. In June the Dutch Supreme Court ruled out prosecution. It thus appears that not all of the notional safeguards may be enforced by the courts.

Johan Legemaate, legal counsel of the Royal Dutch Medical Association, defends the way euthanasia is practised in Holland. He notes that in more than two-thirds of the cases where patients request euthanasia, it is denied, and that in most cases where patients had not formally requested euthanasia and yet received it, there had been previous discussion of the subject. (In most such cases in 1990, according to the report cited above, life was shortened only by a few hours or days. All cases went through an extensive process of review and consultation.) "We feel we have succeeded in creating a large amount of openness and accountability," Mr Legemaate says.

Critics counter, however, that the result is a climate of indifference in which most cases of euthanasia go unreported and patients' rights are being eroded. Euthanasia, they say, so far from giving more freedom to patients, is giving more power over them to doctors.

cancer. She did not want to undergo another series of painful and debilitating treatments with only a 25% chance of surviving. She preferred to choose the time of her death, and asked Dr Quill for barbiturates. He gave them to her and advised her of the amount needed to commit suicide—which she later did. Legally, American doctors can provide patients with drugs that might kill them provided that the drug has a legitimate medical purpose other than suicide. To provide drugs knowing that their likely application will be in suicide is frowned on.

Dr Quill was among the first American doctors to declare openly his role in assisting a death, albeit indirectly. The reaction was muted. Not everyone agreed with his conduct, but there was no rush to condemn it. Giving death a gentle push at a patient's behest does not happen often because the urge to live is usually so strong; but most doctors with long experience of critical care know of cases where it has occurred. A grand jury refused to indict Dr Quill, and in 1992 he and two other doctors published an essay suggesting guidelines for doctor-assisted suicide. The medical establishment remained opposed to the practice, but the taboo of talking about it was at last breached by someone who did not carry the baggage of Mr Kevorkian.

A right to choose

A still more difficult question is whether society should approve, tacitly or otherwise, the next step in the logical sequence, namely the practice of active euthanasia—ie, a doctor administering a substance for no reason other than to cause death. Those who favour legalisation of active euthanasia point to anecdotal evidence from surveys of doctors showing that it already happens. Better to have the decisions made after open discussion with some sort of institutional safeguards, it is argued, than to leave them to the conscience of individual doctors.

Campaigners for voluntary euthanasia argue that some ethical distinctions between what is and is not taboo are already untenable. Withdrawing life-support, for example, is considered a form of passive euthanasia. But it is not really passive. To unplug a machine is a deliberate action.

In the case of Tony Bland, the British football fan, almost three weeks elapsed after the disconnecting of his feeding tubes during which he was left to waste away. It is hard to see why

general mandate and that each such case should go before a court.

Dr Death comes calling

An even more contentious area is "doctor-assisted suicide", in which a doctor helps a patient to take his own life. This has been Mr Kevorkian's speciality. In each of the 20 deaths he facilitated, the patient took the final step in the process—by connecting a hose, say, or pushing a button. Most western countries, and 44 American states, have laws against assisting suicide; in those that do not, such as Switzerland, medical tradition is against it. That record, however, suggests a unanimity absent in practice.

The *Medical Journal of Australia* reported a survey of 354 doctors who had been asked by patients to hasten death* (for footnotes, see final page). Only 107 had done so, but twice as many thought the law should be changed to allow such a thing in certain circumstances. A more recent poll of British doctors, reported in the *British Medical Journal*, found a similar pattern†. Of 273 respondents, 124 had been asked to hasten actively a patient's death; of those, about a third had done so; but almost half of the total sample said they might do so if the practice was legal (see tables).

In America, a widely remarked article in the *New England Journal of Medicine*‡ in 1991 created something of a turning-point in attitudes. Timothy Quill, a former hospice director, told the story of "Diane", who had been diagnosed as having leukaemia. Diane had previously recovered from vaginal that was more compassionate "treatment" than a lethal injection that would have given him, and his family, an equally sure release from their agony.

Nor is it easy to draw a clear line between injecting a dose of pain-killer that is likely to cause death (as some doctors do), and injecting a drug that is certain to kill (which is a crime in most places). In 1992 a British rheumatologist, Nigel Cox, was convicted of attempted murder for giving a lethal injection of potassium cyanide to a pain-wracked patient who had begged him to end her suffering. If Dr Cox had given her a huge dose of pain-killers he would never have been put in the dock.

The case for euthanasia is gaining a more sympathetic hearing as modern medicine and institutional care make dying a more prolonged, impersonal and often agonising business. To see a loved one shrivelled in pain for weeks or months can be a devastating experience for friends and family; but it is one that may become more commonplace as quick and relatively easy cardiac deaths decline as a percentage of deaths in rich countries, and proportionately more people die of cancer and AIDS. Nor may all hospitals be equal to the task of maintaining some measure of decency and comfort for the dying.

Some arguments for euthanasia insist on parallels with abortion, which the American Supreme Court declared to be a legal right on the grounds that the decision to bear a child was a matter of private choice. An American district court made explicit use of this rationale in May when it overturned a statute prohibiting assisted suicide; now under appeal, the case may reach the Supreme Court. This line of argument sees a decision to end one's life as the ultimate act of self-determination. In doing so, it raises legal and philosophical questions about the state of mind of any person taking such a decision; and it probably invites the question of whether such a right, were it to exist, should be restricted to certain classes of person. Could the young, or the healthy, or the clinically depressed, be denied a "right to die" that was conceded to the old or the desperately sick?

A further problem arises in applying this logic of self-determination to cases where the practical issue is not the right to commit suicide, or to be left to die, but to be helped to die by a doctor. A patient does not have a right to demand, say, a voodoo cure

Last rights		%
"In the course of your medical practice, has a patient ever asked you to hasten his or her death?"		
	GPs	Consultants
Had been asked to hasten death	64	52
Had been asked for:		
Passive euthanasia only	13	16
Active euthanasia only	25	11
Passive and active euthanasia	27	25
Total who had been asked for active euthanasia	51	36
Not asked to hasten death	36	48
"Have you ever taken active steps to bring about the death of patient who asked you to do so?"		
	GPs	Consultants
Yes	30	36
No	70	64
"Sometimes I would be prepared to withdraw or withhold a course of treatment from a terminally ill patient, knowing the treatment might prolong the patient's life."		
	GPs	Consultants
Strongly agree	34	45
Agree	54	50
Undecided	5	2
Disagree	5	2
Strongly disagree	1	1
"If a terminally ill patient asked me to bring an end to his or her life, I would consider doing so if it were legal."		
	GPs	Consultants
Strongly agree	10	10
Agree	41	30
Undecided	21	21
Disagree	19	26
Strongly disagree	9	12

Source: *British Medical Journal* May 21st 1994
Totals may not equal 100 because of rounding

from a doctor; it is not obvious that he should have a right to demand death.

The danger of duty

Organised opposition to the cause of voluntary euthanasia comes chiefly from the handicapped, medical associations and some religious groups, including the Roman Catholic church and orthodox Jews. Interest groups for the handicapped are uncomfortable with any form of euthanasia because they fear its use would inevitably be extended to those with long-term disabilities. The underlying fear is that the right to die will become a duty to die, and that society, the principle of euthanasia once established, might tend to categorise some people as expendable. The old, senile, mentally ill and physically helpless could become tempting targets for cost-cutting.

For doctors and nurses, euthanasia is troubling because they are trained to heal and to save life. Doing the opposite, even with the noblest of intentions, runs counter to their oath. Practitioners in hospices that care for

the terminally ill have been at the forefront of medical opposition to euthanasia, arguing that techniques for controlling pain are now so far advanced that fewer people need die in agony. They fear that the availability of euthanasia as an easy option would diminish the incentive to provide compassionate care for those who preferred to let death take its course. Doctors are also worried that practising euthanasia openly would lead some patients to regard them as bringers of death. The BMA thinks it "contrary to the doctor's role deliberately to kill patients, even at their request".

Most medical associations would agree with that as a general statement. In practice, however, things are less clear-cut. On August 16th the Canadian Medical Association voted not to allow doctors any role in active euthanasia or assisted suicide—but by a fairly narrow majority of 93 to 74. In Britain, though Dr Cox was convicted by a criminal court, he was allowed by a regulatory body, the General Medical Council, to retain his practitioner's licence, a sign that his peers did not consider his action monstrous.

For the Christian churches, the issue is equally fraught. Even in western countries where people have lost the habit of going to church on Sundays, Christian values are still influential. One of the central Christian beliefs is that life is a gift from God which individuals guard but do not own; another is that suffering is a wellspring of redemption and, as such, has value in itself.

This idea has proved a source of strength to many sufferers for centuries. But it is possible to respect that belief and yet still to wonder if at some point suffering can become pointless. Must every single possible moment of suffering be extracted as payment for redemption? And should those not attached to this system of belief be subject to its consequences?

The moral muddle

Most people would say no, albeit often hesitantly. But merely coming to that conclusion is not enough to bring societies any closer to defining a new conceptual framework for regulating death and dying. Opinion polls in many western countries have found majority support for allowing assisted suicide and active euthanasia in certain circumstances, but legislators have not judged the trend a sufficiently compelling one for them to make significant changes to existing laws. In the United States, four state legislatures have rejected bills to allow assisted suicide; referendums in California and Washington have found majorities against change. Initiatives in the British and European parliaments have failed. The Canadian parliament, which has defeated four bills on the issue in the past, has formed a Senate committee on euthanasia and assisted suicide to collect opinion.

The result, in many places, is to leave justice in a muddle. Perhaps that is appropriate. Inadvertently, a sensible mean may have been struck. Laws against assisted suicide, it maybe said, are there to express society's unease. At the same time, it is very rare for a practising doctor to be charged with helping a terminally ill patient to die.

"The current law is just about right," says George Annas, an ethicist at the Boston University School of Medicine. "Physicians should understand they are at some risk and so should assist suicide only in very extreme circumstances." He points out the difficulty of creating a better law, particularly one that would be proof against malpractice lawyers: "How do you define the circumstances? What kind of procedural mechanisms would there have to be? It would be such a nightmare."

It is, in fact, not surprising that commissions and parliaments and the public at large should have such difficulty delineating the boundaries of death. To do so means coming to grips not only with the mystery of dying, but also with the meaning of life, and with the relationship between the free will of the individual and the interests of society. To decide not to decide, how-ever, is irresponsible. One of the strongest arguments for more liberal (and more honest) legislation on euthanasia is that it would lighten the burden on doctors who must at present make such terribly difficult decisions alone and without knowing what consequences they may face. In the words of Ian Kennedy, professor of medical law and ethics at King's College, London: "It cannot be fair to doctors to present them with a situation in which they have to guess whether people will subsequently endorse what they have done or whether, if they guess wrong, the law will be applied in all its rigour and they will face a charge of murder."

---

* MJA 1988; 148: 623-627; † BMJ 1994; 308: 1332–1334; ‡NEJM 1991; 324: 691–694

ATTITUDES TOWARD SUICIDAL BEHAVIOR: A REVIEW OF THE LITERATURE

Ellen Ingram and Jon B. Ellis

Ellen Ingram, M.A., is a licensed psychological examiner. Jon Ellis, Ph.D., is a licensed clinical psychologist and assistant professor at East Tennessee State University.

The attitudes people in any given culture [hold] regarding death and suicidal behavior may be viewed as a reflection of that culture's values toward life. This article reviews the literature in the area of societal attitudes toward suicidal behavior. Attitudes include not only how society feels about those who kill themselves but the family members who are left behind as well. Although surveys have shown that many Americans see suicidal people as psychologically disturbed, some groups argue that suicide can be seen as a rational behavior. The idea is postulated that the answer to whether suicide is a rational or irrational act may not be as simple as yes or no.

The opinions that members of a society hold regarding suicidal behavior is a reflection of their values toward human life. These values influence how members of a society are taught to think and behave. Societal attitudes regarding the appropriateness of suicide remain confused and contradictory. Death by suicide affects not only the victim but the victim's family, friends, members of the community, and our entire society. Surviving relatives are thought to be more grief stricken because their loved one willfully took his or her own life, and that they must also deal with more severe and negative attitudes of the people in the community when suicide is the cause of death (Cain & Fast, 1972; Calhoun, Selby, & Selby, 1982; McGinnis, 1987; Range, McDonald, & Anderson, 1987; Range & Thompson, 1986). Suicidal behavior is now viewed as an illness, but it may be a symptom of many illnesses because it is an overt expression of emotions such as rage, guilt, loneliness, shame, sorrow, agony, fear, and hopelessness (McGinnis, 1987).

Douglas (1967) conjectured that suicide was widely condemned in our society and could be understood only by a study of the meaning the self-destructive individual attached to the behavior. The meaning in turn should be studied within the context of the values of a particular society attaches to suicide. Singh, Williams, and Ryther (1986) asserted that the situation itself largely defines the extent to which suicide will be approved as an acceptable alternative to living. Society evaluates the appropriateness in terms of the individual involved and the specific circumstances surrounding the suicide. Community attitudes may even influence suicide rates (de Catanzaro, 1981; Douglas, 1967; Dublin, 1963). Some clinicians suggested that a hardening of attitudes toward suicidal behavior may result in lessening of such behavior (Koller & Slaghuis, 1978). Alternatively, a growing influence that is promoting the acceptance of suicide is the right-to-die movement, which advocates an individual's right to commit suicide particularly when a terminal illness is involved (Klagsburn, 1981).

HISTORICAL OVERVIEW

Some cultures encouraged suicide among certain members of their society, usually for religious purposes, believing in life after death (Siegel, 1988). In the Fiji Islands, suicide was expected of the wives of a chief when he died. The women rushed to kill themselves believing the first to die would become the chief's favorite wife in the spirit world. In India, widows practiced suttee. They threw themselves on their husband's funeral pyre believing they could atone for their husband's sins.

The Chinese regarded suicide as acceptable and honorable, particularly for defeated generals or deposed rulers. The Japanese ritualized suicide in the form of hara-kiri, a long drawn out process of disembowelment. A samurai warrior or a member of the military was bestowed much honor if he died in such a way. Ancient Greek and Roman cities differed greatly in their views of suicide. In Thebes, suicide was strongly condemned, but in other Greek communities tribunals existed to hear the arguments of people who wanted to commit suicide.

During the Middle Ages into the 19th century in Western cultures, society

From *Death Studies,* Volume 16, 1992, pp. 31–43. © 1992 by Taylor & Francis, Inc., 625 Chestnut Street, 8th Floor, Philadelphia, PA, 19106. All rights reserved. Reprinted by permission.

placed negative social sanctions on people who attempted or committed suicide. The sanctions included assigning disgrace to the reputation of the deceased, mutilation of the corpse, hanging the corpse from public gallows, denial of Christian burial, confiscation of the deceased's estate, and excommunication of the deceased from the church.

INFLUENCES ON CURRENT ATTITUDES

The general attitude of the public toward [suicide] remains confused and often contradictory (Kluge, 1975). Today there are two extreme views, amid more moderate views, on suicide. The extreme views range from total acceptance to total rejection of the right of an individual to commit suicide. At the center of the debate is the question of whether people should be allowed the right to die without interference. In its narrowest sense, the question relates to people who are terminally ill or in great pain. In its broadest sense, it extends to any person who wants to die (Klagsburn, 1981). Others regard the right to die as a right to refuse life-sustaining treatment (Weber, 1988). A small number of individuals insist that all persons have the right to control their own bodies even in matters of suicide. Any interference with this right is a violation of fundamental liberties. Szasz (1974) was among the most vocal advocates for the individual's right to commit suicide. He stated, "While suicide is not necessarily morally desirable, it is nonetheless a fundamental inalienable right" (p. 67). Maris (1986) disagreed with Szasz's radical individual autonomy. He pointed out that Szasz has no appreciation for loving the unlovable in our society. He foresaw this view as even contributing to self-destructive behavior.

Most right-to-die advocates make a distinction between a healthy or terminally ill person committing suicide. Advocates argue that medical science has now been able to prolong life artificially to the point that life becomes meaningless. Once the assumption is accepted that there are conditions under which it may be preferable not to sustain life, suicide may be viewed as a reasonable option (Klagsburn, 1981).

Suicide as a Rational Act

Several organizations have been established to promote wider acceptance of the right-to-die movement. Humphry (1987) described the Hemlock Society's position on suicide. Suicide is separated into two types. The first is emotional suicide or irrational self-murder. Their thinking on this type of suicide is to prevent it whenever possible. The second type is justifiable suicide described as rational and planned self-deliverance. They advocate what they call autoeuthanasia. They ethically justify suicide only under certain circumstances. One involves a case of an advanced terminal illness that is causing unbearable suffering to the individual. Another involves a grave physical handicap that is so restrictive that the individual cannot, after due consideration and training, tolerate such a limited existence. This group believes that suicide is ethical only when the person is a mature adult and has made a considered decision. A considered decision is one that was not made at the first knowledge of a life-threatening illness and for which the treating physician's response has been taken into account. Also the person has made plans that do not involve others in criminal liability, and he or she leaves a note stating exactly why he or she is committing suicide. Humphry believed that for many people just knowing how to kill themselves is in itself a great comfort and often extends their lives. They will often renegotiate with themselves the conditions of their dying.

Another group, Concern for the Dying (Sachs, 1987), has furnished thousands of copies of the Living Will document. The Living Will document expresses the desire of an individual to cease medical intervention under certain conditions. The Society for the Right to Die lobbies state legislatures in an effort to protect the right to refuse extraordinary life-preserving measures. Other groups propose schemes for regulating suicidal acts. Collectively, these groups advocate what is called rational suicide. Rational suicide is characterized by a possession of a realistic assessment of the situation by the individual who is faced with the decision to commit suicide. The individual's mental processes are not impaired by psychological illness or distress, and the person's motivation for the decision would be understandable if presented to objective

bystanders (Siegel, 1988). The goals of these groups are for the most part humane, advocating the "right to die with dignity" (Quinnett, 1987).

Opposition to Suicide

Among the opponents, some argue that a person does not have the right to commit suicide regardless of the circumstances. Others believe certain circumstances may be so unbearable that it is understandable why a person commits suicide, but this should be an individual act, and society or the legal system should not encourage this type of behavior. Opponents who hold extreme views argue that life should be preserved regardless of circumstances even in the case of a terminal illness. They believe no one has a right to decide at what point life becomes expendable. They believe condoning any kind of suicide condones them all (Klagsburn, 1981). They argue that there is medical and social justification to intervene and prevent someone from taking his or her life. Suicide is seen as an ambivalent act: Every person who wants to die also wants to live. This view postulates that a person is suicidal only for a short period of time, and if intervention is instigated, the suicidal crisis often passes and the person changes his or her mind.

ACCEPTABILITY OF SUICIDAL BEHAVIOR

Feherman (1989) chaired a 12-member committee that made recommendations to physicians about their responsibility toward terminally ill patients. The committee members agreed that it was not immoral for a physician to assist a terminally ill patient in committing suicide by prescribing sleeping pills and advising the patient of the amount of a lethal dose. Five years before this, the committee had recommended that physicians listen to the final wishes of their dying patients including removal of a feeding tube. Since then, many recommendations of the committee have been adopted by physicians and the court system.

Forty states and the District of Columbia have living will laws that allow people to specify in advance what treatments they would find acceptable in their final days. A New York State Supreme Court Justice ruled in January 1990 that a family did not have to pay

2 years worth of fees ($100,000) to a nursing home for tending a comatose patient after the family had asked to have the feeding tube removed. Less than 6 months later, in June 1990, the U.S. Supreme Court made a ruling by which family members can be barred from ending the lives of long-term comatose relatives who have not made their wishes known conclusively. In the absence of conclusive evidence that a patient does not wish to be sustained by artificial life-saving devices, the states were given broad power to keep such patients on life-saving systems. The court interprets the [C]onstitution that a competent person, as opposed to someone in a coma, is guaranteed the right to refuse medical treatment.

A poll conducted for *Time Magazine*/CNN television network in 1990 found that 80% of those surveyed thought decisions about ending lives of the terminally ill, who cannot decide for themselves, should be made by the patient's family and physician rather than lawmakers. Of the respondents, 81% believed that a physician with an unconscious patient who has left a living will should be allowed to withdraw life-sustaining treatment, and 57% believed physicians should go even further in such cases and [administer] lethal injections or provide a lethal amount of pills (Gibbs, 1990). Public acceptance of the right of an individual with a terminal illness to commit suicide has been growing, and between 1977 and 1983 the percentage of adults in the United States who believe a terminally ill person has a right to commit suicide increased from 39% to almost 50% (Siegel, 1988). Wellman and Wellman (1986) conducted two surveys assessing attitudes toward suicide. In the first surveys, over one half of both men and women believed that no one should be allowed to commit suicide. In the second survey, 70% of both sexes believed no one should be allowed to commit suicide.

Singh (1979) reported that suicide was considered a rational alternative for those who were suffering from an incurable disease by approximately 40% of the respondents in a national survey. Singh et al. (1986) compared four national surveys conducted between 1977 and 1983. The study examined public opinion on suicide in four situations: incurable disease, bankruptcy, family dishonor, and being tired of living. The highest approval rate for suicide was in

the situation in which a person had an incurable disease. In each year an increasing percentage approved of suicide in this situation, from approximately 39% in 1977 to nearly 50% in 1983. There was very little support for a person to commit suicide after having dishonored his or her family or after having gone bankrupt. A person who approved of suicide in the incurable-disease situation would most likely be a college-educated white male under the age of 35 who infrequently attended church services and had a high degree of support for freedom of expression. The approval of suicide was highest in the Pacific region and lowest in the southern regions of the United States. Ginsburg (1971) found a generally punitive and rejecting attitude toward suicidal behavior with little sympathy for those who attempted or completed suicide. Of the respondents, 42% of those who had known someone who had committed suicide felt a person had the right to take his or her own life. Kalish, Reynolds, and Farberow (1974) concluded that respondents to their survey found the victim's situation as well as the victim equally responsible. Johnson, Fitch, Alston, and McIntosh (1980) found that public acceptance of both suicide and euthanasia was highly conditional and limited to certain segments of the population. They found that blacks are less likely to approve of suicide when an individual has an incurable disease than are whites. However, both whites and blacks are equally likely to disapprove of suicide when an individual has dishonored his or her family or because of bankruptcy. Euthanasia is more acceptable to the general white public than is suicide. Men and women are likely to approve of euthanasia with increased education.

Ramsey and Bagley's (1985) findings suggest a more accepting attitude toward suicide than reported in previous studies. Of the respondents, 90% understood the loneliness and depression associated with suicidal behavior.

REACTIONS TO SURVIVORS OF SUICIDE

Survivors who are bereaved because of the death of a loved one by suicide must deal with their personal grief and at the same time deal with community reactions, which have been found to be more

severe and negative than when death is by any other cause (Cain & Fast, 1972; Calhoun et al., 1982). Negative community reactions bring about reduced emotional support (Haim, 1970; Hatton & Valente, 1981; Whitis, 1972) and, at the same time, blame toward the family for the death (Calhoun, Selby, & Faulstich, 1980; Gordon, Range, & Edwards, 1987; Rudestam & Imbroll, 1983). People are more curious about the nature of a suicidal death than a natural death (Rudestam & Imbroll, 1983; Range & Calhoun, in press). Survivors are more likely to experience guilt and have a lengthy psychological resolution of the grief experience (Parks & Weiss, 1983; Rudestam, 1977). Calhoun et al. (1982) found that bereaved survivors of suicide victims reported feeling socially isolated, rejected, and stigmatized. Shneidman (1972) observed that, from all the varied modes of death, suicide brings the greatest stigma on the survivors and produces greater expectations of discomfort in those who must interact with family members (Shepherd & Barraclough, 1974). This reflects what has been termed *ambivalent avoidance* (Whitis, 1972). The most entrenched attitude taken toward suicide is to ignore it (Haim, 1970). Danto (1977) and Danto and Fast (1966) found that the absence of emotional support often reflects the stigma attached to the act of committing suicide (Cain & Fast, 1966). Calhoun, Selby, and Abernathy (1984) investigated reactions of persons who had experienced suicidal bereavement versus bereavement of death resulting from an accident or natural causes. Potential comforters thought that suicide was a more difficult life experience than other modes of death and that they would have difficulty expressing sympathy and would be more uncomfortable at the funeral. These findings were not as pronounced if the comforter was a close friend to the bereaved person. Thus, in this situation, the cause of death may play a lesser role in determining reactions to the survivors.

Calhoun et al. (1986) examined the social rules that govern interactions with bereaved persons. Rules are beliefs by members of a group about whether a specific behavior should or should not be performed in particular situations (Argyle, Furnham, & Graham, 1981). The pattern of the results suggests that the rules for suicide are more constraining. Judgments about the existence of social rules tend to be more inclusive and extreme in a "should not" direction when death is by suicide. They suggested that although individuals may feel greater compassion for the survivors of suicide (Calhoun, Selby, & Steelman, 1983), they may still avoid the situation for fear of violating one of the rules.

Range and Thompson (1986) found that students viewed people in the community as providing mixed messages or unhelpful messages to those who were bereaved as a result of suicide or homicide but as providing helpful messages to those bereaved as a result of other modes of death. Students viewed themselves as being equally helpful regardless of the cause of death. Students viewed those people who were bereaved as a result of homicide as having a more severe reaction than from any other cause of death. Students viewed those who were bereaved as a result of suicide as reacting about the same as those bereaved because of natural or accidental causes. These differences are contrary to the reports of those who have actually been bereaved as a result of suicide (Range & Calhoun, 1985). It was suggested that the students may have overestimated their own helpfulness.

Several researchers found that a child depicted in a scenario as having committed suicide is perceived as having been psychologically unhealthier than if death had occurred in a different way (Calhoun et al., 1980; Ginn, Range, & Hailey, 1988; Kalish, Reynolds, & Farberow, 1974). This [has] also been found to be true of adolescents (Gordon et al., 1987; Range, Goggin, & Cantrell, in press). Range, Bright, and Ginn (1985) found that people in the community thought that suicidal adolescents were more psychologically disturbed than suicidal children. Community members blamed parents of suicidal adolescents less than they blamed parents of suicidal children and expected to like parents of suicidal adolescents more than parents of suicidal children. It seems people react differently depending on the age of the victim. Ginn et al. (1988) reported that subjects did not attribute psychological disturbance to the parents of a child who committed suicide, but Gordon et al. (1987) found that the mother was also viewed as more psychologically disturbed than if the child had died of natural causes. Also more people are opposed to publishing the cause of death in the newspaper when the cause is sui-

cide (Calhoun et al., 1980; Ginn et al., 1988). Gordon et al. (1987) surveyed parents and their children and found that the parents perceived a youth who died of suicide as more psychologically disturbed than did their adolescent children, but parents expected to experience less tension and have less difficulty in expressing sympathy when visiting the survivors than did their adolescent children. It was found that parents may be more supportive to the bereaved than are adolescents.

Bell (1977) found that college students viewed suicidal peers as cowardly, sick, unpleasant, and disreputable and were much more negative in their attitudes toward peers who attempted suicide and lived than toward those who completed suicide. Linehan (1973) reported that college students ascribed traditional male and female qualities to completed suicide as opposed to attempted suicide. College students perceived completed suicide to be more active and potent, and which may explain why Bell (1977) found that students judged peers who attempted suicide and lived more harshly than those who died.

Wellman and Wellman (1986) conducted two surveys with college students to assess gender differences in attitudes toward suicide. Most men and women recognized that people could be suicidal, did not judge them harshly, and were receptive to and supportive of suicidal people. However, men, more so than women, were likely to have harsher attitudes toward suicidal people and were less likely to discuss the subject with them because of the belief that discussing it would precipitate suicide. Men were more likely to deny that suicidal people showed warning signs, believing it was more an impulsive act, and men were more likely to deny the increase in adolescent suicide, believing the media was exaggerating the incidence. The authors emphasized that most men do not have negative attitudes toward suicide, but men are more likely to have negative attitudes than women.

SUMMARY

Attitudes toward suicide have varied throughout time and across cultures. As this review points out, such widespread assumptions as "life is sacred" are open to interpretation. Even the idea that life should be saved at all costs has been questioned. The issues that are confronted by researchers who investigate society's attitudes toward not only the person who kills her or himself but the parents, family, and friends of that person call for a serious examination. The idea that suicide is a rational or irrational act has been argued. Like most societal problems, suicide is probably not as simple as that. Should the suicide of an individual who is suffering from a terminal illness and whose prognosis calls for a short life with intense pain be labeled a rational, well-thought-out act or the behavior of a psychologically disturbed person?

Opponents of rational suicide equate suicide with psychological disturbance. Thus, they argue that suicide is irrational. Anecdotal clinical evidence, as well as research, examined the demographics and characteristics of suicidal individuals and suggested that suicide is often a well-thought-out plan of action that may not be a result of severe psychological disturbance (Fox & Weissman, 1975; Patsiokas, Clum, & Luscomb, 1979).

Thus, society's view of suicidal behavior appears to be mixed. Current attitudes include maintaining life. However, growing movements that have stressed an individual's right to die in certain situations served to move societal attitudes away from a simplistic dichotomy of good or bad.

REFERENCES

Argyle, M., Furnham, A., & Graham, J. (1981). *Social situations.* Cambridge, England: Cambridge University Press.

Bell, D. (1977). Sex and chronicity as variables affecting attitudes of undergraduates toward peers with suicidal behaviors. *Dissertation Abstracts International, 38,* 3380B.

Cain, A., & Fast, I. (1966). The legacy of suicide: Observations on the pathogenic impact of suicide upon marital partners. *Psychiatry, 29,* 406–441.

Cain, A., & Fast, I. (1972). The legacy of suicide: Observations on the pathogenic impact of suicide upon marital partners. In A. C. Cain (Ed.), *Survivors of suicide.* Springfield, IL: Charles C. Thomas.

Calhoun, L., Abernathy, C., & Selby, J. (1986). The rules of bereavement: Are suicidal deaths different? *Journal of Community Psychology, 14,* 213–218.

Calhoun, L., Selby, J. & Abernathy, C. (1984). Suicidal death: Social reactions to bereaved survivors. *Journal of Psychology, 116,* 225–261.

Calhoun, L., Selby, J., & Faulstich, M. (1980). Reactions to the parents of the child's suicide: A study of social impressions. *Journal of Consulting and Clinical Psychology, 48,* 535–536.

Calhoun, L., Selby, J., & Selby, L. (1982). The psychological aftermath of suicide: An analysis of current evidence. *Clinical Psychological Review, 2,* 409–420.

Calhoun, L., Selby, J., & Steelman, J. (1983). *Individual and social elements in acute grief. A collection of funeral directors' impressions of suicidal deaths.* Unpublished manuscript, University of North Carolina, Charlotte.

Danto, B. (1977). Family survivors of suicide. In B. L. Danto & A. H. Kutscher (Eds.) *Suicide and bereavement* (pp. 11–20). New York: MSS Information Corp.

de Catanzaro, D. (1981). *Suicide and self-damaging behavior: A sociobiological perspective.* New York: Academic Press.

Douglas, J. (1967). *The social meaning of suicide.* Princeton: NJ: Princeton University Press.

Dublin L. (1963). *Suicide: A social and statistical study.* New York: Ronald Press.

Feherman, (1989). Ethical recommendations. *New England Journal of Medicine.*

Fox, K., & Weissman, H. (1975). Suicide attempts and drugs: Contradiction between method and intent. *Social Psychiatry, 10,* 31–38.

Gibbs, N. (1990, March 19). Love and let die. *Time,* pp. 62–71.

Ginn, P., Range, L., & Hailey, B. (1988). Community attitudes toward childhood suicide and attempted suicide. *Journal of Community Psychology, 16,* 144–151.

Ginsburg, G. (1971). Public perceptions and attitudes about suicide. *Journal of Health and Social Behavior, 12,* 200–207.

Gordon, R., Range, L., & Edwards, R. (1987). Generational differences in reactions to adolescent suicide. *Journal of Community Psychology, 15,* 268–273.

Haim, A. (1970). *Adolescent suicide.* (A. M. S. Smith, Trans.). New York: International University Press.

Hatton, C. C., & Valente, S. M. (1981). Bereavement group for parents who suffered a suicidal loss of a child. *Suicide and Life-Threatening Behavior, 11,* 141–150.

Humphry, D. (1987). The case for rational suicide [Letter to the editor] *Suicide and Life-Threatening Behavior, 17,* 335–338.

Johnson, D., Fitch, S., Alston, J., & McIntosh, W. (1980). Acceptance of conditional suicide and euthanasia among adult Americans. *Suicide and Life-Threatening Behavior, 10,* 157–166.

Kalish, R., Reynolds, D., & Farberow, N. (1974). Community attitudes toward suicide. *Community Mental Health Journal, 10,* 301–308.

Klagsburn, F. (1981). *Too young to die—youth and suicide.* New York: Houghton Mifflin.

Kluge, E. (1975). *The practice and death.* New Haven, CT: Yale University Press.

Koller, K., & Slaghuis, W. (1978). Suicide attempts 1973–1977 in urban Hobbart: A further five year follow up reporting a decline. *Australian and New Zealand Journal of Psychiatry, 12,* 169–173.

Lampke, R. (1989). AIDS and the allied health care worker: Fears, fantasies, and facts. *Advances in Thanatology, 7,* 92–103.

Linehan, M. (1973). Suicide and attempted suicide: Study of perceived sex differences. *Perceptual and Motor Skills, 37,* 31–34.

Maris, R. (1986). Basic issues in suicide prevention: Resolutions of liberty and love (the Dublin lecture). *Suicide and Life-Threatening Behavior, 16,* 326–334.

McGinnis, J. (1987). Suicide in America—moving up the public agenda. *Suicide and Life-Threatening Behavior, 18,* 18–32.

Parkes, C., & Weiss, R. (1983). *Physical and psychological responses to suicide in the family—recovery from bereavement.* New York: Basic Books.

Patsiokas, A., Blum, G., Luscomb, R. (1983). Cognitive characteristics of suicide attempters. *Journal of Consulting and Clinical Psychology, 47,* 478–484.

Quinnett, P. (1987). *Suicide the forever decision.* New York: Continuum Publishing.

Ramsay, T., & Bagley, C. (1985). The prevalence of suicidal behaviors, attitudes and associated social experiences in an urban population. *Suicide and Life-Threatening Behavior, 15,* 151–167.

Range, L., Bright, P., & Ginn, P. (1985). Public reactions to child suicide: Effects of age and method used. *Journal of Community Psychology, 113,* 288–294.

Range, L., & Calhoun, L. (1985, March). The impact of type of death on the bereavement experience. In L. G. Calhoun (Chair), *Bereavement: Clinical and social aspects.* Symposium conducted at the annual meeting of the Southeastern Psychological Association.

Range, L., Goggin, W., & Cantrell, P. (in press). The false consensus bias as applied to psychologically disturbed adolescents. *Adolescence.*

Range, L., McDonald, D., & Anderson, H. (1987). Factor structure of Calhoun's youth suicide scale. *Journal of Personality Assessment, 51,* 262–266.

Range, L., & Thompson, K. (1986). Community responses following suicide, homicide and other deaths: The perspective of potential comforters. *Journal of Psychology, 121,* 193–198.

Rudestam, K. (1977). Physical and psychological responses to suicide in the family. *Journal of Consulting and Clinical Psychology, 45,* 162–170.

Rudestam, K., & Imbroll, D. (1983). Societal reactions to a child's death by suicide. *Journal of Consulting and Clinical Psychology, 51,* 461–462.

Sachs, A. (1990, November 28). To my family, my physician, my lawyer and all others whom it may concern. *Time,* p. 70.

Shepherd, T., & Barraclough, B. (1974). The aftermath of suicide. *British Medical Journal, 2,* 600–603.

Schneidman, E. S. (1972). Forward. In A. C. Cain (Ed.), *Survivors of suicide* (pp. ix–xi). Springfield, IL: Charles C. Thomas.

Siegel, K. (1988). Rational suicide. In S. Lesse (Ed.), *What we know about suicidal behavior and how to treat it* (pp. 85–102). Northvale, NJ: Jason Anderson.

Singh, B. (1979). Correlates of attitudes toward euthanasia. *Social Biology, 26,* 247–254.

Singh, B., Williams, J., & Ryther, B. (1986). Public approval of suicide: A situational analysis. *Suicide and Life-Threatening Behavior, 16,* 409–418.

Szasz, T. (1974). *The second sin.* London: Routledge and Kegan Paul.

Weber, W. (1988). What right to die? [Letter to the editor]. *Suicide and Life-Threatening Behavior, 18,* 181–188.

Wellman, M., & Wellman, R. J. (1986). Sex differences in peer responsiveness to suicide ideation. *Suicide and Life-Threatening Behavior, 16,* 360–378.

Whitis, P. (1972). The legacy of a child's suicide. In A. C. Cain (Ed.), *Survivors of suicide* (pp. 155–166). Springfield, IL: Charles C. Thomas.

Unit 5

Unit Selections

Key Points to Consider

❖ Describe how the funeralization process can assist in coping with grief and facilitate the bereavement process. Distinguish between grief, bereavement, and funeralization.

❖ Discuss the psychological, sociological, and theological/philosophical aspects of the funeralization process. How do each of these aspects facilitate the resolution of grief?

❖ Describe and compare each of the following processes: burial, cremation, cryonics, and body donation for medical research. What would be your choice for final disposition of your body? Why would you choose this method, and what effects might this choice have upon your survivors (if any)? Would you have the same or different preferences for a close loved one such as a spouse, child, or parent? Why?

 **Links**   **www.dushkin.com/online/**

These sites are annotated on pages 4 and 5.

Decisions relating to the disposition of the body after death often involve feelings of ambivalence—on the one hand, attachments to the deceased might cause one to be reluctant to dispose of the body, on the other hand, practical considerations make the disposal of the body necessary. Funerals or memorial services provide methods for disposing of a dead body, remembering the deceased, and helping survivors accept the reality of death. They are also public rites of passage that assist the bereaved in returning to routine patterns of social interaction. In contemporary America, 79 percent of deaths involve earth burial and 21 percent involve cremation. These public behaviors, along with the private process of grieving, comprise the two components of the bereavement process.

This unit on the contemporary American funeral begins with a general article on the nature and functions of public bereavement behavior by Michael Leming and George Dickinson. Leming and Dickinson provide an overview of the present practice of funeralization in American society including traditional and alternative funeral arrangements. They also discuss the functions of funerals relative to the sociological, psychological, and ethological needs of adults and children.

In the next article, "Psychocultural Influences on African-American Attitudes towards Death, Dying, and Funeral Rites," Ronald Barrett puts death and dying rituals within a pluralistic and multicultural perspective. Then, "How Different Religions Pay Their Final Respects," by William Whalen, discusses commonalities and differences among many religious traditions. Whalen, along with Thomas Lynch ("Burying the Ungrateful Dead"), then demonstrate that the rituals performed at the funeral are often closely tied to the cultural backgrounds and religious values of the people who perform them.

Linda Goldman's report, "We Can Help Children Grieve: A Child-Oriented Model for Memorializing," discusses methods for preparing children to express their grief and to assist them in the process of memorializing.

The remaining two articles by Cynthia Fox ("A Do-It-Yourself Funeral") and Pat Andrus ("A Time to Mourn") concludes this unit by discussing new trends in funeral rituals and services for the bereaved.

Funerals and Burial Rites

The Contemporary American Funeral

Michael R. Leming
St. Olaf College

George E. Dickinson
College of Charleston

Most people use the words *death, grief,* and *bereavement* imprecisely, which can lead to difficulty in communication. The words are closely interrelated, but each has a specific content or meaning. As discussed in chapter 1, death is that point in time when life ceases to exist. *Death* is an event. It can be attached to a certain day, hour, and minute. *Grief* is an emotion, a very powerful emotion. It is triggered or stimulated by death. Although one can have anticipatory grief prior to the death of a significant other, grief is an emotional response to death. *Bereavement* is the state of having lost a significant other to death. Alternative processes—such as denial, avoidance, and defiance—have been shown by psychologists and psychiatrists to be only aberrations of the grief process and, as such, are not viable means of grief resolution.

The decisions about ultimate method of final **disposition** of the body should be determined by the persons in bereavement. Those charged with these decisions will be guided by their personal values and by the norms of the culture in which they live.

With over three fourths of American deaths occurring in hospitals or other institutions for the care of the sick and infirm, the contemporary process of body disposition begins at the time of death when the body is removed from the institutional setting. Most frequently the body is taken to a funeral home. There, the body is bathed, embalmed, and dressed. It is then placed into a casket selected by the family. Typically, arrangements are made for the ceremony, assuming that a ceremony is to follow. The funeral director, in consultation with the family, will determine the type, time, place and day of the ceremony. In most instances, the ceremony will have a religious content (Pine, 1971). The procedure just described is followed in approximately 75 percent of funerals. Alternatives to this procedure will be examined later in this chapter.

Following this ceremony, final disposition of the body is made by either earth burial (79 percent) or cremation (21 percent). (These percentages are approximate national averages and will vary by region.) The bereavement process will then be followed by a period of post-funeral adjustment for the family.

HOW THE FUNERAL MEETS THE NEEDS OF THE BEREAVED

Paul Irion (1956) has described the following needs of the bereaved: reality, expression of grief, social support, and meaningful context for the death. For Irion, the funeral is an experience of significant personal value insofar as it meets the religious, social, and psychological needs of the mourners. Each of these must be met for bereaved individuals to return to everyday living and, in the process, resolve their grief.

The *psychological* focus of the funeral is based on the fact that grief is an emotion. Edgar Jackson (1963) has indicated that grief is the other side of the coin of love. He contends that if a person has never loved the deceased—never had an emotional investment of some type and degree—he or she will not grieve upon death. Evidence of this can easily be demonstrated by the number of deaths that we hear, see, or read about daily that do not have an impact on us unless we have some kind of emotional involvement with those deceased persons. We can read of 78 deaths in a plane crash and not grieve over any of them unless we personally knew the individuals killed. Exceptions to the preceding might include the death of a celebrity or other public figure, when people experience a sense of grief even though there has never been any personal contact.

In his original work on the symptomatology of grief, Erich Lindemann (1944) stressed this concept of grief and its importance as a step in the resolution of grief. He defines how the emotion of grief must support the reality and finality of death. As long as the finality of death is avoided, Lindemann believes, grief resolution is impeded. For this reason, he strongly recommends that the bereaved persons view the dead. When the living confront the dead, all of the intellectualization and avoidance techniques break down. When we can say, "He or she is dead, I am alone, and from this day forward my life will be forever different," we have broken through the devices of denial and avoidance and have accepted the reality of death. It is only at this point that we can begin to withdraw the emotional capital that we have invested in the deceased and seek to create new relationships with the living.

On the other hand, viewing the corpse can be very traumatic for some. Most people are not accustomed to seeing a cold body and a significant other stretched out with eyes closed. Indeed, for some this scene may remain in their memories for a life-time. Thus, they remember the cold corpse, not the warm, responsive person. Whether or not to view the body is not a cut-and-dried decision. Many factors should be taken into account when this decision is made.

Grief resolution is especially important for family members, but others are affected also—the neighbors, the business community in some instances, the religious community in most instances, the health care community, and the circle of friends and associates (many of whom may be unknown to the family). All of these groups will grieve to some extent the death of their relationship with the deceased. Thus, many people are affected by the death. These affected persons will seek not only a means of expressing their grief over the death, but also a network of support to help cope with their grief.

Sociologically, the funeral is a social event that brings the chief mourners and the members of society into a confrontation with death. The funeral becomes a vehicle to bring persons of all walks of life and degrees of relationship to the deceased together for expression and support. It is for this reason that in our contemporary culture the funeral becomes an occasion to which no one is invited but to which all may come. This was not always the case, and some cultures make the funeral ceremony an "invitation only" experience. It is perhaps for this reason that private funerals (restricted to the family or a special list of persons) have all but disappeared in our culture. (The possible exception to this statement is a funeral for a celebrity—where participation by the public is limited to media coverage.)

At a time when emotions are strong, it is important that human interaction and social support become high priorities. A funeral can provide this atmosphere. To grieve alone can be devastating because it becomes necessary for that lone person to absorb all of the feelings into himself or herself. It has often been said that "joy shared is joy increased"; surely grief shared is grief diminished. People need each other at times when they have intense emotional experiences.

A funeral is in essence a onetime kind of "support group" to undergird and support those grieving persons. A funeral provides a conducive social environment for mourning. We may go to the funeral home either to visit with the bereaved or to work through our own grief.

Most of us have had the experience of finding it difficult to discuss a death with a member of the family. We seek the proper atmosphere, time, and place. It is during the funeral, the wake, the shivah, or the visitation with the bereaved that we are provided with the opportunity to express our condolences and sympathy comfortably.

Anger and guilt are often deeply felt at the time of death and will surface in words and actions. They are permitted within the funeral atmosphere as honest and candid expressions of grief, whereas at other times they might bring criticism and reprimand. The funeral atmosphere says in essence, "You are okay, I am okay; we have some strong feelings, and now is the time to express and share them for the benefit of all." Silence, talking, feeling, touching, and all means of sharing can be expressed without the fear of their being inappropriate.

Another function of the funeral is to provide a *theological* or *philosophical* perspective to facilitate grieving and to provide a context of meaning in which to place one of life's most significant experiences. For the majority of Americans, the funeral is a religious rite or ceremony (Pine, 1971). Those grievers who do not possess a religious creed or orientation will define or express death in the context of the values that the deceased and the grievers find important. Theologically or philosophically, the funeral functions as an attempt to bring meaning to the death and life of the deceased individual. For the religiously oriented person, the belief system will perhaps bring an understanding of the afterlife. Others may see only the end of biological life and the beginning of symbolic immortality created by the effects of one's life on the lives of others. The funeral should be planned to give meaning to whichever value context is significant for the bereaved.

"Why?" is one of the most often asked questions upon the moment of death or upon being told that someone we know has died. Though the funeral cannot provide the final answer to this question, it can place death within a context of meaning that is significant to those who mourn. If it is religious in context, the theology, creed, and articles of faith confessed by the mourners will give them comfort and assurance as to the meaning of death. Others who have developed a personally meaningful philosophy of life and death will seek to place the death in that philosophical context.

Cultural expectations typically require that we dispose of the dead with ceremony and dignity. The funeral can also ascribe importance to the remains of the dead.

THE NEEDS OF CHILDREN AND THEIR ATTENDANCE AT FUNERALS

For children, as well as for their elders, the funeral ceremony can be an experience of value and significance. At a very early age, children are interested in any type of family reunion, party, or celebration. To be excluded from the funeral may create questions and doubts in the minds of children as to why they are not permitted to be a part of an important family activity.

Another question to be considered when denying the child an opportunity to participate in postdeath activities is what goes through the child's mind when such participation is denied. Children deal with other difficult situations in life, and when denied this opportunity, many will fantasize. Research suggests that these fantasies may be negative, destructive, and at times more traumatic than the situation from which the children are excluded.

Children also should not be excluded from activities prior to the funeral service. They should be permitted to attend the visitation, wake, or shivah. (In some situations it would be wise to permit children to confront the deceased prior to the public visitation.) It is obvious that children should not be forced into this type of confrontation, but, by the same token, children who are curious and desire to be involved should not be denied the opportunity.

Children will react at their own emotional levels, and the questions that they ask will usually be asked at their level of comprehension. Two important rules to follow: Never lie to the child, and do not overanswer the child's question.

At the time of the funeral, parents have two concerns about their child's behavior at funerals. The first concern is that the child will have difficulty observing the grief of others—particularly if the child has never seen an adult loved one cry. The second concern is that parents themselves become confused when the child's emotional reactions may be different than their own. If the child is told of a death and responds by saying, "Oh, can I go out and play?" the parents may interpret this as denial or as a suppressed negative reaction to the death. Such a reaction can increase emotional concern by the parents. However, if the child's response is viewed as only a first reaction, and if the child is provided with loving, caring, and supportive attention, the child will ordinarily progress into an emotional resolution of the death.

The final reasons for involving children in postdeath activities are related to the strength and support that children give other grievers. They often provide positive evidence of the fact that life goes on. In other instances, because they have been an important part of the life of the deceased, their presence is symbolic testimony to the immortality of the deceased. Furthermore, it is not at all unusual for children to change the atmosphere surrounding bereavement from one of depression and sadness to one of laughter, verbalization, and celebration. Many times children do this by their normal behavior, without any understanding of the kind of contribution being made.

Psychocultural Influences on African-American Attitudes towards Death, Dying and Funeral Rites

Ronald K. Barrett

. . .

THE AMERICAN FUNERAL RITES

An historical and retrospective look at the American funeralization process over a four-hundred-year period reveals a number of changes and evolving traditions, demonstrating causality and coincidence in the evolution of the contemporary American funeral industry [24]. In the early years of our country the abundance of lumber and land allowed people to build large homes to shelter often large, extended families. Many of their ceremonial occasions were held in the home. The 1880s characterized the undertaker as a tradesman and merchant who supplied materials and funeral paraphernalia (i.e., caskets, carriages, door badges and scarfs, special clothing, memorial cards, chairs, candles, and other ornaments). By the end of the 19th century the undertakers began to assume a much larger role—assisting more with the deposition of the dead. After the Civil War, embalming became increasingly a conventional American custom, and most states required funeral directors and embalmers to be certified by state licensing. In the 1880s the National Funeral Directors Association began to regulate the profession and established minimum standards of service. With the advent of smaller houses and increasing urbanization, the funeral "parlour" became the place for the preparation of the dead, replacing the family parlor. Although the one-room funeral parlor became the substitute ceremonial room as people no longer used their homes, the custom of survivors sitting up in a vigil with the dead until burial, called the "wake," was often held in the family parlor [15].

The contemporary funeralization process is initialized by the authorization of the funeral home, which removes the body from the place of death. Frequently, upon removing the body, the funeral home begins to prepare the body via bathing, embalming, and dressing. Afterwards it is placed in a casket selected by the family. The traditional wake is an opportunity for members of the community to "pay their respects" and visit with the family prior to the formal funeral service. The preference for viewing or having the body present is optional. Similarly, arrangements for the ceremony and the details of the funeral ritual (i.e., time, place, type of service, etc.) vary and often depend upon family preferences, religion, and ethnicity. In most contemporary American funerals a public rite or ceremony with a religious content is typical in 75 percent of funerals [24]. Following the funeral ceremony, the final disposition of the body is made. The survivors must choose between either burial (85%), cremation (10%), or entombment (5%) [9].[1]

THE AFRICAN PERSPECTIVE ON DEATH AND FUNERAL RITES

The African cultural heritage provides enormous resources for understanding of life and death. According to Opuku [25], these resources are the product of many centuries of experienced and mature reflection and represent Africa's own insights into the meaning and significance of life and death.

According to Chief Musamasli Nangol, the traditional African belief is that in the beginning God intended man to live forever [26]. African scholar and writer John B. Mbiti supports this view [27]. According to Mbiti, there

---

[1]The percentages are based on national averages and may vary by geographic region.

From *Personal Care in an Impersonal World: A Multidimensional Look at Bereavement,* edited by John D. Morgan, 1993, pp. 216–230. © 1993 by Baywood Publishing Company, Inc. Reprinted by permission.

are hundreds of myths in Africa concerning ideas about the origin of death—some documented and researched, others are unrecorded and undocumented. According to traditional African beliefs, God gave the first men one or more of the three gifts of immortality, resurrection, and the ability to become young again. But all three gifts were somehow lost and death came into the world. There are many different explanations as to how the loss took place and how death came about [28].

The variation in myths reflects a general belief that death came about by mistake, but has since remained due to some blame laid upon people themselves (especially women), animals, and, in some cases, evil spirits or monsters. Death therefore spoiled the original paradise of men, separating God from men and bringing many associated sorrows and agonies to men. While there are many variations in beliefs about the origin of death there are no myths in Africa about how death might one day be overcome or removed from the world [27].

Death was accepted as one of the rhythms of life, firmly integrated into the totality of life as an unalterable sequence. Life without death was viewed as clearly contrary to our nature as human beings [25]. A traditional Asante myth illustrates this traditional African view. The Asante believe that when the early human beings started experiencing death, they pleaded with God to put a stop to death. Their request was granted and for three years no one died; however, strangely enough, no one gave birth to a child during this time. The people found this situation unbearable and again pleaded with God, this time to grant them the ability to have children even if it meant accepting death also. Consequently, among the Asante, death and birth are complementary—death taking away members from the society, while birth compensates for the losses death inflicts on the community [25].

Therefore, the traditional African attitude towards death is positive and accepting and comprehensively integrated into the totality of life. Life in the African cultural tradition is so whole that death does not destroy its wholeness. Death becomes, therefore, a prolongation of life. And, instead of a break between life and death, there is continuity between the two [29, p. 138]. According to Mbiti, death is regarded as a journey to man's original place as home, and not as an end or an annihilation [30, p. 157]. The deceased goes to join the ancestors, to live in the land of the spirits ("living dead").

This means that the relationship between the living and the "living dead," as Mbiti describes them, remains unbroken and that the community of the living and the community of the "living dead" experience a reciprocal permeability characterized by a constant interaction between the two communities. This wholeness of life expresses itself in the fact that the African family as community is made up of the living as well as the dead. Therefore, the belief in a supernatural or extra-human dimension of the family and community is an extension of the traditional African belief system and world view of life and death [25].

The traditional African funeral rites and ritual reflect a view of death as sorrowful and important. Even though death is accepted as part of life, it is regarded as impolite to state bluntly that someone is dead. It reflects good breeding and courteous comportment to refer to the death of someone in euphemistic terms (i.e., "has gone home," "has joined the ancestors," etc.). Throughout the mourning period, which may last up to three moons, the close relatives of the deceased may not do any work. These tasks are eagerly performed by distant relatives and community friends. Women tend to wail, while men sing and dance, often in praise of the departed one. According to African customs, men are not to cry in front of women because they would appear weak before the very group they are to protect. It is therefore reasonable to assume the traditional funeral masks worn by men may have served as a cover of facial affect as well as a funeral ritual ornament. The body of the deceased is displayed either inside the house or outside on a veranda for public view. The body is displayed until all the relatives have gathered and paid their respects. Any relative who fails to show up for the funeral is often accused or suspected of having bewitched the deceased. A failure to acknowledge the dead is a social offense which is punishable in some communities. Traditional African customs require that gifts of money be

Cultural Groups	Orientation		Life View		Ritual Priority		Funeral Social Sig.		Investment		Funeral Disposition
	Avoid	Accept	Life-Death	Death-Birth	Primary	Secondary	Low	High	Low	High	
AFRICAN		✓		✓	✓			✓		✓	GROUND BURIAL
AFRICAN-AMERICAN		✓		✓	✓			✓		✓	GROUND BURIAL

Figure 1. Comparative and descriptive model of traditional African and African-American Funeral Rites.

given to the family of the deceased to help defray funeral expenses [25].

The African funeral rites vary according to the social status and importance of the deceased. The funeral for children and unmarried people is usually simple and often attended by only close relatives, whereas the funeral for a chief or a king could take on the significance of a national affair requiring much preparation, pomp, and expense [27]. African customs vary considerably in terms of the extent and methods used to prepare the body—sometimes ritually and other times without formality. Generally, the disposal of the body takes place the same day or the next day due to the effects of the tropical heat that accelerate decomposition. In most parts of Africa the traditional ground burial is most commonly favored, although there are vast variations in terms of place of burial, position of the grave, the position of the body in the grave, and grave markings [25–27].

Often after the initial shock of a death and the customary funeral rites, the atmosphere of sadness is soon replaced by laughter and the sharing of funny stories about the dead. When the deceased is a person of note, such as a chief or king, the burial often assumes a carnival atmosphere accompanied with music from drums, dancing, and food for the assembled mourners. Often, the funeral festivities may go on for some time until the community agrees that the important person has been properly acknowledged and properly escorted to the next world. According to custom and tradition, a child of the same sex as the deceased will be born into the family and, according to African custom and tradition, given the name of the deceased—honoring the deceased and symbolizing the wholeness of life [25, 26, 31].

THE AFRICAN-AMERICAN PERSPECTIVE ON DEATH AND FUNERAL RITES

The African-American contemporary response to death is intimately connected and deeply rooted in the traditional African tradition, yet tempered by the American sociocultural experience [32]. Much has been written about the traditional African response to death, yet very few people have acknowledged the African-American response. The African-American funeralization practices and customs have evolved over centuries, reflecting a characteristic disposition and tradition rich in cultural symbolism and customs deeply rooted in and resembling the African experience (see Figure 1).

The earliest, most authoritative work on African-American attitudes towards death and dying is contained in a classic cross-cultural study by Kalish and Reynolds [3]. In this largest study of its type, the researchers examine 100 or more persons in four ethnic groups (African-American, Japanese-American, Mexican-

American, and Anglo). Inevitably, a number of ethnic differences were found.

To be an African-American in America is to be part of a history told in terms of contact with death and coping with death. For the Black race in the era of slavery, death or other forms of personal loss could come at any time, at any age, randomly, and often at the whim of someone else [3]. According to Chapman, African-American artists reflect this history in artistic expression in music, spirituals, poetry, novels, drama, and visual arts [34]. Kalish and Reynolds' survey data indicate that contemporary Black Americans also have significantly more contact with homicide, accidents, and war-time deaths than any other group.

The American sociocultural attitudes and behavior in response to death have been termed "death-avoiding" [1] and "death denying" [18, 20]. However, African-Americans tend to be more accepting and less fearful of death than the three other ethnic groups studied [3]. In a study by Myers, Wass, and Murphey, elderly African-Americans showed a higher level of fear towards death than elderly whites [34]. However, researchers [2, 3] argue that devout and true believers can cope with death more effectively than those with vague or ambivalent views. Kalish and Reynolds report findings that African-Americans perceive themselves as more religious than Anglos and tend to rely on their belief systems more in times of crisis and need [3]. This observation lends more support to the perception of Blacks as less fearful of death than Anglos [35].

The various art forms (i.e., music, literature, theatre, and visual arts, etc.) mirror the attitudes of African-Americans towards death [36]. A consistent theme of death is reflected and often connected to a sense of solace in a theology and belief in the afterlife and promise of a better life [33]. Similarly, another study conducted in

CULTURAL GROUPS	ORIENTATION	
	AVOIDANCE	ACCEPTANCE
AFRICAN		Opuku (1989) Nangol (1986) Mbiti (1975) Parinder (1976)
AFRICAN-AMERICAN	Myers, Wass & Murphy (1980)	Kalish and Reynolds (1981) Martin & Wrightsman (1965) Lewis (1971) Nichols (1989) Fenn (1989) Connor (1989)
AMERICAN	Rando (1984) Kübler-Ross (1969) Leming and Dickinson (1985) Kavanaugh (1972) Feifel (1959) Feifel (1971) Mitford (1963) Kastenbaum and Aisenberg (1972)	

Figure 2. Cultural influences on attitudes towards death.

Detroit showed that African-Americans, substantially more than Anglos, believed that people should live as long as they can, and that helplessness, but not pain and suffering, would justify dying [37]. Kalish and Reynolds report findings that African-Americans are more likely than Anglos to disapprove of allowing people who want to die to do so [3]. The basic premise appears to hold true: whether it is their religiousness or their survival ordeal, African-Americans express a high acceptance of life and death [3].

Elaine Nichols' *The Last Miles of the Way* is the most comprehensive and authoritative documented anthropological study of African-American cultural traditions and funeral rituals in the southeastern United States (i.e. the South Carolina low-lands) [32]. Nichols' work supports and carefully documents the African cultural origin of many African-American beliefs, traditions, and practices in funeral rites. Nichols' efforts also illustrate and detail the intricate symbolism of burials and grave markings. Fenn also supports Nichols' thesis of African cultural roots in grave markings as Fenn documents methods and symbolism rooted in African Kongo traditions [38]. An anthropological analysis of African-American mortuary practices by Conner [39], also supports Elaine Nichols' classic and insightful scholarly work.[2] While a number of aspects of Nichols' findings may be unique to the southeastern region of the United States (i.e., South Carolina), striking similarities in the African-American experience in other regions lend support to the generalizability of similar cultural influences and behaviors in the subculture of the African-American experience.

The available research [3, 39, 40] provides documented support of the thesis that many of the attitudes, beliefs, and traditions regarding funeral rites, death and dying are deeply rooted in African cultural traditions. The African-American attitudes, beliefs, and funeral rites are also significantly influenced by American attitudes, beliefs, and cultural traditions regarding death, dying, and funeral rites. These studies make a significant contribution to our knowledge and understanding of the African-American experience; however, more research and study is needed to understand better death-related behaviors and also provide needed documentation of a very important and regarded sacred psychocultural complex tradition.

African-American attitudes toward funeral rites have remained for too long largely undocumented and lacking in systematic study and observation. Halloween Lewis' [41] analysis of the role of the church and religion in the life of southern Blacks suggests that the religious connection took on special meaning in funeral customs. Lewis notes variations occurring according to the com-

---

[2]Elaine Nichols' unprecedented anthropological work involved the procurement and analysis of physical evidence and cultural artifacts obtained from both library research and private individual collectors that are a part of a special exhibit in the South Carolina State Museum scheduled for a national tour.

CULTURAL GROUPS	LIFE VIEW	
	LIFE-DEATH	DEATH-BIRTH
AFRICAN		Opuku (1989) Mbiti (1969) Methuh (1982) Mulago (1969)
AFRICAN-AMERICAN		Lomax (1970) Chapman (1968) Nichols (1989) Fenn (1989) Conner (1989)
AMERICAN	Rando (1984) Leming and Dickinson (1985) Kastenbaum and Aisenberg (1972) Kearl (1989) Ranum (1974)	

Figure 3. Cultural influences on attitudes towards death.

CULTURAL GROUPS	RITUAL PRIORITY		FUNERAL SOCIAL SIG.	
	PRIMARY	SECONDARY	LOW	HIGH
AMERICAN	Opuku (1969) Mbiti (1969) Nangol (1969)			Opuku (1989) Mbiti (1969) Nangol (1969)
AFRICAN-AMERICAN	Kalish and Reynolds (1981) Chapman (1968) Nelson (1971) Carter (1971) Nichols (1989) Fielding (1989) Fenn (1989) Conner (1989)			Kalish and Reynolds (1981) Chapman (1968) Nelson (1971) Carter (1971) Nichols (1989) Fielding (1989) Fenn (1989) Conner (1989)
AMERICAN	Mitford (1963)	Reather (1971) Kübler-Ross Gorer (1955)	Reather (1971) Gorer (1955) Harmer (1971)	Mitford (1963) Fulton (1965)

Figure 4. Cultural influences on attitudes towards death.

CULTURAL GROUPS	INVESTMENT		FUNERAL DISPOSITION
	LOW	HIGH	
AFRICAN		Opuku (1989) Nangol (1986) Mbiti (1975)	Ground Burial Opuku (1989) Nangol (1986) Mbiti (1975) Fenn (1989) Nichols (1989)
AFRICAN-AMERICAN		Kalish and Reynolds (1981) Nichols (1989) Fenn (1989) Conner (1989) Fielding (1989)	Ground Burial Kalish and Reynolds (1981) Nichols (1989) Fenn (1989) Conner (1989) Fielding (1989)
AMERICAN		Mitford (1963) Raether (1971) De Spelder and Strickland (1987) Tegg (1876)	Ground Burial Cremation (10%) Emtombment (5%) Leming and Dickinson (1985)

Figure 5. Cultural influences on attitudes towards death.

munity reputation of the deceased, family wishes, and local church practices. As is common among Protestants, most African-American Protestant churches have no formally prescribed funeral ritual dictated by church hierarchy. Local church custom is followed [42]. According to the denominational procedure outlined in Habenstein and Lamers [8], the only generalizations that can really be made are: 1) that family members can select the equipment, music, participants, and place of service without dogmatic restriction, and 2) that the minister leads the procession from church to the funeral coach and from the coach to grave site, positioning himself at the head of the grave. This leaves room for considerable variation [3].

While regional and denominational backgrounds influencing the African-American funeral rites vary, there are some striking similarities linked to traditional African-American beliefs and traditions. In a social context where people are treated like objects and with minimal respect, and the channels by which respect can be achieved are blocked, it is understandable for victims to desperately seek a way to affirm themselves and confirm some sense of self-worth and positive self-identity [3]. African-American funerals in the African-American subculture represent a posthumous attempt for dignity and esteem denied and limited by the dominant culture [32, 40]. Funerals in the African-American experience historically are "primary rituals" of symbolic importance. Kalish and Reynolds'[3] survey reveals that African-Americans were more likely to have taken out life and burial insurance than any other group surveyed [3]. It appears that funeral pre-arrangements, wills, and insurance represent psychological readiness, as these are the most practical arrangements that people can make for death. As expected, Kalish and Reynolds report that older African-Americans are more likely to have made death arrangements than middle-aged or younger adults [3].

The African-American mourners, like the African mourners, were more likely to depend upon the church and the community (extended family) for support during bereavement and mourning [40]. Unlike the other ethnic groups surveyed, African-Americans were more likely to rely on friends, church members, neighbors, and non-relatives for practical assistance consistent with the finding that devout believers had less death anxiety, those active in churches had more traditional sources of spiritual and social support [3].

The social support of family and friends is important to those in mourning. Since a death is a significant event and the funeral is an important social occasion, social expectations require participation and some expression of condolence. It is a standard custom that if one cannot attend the funeral, flowers or other expressions of con-

dolences should be sent. The African-American funeral is indeed a primary ritual and a focal occasion with a big social gathering after the funeral and the closest thing to a family union that might ever take place [32, 40, 43].

Kalish and Reynolds [3] report that the great majority of African-American respondents expressed opposition to elaborate funerals; did not expect friends to participate in covering funeral costs; preferred a funeral with only close friends and relatives; desired African-American clergymen and funeral directors; did not want a wake; wanted the funeral in the church; did not oppose an autopsy; and wanted to be buried. Overall, the African-American funeral is an important event characterized by a programmed atmosphere that is official, ritualistic, serious, and dignified.

ACKNOWLEDGMENTS

The author wishes to acknowledge Luvenia Morant Addison; Dorothy Addison Barrett; Deborah Freathy, Graduate Research Assistant, Loyola Marymount University; Elaine Nichols, Curator, South Carolina State Museum; Harri Close, President, National Funeral Directors & Morticians Association, Inc.; John Hill, III, Chief Administrator, Angelus Funeral Home; Chief Medical Examiner and Staff, Los Angeles County Coroners Office.

REFERENCES

1. R. Kastenbaum and B. R. Aisenberg, The *Psychology of Death*, Springer, New York, 1972.
2. E. Kübler-Ross, *On Death and Dying*, Macmillan, New York, 1969.
3. R. Kalish and D. Reynolds, *Death and Ethnicity: A Psychocultural Study*, Baywood, Amityville, New York, 1981.
4. J. Choron, *Death and Western Thought*, The Macmillan Company, New York, 1963.
5. R. Huntington and P. Metcalf, *Celebration of Death: The Anthropology of Mortuary Ritual*, Cambridge, Cambridge, 1979.
6. D. C. Rosenblatt, Grief in Cross-Cultural and Historical Perspective, in *Death and Dying*, P. F. Pegg and E. Metza (eds.), Pitman Press, London, 1981.
7. M. McGoldrick, P. Hines, E. Lee, and G. H. Preto, Mourning Rituals: How Culture Shapes the Experience of Loss, *Networker*, 1986.
8. W. R. Habenstein and M. W. Lamers, *Funeral Customs the World Over*, Bulfin, Milwaukee, 1963.
9. R. M. Leming and E. G. Dickinson, *Understanding Dying, Death, and Bereavement*, Holt, Rinehart and Winston, New York, 1985.
10. R. P. Cuzzort and W. E. King, *Twentieth Century Social Thought*, Holt, Rinehart and Winston, New York, 1980.
11. J. R. Averill, Grief: Its Nature and Significance, *Psychological Bulletin*, 70:61, 1968.
12. E. Durkheim, *The Elementary Forms of Religious Life*, Macmillan, New York, 1915.
13. M. C. Kearl, *Endings—A Sociology of Death and Dying*, Oxford, New York, 1989.
14. C. Geerty, *The Interpretations of Cultures: Selected Essays*, Basic Books, New York, 1973.
15. L. A. DeSpelder and L. A. Strickland, *The Last Dance: Encountering Death and Dying*, Mayfield, Mountain View, California, 1987.
16. A. M. Hocart, Death Customs, in *Encyclopedia of the Social Sciences 5*, E. R. A. Seligman and A. Johnson (eds.), Macmillan, New York, 1937.
17. P. G. Mandelbaum, Social Issues of Funeral Rites, in *The Meaning of Death*, H. Feifel (ed.), McGraw-Hill, New York, 1959.

---

[3]The term "primary ritual" is used in this context to refer to an event of primary, major importance in that social context. (Contrastingly, a "secondary ritual" is an event of lesser social priority or significance—informal gatherings, family meetings, local holidays, etc.)

18. T. A. Rando, *Grief, Dying and Death,* Research Press Co., Champaign, Illinois, 1984.
19. R. E. Kavanaugh, *Facing Death,* Penguin, Baltimore, Maryland, 1971.
20. H. Feiffel, The Meaning of Death in American Society: Implications for Education, 1971.
21. G. Gorer, *Death, Grief & Mourning,* Crescent Press, London, 1965.
22. H. Feifel, *The Meaning of Death,* McGraw-Hill, New York, 1959.
23. J. Mitford, *The American Way of Death,* Simon and Schuster, New York, 1963.
24. H. C. Raether, The Place of the Funeral: The Role of the Funeral Director in Contemporary America, *Omega,* 2, pp. 136–149, 1971.
25. K. A. Opuku, African Perspectives on Death and Dying, in *Perspectives on Death and Dying,* A. Berger, P. Badham, J. Berger, V. Cerry, and J. Beloff (eds.) The Charles Press, Philadelphia, 1989.
26. C. M. Nangoli, *No More Lies About Africa,* African Heritage, East Orange, New Jersey, 1988.
27. J. S. Mbiti, *Introduction to African Religion,* Heinemann, London, 1975.
28. E. G. Parinder, *African Mythology,* Paul Hamlyn, London, 1967.
29. V. Mulago, Vital Participation: The Cohesive Principle of the Bantu Community, in *Biblical Revelation and African Beliefs,* K. Dickson and P. Ellingworth (eds.), Butterworth, London, 1979.
30. J. S. Mbiti, *African Religions and Philosophy,* Heinemann, London, 1969.
31. I. E. Metuh, *God and Man in African Religion: A Case of the Igbo of Nigeria,* G. Chapman, London, 1982.
32. E. Nichols (ed.), *The Last Miles of the Way: African American Homegoing Traditions 1890–Present,* Dependable, Columbia, South Carolina, 1989.
33. A. Chapman (ed.), *Black Voices: An Anthology of Afro-American Literature,* New American Library, New York, 1968.
34. J. E. Myers, H. Wass, and M. Murphey, Ethnic Differences in Death Anxiety among the Elderly, *Death Education,* 4, pp. 237–244, 1980.
35. D. S. Martin and L. Wrightsman, The Relationship between Religious Behaviour and Concern about Death, *Journal of Social Psychology,* 65, pp. 317–323, 1965.
36. A. Lomax, The Homogeneity of African-Afro-American Musical Style, in *Afro-American Anthropology,* N. E. Whitten and J. F. Szwed (eds.), Free Press, New York, 1970.
37. R. Koenig, N. S. Goldner, R. Kresojevich, and G. Lockwood, Ideas About Illness of Elderly Black and White in an Urban Hospital, *Aging and Human Development,* 2, pp. 217–225, 1971.
38. E. A. Fenn, Honouring the Ancestors: Kongo-American Graves in the American South, in *The Last Miles of the Way,* E. Nichols (ed.), Dependable, Columbia, South Carolina, 1989.
39. C. Connor, Archaeological Analysis of African-American Mortuary Behaviour, in *The Last Miles of the Way,* Dependable, Columbia, South Carolina, 1989.
40. H. U. Fielding, Mourning and Burying the Dead: Experiences of a Lowcountry Funeral Director, in *The Last Miles of the Way,* Dependable, Columbia, South Carolina, 1989.
41. H. Lewis, Blackways of Kent: Religion and Salvation, in *The Black Church in America,* H. M. Nelson, et al. (eds.), Basic Books, New York, 1971.
42. H. M. Nelson, et al. (eds.), *The Black Church in America,* Basic Books, New York, 1971.
43. W. B. Carter, Suicide, Death, and Ghetto Life, *Life-Threatening Behaviour,* L. 1971.

BIBLIOGRAPHY

Abrahamson, H., *The Origin of Death: Studies in African Mythology,* Almgvist, Uppsala, 1951.
Balandier, G. and Maguet, J. *Dictionary of Black African Civilization,* Leon Amiel, New York, 1974.
Boulby, J., Process of Mourning, *International Journal of Psycho-Analysis,* 43, pp. 314–340, Grune and Statton, New York. Reprinted in G. E. Daniels (ed.), 1965, *New Perspectives in Psychoanalysis,* 1961.
Feifel, H., The Taboo on Death, *The American Behavioral Scientist,* 6, 1963.
Fulton, R., The Sacred and the Secular: Attitudes of the American Public toward Death, Funerals, and Funeral Directors, in *Death and Identity,* R. Fulton (ed.), Wiley, New York, 1965.
Goody, J., *Death, Property, and the Ancestors: A Study of the Mortuary Customs of the LoDagaa of West Africa,* Stock, London, 1962.
Harmer, R., Funerals, Fantasy, and Flight, *Omega,* 2, pp. 127–135, 1971.
Idowu, E. B., *African Traditional Religion,* SCM Press, London, 1973.
Jackson, M., The Black Experience with Death: A Brief Analysis through Black Writings, *Omega,* 3, pp. 203–209, 1972.
Kopytoff, E., Ancestors as Elders in Africa, *Africa,* 41, 1971.
Kutscher, A. H., *Death and Bereavement,* Charles C. Thomas, Springfield, Illinois, 1969.
Lindemann, E., Symptomatology and Management of Acute Grief, *American Journal of Psychiatry,* 101. Reprinted in R. Fulton (ed.) (1965) *Death and Identity,* Wiley, New York, 1944.
Lend, F. H., Why Do We Weep? *Journal of Social Psychology,* 1, 1930.
Opuku, K. A., Death and Immortality in the African Religious Heritage, in *Death and Immortality in the Religions of the World,* P. Badham and L. Badham (eds.), Paragon, New York, 1987.
Parinder, E. G., *African Traditional Religion,* SPCK, London, 1962.
Pinkney, A., *Black Americans,* Prentice Hall, Englewood Cliffs, New Jersey, 1969.
Ranum, P. M., *Western Attitudes toward Death: From the Middle Ages to the Present,* Johns Hopkins University Press, Baltimore, 1974.
Tegg, W., *The Last Act Being the Funeral Rites of Nations and Individuals,* William Tegg & Co., London, 1876.
Thomas, L. R., Litany of Home—Going—Going Forth: The African Concept of Time, Eternity and Social Ontology, in *The Last Miles of the Way,* E. Nichols, Dependable, Columbia, South Carolina, 1989.
Zahan, D., The *Religion, Spirituality, and Thought of Traditional Africa,* E. Martin and L. M. Martin (trans.), University of Chicago, Chicago, 1979.

How different religions pay their final respects

From mummies to cremation to drive-up wakes, funeral rituals reflect religious traditions going back thousands of years as well as up-to-the-minute fads.

William J. Whalen

Most people in the United States identify themselves as Protestants; thus, most funerals follow a similar form. Family and friends gather at the funeral home to console one another and pay their last respects. The next day a minister conducts the funeral service at the church or mortuary; typically the service includes hymns, prayers, a eulogy, and readings from the Bible. In 85 percent of the cases today, the body is buried after a short grave-side ceremony. Otherwise the body is cremated or donated to a medical school.

But what could be called the standard U.S. funeral turns out to be the funeral of choice for only a minority of the rest of the human race. Other people, even other Christians, bury their dead with more elaborate and, to outsiders, even exotic rites.

How your survivors will dispose of your body will in all likelihood be determined by the religious faith you practiced during your life because funeral customs reflect the theological beliefs of a particular faith community.

For example, the Parsi people of India neither bury nor cremate their dead. Parsis, most of whom live in or near Bombay, follow the ancient religion of Zoroastrianism. Outside Bombay, Parsis erected seven Towers of Silence in which they perform their burial rites. When someone dies, six bearers dressed in white bring the corpse to one of the towers. The Towers of Silence have no roofs; within an hour, waiting vultures pick the body clean. A few days later the bearers return and cast the remaining bones into a pit. Parsis believe that their method of disposal avoids contaminating the soil, the water, and the air.

Out of the ashes

The Parsis' millions of Hindu neighbors choose cremation as their usual burial practice. Hindus believe that as long as the physical body exists, the essence of the person will remain nearby; cremation allows the essence, or soul, of the person to continue its journey into another incarnation.

Hindus wash the body of the deceased and clothe it in a shroud decorated with flowers. They carry the body to a funeral pyre, where the nearest male relative lights the fire and walks around the burning body three times while reciting verses from Hindu sacred writings. Three days later someone collects and temporarily buries the ashes.

On the tenth day after the cremation, relatives deposit the ashes in the Ganges or some other sacred river. The funeral ceremony, called the *Shraddha,* is then held within 31 days of the cremation. Usually the deceased's son recites the prayers and the invocation of ancestors; that is one reason why every Hindu wants at least one son.

Prior to British rule in India, the practice of suttee was also common.

Reprinted with permission from *U.S. Catholic,* September 1990, pp. 29-35. © 1990 by U.S. Catholic, 205 West Monroe Street, Chicago, IL 60606.

Suttee is the act of a Hindu widow willingly being cremated on her husband's funeral pyre. Suttee was outlawed by the British in 1829, but occasionally widows still throw themselves into the flames.

Like the Hindus, the world's Buddhists, who live primarily in China, Japan, Sri Lanka, Myanmar, Vietnam, and Cambodia, usually choose cremation for disposing a corpse. They believe cremation was favored by Buddha. A religious teacher may pray or recite mantras at the bedside of the dying person. These actions are believed to exert a wholesome effect on the next rebirth. Buddhists generally believe that the essence of a person remains in an intermediate state for no more than 49 days between death and rebirth.

While Hindus and Buddhists prescribe cremation, the world's 900 million Muslims forbid cremation. According to the Qu'ran, Muhammad taught that only Allah will use fire to punish the wicked.

If a Muslim is near death, someone is called in to read verses from the Qu'ran. After death, the body is ceremonially washed, clothed in three pieces of white cloth, and placed in a simple wooden coffin. Unless required by law, Muslims will not allow embalming. The body must be buried as soon as possible after death—usually within 24 hours. After a funeral service at a mosque or at the grave side, the body is removed from the coffin and buried with the head of the deceased turned toward Mecca. In some Muslim countries the women engage in loud wailing and lamentations during the burial.

Some Islamic grave sites are quite elaborate. The Mogul emperor Shah Jahan built the world-famous Taj Mahal as a mausoleum for his wife and himself. The Taj Mahal, which is one of the finest examples of Islamic architecture, was finished in 1654. It took 20,000 workers about 22 years to complete the project.

The Baha'i faith, which originated in Persia in the nineteenth century as an outgrowth of the Shi'ite branch of Islam, also forbids cremation and embalming and requires that the body not be transported more than an hour's journey from the place of death. Because Bahaism has no ordained clergy, the funeral may be conducted by any member of the family or the local assembly. All present at the funeral must stand during the recitation of the Prayer for the Dead composed by Baha'u'llah. Several million Baha'is live in Iran, India, the Middle East, and Africa; and an estimated 100,000 Baha'is live in the United States.

In Judaism, the faith of some 18 million people, the Old Testament only hints at belief in an afterlife; but later Jewish thought embraced beliefs in heaven, hell, resurrection, and final judgment. In general, Orthodox Jews accept the concept of a resurrection of the soul and the body while Conservative and Reform Jews prefer to speak only of the immortality of the soul.

Orthodox Judaism prescribes some of the most detailed funeral rites of any religion. As death approaches, family and friends must attend the dying person at all times. When death finally arrives, a son or the nearest relative closes the eyes and mouth of the deceased and binds the lower jaw before rigor mortis sets in. Relatives place the body on the floor and cover it with a sheet; they place a lighted candle near the head.

Judaism in its traditional form forbids embalming except where required by law. After a ritual washing, the body is covered with a white shroud and placed in a wooden coffin. At the funeral, mourners symbolize their grief by tearing a portion of an outer garment or wearing a torn black ribbon. The Orthodox discourage flowers and ostentation at the funeral.

The Jewish funeral service includes a reading of prayers and psalms, a eulogy, and the recitation of the Kaddish prayer for the dead in an Aramaic dialect. Like other Semitic people, Jews forbid cremation. Orthodox Jews observe a primary mourning period of seven days; Reform Jews reduce this period to three days. During the secondary yearlong mourning period, the Kaddish prayer is recited at every service in the synagogue.

Dearly beloved

Christianity, the world's largest religion, carries over Judaism's respect for the body and firmly acknowledges resurrection, judgment, and eternal reward or punishment.

These Christian beliefs permeate the liturgy of a Catholic funeral. Older Catholics remember the typical funeral of the 1940s and '50s: the recitation of the rosary at the wake, the black vestments, the Latin prayers. They probably recall the "Dies Irae," a thirteenth-century dirge and standard musical piece at Catholic funerals prior to the liturgical changes of the Second Vatican Council in the 1960s.

Nowadays, those attending a Catholic wake may still say the rosary, but often there is a scripture service instead. The priest's vestments are likely to be white or violet rather than black. Prayers tend to emphasize the hope of resurrection rather than the terrors of the final judgment.

As death approaches, the dying person or the family may request the sacrament of the Anointing of the Sick. Once called Last Rites or Extreme Unction, this sacrament is no longer restricted to those in imminent danger of death; it is regularly administered to the sick and the elderly as an instrument of healing as well as a preparation for death.

Sacred remains

The Catholic Church raises no objections to embalming, flowers, or an open casket at a wake. At one time Catholics who wished to have a church funeral could not request cremation. In 1886 the Holy Office in Rome declared that "to introduce the practice (of cremation) into Christian society was un-Christian and Masonic in motivation." Today Catholics may choose the option of cremation over burial "unless," according to canon law, "it has been chosen for reasons that are contrary to Christian teaching."

The church used to deny an ecclesiastical burial to suicides, those killed in duels, Freemasons, and members of the ladies' auxiliaries of Masonic lodges. Today the church refuses burial only to "notorious apostates, heretics, and schismatics" and to "sinners whose funerals in church would scandalize the faithful." Catholics who join Masonic lodges no longer incur excommunication, although they still may not receive Communion.

The church has also softened its position on denying funeral rites to suicides. Modern pastoral practice is based on the understanding that anyone finding life so unbearable as to end it voluntarily probably was acting with a greatly diminished free will.

For Roman Catholics, the Mass is the principal celebration of the Christian funeral; and mourners are invited to receive the Eucharist. Most Protestant denominations, except for some Lutherans and Episcopalians, do not incorporate a communion service into their funeral liturgies. The Catholic ritual employs candles, holy water, and incense but does not allow non-Christian symbols, such as national flags or lodge emblems, to rest on or near the coffin during the funeral. In many parishes the pastor encourages the family members to participate where appropriate as eucharistic ministers, lectors, and singers. In the absence of a priest, a deacon can conduct the funeral service but cannot preside at a Mass of Christian burial.

The revised funeral liturgy of the Catholic Church is meant to stress God's faithfulness to people rather than God's wrath toward sinners. The Catholic Church declares that certain men and women who have lived lives of such heroic virtue that they are indeed in heaven are to be known as saints. The church also teaches that hell is a reality but has never declared that anyone, even Judas, has actually been condemned to eternal punishment.

Unlike Protestant churches, Catholicism also teaches the existence of a temporary state of purification, known as purgatory, for those destined for heaven but not yet totally free from the effects of sin and selfishness. At one time some theologians suggested that unbaptized babies spent eternity in a place of natural happiness known as limbo, but this was never church doctrine and is taught by few theologians today.

At the committal service at the grave site, the priest blesses the grave and leads the mourners in the Our Father and other prayers for the repose of the soul of the departed and the comfort of the survivors. Catholics are usually buried in Catholic cemeteries or in separate sections of other cemeteries.

Dressed for the occasion

The funeral rite in the Church of Jesus Christ of Latter-day Saints, which is the fastest growing church in the United States, resembles the standard Protestant funeral in some ways; but one significant difference is in the attire of the deceased. Devout Mormons receive the garments of the holy priesthood during their endowment ceremonies when they are teens. These sacred undergarments are to be worn day and night throughout a Mormon's life. When a Mormon dies, his or her body is then attired in these garments in the casket. At one time Mormon sacred garments resembled long johns, but they now have short sleeves and are cut off at the knees. The garments are embroidered with symbols on the right and left breasts, the navel, and the right knee, which remind the wearer of the oaths taken in the secret temple rites.

Mormons who reached their endowments are also clothed in their temple garb at death. For the men, this includes white pants, white shirt, tie, belt, socks, slippers, and an apron. Just before the casket is closed for the last time, a fellow Mormon puts a white temple cap on the corpse. If the deceased is a woman, a high priest puts a temple veil over her face; Mormons believe the veil will remain there until her husband calls her from the grave to resurrection. Mormons forbid cremation.

Freemasons conduct their own funeral rites for a deceased brother, and they insist that their ceremony be the last one before burial or cremation. Thus, a separate religious ceremony often precedes the Masonic rites. Lodge members will bury a fellow Mason only if he is a member in good standing and he or his family has requested the service.

All the pallbearers at the Masonic services must be Masons, and each wears a white apron, white gloves, a black band around his left arm, and a sprig of evergreen or acacia in his left lapel. The corpse is clothed in a white apron and other lodge regalia.

Masonry accepts the idea of the immortality of the soul but makes no reference to the Christian understanding of the resurrection of the soul and the body. The Masonic service speaks of the soul's translation from this life to that "perfect, glorious, and celestial lodge above" presided over by the Grand Architect of the Universe.

In memorium

Other small religious groups have much less elaborate and formalized funeral services. Christian Scientists, for example, have no set funeral rite because their founder, Mary Baker Eddy, denied the reality of death. The family of a deceased Christian Scientist often invites a Christian Science reader to present a brief service at the funeral home.

Unitarian-Universalists enroll many members who would identify themselves as agnostics or atheists. Therefore, in a typical Unitarian Universalist funeral service, the minister and loved ones say little about any afterlife but extol the virtues and good works of the deceased.

Salvation Army officers are buried in their military uniforms, and a Salvationist blows taps at the grave side. In contrast, the Church of Christ, which allows no instrumental music during Sunday worship, allows no organs, pianos, or other musical instruments at its funerals.

The great variety of funeral customs through the ages and around the world would be hard to catalog. The Egyptians mummified the bodies of royalty and erected pyramids as colossal monuments. Viking kings were set adrift on blazing boats. The Soviets mummified the body of Lenin, and his tomb and corpse have become major icons in the U.S.S.R.

In a funeral home in California, a drive-up window is provided for mourners so that they can view the remains and sign the book without leaving their cars. In Japan, where land is scarce, one enterprising cemetery owner offers a time-share plan whereby corpses are displaced after brief burial to make room for the next occupant. Complying with the wishes of the deceased, one U.S. undertaker once dressed a corpse in pajamas and positioned it under the blankets in a bedroom for viewing.

The reverence and rituals surrounding the disposal of the body reflect religious traditions going back thousands of years as well as up-to-the-minute fads. All of the elements of the burial—the preparation of the body, the garments or shroud, the prayers, the method of disposal, the place and time of burial—become sacred acts by which a particular community of believers bids at least a temporary farewell to one of its own.

BURYING THE UNGRATEFUL DEAD

Thomas Lynch

Thomas Lynch is an undertaker in Milford, Michigan, and is the author of Grimalkin & Other Poems, *published in England by Random House.*

Every year I bury one hundred and fifty of my townspeople. Another dozen or two I take to the crematory to be burned. I sell caskets, burial vaults, and urns for the ashes. I have a sideline in headstones and monuments. I do flowers on commission. I rent my building: eleven thousand square feet, furnished and fixtured with an abundance of pastel and chair rail and crown moldings. The whole mess is mortgaged and remortgaged well into the next century. My modes of transport include a hearse, a limo, two Fleetwoods, and a minivan with darkened windows, which our price list calls a service vehicle and which everyone in town calls the Dead Wagon.

They die around the clock here, without apparent preference for a day of the week or month of the year; there is no clear favorite among the seasons. Nor does the alignment of the stars, the fullness of the moon, or the liturgical calendar have very much to do with it. They go off upright or horizontally, in Chevrolets and nursing homes, in bathtubs, on the interstates, in ERs, ORs, BMWs. And while it may be that we assign more equipment and more importance to deaths that occur in places marked by initials—ICU being somehow better than Greenbriar Convalescent Home—it is also true that the dead don't care. In this way, the dead I bury and burn are like the dead before them, for whom time

and space have become mortally unimportant. This loss of interest among the dying is one of the first sure signs that something serious is about to happen. The next thing is they quit breathing.

Nor does *who* matter much either. To say, "I'm okay, you're okay, but him, he's dead!" is, for the living, a kind of comfort. It is why we drag rivers and comb plane wrecks. It is why MIA is more painful than DOA. It is why we have open caskets and classified obits. Knowing is better than not knowing, and knowing it is you is terrifically better than knowing it is me. Once I'm the dead guy, whether you're okay or he's okay won't interest me, because the dead don't care.

Of course, the living, bound by their adverbs and their actuarials, still do. That's the reason I'm in business. The living are careful and often caring. The dead are careless, or maybe it's care-less. Either way, they don't care. These are unremarkable and verifiable truths.

My former mother-in-law, herself an unremarkable and verifiable truth, was always fond of holding forth with Cagneyesque bravado—to wit: "When I'm dead, just put me in a box and throw me in a hole." But whenever I reminded her that we did, in effect, do that with everyone, the woman grew sullen and a little cranky. Later, over meatloaf and green beans, she would invariably burst forth with: "When I'm dead, just cremate me and scatter the ashes."

My former mother-in-law was trying to make carelessness sound like fearlessness. My kids would stop eating and look at each other. The kids' mother would whine: "Oh, Mom, don't talk like that." I'd take out my lighter and begin to play with it.

In the same way, the priest that married me to this woman's daughter—a man who loved golf and gold chalices and vestments made of Irish linen; a man who drove a great black car with a wine-red interior—this same fellow, leaving the cemetery one day, felt called upon to instruct me thus: "No bronze coffin for me. No sir! No orchids or roses or limousines. The plain pine box is the one I want, a quiet Low Mass, and the pauper's grave. No pomp and circumstance."

He wanted to be an example of simplicity, of prudence, of piety and austerity. When I told him that he needn't wait, that he could begin his ministry of good example even today, that he could quit the country club and trade his luxury sedan for a used Chevette, that free of his Florsheims and cashmeres and prime ribs he could become the very incarnation of Saint Francis himself or Anthony of Padua—when I told the priest who had married me these things, he said nothing at all, but turned his wild eye on me in the way that

the cleric must have looked on Sweeney years ago, before he cursed him, irreversibly, into a bird.

What I was trying to tell the fellow was, of course, that being a dead saint is no more worthwhile than being a dead philodendron. Living is the rub, and always has been. Living saints still feel the flames and stigmata, the ache of chastity and the pangs of conscience. Once dead, they let their relics do the leg-work, because, as I was trying to tell this priest, the dead don't care.

And that is the truth, abundantly self-evident, that seems, now that I think of it, the one most elusive to my old in-laws, to the parish priest, and to perfect strangers who are forever accosting me in barbershops and in cocktail bars and at parent-teacher conferences, hell-bent or duty-bound on telling me what it is they want done with them when they are dead.

I say, Give it a rest. Once you are dead, call it a day, and let the old man or the missus or the thankless kids decide whether you are to be buried or burned or blown out of a cannon or left to dry out in a ditch. It's not your day to watch.

We Can Help Children Grieve:
A Child-Oriented Model for Memorializing

Linda Ellen Goldman

On a family vacation Andrew died suddenly of a rare virus. Family and friends were shocked by this unexpected death. Andrew was six years old and had just completed kindergarten. The shock of his death needed to be recognized and processed before the overwhelming feeling of loss for Andrew could be honored. A special child-oriented memorial service was a vehicle for expression of this complicated grief.

Preparing the community and school

Andrew's parents wrote a letter explaining the facts of Andrew's death and the events surrounding his illness. It was mailed to every parent of a child at Andrew's school before Andrew's parents returned home from the vacation. The head of Andrew's school included with this letter an additional letter with information and

Linda Ellen Goldman, M.S., a certified grief counselor and certified grief educator specializing in working with children and grief, is codirector of counseling for children at the Center for Loss and Grief Therapy in Kensington, Maryland. She is the author of two books on helping children with grief issues, a frequent lecturer, and private-practice therapist. In addition, she is a member of the continuing education faculty of the University of Maryland School of Social Work and a consultant to Head Start.

Parents and children need to know the facts about a loss. This information lessens fear and creates a foundation from which to grieve.

resources on children and grief. Prior to the opening of school, the faculty met and discussed appropriate ways to work with children and their grief. Counseling was available to children at school.

Preparing concerned parents

A meeting was held at Andrew's school for all concerned parents and faculty. Information and appropriate resources were presented on how young children grieve. Adults expressed their own feelings, fears, and vulnerabilities, and they shared information about how Andrew's death was affecting the children. Parents were given suggestions about how to help the children grieve and prepare them for the memorial service planned for Andrew. The ideas included the following:

1. Give the facts of Andrew's death.

2. Share your feelings of grief.

3. Allow your children to express their feelings and to commemorate Andrew through drawings and stories.

4. Describe what will happen at the memorial service.

5. Invite your child to join you in coming to the service, but don't insist that she come.

6. Explain that children can participate if they feel like it by telling a story about Andrew or something special they remember. They can share artwork or poetry or join in singing. They do not have to participate if they don't feel like it.

7. Tell your child that there will be people there he knows.

8. Be prepared to leave with your child if she feels uncomfortable.

9. Let your children know that people may be sad and cry and *they* themselves may be sad and cry. That's OK. They may not feel sad and may not cry. That's OK, too.

10. Read resources written for parents, such as those mentioned at the end of this article.

11. Read to children to help prepare them and to answer questions—see the suggested books [in the box "Books to Read"].

12. Encourage your children to ask questions.

From *Young Children*, September 1996, pp. 69-73. © 1997 by the National Association for the Education of Young Children (NAEYC). Reprinted by permission.

We can define death to the young child in the following way: "When someone dies his or her body stops working. No matter how hard the doctors and nurses try, they can't make the body work again. Usually people die when they are very, very, very old or very, very, very sick, or when something so bad has happened to someone that the doctors and nurses can't make the body work anymore."

The child's view of death

1. Young children ages three through six often think that **death is reversible,** and they imagine that their loved one will return after death.

Joey, age four, asked his mom, "Why can't God bring our baby back from heaven, give him back to the doctors, and then the doctors can fix him and send him home?"

2. Alice, age three, sat at her mother's funeral and whispered to her dad, "I bet Mom is sleeping in God's bed right now." Children believe that **death is sleep.**

3. Five-year-olds **may ask for facts and details of the death.** "How did Megan die? Who was with her? Where did she go?"

4. They may also **ask about the nature of death and what happens after someone dies.** "Can Megan see me?" "What does she have for dinner?" and "Can she watch TV in heaven?"

5. Three- to five-year-olds often **take language literally** and many common clichés confuse young children, inhibiting their ability to grieve. The following are a few inappropriate clichés:

"God loved Grandpa so much that he took him with him to heaven." (Three-year-old Tom thinks, "Why doesn't God love me?")

"Mom's watching over me." (Five-year-old Alice thinks, "I can't do anything without Mom seeing me.")

"Dad went on a long trip." (Four-year-old Susan questions, "Why didn't he take me?")

"Grandma went to sleep." (Three-year-old Sam wonders, "Will I die when I go to sleep, too?")

Alex, age four, began to have terrifying nightmares after the death of his alcoholic dad. His grandmother was telling him that "Dad is watching over you in heaven," and Alex was very frightened. His dad had been punitive and physically abusive. Alex visualized him being able to see and hear everything because he had taken his grandmother's words literally.

6. **Magical thinking and egocentricity** is another component of the young child's view of death. Five-year-old Joshua began bed-wetting after his older sister Karen was killed by a drunk driver. He had become clingy and fearful and had refused to play with other children. One night before bed he confided to his mom,

"I know it's my fault that Karen died. We had a fight that day, and I told her I hated her; she was a bad sister, and I wished she was dead. I know my words made her die!"

Children often feel that their thoughts and words can magically cause things to happen. This was a perfect opportunity for Mom to explain the facts to Josh about how his sister died.

"Your sister was killed by a drunk man in a car accident. Your words did not cause her death. Karen knows you love her, and I know we will miss her very much."

Preparing the memorial service

While Andrew's parents went through all the pain, anguish, and stages of deep personal grief to be expected under such tragic circumstances, they summoned their love for their son Andrew to help them create a loving tribute to his life. In so doing, their own grief process was enriched as was the grief process of all others who were involved with the memorial service.

Andrew's parents prepared a very child-oriented memorial service to celebrate Andrew's life as well as to commemorate his death. They told other parents what the ceremony would be like, so that these parents, in turn, could tell their children what to expect. A notice also was put in the school newspaper.

So many times at the Center for Loss and Grief Therapy, I have received calls from parents asking if children should come to a funeral or memorial service. Breaking this silence on children and funerals and memorial services by *including children* is an idea whose time has come. The memorial service and funeral can become a shared family experience. To include young children in these experiences we need to understand the young child's vision of death (see box "The child's view of death").

The memorial service

Andrew's memorial service served as a model for me of what is possible when parents choose to commemorate and honor the dignity of their

Ways children can commemorate:

- Plant a flower or tree.

- Send a balloon.

- Blow bubbles.

- Light a candle.

- Say a prayer.

- Create a mural or collage about the life of the person who died.

- Make cookies or cake.

- Make a memory gift for the child's family.

- Write a poem, story, or song about the loved one who died.

- Talk into a tape recorder or make a video of memories.

child's life, with a true respect for all children.

While there certainly was sadness, the service held a warmth and invited an openness that allowed children of all ages, adult friends, family members, coworkers of Andrew's parents, school representatives, and Andrew's parents themselves to freely and spontaneously participate. People of all ages told stories, sang songs, and read poetry acknowledging Andrew's wonderful life.

Children and adults sat on the floor. Chairs were set up in the back of the room for those who preferred them. Families were together. Children could lie down, stand up, or leave. They did not have to participate—they could if they wanted to. They could go outside or blow bubbles or play. Children made their own choices as long as the service

was respected. A parent or caring adult was prepared to leave with any child who wanted to.

Children shared their thoughts, feelings, pictures, poetry, and stories. Artwork and stories were displayed on tables and walls. They told of memories and love and sorrow for their friend Andrew. Some children shared their photo collections about special times with Andrew. Andrew's dad read memories of Andrew for a child who was hesitant to speak. Andrew's adult friends and relatives also shared memories. Andrew's class offered gifts for his parents—a quilt with each child's handprints on it and a photo album of the kindergarten year.

Community support was very meaningful. Andrew's principal spoke of his memories of Andrew. Andrew's parents shared their love

for their son and experiences with him. They told funny stories about Andrew and had made a booklet of favorite poems and prayers for each family to take home. Some children's words were included. Andrew's good friend Chris, age seven, wrote, "Andrew is in my heart." His mom had been crying and Chris wanted to know why. She explained she was sad because she would never be able to see Andrew again. "Don't worry," Chris replied. "I can see Andrew whenever I want, because he is always in my heart."

His teachers and friends sang many of Andrew's favorite songs. They invited the children and their families to join in if they felt comfortable. Songs included "The Earth Is Mine," "When the Rain Comes Down," "I'm Being Eaten by a Boa Constrictor," and "The Garden Song."

Four-year-old Mary was sad at school one day and explained to her teacher that she missed her dog Lucky who was recently killed by a car. Her teacher handed her a toy telephone and suggested she call him and tell him how she feels. Mary sat down, dialed a number, and began speaking. "I love you, Lucky. I miss you so much. I hope you are OK and having fun and that God plays ball with you every day."

At the very end of the service people held hands and sang "Friends, Friends."

After the service

After the service the children were invited to make commemorations of Andrew if they wanted. There was a crafts table where children could draw pictures, write letters, or share stories about Andrew. Bubbles were provided. Children could take them outside to blow in remembrance of Andrew.

"Memory bags" were given to each child who attended—bags filled with treats (like stickers and a piece of candy) that Andrew's parents felt he would have liked to give to his friends. The room was filled with photos of Andrew and his family and friends, Andrew's artwork, and the artwork of Andrew's friends. The children could walk through the room freely and experience Andrew's life visually. Andrew's favorite toys and books were on display.

The children who attended Andrew's memorial service appeared to gain a great gift, the gift of inner strength. Participating with adults in a community remembrance of their

---

Books to Read

For teachers and parents

Breaking the Silence: A Guide to Help Children with Complicated Grief by Linda Goldman. 1996. Washington, DC: Taylor & Francis. For adults to help children with *complicated* grief issues of suicide, homicide, AIDS, violence, and abuse. It includes guidelines for educators, national resources, an annotated bibliography, and a chapter on a child-oriented memorial service.

Good Grief: Helping Groups of Children When a Friend Dies by Sandra Fox. 1988. Boston: New England Association for the Education of Young Children. A pioneering book that is an excellent source of information for adults working with children whose friends have died. Defines death for young children with clarity and simplicity.

The Grieving Child by Helen Fitzgerald. 1992. New York: Simon & Schuster. A comprehensive guide for parents to use in helping children with their grief. It is written clearly, in a very practical style, and with many useful suggestions.

Life and Loss: A Guide to Help Grieving Children by Linda Goldman. 1994. Washington, DC: Taylor & Francis. A resource for working with children and *normal* grief. It provides practical information, resources, hands-on activities, and an annotated bibliography.

Thank You for Coming to Say Good-Bye by Janice Roberts and Joy Johnson. 1994. Omaha, NE: Centering Corporation. An excellent source of information to help caring adults involve children in funeral services.

For children

Aardy Aardvark Finds Hope by Donna O'Toole. 1988. Burnesville, NC: Mt. Rainbow Publications. (ages 5–8). In this story of grief for young children, animals are used to show the pain, sadness, and hope that is felt after the death of a loved one.

About Dying by Sarah Stein. 1974. New York: Walker & Co. (ages 3–6). Contains a simple text and photographs to help young children understand death and memorializing.

The Frog Family's Baby Dies by Jerri Oehler. 1978. Durham, NC: Duke University Medical Center. (ages 3–6). A coloring book for very young children discussing feelings after a death in the family.

So Much to Think About by Fred Rogers. 1991. Pittsburgh, PA: Family Communications, Inc. (ages 3–6). An excellent activity book for young children that allows them hands-on ways to commemorate the death of someone they have loved.

Tell Me Papa by Joy and Marv Johnson. 1990. Omaha, NE: Centering Corporation. (ages 5–8). A book that talks in very simple and clear language about

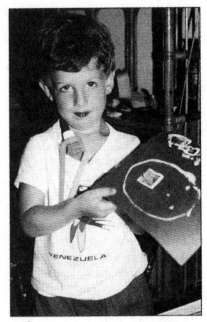

Andrew

death, funerals, and how children feel about both.

You Hold Me and I'll Hold You by Jo Carson. 1992. New York: Orchard. (ages 5–8). A simple story for young children about a young girl's feelings of wanting to hold and be held at a memorial service.

Young children learn through play and grieve through play. Role-playing, puppets, artwork, clay, and sand-table work are a few of the many ways they can imagine, pretend, and engage in meaningful activities that allow them to act out or project their grief feelings without having to directly verbalize them.

Young children need to know the facts of death in an age-appropriate way. They usually imagine far worse and have a sense that they are being lied to when they are not told the truth.

friend gave them a way to honor Andrew's life. Knowing how to honor Andrew's life gives these children a way to value and respect their own lives. We hope this will help them be a little better prepared for other life and death experiences they will face. For sadly, sooner or later, we all must face the ending of a life.

For further reading

Essa, E.L., & C.I. Murray. 1994. Research in review. Young children's understanding and experience with death. *Young Children* 49 (4): 74–81.

Furman, E. 1990. Plant a potato—learn about life (and death). *Young Children* 46 (1): 15–20.

Hofschield, K. 1991. The gift of a butterfly. *Young Children* 46 (3): 3–6.

MacIsaac, P., & S. King. 1989. What did you do with Sophie, teacher? *Young Children* 44 (2): 37–38.

Riley, S.S. 1989. Pilgrimage to Elmwood cemetery. *Young Children* 44(2): 33–36.

Children's Voices

The following excerpts reflect the thoughts, feelings, and memories of children who knew and loved Andrew. They appeared in a booklet made for Andrew's first anniversary memorial, entitled *"We Remember Andrew."*

This is a drawing that Andrew made at age four-and-a-half on one of his favorite themes: a knight with a sword.

Elyssa

"Andrew, you were a good friend. When we played the chace [chase] game it was really fun. One day Paige came over and she said that you dide [died]. I did not want to bleav [believe] her but my Mom came into my room She got a letter and said that is was tror [true]. You were such a good friend. I wish you were here your teacher wood [would] be Sharan. You wood [would] be with me Elyssa we did so much things together. I am the one uuw [you] made up huugy [huggy] but I want to end it but nothing is the same with out you

This Pache [page] is dedicadid [dedicated] to one of my Best Friends Andrew Love Elyssa."

Christina

"One day Christina, Andrew's five-year-old cousin, and I (Andrew's mom) were driving in the car. She looked at me and sighed, 'If I only had one wish, do you know what it would be? I would wish for a machine with a button on it. When I pressed the button, it would bring kids back from being dead. Then cousin Andrew would be alive. Don't you think that's a good wish?' "

Adam

"Seven-year-olds ask difficult questions. Recently, Adam asked his mother Joanne who her best friend was. She replied that she didn't have one best friend, rather she liked this person for this reason, and that person for that reason. Then she asked Adam who his best friend was. He named a friend from the neighborhood and one from his class. Then he paused, 'And Andrew . . . I didn't mind when he called me names. In fact, I kind of liked it.' Joanne says that Adam sometimes asks if the doctors will ever find out why his friend got sick and died."

Christy

"Before the Memorial Service, Christy and his mother were talking about Andrew. He had a theory about what happened to his friend: 'When you die, your body goes to the ground and makes trees. And your dreams go to heaven and they come back and get born again in other people.' "

A Do-It-Yourself Funeral

Clyde Spivey, like more and more people, chose to bypass the American way of death.

Cynthia Fox

For 50 years the amiable Clyde Spivey favored a girl who seemed his opposite: that wild redhead Nancy Sharpe. Their childhood pastimes appeared to say it all. She picked off rattlesnakes in ponds with a sawed-off shotgun; he skipped class to stoke coals with the janitor. When Nancy was 18 and ran off with another boy, it seemed fitting that Clyde would enter the Air Force and earn a Good Conduct Medal. But he also led police on high-speed chases through three Texas counties, cruising to safety through base gates. "I was a Texas Ranger," he would joke later, with a slow smile that friends said was like "prying open an oyster" but that strangers found so Bobby Kennedyesque they would stop him on the street to shake his hand.

In an era of white gloves and bow ties, Nancy flew in the face of convention. Clyde was never far behind, which may explain why, hearing she was divorced with two children at 23, he stood in her driveway until she promised to marry him. It may also explain why, 34 years later, he stood in his living room watching a heaven-blue coffin tumble through his front door.

"Sheesh," he said when it disappeared into a back room. Moving slowly, as a result of pancreatic cancer, he tacked up a sign reading RESTRICTED AREA. "This won't be an open casket deal," he said firmly.

"No," said Nancy, "but if I get mad at you tonight, you'll have somewhere to go."

"At least it'll be closure," Clyde said.

He calmly began vacuuming the hall.

The Spiveys of Durham, N.C., had decided to do Clyde's funeral themselves, from his death to the first shovel of dirt on his grave. It was an iconoclastic choice in what has become an age of identical McEverything, but the Spiveys weren't alone. Lisa Carlson, executive director of the Funeral and Memorial Societies of America and author of *Caring for the Dead*, fields 200 calls a year from people interested in bypassing funeral homes. Some 90 casket companies selling directly to consumers have sprung up in the wake of a 1994 Federal Trade Commission ruling that bars funeral homes from penalizing customers who shop around for coffins. More and more people are taking advantage of a well-kept secret: In most states, it is legal to bury the dead without mortuaries, cemeteries or embalming.

One reason for all this is that funeral and burial costs, which average $8,000 nationwide ($5,400 for the funeral alone), have been rising 5 percent a year, partly because three megaparlors—Stewart Enterprises, the Loewen Group and Service Corporation International—now control more than a quarter of the U.S. market. (In England funeral costs average $1,650; in France they're $2,200.) The hospice movement has also stimulated interest. So has the growing realization that, as James Farrell wrote in *Inventing the American Way of Death*, "the price we pay for paying our last respects in the American way of death is the price of our personality."

Clyde had plenty of that. By age 58, there was nothing McAnything about him. When Nancy bought a computer for the local TV guide they ran from their home for 19 years, he vowed never to touch "that thing." Never did. After a triple bypass in 1987, he was at work in a week, muttering about "the most expensive trip I ever took"—the $350 ambulance ride. He liked his wife, red suspenders, Dr Pepper and leaving people guessing. A sign in his office read: IF YOU CAN'T STUN 'EM WITH YOUR BRILLIANCE, BAFFLE 'EM WITH YOUR BULLSHIT.

So when his doctor gave him one to three months to live last May, he said, "No hospitals." And when Nancy came home with tales of funeral chains that can jack up prices 1,000 percent with bizarre devices like $1,000 "sealers" (actually $35 rubber gaskets that are supposed to preserve loved ones, but which mausoleum operators say can cause them to explode), exorbitant "basic service" fees, and countless bills for everything from hairstyling ($75) to makeup ($75), his reaction was in keeping with All Things Clyde.

First he went with Nancy to a mortuary. But when he asked for the cheapest casket and got the classic answer—"Not in stock"—he helped Nancy make the loneliest decision of her life. He may have dropped a few hundred on red cowboy boots in his day, but he had never paid $75 for a haircut, and he wasn't much for getting blown up. And makeup? "What does a funeral director do but stand there looking at you, anyway? Make sure the tent poles don't fall?" After Nancy found out that North Carolina doesn't require a mortuary, Clyde said, "Let's do it ourselves," and he paid $600 for a coffin that would have cost him $2,000 in a funeral home.

Until casket day, everything had gone smoothly enough. They had battled neighbors who said it was unhealthy to deal with death this way and officials who erroneously told them it was against the law. Clyde had a moment of squeamishness ("You and some nurse are cleaning me up after? You'll drown me"), but it passed. He had fended off neighbors with a quiet "Death is a fact of life."

Today, however, something was bothering Clyde. When Nancy told a hospice nurse she feared high morphine doses because when people go on them "they're gone"—and was told he had been taking them for weeks—Clyde, ironing shirts, merely raised an eyebrow as Nancy sank into a chair. But later, in the kitchen, he observed his children: Warren, 41, Nancy's son from her first marriage, a sporadically employed construction supervisor married four times; Carole, 39, his stepdaughter, married twice, now supporting a man no one much approved of; Clyde Eric, 29, a born father as good-natured as his namesake, if wilder than his mother. While all knew that Clyde Eric had settled down when his daughter Haley was conceived, they also knew he had started partying again when told about the cancer. They all brought gifts—Warren, gospel music; Carole, a map pinpointing the star she had registered in his name; Clyde Eric, dinner fixings. Even Carole's son Jacob was there, which was something, seeing as he had stayed away when his great-grandmother died.

A week earlier, perusing the funeral album Nancy was making, Clyde had said: "My kids have me tore up. I pushed too hard. I really expected them to do better than I did." They had taken up half his ways, he thought, flying in the face of things, without taking up the other half, shouldering consequences. "And now there's this . . . We've had family meetings about the cancer, because mine never talked about death. Never saw my parents or brother die. So I'm trying to make them talk, handle things—something . . . poor babies."

Home funerals often "start as a money thing and turn into something else," Lisa Carlson says. The Natural Death Care Project of Sebastopol, Calif., which helps families make personalized caskets, calls do-it-yourself funerals journeys that can "connect the hearts of those who are present to a universalizing whole." Clyde wasn't sure about that. Prompted by the invitation to honesty implied by the whole deal, a neighbor had nudged her children forward like a stage mother. "I'm sad you're going to die," one said. "Me too," said the other. Clyde nodded. "Yep," he replied. When more was apparently required, he added, uncomfortably, "It's too bad."

Sheesh.

And this funeral book he was supposed to write in? After weeks of deliberation, this is what he dredged up for his wife of 34 years: "I love you and I'm sorry I'm so stubborn."

Nope. He didn't know from "universalizing wholes."

He did know, however, that his kids were afraid of life. And why hadn't he been there for his parents' families in death? Had he been afraid of something too?

Since the illness, he had begun attending alcohol-free hootenannies. Banjos going at each other, no secrets and nothing to fear, just tobacco fields flat as Texas and people unexpectedly busting into clog dances everywhere. Maybe this crazy home funeral could bust them all up a bit, like that. Bring about some unexpected things.

Yet into the kitchen now came Warren, who, in a mood, had said he might miss the funeral because of a fishing tournament. In came Carole, who'd been staying away lately, admitting she was afraid of the dying, the talk. In came the jubilant baby Haley, riding Aunt Carole's hip, wearing sunglasses. Clyde tidied up his isosorbide, Toprol XL, Compazine, Valium, Advil, erythromycin—30 pills a day. The nurse had just added a 31st ritual: a swab for his neck so he could avoid death rattles at the end. Coffins, death rattles, babies holding babies. "Eaten anything?" he asked lightly, rising to make eggs.

That night, Clyde Eric, Carole and her kids read Bible verses into a tape recorder for the funeral. They went outside to smoke, their words lost in a symphony of crickets and tree frogs. "When Mama's daddy died, it was like someone grabbed the moon out of the sky," said Carole, brushing away a slug. She watched her 11-year-old look in vain through a telescope for his granddaddy's star.

A week later, a scare. Clyde threw up a cup of blood, cancer having pierced an organ. The family gathered, then scattered the next morning when Clyde serenely rose to pick up the TV guides from the printer's. In a nearby "honey pot," Clyde Eric fished for crappies and reminisced about his childhood, which involved, among other things, spray-painting cows pink.

That night, as Clyde, a practiced audience, lowered and hoisted an eyebrow, Nancy reenacted her day. Today's problem: the refusal of the Greensboro News & Record's obit desk to take hospice's word for a death. This had followed the health department's contention that it couldn't issue a death certificate if Clyde died on a weekend, and the claim of Guilford Memorial Park, the Loewen-owned cemetery where the family has prepaid plots, that the law required a funeral director. "Oh,"

Nancy said, throttling a pillow, "they're messing with the wrong redhead."

Clyde Eric had haunted the house for weeks, doing chores. Now, as he changed Haley's diapers, he went into high Spivey gear. Remember the L.A. trip? The old CB? "Tell the one about . . ." he said repeatedly, with his father's half-smile. Nancy threw a magazine at him and hit Clyde instead. "Now what did you do that for?" Clyde said, strapping his old Roy Rogers cap guns to his hips and soft-shoeing around the room. When he remembered an errand, his son said, "I can drive you." Clyde considered him. "Yes, Sunshine. You're always there."

"This one," Clyde said later, when asked which was the best year of his life. But at bedtime he stood in the kitchen with one arm around Nancy, his forehead touching hers as she sobbed.

August was a bad month. Warren left the house angry and didn't return. Carole stayed away a lot, frightened off again, and Clyde Eric was in turmoil: The mother of his child had left him. Clyde bought a power mower, taking pleasure in ferrying a visitor around the yard. But he also went from 360 milligrams of morphine daily to over 670, from 140 pounds to 90. One night, toward the end of the month, he began running in circles, in his underwear and his fanny pack of morphine, huddled over his fists as if racing a car around the dark house. The next day he didn't get up.

Then something unexpected: Without discussion, Clyde Eric, Jacob and the baby moved in. For the next two weeks, while Nancy was ill with bronchitis, it was the boys who tended the near-mute Clyde around the clock, regulating his morphine, carrying him to the bathroom as delicately as if leading him in a minuet. He was skeletal and uncoordinated, puppetlike, but he fought their help. They fought back. Hour after hour, he'd point above his head, a terrorized look on his face; hour after hour, Clyde Eric rushed from one room to another, changing his daughter's diapers, changing his dad's.

On September 13 they were joined by Carole, who spent a day and a night wrapped in a quilt, stroking her father's hair and talking in a bedtime-story voice. The next day, Warren came home. All searched Clyde's face, seeking evidence that he was still there. When a neighbor chirped, "Seen any angels yet, honey?" they got their answer. An eyebrow rose high on his face. "There he is!" Carole said. When Nancy came in, he pushed up his lips like a volcano: kiss.

Warren stayed with Clyde all night. The next day the hospice nurse visited, then tiptoed into Nancy's room. Nancy rushed out and lay beside her husband, pushing aside the baby dinosaur blanket covering him. The room filled with stunned family, so silent the oxygen machine was heard slurping. Clyde had died in one of the few moments he'd been alone since May.

Then another unexpected thing. The plan was for Nancy and the nurse to handle Clyde's death. But it was Warren who took his father's suit out of a closet, and Clyde Eric

who hastily polished his boots. Once started, they just kept going. Warren clipped his father's eyebrows; Clyde Eric brought in a tub. Warren washed Clyde's face and chest, as Clyde Eric and Jacob held his fragile body. "Mama, we need his Sunday belt," Clyde Eric said, sending Nancy running. The boys dressed their father, placing his arms through the shirt, vest and jacket gingerly, as if not to awaken him. Warren tied his father's tie; Clyde Eric slipped the boots on. When done, all three raised paper cups to Clyde, then headed for the back room to get the coffin that had been stashed there months before. They placed it on a stand in the living room and fixed its cotton batting the way they would make a bed.

Later, they carried Clyde to the coffin. Clyde Eric cried as he folded his father's hands, then leaned over, smiling as if listening to him say something ornery. When Nancy announced that she didn't want her husband's mouth open, they tied a handkerchief around his head like a bonnet and placed a teddy bear under his chin. They closed the lid, draped it in the serviceman's American flag and stood still, looking around the house that no longer had Clyde Spivey in it, yet did.

The boys climbed into sleeping bags beside their father. "I've never seen anything like it," said the nurse as she left.

The next day, Nancy and Clyde Eric picked up a death certificate from the health department, which Nancy says had stopped objecting when told that *LIFE* was doing a story. They got it signed by the doctor, then went to the local papers, which took the obits. (The Greensboro editor had caved in after Nancy called the company that owns the paper to protest.) They gave another copy to cemetery head Merle Neal, who had agreed to a burial without a funeral director after Corrine Culbreth, executive director of the state Board of Mortuary Science, explained the law to her. "She should know better," Culbreth said. "She is a licensed funeral director."

At seven the following evening, 40 friends gathered in the Spiveys' living room. Next to the coffin, which had toys scattered at its base, was a crib with the baby dinosaur blanket crumpled inside.

The next day the men in Clyde's life loaded the coffin into a friend's van. At the cemetery, they carried it to the burial site, then sat in the tent Clyde had joked about when the whole hootenanny began. (Tent poles held.) After playing the tape of family Bible readings, Nancy grabbed a shovel and tossed a pile of dirt into the air. She looked vibrant against the McCemetery green. She was dressed in her husband's favorite color, the red of her hair.

The most complete guide to DIYs can be found in Lisa Carlson's *Caring for the Dead* (Upper Access, 1998). For more information, contact FAMSA at 800-765-0107 or www.funerals.org/famsa; R.E. Markin, author of *The Affordable Funeral*, at 757-427-0220; Father Henry Wasielewski at 602-253-6814.

A Time to Mourn

by Pat Andrus, MS, CFLE, CGC

We often say that our industry is dedicated to helping people in their time of greatest need. Yet for many who lose a loved one, that time comes days, weeks, months or even years after the funeral and burial ceremonies end. A birthday, an anniversary or simply a rainy Monday morning can bring on intense feelings of grief and depression. In response, many cemeteries and funeral homes provide aftercare services ranging from newsletter mailings to intensive counseling. Since its inception six years ago, The Mourning After Program at Martin and Castille Funeral Home in Lafayette, Louisiana, has become one of the most comprehensive and successful aftercare programs in the industry.

My day began with a 7:30 a.m. photo shoot and planning meeting for an upcoming community training event on therapeutic intervention for grieving children and teens, followed by a two-hour session with a new client whose mother died six weeks ago. Next, I headed to a local hospital for an in-service brown bag luncheon with the social workers on staff, where I discussed various skills for handling bereaved families. This was followed by a 30-minute private debriefing with one social worker struggling with reactions to the tragic death of a toddler run over as his father backed out of the family's driveway.

Next, I returned to my office, where I attended a staff meeting, proofread a flier produced for The Grief Center of Southwest Louisiana and checked the production progress of the funeral home's fall 1996 newsletter. Finally, at 3 p.m., I settled in at my computer to begin work on this article.

Since being named director of The Mourning After Program at Martin and Castille Funeral Home in 1990, I have never had a boring, routine day. I have at times felt overwhelmed and overloaded, but I have always enjoyed the diversity of my job and the challenge of finding new avenues to respond to the needs of our families and community.

The Mourning After Program

The primary purpose of The Mourning After Program is to provide education, support and referral resources to the families we serve and our community at large. It is the most extensive aftercare program in the Lafayette area; each year it serves more than 450 families as well as an additional 600 to 1,000 individuals through in-service programs, presentations and training sessions.

As coordinator, I am the only employee who is devoted full-time to the program, though all funeral home staff participate at some level. In addition, university interns play a vital role in planning and administering certain events.

Some of the primary components of the program are as follows:
- individual grief education, counseling and community referrals;
- follow-up home visits;

- a resource reference library;
- community outreach and grief seminars; and
- a quarterly newsletter.

Education, counseling and referrals. Educating people about the process of grief and bereavement usually is the most important part of our services. Counseling comes afterward, as we help clients define other resources and make choices for themselves. In some ways, education and counseling come together much like beaten egg whites folded into waffle batter. The two become one to make the perfect waffle. Without either part, the batter is flat and is of lesser quality and flavor.

Individuals and families grieving losses from any area of life are welcome to contact The Mourning After Program. Our families often return to us near anniversary times or when some other event triggers their old pain anew. They know they are welcome to ask questions without fear of being judged. The number of calls we receive from "outside" fluctuates with the holidays, the start of school after summer vacations or when tragedy strikes in smaller communities.

During counseling sessions, I provide a listening ear, resource information and education regarding the grief process, and I help the client define his or her needs. Primarily, people want to know they are all right and are experiencing their pain in acceptable ways. They want to know they are not going crazy even though they find themselves in a crazy situation. Reading sensitively written literature, attending seminars and support groups or watching a film on grief often provides the needed reassurance and comfort.

I usually schedule one or two visits with interested clients and then refer those with complicated or unresolved grief issues to local licensed counselors and social workers. They are responsible for making their own arrangements for private counseling with these professionals.

In addition to providing referrals through our counseling sessions, Martin and Castille produces a "Directory of Support Services for the Bereaved." This free 25-page pamphlet offers listings for support groups, educational programs, grief coun-

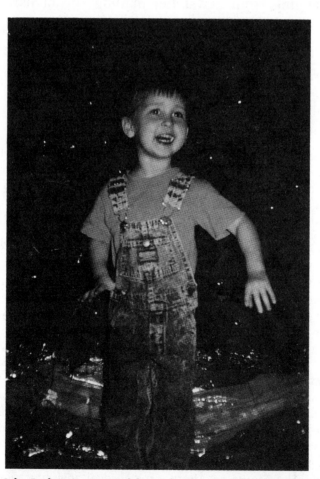

Jake Barber, age 4, participates in The Mourning After Program's Small Remembrances program, a children's memorial service held each December at the funeral home.

selors in private practice and a speakers bureau as well as other information. The funeral home publishes the directory as a joint project with a local hospital, which helps reduce costs. This service has proved effective in building credibility and referrals for both the funeral home and the hospital.

Home visits. In addition to providing counseling at our offices, we sometimes schedule home visits with Martin and Castille clients. This may include delivering the remaining paperwork and the death certificate or handling insurance signature requests. When possible, I take the time to discuss grief and bereavement issues, family needs and changes, and concerns regarding financial resources.

In the last several years, the number of home visits we have been able to conduct has diminished drastically due to time constraints. However, our president, vice president, funeral directors and office staff continue to screen the families we serve and recommend home visits for those they feel would find this service most beneficial. This often includes those who are ill, those who are uneasy about returning to the funeral home and those who specifically request a home visit.

Occasionally the funeral directors conduct initial home visits by delivering paperwork and the funeral register book, and they routinely make care calls by phone at regular intervals after the funeral. In addition, all families we serve receive a folder of materials that includes general grief information, special topic information specific to their loss, and introductory materials to The Mourning After Program.

Recently an elderly widow brusquely requested that the funeral home deliver her paperwork to her home as she didn't drive much and had no one to help her. She said she wanted no company cars with insignia in her driveway and was specific about the way the funeral director should act when going to see her. The executive secretary preparing her paperwork, concerned that the woman was perhaps paranoid or lived as a hermit, asked me to conduct a home visit.

Upon arriving at the woman's home, located in a prominent neighborhood, I found she had triple locks and a dog kennel guarding her entrance. At first, she refused to open the door, but after speaking with me for several minutes, she cracked it slightly. Ultimately she invited me in. We chatted for two hours in her small, cramped kitchen. To control expenses and the need for cleaning and to allow her to spend the maximum amount of time caring for her dying husband, she had closed off the remainder of the house.

This brilliant woman shared her history of world travel, university teaching and musical talents as well as her romantic marriage. She shared the pain of early childhood inadequacies and the breakdown of her family. She discussed the difficulties of having her only stepson live in a distant state and her fears of social service agencies and counselors. She described how overwhelmed she felt by her lack of control in her husband's death and her sense of guilt and helplessness in being unable to keep him alive.

By the end of our visit, she had invited me to come back, agreed she would call me to pick up groceries occasionally, complimented our funeral home services and spoke of planning her own prearrangements with us. Our gift to her was someone who could fully listen to her, hear her pain and fear, serve as a resource and be available to her during her bereavement. Her gift to me was helping me fall asleep that night knowing my work makes a difference.

The Olive Branch Library. Our library offers a well-stocked selection of books, magazines, journals, pamphlets and VHS tapes geared toward grief management and coping with loss. We regularly add new materials, basing our selection on factors such as specific death topics, reading/listening levels, target audience age or overall usefulness to our market. Our children's materials and general grief information have proved most popular.

The Olive Branch, which is housed in the funeral home conference room, is open for use during our business hours. The public is welcome to browse through the materials, preferably with an appointment time. They can check out items of interest. Unfortunately, some items

Helping Yourself Through Grief

The Mourning After Program's newsletter, *A Comforting Voice,* provides information on Martin & Castille services as well as general grief management. The following advice on handling grief is excerpted from the spring/summer 1996 edition.

- Allow yourself plenty of time to heal. It takes much longer than we want to realize . . . months, not days, and yes, years in many instances.
- Acknowledge your losses. They are important.
- Cry if you need to cry. Sometimes arranging a special time and place eases our embarrassment about crying in public. Not all of us cry alike . . . some tears come as sobs, some as sighs, some are silent.
- Set small goals. Over and over again, set small goals. Baby steps become achievements and accomplishments.
- Exercise helps us sleep better.
- Find your sense of humor. Hang on tight!
- Keeping a diary or journal gives us a place to jot down thoughts and memories. Sometimes it may only be a reminder to do a task. Sometimes it's what I am afraid to voice aloud quite yet.
- Eating nutritiously is helpful, even though we don't have time or energy to cook. Just try to increase fruits and vegetables, pastas, rice, breads and other carbohydrates. Lower fats, gravies, sauces and desserts.
- Decrease alcohol and drug consumption. Drugs and alcohol mask the pain for awhile but cannot remove the pain from us.
- Accept and give out hugs.
- Have a physical checkup with a trusted physician. Review prescribed medications with a physician familiar with the grief process. Not all doctors truly understand the process or how to treat grief effectively.
- Water is necessary for our stressed bodies. Substitute water and/or fruit juice for caffeinated drinks. Decreasing the use of carbonated beverages eases digestion.

- Postpone major decisions such as selling your home, changing jobs, divorcing your spouse. Get some qualified guidance on major decision making.
- Consider participating in a support group. Family and friends may not understand the need to retell our story over and over.
- Tell others what you want from them: help, emotional support, time shared, etc.
- Seek spiritual guidance. Having a crisis in faith is not unusual in grief.
- Check out advice. Accepting the imperfections of others means realizing I have imperfections too. We all give and get bad advice at times.
- Expand your vocabulary of feeling words. Reach past the usual ones: bad, sad, glad and mad.
- Use music, art, philosophy, religion, gardening, games, nature walks, reading, writing and volunteer work to gain comfort, relief and understanding.
- Seek professional counseling to work on specific issues, questions, bothersome ideas, or just to sort things out. There's strength in knowledge.
- Realize suicidal thoughts are an intense reaction to the pain of bereavement. Reach out for help immediately.
- Make plans for the tough times like weekends, holidays, evenings, anniversaries, birthdays and other special occasions.
- Planning a ritual can help us release emotion around specific loss and gain a sense of closure. Rituals may be simple or elaborate, individual or group-oriented, personal or public.
- Recognize your impatience for what it is—a desire to be better. Just as it takes time for bread to bake, we must allow ourselves to rise, be punched down and rise again. Otherwise the product is hard and tasteless, never having developed fully.

—Pat Andrus

never find their way back to us in spite of phone calls and careful monitoring, so we purchase multiple editions of the most popular materials. When families contact us to request books, I usually meet and speak with them about their specific needs.

In addition to helping those who are dealing with grief, the library serves as a general education resource for the community. We see an influx of students around term-paper time each semester.

Community work. Our community work is a key ingredient in the success of Martin and Castille Funeral Home. Professionals in our community such as school counselors and hospital social workers turn to us for guidance, education and resource identification. Families often choose our funeral home based on the recommendations of such professionals or simply because they know we have The Mourning After Program.

By collaborating with other agencies, hospitals and organizations, we demonstrate our high ethical standards and achieve shared success. We hold yearly grief seminars, inviting the public to hear major speakers such as Dr. Alan Wolfelt and Dr. Rabbi Earl Grollman.

As trainer/facilitator, I regularly conduct series such as "Adjusting to Widowhood" and "When Grief Hits Home: The Death of Your Parent." I offer frequent presentations to support groups such as Widowed Persons Service groups, Compassionate Friends and church bereavement groups. In addition, I have participated in special programs for the Louisiana Ministerial Alliance; the local Older Americans Conference; university nursing, sociology and consumer health classes; and social service agency staffs. Finally, I conduct a number of in-service training sessions for nurses, social workers, police, teachers, school counselors, emergency personnel and nursing home staffs.

As a state vice president and long-time local volunteer with the Louisiana chapter of the American Heart Association, I have worked to identify ways Martin and Castille can work with this influential group to integrate programming and fundraising efforts. For example, by coordinating efforts for the more than 7,000 individuals in our Spanish-speaking community to receive free cholesterol and blood pressure screenings as well as health and nutrition lessons, I established Martin and Castille as the firm that helps them live better lives. This fits hand-in-hand with our funeral home's tag line, "Helping you through life."

Another group in which I am active is The Grief Center of Southwest Louisiana, which began in 1991 as a discussion and debriefing group for those working in the bereavement field and became incorporated in January 1996. Through this organization, Martin and Castille, Lafayette General Medical Center and the Diocese of Lafayette Office of Justice and Peace recently hosted a program to train community bereavement personnel on working with children and traumatic grief issues. The center plans to offer initial group and individual services to grieving children by early spring 1997.

The Grief Center of Southwest Louisiana builds on Martin and Castille's "Small Remembrances" program, special children's memorial services held at the funeral home in early December. "Small Remembrances" allows more than 200 children and their adult caretakers to participate in an educational lesson and candle-lighting ceremony in honor of the loss of a pet or family member through death, divorce, relocation or other causes.

Co-sponsoring events with other organizations and community groups allows everyone concerned to stretch their advertising dollars and spread the workload. Since The Mourning After Program is not an income-producing enterprise, this business-to-business networking proves highly effective in maintaining our reputation as a well-respected asset to the community. In addition, we have become involved in several co-sponsorships with leading television stations, allowing us to build a rapport with the media on both personal and professional levels.

> **People want to know they are all right and are experiencing their pain in acceptable ways. They want to know they are not going crazy even though they find themselves in a crazy situation.**

A Comforting Voice **newsletter.** The production of our quarterly newsletter is an excellent tool for reaching individuals, families, support groups and professionals. By carefully balancing articles, we repeat grief education themes through new words and formats. The newsletter also announces upcoming events, invites participation, and encourages the use of our resources.

This year we are shifting from a quarterly newsletter to Spring/Summer and Fall/Winter editions with a Special Holiday Issue. This allows us to massage our budget a bit, creates a special edition that can be used for two to three years worth of mailings and adds a new look to our six-year-old newsletter style.

Aftercare and You

Not all cemetery and funeral home aftercare programs are as extensive or involved in the community as ours has become. But if you have not already begun considering ways to offer aftercare, now is the time.

Aftercare programs can take many paths, which can be used effectively on their own or in conjunction with one another. Grief seminars, sensitive literature, support groups, bereavement education groups, counseling, newsletters, information and referral services all offer distinct possibilities for aftercare.

One thing these programs have in common is that they offer dual benefits: They help your clients while at the same time helping your business. Martin and Castille has found that name recognition and free publicity for the funeral home abound because of the work we do. The Mourning After Program—and therefore the funeral home—are recognized by mental health, social service and medical professionals as the grief experts in the region. Media interviews on specific topics such as grief during the holidays and coverage of our many community-based events provide public broadcasting of our name and services at no monetary cost.

School teachers, administrators and counselors respect our leadership and gratefully use our resource library. This in turn opens the door for me to work within their systems. After one presentation, an elementary school counselor wrote, "Thank you for coming to work with my students. I feel it helped a group of students that might not have 'tapped into' these feelings, otherwise."

Community reaction to our presentations offers clear evidence that word-of-mouth is the best form of advertising. By consistently interacting within the health fields, we receive recognition from many. We have been told we have heart . . . are wise . . . are blessings to our community . . . have shared insights . . . have responded to someone's great need . . . and offered assistance at just at the right time. This type of feedback offers benefits not only in the form of increased business but also in the form of our own professional development and gratification.

Family members and friends of the deceased often express relief in realizing their emotions and behaviors, while scary, are normal reactions to grief. One of our most moving letters came from a woman whose husband had committed suicide a year and a half earlier, leaving her to rear their two-year-old daughter. "I was laying here thinking about . . . the many times you saved my life," she wrote. "I can't thank you enough for your help. [My daughter] has been asking for her daddy, so I finally found the strength to say, 'Daddy died and he's never coming back.' That was hard but I did it."

I think Wes Castille, our vice president, expressed it best. When asked his views on the greatest benefit of The Mourning After Program to our funeral home, he answered, "Yes, it has drawn attention and recognition to us as a funeral home. More importantly, our own empathy has heightened. We have broadened our horizons for what we are about. And we have increased the public's and our own personal awareness of how grief affects our community at large."

The value of providing aftercare services far outweighs the cost and effort. It can be the highest form of marketing and public relations. The good we do in our area has led to a shift in the market share for us. In addition, while our program stays separate from preneed sales, it does present an opportunity to encourage those we serve to consider prearrangement. I am always willing to help connect clients or community persons with a funeral director, and I consistently encourage prearrangement as a wise decision and even a form of stress management.

Finally, I believe aftercare programs can help revitalize our entire industry, bringing it back full circle to one that is viewed as compassionate and life-supporting. Through aftercare, your firm has the power to help the cemetery and funeral industry become a positive force in today's society.

Pat Andrus is director of The Mourning After Program at Martin and Castille Funeral Home in Lafayette, Louisiana. She is certified as a family life educator and grief counselor.

Unit 6

Key Points to Consider

❖ Discuss how the seven stages of grieving over death can also be applied to losses through divorce, moving from one place to another, or the amputation of a limb (arm or leg). What is the relationship between time and the feelings of grief experienced within the bereavement process?

❖ Describe the four necessary tasks of mourning. What are some of the practical steps one can take in accomplishing each of these tasks? How can one assist friends in bereavement?

❖ How can one know if one is experiencing "normal" bereavement or "abnormal" bereavement? What are some of the signs of aberrant bereavement? What could you do to assist people experiencing abnormal grief symptoms?

 **Links**

www.dushkin.com/online/

36. **Bereaved Families of Ontario Support Center**
    http://www.inforamp.net/~bfo/index.html
37. **The Compassionate Friends**
    http://www.compassionatefriends.org
38. **GriefNet**
    http://rivendell.org
39. **Widow Net**
    http://www.fortnet.org/WidowNet/

These sites are annotated on pages 4 and 5.

In American society many people act as if the process of bereavement is completed with the culmination of public mourning related to the funeral or memorial service and the final disposition of the dead. For those in the process of grieving, the end of public mourning only serves to make the bereavement process a more individualized, subjective, and private experience. Private mourning for most people, while more intense at its beginning, continues throughout their lifetime. The nature and intensity of this experience is influenced by the relationship of the mourner to the deceased, the age of the mourner, and the social context in which bereavement takes place.

This unit on bereavement begins with two general articles on the bereavement process. The first article, by Michael Leming and George Dickinson, describes and discusses the active coping strategies related to the bereavement process, disenfranchised grief, and the four tasks of bereavement. The next article, "Learning to Mourn" by Nancy Wartik, explains the universal stages of grieving and provides ways to assist those who mourn. Then, Kenneth Doka ("Disenfranchised Grief") provides assistance for caregivers in dealing with the needs of bereaved survivors who cannot acknowledge their grief publicly. The fourth unit article, by Therese Rando ("The Increasing Prevalence of Complicated Mourning: The Onslaught Is Just Beginning")

illustrates the principles described by Leming and Dickinson by providing a critique of America's health care industry for its lack of involvement in the post-death grieving experience. This article discusses many different types of death and the respective influences upon the bereaved while suggesting strategies for active coping with grief.

The remaining articles of this unit focus upon child, adolescent, and adult bereavement and coping strategies. The first of these articles, written by Linda Goldman, deals with children and bereavement and provides very practical strategies for assisting children to memorialize and mourn the deaths of significant others. In the next article, "Living with Loss: A Group for Bereaved College Students," we learn of a newly created bereavement group on the campus of the Indiana University of Pennsylvania that assists students in understanding and coping with the bereavement process. The last two articles provide other intervention strategies for adult grievers. Judith Larson's essay is concerned with the relationship between grief and depression and attempts to provide a context for distinguishing various aspects of the two experiences. Finally, "GriefTips: Help for Those Who Mourn," by James Miller, provides a number of very practical coping strategies that grievers have found helpful in living with loss and bereavement.

The Grieving Process

Michael R. Leming
St. Olaf College

George E. Dickinson
College of Charleston

Grief is a very powerful emotion that is often triggered or stimulated by death. Thomas Attig makes an important distinction between grief and the grieving process. Although grief is an emotion that engenders feelings of helplessness and passivity, the process of grieving is a more complex coping process that presents challenges and opportunities for the griever and requires energy to be invested, tasks to be undertaken, and choices to be made (Attig, 1991, p. 387).

Most people believe that grieving is a diseaselike and debilitating process that renders the individual passive and helpless. According to Attig (1991, p. 389):

> It is misleading and dangerous to mistake grief for the whole of the experience of the bereaved. It is misleading because the experience is far more complex, entailing diverse emotional, physical, intellectual, spiritual, and social impacts. It is dangerous because it is precisely this aspect of the experience of the bereaved that is potentially the most frustrating and debilitating.

Death ascribes to the griever a passive social position in the bereavement role. Grief is an emotion over which the individual has no control. However, understanding that grieving is an active coping process can restore to the griever a sense of autonomy in which the process is permeated with choice and there are many areas over which the griever does have some control. . . .

Coping With Grief

The grieving process, like the dying process, is essentially a series of behaviors and attitudes related to coping with the stressful situation of changing the status of a relationship. . . . Many have attempted to understand coping with dying as a series of universal, mutually exclusive, and linear stages. However, because most will acknowledge that not all people will progress through the stages in the same manner, we will list a number of coping strategies used as people attempt to resolve the pain caused by the loss of a significant relationship.

Robert Kavanaugh (1972) identifies the following seven behaviors and feelings as part of the coping process: shock and denial, disorganization, volatile emotions, guilt, loss and loneliness, relief, and reestablishment. It is not difficult to see similarities between these behaviors and Kübler-Ross's five stages (denial, anger, bargaining, depression, and acceptance) of the dying process. According to Kavanaugh (1972, p. 23), "these seven stages do not subscribe to the logic of the head as much as to the irrational tugs of the heart—the logic of need and permission."

SHOCK AND DENIAL

Even when a significant other is expected to die, at the time of death there is often a sense in which the death is not real. For most of us our first response is, "No, this can't be true." With time our experience of shock diminishes, but we find new ways to deny the reality of death.

Some believe that denial is dysfunctional behavior for those in bereavement. However, denial not only is a common experience among the newly bereaved, but also serves positive functions in the process of adaptation. The main function of denial is to provide the bereaved with a "temporary safe place" from the ugly realities of a social world that offers only loneliness and pain.

With time the meaning of loss tends to expand, and it may be impossible for one to deal with all of the social meanings of death at once. For example, if my wife dies, not only do I lose my spouse, but also I lose my best friend, my sexual partner, the mother of my children, a source of income, the person who writes the Christmas cards, and so on. Denial can protect me from some of the magnitude of this social loss, which may be unbearable at one point in time. With denial, I can work through different aspects of my loss over time.

DISORGANIZATION

Disorganization is that stage in the bereavement process in which one may feel totally out of touch with the reality of everyday life. Some go through the 3-day time period just prior to the funeral as if on "automatic pilot" or "in a daze."

Excerpted from *Understanding Dying, Death, and Bereavement* by Michael R. Leming and George E. Dickinson, Fort Worth, TX: Holt, Rinehart, and Winston, pp. 476-487. © 1998 by Holt, Rinehart, and Winston. Reprinted by permission.

Nothing normal "makes sense," and they may feel that life has no inherent meaning. For some, death is perceived as preferable to life, which appears to be devoid of meaning.

This emotional response is also a normal experience for the newly bereaved. Confusion is normal for those whose social world has been disorganized through death. When my father died, my mother lost not only all of those things that one loses with a death of a spouse, but also her caregiving role—a social role and master status that had defined her identity in the 5 years that my father lived with cancer. It is only natural to experience confusion and social disorganization when one's social identity has been destroyed.

VOLATILE REACTIONS

Whenever one's identity and social order face the possibility of destruction, there is a natural tendency to feel angry, frustrated, helpless, and/or hurt. The volatile reactions of terror, hatred, resentment, and jealousy are often experienced as emotional manifestations of these feelings. Grieving humans are sometimes more successful at masking their feelings in socially acceptable behaviors than other animals, whose instincts cause them to go into a fit of rage when their order is threatened by external forces. However apparently dissimilar, the internal emotional experience is similar.

In working with bereaved persons over the past 15 years, I have observed that the following become objects of volatile grief reactions: God, medical personnel, funeral directors, other family members, in-laws, friends who have not experienced death in their families, and/or even the person who has died. I have always found it interesting to watch mild-mannered individuals transformed into raging and resentful persons when grieving. Some of these people have experienced physical symptoms such as migraine headaches, ulcers, neuropathy, and colitis as a result of living with these intense emotions.

GUILT

Guilt is similar to the emotional reactions discussed earlier. Guilt is anger and resentment turned in on oneself and often results in self-deprecation and depression. It typically manifests itself in statements like "If only I had . . . ," "I should have . . . ," "I could have done it differently . . . ," and "Maybe I did the wrong thing." Guilt is a normal part of the bereavement process.

From a sociological perspective, guilt can become a social mechanism to resolve the **dissonance** that people feel when unable to explain why someone else's loved one has died. Rather than view death as something that can happen at any time to any one, people can **blame the victim** of bereavement and believe that the victim of bereavement was in some way responsible for the death—"If he had been a better parent, the child might not have been hit by the car," or "If I had been married to him I might also have committed suicide," or "No wonder he died of a heart attack, her cooking would give anyone high cholesterol." Therefore, bereaved persons are some-

times encouraged to feel guilt because they are subtly sanctioned by others' reactions.

LOSS AND LONELINESS

As we discussed earlier, loss and loneliness are the other side of denial. Their full sense never becomes obvious at once; rather, each day without the deceased helps us to recognize how much we needed and depended upon those persons. Social situations in which we expected them always to be present seem different now that they are gone. Holiday celebrations are also diminished by their absence. In fact, for some, most of life takes on a "something's missing" feeling. This feeling was captured in the 1960s love song "End of the World."

> Why does the world go on turning?
> Why must the sea rush to shore?
> Don't they know it's the end of the world
> 'Cause you don't love me anymore?

Loss and loneliness are often transformed into depression and sadness fed by feelings of self-pity. According to Kavanaugh (1972, p. 118), this effect is magnified by the fact that the dead loved one grows out of focus in memory—"an elf becomes a giant, a sinner becomes a saint because the grieving heart needs giants and saints to fill an expanding void." Even a formerly undesirable spouse, such as an alcoholic, is missed in a way that few can understand unless their own hearts are involved. This is a time in the grieving process when anybody is better than nobody and being alone only adds to the curse of loss and loneliness (Kavanaugh, 1972, p. 118).

Those who try to escape this experience will either turn to denial in an attempt to reject their feelings of loss or try to find surrogates—new friends at a bar, a quick remarriage, or a new pet. This escape can never be permanent, however, because loss and loneliness are a necessary part of the bereavement experience. According to Kavanaugh (1972, p. 119), the "ultimate goal in conquering loneliness" is to build a new independence or to find a new and equally viable relationship.

RELIEF

The experience of relief in the midst of the bereavement process may seem odd for some and add to their feelings of guilt. My mother found relief in the fact that my father's battle with cancer had ended, even though this end provided her with new problems. I have observed a friend's relief 6 months after her husband died. This older friend of mine was the wife of a minister, and her whole life before he died was his ministry. With time, as she built a new world of social involvements and relationships of which he was not a part, she discovered a new independent person in herself whom she perceived was a better person than she had ever been.

Although relief can give rise to feelings of guilt, like denial, it can also be experienced as a "safe place" from the pain, loss, and loneliness that are endured when one is grieving. According to Kavanaugh (1972, p. 121):

The feeling of relief does not imply any criticism for the love we lost. Instead, it is a reflection of our need for ever deeper love, our quest for someone or something always better, our search for the infinite, that best and perfect love religious people name as God.

REESTABLISHMENT

As one moves toward reestablishment of a life without the deceased, it is obvious that the process involves extensive adjustment and time, especially if the relationship was meaningful. It is likely that one may have feelings of loneliness, guilt, and disorganization at the same time and that just when one may experience a sense of relief something will happen to trigger a denial of the death. What facilitates bereavement and adjustment is fully experiencing each of these feelings as normal and realizing that it is hope (holding the grieving person together in fantasy at first) that will provide the promise of a new life filled with order, purpose, and meaning.

Reestablishment never occurs all at once. Rather, it is a goal that one realizes has been achieved long after it has occurred. In some ways it is similar to Dorothy's realization at the end of *The Wizard of Oz*—she had always possessed the magic that could return her to Kansas. And, like Dorothy, we have to experience our loss before we really appreciate the joy of investing our lives again in new relationships.

The Four Tasks of Mourning

In 1982 J. William Worden published *Grief Counseling and Grief Therapy,* which summarized the research conclusions of a National Institutes of Health study called the Omega Project (occasionally referred to as the Harvard Bereavement Study). Two of the more significant findings of this research, displaying the active nature of the grieving process, are that mourning is necessary for all persons who have experienced a loss through death and that four tasks of mourning must be accomplished before mourning can be completed and reestablishment can take place.

According to Worden (1982, p. 10), unfinished grief tasks can impair further growth and development of the individual. Furthermore, the necessity of these tasks suggests that those in bereavement must attend to "grief work" because successful grief resolution is not automatic, as Kavanaugh's (1972) stages might imply. Each bereaved person must accomplish four necessary tasks: (a) accept the reality of the loss, (b) experience the pain of grief (c) adjust to an environment in which the deceased is missing, and (d) withdraw emotional energy and reinvest it in another relationship (Worden, 1982).

ACCEPT THE REALITY OF THE LOSS

Especially in situations when death is unexpected and/or the deceased lived far away, it is difficult to conceptualize the reality of the loss. The first task of mourning is to overcome the natural denial response and realize that the person is dead and will not return.

Bereaved persons can facilitate the actualization of death in many ways. The traditional ways are to view the body, attend the funeral and committal services, and visit the place of final disposition. The following is a partial list of additional activities that can assist in making death real for grieving persons.

1. View the body at the place of death before preparation by the funeral director.
2. Talk about the deceased and the circumstances surrounding the death.
3. View photographs and personal effects of the deceased.
4. Distribute the possessions of the deceased among relatives and friends.

EXPERIENCE THE PAIN OF GRIEF

Part of coming to grips with the reality of death is experiencing the emotional and physical pain caused by the loss. Many people in the denial stage of grieving attempt to avoid pain by choosing to reject the emotions and feelings that they are experiencing. Some do this by avoiding places and circumstances that remind them of the deceased. I know of one widow who quit playing golf and quit eating at a particular restaurant because these were activities that she had enjoyed with her husband. Another widow found it extremely painful to be with her dead husband's twin, even though he and her sister-in-law were her most supportive friends.

J. William Worden (1982, pp. 13–14) cites the following case study to illustrate the performance of this task of mourning:

> One young woman minimized her loss by believing her brother was out of his dark place and into a better place after his suicide. This might have been true, but it kept her from feeling her intense anger at him for leaving her. In treatment, when she first allowed herself to feel anger, she said, "I'm angry with his behavior and not him!" Finally she was able to acknowledge this anger directly.

The problem with the avoidance strategy is that people cannot escape the pain associated with mourning. According to Bowlby (cited by Worden, 1982, p. 14), "Sooner or later, some of those who avoid all conscious grieving, break down—usually with some form of depression." Tears can afford cleansing for wounds created by loss, and fully experiencing the pain ultimately provides wonderful relief to those who suffer while eliminating long-term chronic grief.

ADJUST TO AN ENVIRONMENT IN WHICH THE DECEASED IS MISSING

The third task, practical in nature, requires the griever to take on some of the social roles performed by the deceased, or to find others who will. According to Worden (1982, p. 15), to abort this task is to become helpless by refusing to develop the skills necessary in daily living and by ultimately withdrawing from life.

I knew a woman who refused to adjust to the social environment in which she found herself after the death of her husband. He was her business partner, as well as her best and only friend. After 30 years of marriage, they had no children, and she had no close relatives. She had never learned to drive a car. Her entire social world had been controlled by her former husband. Three weeks after his funeral she went into the basement and committed suicide.

The alternative to withdrawing is assuming new social roles by taking on additional responsibilities. Extended families who always gathered at Grandma's house for Thanksgiving will be tempted to have a number of small Thanksgiving dinners after her death. The members of this family may believe that "no one can take Grandma's place." Although this may be true, members of the extended family will grieve better if someone else is willing to do Grandma's work, enabling the entire family to come together for Thanksgiving. Not to do so will cause double pain—the family will not gather, and Grandma will still be missed.

The final task of mourning is a difficult one for many because they feel disloyal or unfaithful in withdrawing emotional energy from their dead loved one. One of my family members once said that she could never love another man after her husband died. My twice-widowed aunt responded, "I once felt like that, but I now consider myself to be fortunate to have been married to two of the best men in the world."

Other people find themselves unable to reinvest in new relationships because they are unwilling to experience again the pain caused by loss. [A] quotation from John Brantner . . . provides perspective on this problem: "Only people who avoid love can avoid grief. The point is to learn from it and remain vulnerable to love."

However, those who are able to withdraw emotional energy and reinvest it in other relationships find the possibility of a newly established social life. Kavanaugh (1972, pp. 122–123) depicts this situation well with the following description.

At this point fantasies fade into constructive efforts to reach out and build anew. The phone is answered more quickly, the door as well, and meetings seem important, invitations are treasured and any social gathering becomes an opportunity rather than a curse. Mementos of the past are put away for occasional family gatherings. New clothes and new places promise dreams instead of only fears. Old friends are important for encouragement and permission to rebuild one's life. New friends can offer realistic opportunities for coming out from under the grieving mantle. With newly acquired friends, one is not a widow, widower, or survivor—just a person. Life begins again at the point of new friendships. All the rest is of yesterday, buried, unimportant to the now and tomorrow.

LEARNING TO MOURN

By Nancy Wartik

Changing the way America copes with grief

When her 37-year-old husband, Brian, was diagnosed with an advanced case of the skin cancer melanoma, Cathy Adams went into shock. Over the next 10 months she lived in continual fear and panic. When Brian died on Christmas Eve, 1992, leaving her with two young children, "I went numb," she says. "In some ways it was a relief, just to know that was the end of it."

Numbness turned to anger, Adams says, "at everyone and everything"—even God. "I tried to go to church once after Brian died, but I had to leave. I kept thinking, 'How can I accept this?' " Real sorrow didn't strike for almost a year. "The first few months, I didn't feel sad. Then it really hit me."

Plagued by money woes, the demands of single parenting and the desertion of friends who couldn't cope with the enormity of her loss, Adams fell into despair. "Putting one foot in front of the other was as much as I could do," she says. "I had days where I'd break down and just cry all day long. Everything looked black."

Eventually her depression was treated with medication, and Adams moved with her children to a town less haunted by old memories. "I'd never have believed I could go through something like this and come out feeling normal, but I do," says Adams, now 40. "No matter how bad something seems, I've learned you can get the strength to go through it. But that's what you have to do—go *through*. You can't go around, you can't run away; you've got to go through."

The journey into grief after someone we love has died is a voyage as ancient as human history, and one that most of us will inevitably take. Not every death provokes grief, of course, nor is grief felt only after a death; we mourn many losses over a lifetime. But the pain of bereavement, striking as it does at so many levels—psychological, physical, social—is one of the most taxing experiences we will ever struggle with. In describing the process more than 75 years ago, Sigmund Freud coined the phrase "grief work." Arduous as grief work is, it's the only hope for real healing after loss, ultimately offering a chance for emotional growth.

Yet in a society where the realities of aging and mortality are often denied—"Death," historian Arnold Toynbee once observed, "is un-American"—the subject of grief has largely been shunned. Those who suffer loss are plunged into bereavement with little idea of what to expect and no way to know if their experience is normal. Believing their strong emotions to be unacceptable, they deny grief even to themselves or mourn in silence.

"Unfortunately, Jackie Kennedy became the model for so many of us, with her stalwart behavior" after her husband's assassination, notes psychologist Catherine Sanders. Dr. Sanders, the author of *Surviving Grief and Learning to Live Again*, lost her 17-year-old son in a waterskiing accident. "So often, bereaved people I've talked with have said they truly tried to emulate Mrs. Kennedy and behave very bravely, never breaking down in public, never sharing. But sharing and breaking down are part of grief."

From *American Health*, May 1996, pp. 76-79, 96. © 1996 by Nancy Wartik. Reprinted by permission.

Some experts say mourning has never been harder. "Increased mobility means we're not always living near family when we experience a death," says Dr. Therese A. Rando, clinical director for the Institute for the Study and Treatment of Loss in Warwick, R.I., and the author of *How to Go On Living When Someone You Love Dies*. "Because most people in the U.S. now die in hospitals, we're not as familiar with death to begin with. And there's a decline in religion and in the rituals—wakes, funerals—that are psychologically important for survivors."

Three Stages of Grief

Grief is not a single emotion, but a series of phases through which a mourner passes. Broadly speaking, there are three. In the first, a person may feel shock, followed by numbness, denial, a dazed sense; he or she may irrationally look for the loved one to return. Such responses serve to cushion the blow of loss until the mind adjusts to reality.

In the next stage, a bereaved person confronts the death. This is the deepest, most intense phase of grief. "Intellectually, we know our loved ones are not coming back," says Sanders, "yet it seems impossible to let them go. We remain in emotional conflict until we can finally release them." The final stage is a time of healing, the point when the griever turns a corner and begins to adjust to life without the departed.

Progression through these stages is rarely neat and orderly. Often they repeat themselves in cycles of diminishing intensity. "Tonight all the hells of young grief have opened again," wrote British author C.S. Lewis in his classic 1961 book, *A Grief Observed*, which chronicled his responses after his wife died of cancer. "[In] grief nothing 'stays put.' One keeps on emerging from a phase, but it always recurs. Round and round. Everything repeats."

Sometimes after a death, people freeze their most disturbing emotions until months or years later. In *Motherless Daughters*, Hope Edelman tells of thinking she'd overcome the loss of her mother at 17, only to find herself at age 24 prostrate with longing for her. Grief, Edelman writes, is "not linear. It's not predictable. It's anything but smooth and self-contained.... Grief goes in cycles, like the seasons, like the moon."

> # Grief is a series of phases we must pass through.

Universal Anger

Throughout the mourning process, a survivor may be besieged by a confusing slew of emotions. Anger is almost universal. "It's much more pronounced in some cases, but there's always a kind of resentment at the person for dying and leaving you alone," says Dr. Calvin Frederick, a medical psychologist at UCLA. Dr. Earl Grollman, the author of *Living When a Loved One Has Died*, adds that most survivors experience guilt: "Very few escape without saying, 'I should have been more loving,' without blaming themselves for something they did or didn't do." People may also feel guilty at experiencing relief after a death—say, following a lingering illness. And anxiety, despair and depression are common emotions.

Grief can also cause physical symptoms such as insomnia, stomach problems, fatigue or dizziness. Studies have even found higher than normal mortality rates among those who've recently lost a spouse, as well as a link between bereavement and decreased immune function.

And grief may cause people to question their sanity. After his mother died in 1994, President Clinton reported repeatedly picking up a phone to call her, a fairly typical slip. In addition, normal routines may become impossible. "People drive by a red light and can't recall if it means stop or go," says Grollman. "They go to make a bank deposit and forget how. People worry they're going crazy. They're not. It takes time and effort to regain the ability to function more effectively after a loved one dies."

"Friends will say, 'You have to get out more, stay busy.' That's usually the opposite of what the person needs," says Sanders. "They're exhausted and fatigued. They just need someone to stay with them and listen."

Occasionally a griever has a vivid encounter with the deceased. "Some people have visions or hear the voice of the dead person," says Dr. Sidney Zisook, a University of California at San Diego (UCSD) psychiatrist. "They may not want to admit it, for fear it

Resource Box

Reaching out for support can ease the pangs of grief. The following organizations can help.

• **Widowed Persons Service**
American Association of Retired Persons
601E St. NW
Washington, DC 20049
202-434-2260
Connects anyone who has lost a spouse with programs around the country offering information and support.

• **The Compassionate Friends**
P.O. Box 3696
Oak Brook, IL 60522-3696
708-990-0010
Provides information and connects bereaved parents and siblings to support groups throughout the country.

• **Grief Recovery Helpline**
800-445-4808
People trained in grief recovery counseling speak with callers Monday to Friday, 9 a.m. to 5 p.m. Pacific time (the lines are very busy, so be persistent).

• **National Self-Help Clearinghouse**
25 West 43rd St., Suite 620
New York, NY 10036
212-354-8525
Provides names of a wide variety of bereavement support groups.

will seem as if they're losing their mind. But is hearing a voice during bereavement a psychotic symptom? Of course you hear the voice of someone you spent 40 years with."

Taking Mourning's Measure

Once it was assumed mourning lasted only six months to a year. But such constraints are unrealistic at best, suggesting that those who don't let go quickly enough are maladjusted. "Grief has no timetable," says Grollman. "It's like fingerprints or snowflakes: different for each person. Resolving grief almost always takes longer than people expect. If it's the death of your child, it's the death of your future. If your parent has died, it's the death of your past. With a spouse, the death of the present."

A wide range of factors determine the course of bereavement, including the mourner's ethnic and religious background, the quality of his or

her relationship to the deceased, and the role the deceased played in the mourner's life. Age affects the mourning process (though adults need to recognize that children grieve deeply too), as does gender. A 1993 study of bereaved spouses showed widowers to be more disturbed, and for longer, than widows. "Men are more often dependent on wives to provide their emotional support," asserts study author Dr. Leon Levy, chairman of psychology at the University of Maryland in Baltimore County. "A spouse's death is in many respects a greater loss for men."

Certain circumstances prolong mourning. Rando cites seven: the death of a child; sudden death leaving no time to prepare; a death perceived as preventable, as with suicide; a death occurring after a long illness such as cancer; a difficult, ambivalent or overly dependent relationship between the mourner and the deceased; a lack of social support in the griever's life; and a griever's preexisting mental illness (such as depression) or extreme life stresses (such as a divorce or job loss).

A child's death is perhaps the hardest loss a person can suffer. Not only is it an appalling violation of the natural order, but it also leaves most bereaved parents feeling intense guilt at not having better protected their offspring. "It's a pain that only people who have been through can relate to," says Don Fiegel, a Williamsville, N.Y., pharmacist whose daughter Claudia died at age 20, four months after being diagnosed with ovarian cancer. "It's indescribable, a gut-wrenching, soul-tearing pain."

After Claudia died, Fiegel withdrew from his surviving children and his wife. "I kept it all in, sat by myself at night and cried. I had no empathy, no sense of direction. I started to drink quite heavily. I'd come home late, or not until morning. My wife told me in no uncertain terms that I had to stop. But I didn't give a damn. I didn't care about anything." It took more than three years, until Fiegel joined a support group for grieving parents, before his healing process truly began.

"Unfinished business" between the survivor and the deceased can complicate grief. When her father had a fatal heart attack at 56, Diana Willensky, now an Associate Editor at AMERICAN HEALTH, was 24. He and her mother had divorced years earlier. "I'd always been disappointed that my father didn't know me better, that we hadn't been closer," she says, "but I assumed we'd have time to do that in the future. After he died, I realized we'd never have that chance. It was a huge regret, and it made his death even more upsetting."

Dealing With the Emotions

Understandably, many people want a way to fast-forward through grief. Though there are no shortcuts, bereavement is often harder than it needs to be, because people lack knowledge of what they're facing or of how to prepare.

If a death is anticipated, family members or friends should try to speak frankly with the dying person beforehand. "Sometimes when a person is dying, people withdraw," says Dr. Dorothea Lack, a San Francisco psychologist specializing in bereavement. "But if there are things left unsaid or undone and you can bring them to completion, you don't wind up with unresolved doubts and conflicts."

For many people, giving in to their feelings about the death is the hardest aspect of grieving. Men in particular may resist breaking down, and they have fewer outlets for expressing grief. "If a couple loses a child, people will ask the husband, 'How's your wife?' " says Grollman. "Men have been told that big boys don't cry. So they camouflage grief with alcohol abuse, or it comes out in physical problems like headaches or backaches. They don't feel free to feel."

Yet dealing with the emotions provoked by a death is crucial. Trying to escape from the process will take a heavy toll in the end. "You can try to avoid thinking about the loss, or cut yourself off from your feelings when you do think of it," says Rando. "You can try to minimize the loss or keep yourself so busy you'll never notice it. But all of those things will cost you. If you don't pay now, you're going to pay later."

Funerals and mourning rites, sometimes maligned as superficial or outmoded ceremonies, help catalyze grief. In traditional Judaism, for instance, mourners sit shivah (Hebrew for "seven") for a week, during which they're not supposed to leave home or work or engage in pleasurable activities of any kind. "It's a very sensible, therapeutic device," says Irene Nathan of Chicago, who has survived the deaths of her husband and four siblings. "It's a whole week dedicated to the memory of the departed one. You mourn as much as you can; you just get it out, cry. It's grief at its utmost depths." Experts urge those who are grieving not to give short shrift to memorial ceremonies.

Emotional support is also crucial, though friends and relatives aren't always adept at reaching out. They may not realize how long grief can take to resolve. Or they may not perceive a loss as meaningful, though it leaves a great void in the griever's life. Not everyone understands, for instance, how devastating the death of a friend, a newborn child or even a pet can be. "People may denigrate the death of a pet, saying 'It was only an animal,' " says Rando, "but there's evidence that it can hurt as profoundly as losing a family member."

Tragedies such as suicide or the death of a child may dampen support from friends. "Lots of the things said to the bereaved are signals for them not to share how they really feel," says Dr. Dennis Klass, a bereavement specialist who chairs the religion department at Webster University in St. Louis. "When people say 'You're so strong; you're handling this so well,' what they're really saying is 'I don't want to know how bad it is. It scares me.' "

For the bereaved, the best approach is simply to ask family or friends for help. Alternatively, there are support groups addressing specific types of loss, from the death of a sibling to that of a pet. Such groups allow grievers to connect with others who understand exactly what they're going through.

When a griever becomes "stuck" in mourning, a counselor or psychologist specializing in bereavement may be helpful. Signs that mourning has gone awry include physical symptoms (fatigue, aches and pains) in the absence of emotional distress; uncontrollable anger or guilt; heavy use of drugs or alcohol; and extreme social withdrawal or suicidal feelings.

Chronic depression can also signal that a griever is in real trouble. Some degree of depression is normal in mourning, but severe, ongoing mood disorder is not. UCSD's Zisook has found that two months after losing a spouse, one in four people is clinically depressed; many could benefit from professional help. "We've tended not to bother treating depressive illness when it's part of bereavement," notes Zisook. "We've discounted it as just part of grief. That's been destructive to people's recovery. Depression after bereavement needs to be treated as seriously as at any other time."

When the Worst Is Over

To those in the midst of it, grief seems endless. But it does pass. "You wake up one morning," says Don Fiegel, "and all of a sudden that specter isn't there. Or you take two steps forward and only one back. That's when you know you're coming around."

Freud saw the goal of grief work as cutting ties to the dead in order to form new bonds. Today psychologists realize that people shouldn't break all connections to someone they've deeply loved. "I've seen people come to support groups," says Klass, "and say, 'I lost a child 40 years ago. People told me to forget about it and move on, but I've remembered that child every day of my life.' "

Such responses are now viewed as appropriate, even beneficial, as long as they don't prevent the person from forming new attachments or interests. "I remember a mother who lost her son to cancer and was trying to stop smoking," Klass notes. "I asked how she was doing, and she said, 'He's helping me quit. Every time I want to reach for a cigarette, I'll think of him and he helps me.' "

Recovery from grief doesn't mean a resumption of life exactly as it was, however. Just as a deep wound leaves a bodily scar, emotional scar tissue is permanent, even when a person has moved on to a new life or love. From time to time over the years, the scar will ache. Yet many people deeply touched by grief change in remarkably positive ways. They develop new empathy for others who suffer loss or learn to deal more effectively with people or situations.

"My father's death taught me that you can't assume you'll have time to make a relationship what you want it to be," says Willensky. "It really pushes me to tackle problems I might not try to deal with otherwise. I didn't have the opportunity to do that with my father, but it's something I have more control over now."

For her part, Cathy Adams says, "I've found I don't feel afraid of things anymore. I know how to handle them. It's not that I feel that nothing can hurt me again; I know lots of things can. But whatever they are, I know that I have the strength to get through them."

Nancy Wartik is a Contributing Editor at AMERICAN HEALTH.

Disenfranchised Grief

KENNETH J. DOKA

KEN DOKA, PH.D., is a professor of gerontology at the College of New Rochelle in New York. He became interested in the study of death and dying quite inadvertently. Scheduled to do a practicum in a facility that housed juvenile delinquents, he discovered that his supervisor had changed the assignment. Instead, Doka found himself counseling dying children and their families at Sloan-Kettering, a major cancer hospital in New York. This experience became the basis of two graduate theses, one in sociology entitled "The Social Organization of Terminal Care in Two Pediatric Hospitals," and the other in religious studies entitled "Pastoral Counseling to Dying Children and Their Families." (Both were later published.) His doctoral program pursued another longstanding interest: the sociology of aging. In 1983, Dr. Doka accepted his present position at the College of New Rochelle where he specializes in thanatology and gerontology.

Active in the Association for Death Education and Counseling since its beginnings, Dr. Doka was elected its president in 1993. In addition to articles in scholarly journals, he is the author of *Death and Spirituality* (with John Morgan, 1993), *Living with Life-Threatening Illness* (1993) and *Disenfranchised Grief: Recognizing Hidden Sorrow* (1989), from which the following selection is excerpted. His work on disenfranchised grief began in the classroom when a graduate student commented, "If you think widows have it rough, you ought to see what happens when your ex-spouse dies."

Introduction

Ever since the publication of Lindemann's classic article, "Symptomatology and Management of Acute Grief," the literature on the nature of grief and bereavement has been growing. In the few decades following this seminal study, there have been comprehensive studies of grief reactions, detailed descriptions of atypical manifestations of grief, theoretical and clinical treatments of grief reactions, and considerable research considering the myriad variables that affect grief. But most of this literature has concentrated on grief reactions in

socially recognized and sanctioned roles: those of the parent, spouse, or child.

There are circumstances, however, in which a person experiences a sense of loss but does not have a socially recognized right, role, or capacity to grieve. In these cases, the grief is disenfranchised. The person suffers a loss but has little or no opportunity to mourn publicly.

Up until now, there has been little research touching directly on the phenomenon of disenfranchised grief. In her comprehensive review of grief reactions, Raphael notes the phenomenon:

> There may be other dyadic partnership relationships in adult life that show patterns similar to the conjugal ones, among them, the young couple intensely, even secretly, in love; the defacto relationships; the extramarital relationship; and the homosexual couple.... Less intimate partnerships of close friends, working mates, and business associates, may have similar patterns of grief and mourning.

Focusing on the issues, reactions, and problems in particular populations, a number of studies have noted special difficulties that these populations have in grieving. For example, Kelly and Kimmel, in studies of aging homosexuals, have discussed the unique problems of grief in such relationships. Similarly, studies of the reactions of significant others of AIDS victims have considered bereavement. Other studies have considered the special problems of unacknowledged grief in prenatal death, [the death of] ex-spouses, therapists' reactions to a client's suicide, and pet loss. Finally, studies of families of Alzheimer's victims and mentally retarded adults also have noted distinct difficulties of these populations in encountering varied losses which are often unrecognized by others.

Others have tried to draw parallels between related unacknowledged losses. For example, in a personal account, Horn compared her loss of a heterosexual lover with a friend's loss of a homosexual partner. Doka discussed the particular problems of loss in nontraditional relationships, such as extramarital affairs, homosexual relationships, and cohabiting couples.

This article attempts to integrate the literature on such losses in order to explore the phenomenon of disenfranchised grief. It will consider both the nature of disenfranchised grief and its central paradoxical problem: the very nature of this type of grief exacerbates the problems of grief, but the usual sources of support may not be available or helpful.

The Nature of Disenfranchised Grief

Disenfranchised grief can be defined as the grief that persons experience when they incur a loss that is not or cannot be openly acknowledged, publicly mourned, or socially supported. The concept of disenfranchised grief recognizes that societies have sets of norms—in effect, "grieving rules"—that attempt to specify who, when, where, how, how long, and for whom people should grieve. These grieving rules may be codified in personnel policies. For example, a worker may be allowed a week off for the death of a spouse or child, three days for the loss of a parent or sibling. Such policies reflect the fact that each society defines who has a legitimate right to grieve, and these definitions of right correspond to relationships, primarily familial, that are socially recognized and sanctioned. In any given society these grieving rules may not correspond to the nature of attachments, the sense of loss, or the feelings of survivors. Hence the grief of these survivors is disenfranchised. In our society, this may occur for three reasons.

1. The Relationship Is Not Recognized

In our society, most attention is placed on kin-based relationships and roles. Grief may be disenfranchised in those situations in which the relationship between the bereaved and deceased is not based on recognizable kin ties. Here the closeness of other non-kin relationships may simply not be understood or appreciated. For example, Folta and Deck noted, "While all of these studies tell us that grief is a normal phenomenon, the intensity of which

corresponds to the closeness of the relationship, they fail to take this (i.e., friendship) into account. The underlying assumption is that closeness of relationship exists only among spouses and/or immediate kin." The roles of lovers, friends, neighbors, foster parents, colleagues, in-laws, stepparents and stepchildren, caregivers, counselors, co-workers, and roommates (for example, in nursing homes) may be long-lasting and intensely interactive, but even though these relationships are recognized, mourners may not have full opportunity to publicly grieve a loss. At most, they might be expected to support and assist family members.

Then there are relationships that may not be publicly recognized or socially sanctioned. For example, nontraditional relationships, such as extramarital affairs, cohabitation, and homosexual relationships have tenuous public acceptance and limited legal standing, and they face negative sanctions within the larger community. Those involved in such relationships are touched by grief when the relationship is terminated by the death of the partner, but others in their world, such as children, may also experience grief that cannot be acknowledged or socially supported.

Even those whose relationships existed primarily in the past may experience grief. Ex-spouses, past lovers, or former friends may have limited contact, or they may not even engage in interaction in the present. Yet the death of that significant other can still cause a grief reaction because it brings finality to that earlier loss, ending any remaining contact or fantasy of reconciliation or reinvolvement. And again these grief feelings may be shared by others in their world such as parents and children. They too may mourn the loss of "what once was" and "what might have been." For example, in one case a twelve-year-old child of an unwed mother, never even acknowledged or seen by the father, still mourned the death of his father since it ended any possibility of a future liaison. But though loss is experienced, society as a whole may not perceive that the loss of a past relationship could or should cause any reaction.

2. The Loss Is Not Recognized

In other cases, the loss itself is not socially defined as significant. Perinatal deaths lead to strong grief reactions, yet research indicates that many significant others still perceive the loss to be relatively minor. Abortions too can constitute a serious loss, but the abortion can take place without the knowledge or sanctions of others, or even the recognition that a loss has occurred. It may very well be that the very ideologies of the abortion controversy can put the bereaved in a difficult position. Many who affirm a loss may not sanction the act of abortion, while some who sanction the act may minimize any sense of loss. Similarly, we are just becoming aware of the sense of loss that people experience in giving children up for adoption or foster care, and we have yet to be aware of the grief-related implications of surrogate motherhood.

Another loss that may not be perceived as significant is the loss of a pet. Nevertheless, the research shows strong ties between pets and humans, and profound reactions to loss.

Then there are cases in which the reality of the loss itself is not socially validated. Thanatologists have long recognized that significant losses can occur even when the object of the loss remains physically alive. Sudnow for example, discusses "social death," in which the person is alive but is treated as if dead. Examples may include those who are institutionalized or comatose. Similarly, "psychological death" has been defined as conditions in which the person lacks a consciousness of existence, such as someone who is "brain dead." One can also speak of "psychosocial death" in which the persona of someone has changed so significantly, through mental illness, organic brain syndromes, or even significant personal transformation (such as through addiction, conversion, and so forth), that significant others perceive the person as he or she previously existed as dead. In all of these cases, spouses and others may experience a profound sense of loss, but that loss cannot be publicly acknowledged for the person is still biologically alive.

3. The Griever Is Not Recognized

Finally, there are situations in which the characteristics of the bereaved in effect disenfranchise their grief. Here the person is not socially defined as capable of grief; therefore, there is little or no social recognition of his or her sense of loss or need to mourn. Despite evidence to the contrary, both the very old and the very young are typically perceived by others as having little comprehension of or reaction to the death of a significant other. Often, then, both young children and aged adults are excluded from both discussions and rituals.

Similarly, mentally disabled persons may also be disenfranchised in grief. Although studies affirm that the mentally retarded are able to understand the concept of death and, in fact, experience grief, these reactions may not be perceived by others. Because the person is retarded or otherwise mentally disabled, others in the family may ignore his or her need to grieve. Here a teacher of the mentally disabled describes two illustrative incidences:

> In the first situation, Susie was 17 years old and away at summer camp when her father died. The family felt she wouldn't understand and that it would be better for her not to come home for the funeral. In the other situation, Francine was with her mother when she got sick. The mother was taken away by ambulance. Nobody answered her questions or told her what happened. "After all," they responded, "she's retarded."

The Special Problems of Disenfranchised Grief

Though each of the types of grief mentioned earlier may create particular difficulties and different reactions, one can legitimately speak of the special problem shared in disenfranchised grief.

The problem of disenfranchised grief can be expressed in a paradox. The very nature of disenfranchised grief creates additional problems for grief, while removing or minimizing sources of support.

Disenfranchising grief may exacerbate the problem of bereavement in a number of ways. First, the situations mentioned tend to intensify emotional reactions. Many emotions are associated with normal grief. Bereaved persons frequently experience feelings of anger, guilt, sadness and depression, loneliness, hopelessness, and numbness. These emotional reactions can be complicated when grief is disenfranchised. Although each of the situations described is in its own way unique, the literature uniformly reports how each of these disenfranchising circumstances can intensify feelings of anger, guilt, or powerlessness.

Second, both ambivalent relationships and concurrent crises have been identified in the literature as conditions that complicate grief. These conditions can often exist in many types of disenfranchised grief. For example, studies have indicated the ambivalence that can exist in cases of abortion, among ex-spouses, significant others in nontraditional roles, and among families of Alzheimer's disease victims. Similarly, the literature documents the many kinds of concurrent crises that can trouble the disenfranchised griever. For example, in cases of cohabiting couples, either heterosexual or homosexual, studies have often found that survivors experience legal and financial problems regarding inheritance, ownership, credit, or leases. Likewise, the death of a parent may leave a mentally disabled person not only bereaved but also bereft of a viable support system.

Although grief is complicated, many of the factors that facilitate mourning are not present. The bereaved may be excluded from an active role in caring for the dying. Funeral rituals, normally helpful in resolving grief, may not help here. In some cases the bereaved may be excluded from attendance. In other cases they may have no role in planning those rituals or in deciding whether even to have them. Or in cases of divorce, separation, or psychosocial death, rituals may be lacking altogether.

In addition, the very nature of the disenfranchised grief precludes social support. Often there is no recognized role in which mourners can assert the right to mourn and thus receive such support. Grief may have to remain private. Though they may have experienced an intense loss, they may not be given time off from work, have the opportunity to verbalize the loss, or receive the expressions of sympathy and support characteristic in a death. Even traditional sources of solace, such as religion, are unavailable to those whose relationships (for example, extra-marital, cohabiting, homosexual, divorced) or acts (such as abortion) are condemned within that tradition.

Naturally, there are many variables that will affect both the intensity of the reaction and the availability of support. All the variables—interpersonal, psychological, social, physiological—that normally influence grief will have an impact here as well. And while there are problems common to cases of disenfranchised grief, each relationship has to be individually considered in light of the unique combinations of factors that may facilitate or impair grief resolution.

Implications

Despite the shortage of research on and attention given to the issue of disenfranchised grief, it remains a significant issue. Millions of Americans are involved in losses in which grief is effectively disenfranchised. For example, there are more than 1 million couples presently cohabiting. There are estimates that 3 percent of males and 2–3 percent of females are exclusively homosexual, with similar percentages having mixed homosexual and heterosexual encounters. There are about a million abortions a year; even though many of the women involved may not experience grief reactions, some are clearly "at risk."

Disenfranchised grief is also a growing issue. There are higher percentages of divorced people in the cohorts now aging. The AIDS crisis means that more homosexuals will experience losses in significant relationships. Even as the disease spreads within the population of intravenous drug users, it is likely to create a new class of both potential victims and disenfranchised grievers among the victims' informal liaisons and nontraditional relationships. And as Americans continue to live longer, more will suffer from severe forms of chronic brain dysfunctions. As the developmentally disabled live longer, they too will experience the grief of parental and sibling loss. In short, the proportion of disenfranchised grievers in the general population will rise rapidly in the future.

It is likely that bereavement counselors will have increased exposure to cases of disenfranchised grief. In fact, the very nature of disenfranchised grief and the unavailability of informal support make it likely that those who experience such losses will seek formal supports. Thus there is a pressing need for research that will describe the particular and unique reactions of each of the different types of losses; compare reactions and problems associated with these losses; describe the important variables affecting disenfranchised grief reactions; assess possible interventions; and discover the atypical grief reactions, such as masked or delayed grief, that might be manifested in such cases. Also needed is education sensitizing students to the many kinds of relationships and subsequent losses that people can experience and affirming that where there is loss there is grief.

THE INCREASING PREVALENCE OF COMPLICATED MOURNING: THE ONSLAUGHT IS JUST BEGINNING*

Therese A. Rando, Ph.D.

Warwick, Rhode Island

ABSTRACT

In this article, complicated mourning is operationalized in relation to the six "R" processes of mourning and its seven high-risk factors are identified. The main thesis is that the prevalence of complicated mourning is increasing today due to a number of contemporary sociocultural and technological trends which have influenced 1) today's types of death; 2) the characteristics of personal relationships severed by today's deaths; and 3) the personality and resources of today's mourner. Additionally, specific problems in both the mental health profession and the field of thanatology further escalate complicated mourning by preventing or interfering with requisite treatment. Thus, complicated mourning is on the rise at the precise time when caregivers are unprepared and limited in their abilities to respond. New treatment policies and models are mandated as a consequence.

In the 1990s, the mental health profession (a term herein broadly used to encompass any caregiver whose work places him/her in the position of ministering to the mental health needs of another) and the thanatological community are at a crucial crossroads. Current sociocultural and technological trends in American society are directly increasing the prevalence of complicated mourning at the precise point in time at which the mental health profession is particularly both unprepared and limited in its abilities to respond to the needs created. Thanatology has a pivotal role to play in identifying this crisis, delineating the problems to be addressed, and advocating for the development of new policies, models, approaches, and treatments appropriate to today's grim realities. Failure of either profession to recognize these realities is bound to result not only in inadequate care for those who require it, but to place our society at greater risk for the serious sequelae known to emanate from untreated complicated mourning [1].

After a brief review of complicated mourning, this article will: 1) identify the high-risk factors for complicated mourning; 2) delineate the sociocultural and technological trends ex-

acerbating these factors, which in turn increase the prevalence of complicated mourning; 3) indicate the problems inherent in the mental health profession that interfere with proper response to complicated mourning and to its escalation; and 4) point out the pitfalls for addressing complicated mourning that reside in the field of thanatology today. The focus on this article is restricted to raising awareness of the problem and discussing its determinants.

COMPLICATED MOURNING

Historically, there have been three main difficulties in defining complicated mourning. The first stems from the imprecise and inconsistent terminology employed. The very same grief and mourning phenomena have been described at various times and by various authors as "pathological," "neurotic," "maladaptive," "unresolved," "abnormal," "dysfunctional," or "deviant," just to name some of the designations used. Communication has been hampered by a lack of semantic agreement and consensual validation. This author's preference is for the term "complicated mourning." Such a term suggests that mourning is a series of processes which in some way have become complicated, with the implication being that what has become complicated can be uncomplicated. It avoids the pejorative tone of many of the other terms. Additionally, there is no insinuation of pathology in the mourner. Heretofore, complications typically have been construed to arise from the deficits of the person experiencing the bereavement. The term "complicated" avoids the assumption that the complications necessarily stem from the mourner him or herself. This is quite crucial because it is now well-documented that there are some circumstances of death and some postdeath variables that in and of themselves complicate mourning regardless of the premorbid psychological health of the mourner.

A second difficulty stems from the lack of objective criteria for what constitutes complicated mourning. Unlike the analogous medical situation in which the determination of pathology is more readily discerned and defined (e.g., the diagnosis of a broken bone usually can be easily agreed upon by several physicians

*This article is adapted from a keynote address of the same name presented at the 13th Annual Conference of the Association for Death Education and Counseling, Duluth, Minnesota, April 26–28, 1991 and from the author's book, *Treatment of Complicated Mourning*, Research Press, Champaign, Illinois, 1993.

following viewing of an x-ray), the phenomena in mourning tend not to be so concrete or unarguable. For instance, a woman hearing her deceased husband's voice in some circumstances is quite appropriate, whereas in others it reflects gross pathology.

The third and related difficulty is found because mourning is so highly idiosyncratic. It is determined by a constellation of thirty-three sets of factors circumscribing the loss and its circumstances, the mourner, and the social support received. No determination of abnormality technically ever can be made without taking into consideration the sets of factors known to influence any response to loss [2]. What may be an appropriate response in one circumstance for an individual mourner may be a highly pathological response for a different mourner in other circumstances. For this reason, it appears most helpful to look at complications in the mourning processes themselves rather than at particular symptomatology.

With this as a premise, complicated mourning can be said to be present when, taking into consideration the amount of time since the death, there is a compromise, distortion, or failure of one or more of the six "R" processes of mourning [1]. The six "R" processes of mourning necessary for healthy accommodation of any loss are:

1. Recognize the loss
   • Acknowledge the death
   • Understand the death
2. React to the separation
   • Experience the pain
   • Feel, identify, accept, and give some form of expression to all the psychological reactions to the loss
   • Identify and mourn secondary losses
3. Recollect and reexperience the deceased and the relationship
   • Review and remember realistically
   • Revive and reexperience the feelings
4. Relinquish the old attachments to the deceased and the old assumptive world
5. Readjust to move adaptively into the new world without forgetting the old
   • Revise the old assumptive world
   • Develop a new relationship with the deceased
   • Adopt new ways of being in the world
   • Form a new identity
6. Reinvest

In all forms of complicated mourning, there are attempts to do two things: 1) to deny, repress, or avoid aspects of the loss, its pain, and the full realization of its implications for the mourner; and 2) to hold onto, and avoid relinquishing, the lost loved one. These attempts, or some variation thereof, are what cause the complications in the "R" processes of mourning.

Complicated mourning may take any one or combination of four forms: symptoms, syndromes, mental or physical disorder, or death [1].

Complicated mourning symptoms refer to any psychological, behavioral, social, or physical symptom—alone or in combination—which in context reveals some dimension of

compromise, distortion, or failure of one or more of the six "R" processes of mourning. They are of insufficient number, intensity, and duration, or of different type, than are required to meet the criteria for any of the other three forms of complicated mourning discussed below.

There are seven *complicated mourning syndromes* into which a constellation of complicated mourning symptoms may coalesce. They may occur independently or concurrently with one another. Only if the symptoms comprising them meet the criteria for the specific syndrome is there said to be a complicated mourning syndrome present. If only some of the symptoms are present, or there is a combination of symptoms from several of the syndromes but they fail to meet the criteria for a particular complicated mourning syndrome, then they are considered complicated mourning symptoms. The reader should be advised that a syndrome is not necessarily more pathological than a group of symptoms which clusters together but does not fit the description of one of the complicated mourning syndromes. Sometimes just a few complicated mourning symptoms—depending upon which they are—can be far more serious than the complicated mourning syndromes. With the exception of death, severity is not determined by the form of complicated mourning.

The seven syndromes of complicated mourning include three syndromes with problems in expression (i.e., absent mourning, delayed mourning and inhibited mourning); three syndromes with skewed aspects (i.e., distorted mourning of the extremely angry or guilty types, conflicted mourning, and unanticipated mourning); and the syndrome with a problem in ending (i.e., chronic mourning).

The third form that complicated mourning may take is of a *diagnosable mental or physical disorder.* This would include any DSM-III-R [3] diagnosis of a mental disorder or any recognized physical disorder that results from or is associated with a compromise, distortion, or failure of one or more of the six "R" processes of mourning. *Death* is the fourth form which complicated mourning may take. The death may be consciously chosen (i.e., suicide) or it may stem from the immediate results of a complicated mourning reaction (e.g., an automobile crash resulting from the complicated mourning symptom of driving at excessive speed) or the long-term results of a complicated mourning reaction (e.g., cirrhosis of the liver secondary to mourning-related alcoholism). The latter two types of death may or may not be subintentioned on the part of the mourner.

GENERIC HIGH-RISK FACTORS FOR COMPLICATED MOURNING

Clinical and empirical evidence reveals that there are seven generic high-risk factors which can predispose any individual to have complication in mourning [1]. These can be divided into two categories: factors associated with the specific death and factors associated with antecedent and subsequent variables.

Factors associated with the death which are known especially to complicate mourning include: 1) a sudden and unanticipated death, especially when it is traumatic, violent, mutilating, or random; 2) death from an overly-lengthy illness; 3) loss of a child; and 4) the mourner's perception of preventability. Antecedent and subsequent variables that tend to complicate mourning include: 1) premorbid relationship with the deceased which has been markedly angry or ambivalent or markedly dependent; 2) the mourner's prior or concurrent mental health problems and/or unaccommodated losses and stresses; and 3) the mourner's perceived lack of social support.

To the extent that any bereaved individual is characterized by one or more of these factors, that individual can be said to be at risk for the development of complications in one or more of the six "R" processes of mourning, and hence at risk for complicated mourning.

SOCIOCULTURAL AND TECHNOLOGICAL TRENDS EXACERBATING THE HIGH-RISK FACTORS AND INCREASING THE PREVALENCE OF COMPLICATED MOURNING

Social change, medical advances, and shifting political realities have spawned the recent trends that have complicated healthy grief and mourning.

Social change, occurring at an increasingly rapid rate, encompasses such processes as urbanization; industrialization; increasing technicalization; secularization and deritualization (particularly the trend to omit funeral or memorial services and not to view the body); greater social mobility; social reorganization (specifically a decline in—if not a breakdown of—the nuclear family, increases in single parent and blended families, and the relative exclusion of the aged and dying); rising societal, interpersonal, and institutional violence (physical, sexual, and psychological); and unemployment, poverty, and economic problems. Consequences include social alienation; senses of personal helplessness and hopelessness; parental absence and neglect of children; larger societal discrepancies between the "haves" and the "have nots"; and epidemic drug and alcohol abuse, physical and sexual abuse of children and those without power (e.g., women and the elderly), and availability of guns. All of these sequelae have tended to increase violence even more, to sever or severely damage the links between children and adults, and to expose individuals to more traumatic and unnatural deaths.

Medical advances have culminated in lengthier chronic illnesses, and increased age spans, altered mortality rates, and intensified bioethical dilemmas. These trends, plus those involving social change, accompany contemporary political realities of increasing incidence of terrorism, assassination, political torture, and genocide, which get played out against the ever-present possibility of ecological disaster, nuclear holocaust, and megadeath to impact dramatically and undeniably on today's mourner [4–6].

VIOLENCE: A PARTICULARLY MALIGNANT TREND

Any commentary on present-day trends would be negligent if it did not elaborate somewhat upon the phenomenon of violence in today's society. Violence contributes significantly to the increasing prevalence of complicated mourning, and is associated with most of its generic high-risk factors. One crime index offense occurs every two seconds in the United States, with one violent crime occurring every nineteen seconds [7]. Violent crime has risen to the extent that in April 1991 Attorney General Richard Thornburgh issued the statement that "a citizen of this country is today more likely to be the victim of a violent crime than of an automobile accident" [8]. The U.S. Department of Justice estimates that five out of six of today's twelve-year-olds will become victims of violent crime during their lifetimes [9], with estimates for the lifetime chance of becoming a victim of homicide in the United States ranging from one out of 133 to one out of 153 depending upon the source of the statistics [10]. One category of homicide—murder by juvenile—is increasing so rapidly that it is now being termed "epidemic" by psychologist and attorney Charles Ewing [11], an authority on child perpetrators of homicide.

Other types of crime and victimization are on the rise in the United States. The National Victim Center Overview of Crime and Victimization in America [12] provides some of the horrifying statistics:

- Wife-beating results in more injuries that require medical treatment than rape, auto accidents, and muggings combined.
- More than one out of every 200 senior citizens is the victim of a violent crime each year, making a total of 155,000 elderly Americans who are attacked, robbed, assaulted, and murdered every year—435 each day.
- New York City has reported an eighty percent increase in hate-motivated crimes since 1986, with seventy percent of them perpetrated by those under age nineteen.
- One in three women will be sexually assaulted during her lifetime.
- Every forty-seven seconds a child is abused or neglected.

Certainly, society not only condones, but escalates, violence. Books, movies, music videos, and songs perpetuate the belief that violence is not merely acceptable, but exciting. Books focusing on real-life serial killers; escalating movie violence associated with anatomically precise and sexually explicit images; and music portraying hostility against women, murder, and necrophilia are routine. According to Thomas Radecki, Research Director for the National Coalition on Television Violence, by the age of 18 the average American child will have seen 200,000 violent acts on television, including 40,000 murders [13]. Children's programming now averages twenty-five violent acts per hour, which is up fifty percent from that in the early 1980s [14]. The recently popular children's movie, *Teenage Mutant Ninja Turtles,* had a total of 194 acts of violence primarily committed by the "heroes" of the film, which was the most violent film ever to be given a "PG" rating [15]. In the week of March 11, 1990, *America's Funniest Home Videos* became the highest-rated series on television. Some of the stories on that program that viewers found particularly amusing included a child getting hit in the face with a shovel, seven women falling off a bench, a man getting hit by a glider, and a child bicycling into a tree [15]. All of this provides serious concerns given the twenty-year research of Leonard Eron and L. Rowell Huesmann, who found that children who watch significant amounts of TV violence at the age of eight were consistently more likely to commit violent crimes or engage in spouse abuse at age thirty [13]. These researchers determined that heavy exposure to media violence is one of the major causes of aggressive behavior, crime, and violence in society.

Other forms of violence are increasing as well. Reports of abused and neglected children continue to rise. They reached 2.5 million in 1990, an increase of 30.7 percent since 1986, and 117 percent in the past decade [16]. One out of three girls, and one out of seven boys, are sexually abused by the time they reach eighteen [17]. In the United States, when random studies are conducted without the inclusion of high-risk groups, one in eight husbands has been physically aggressive with his wife in the preceding twelve months [18]. At least 2,000,000 women are severely and aggressively assaulted by their partners in any twelve-month period [18]. It is a myth that what has been termed "intimate violence" is confined to mentally disturbed individuals. While ten percent of offenders do sustain some form of psychopathology, ninety percent of offenders do not look any different than the "normal" individual [19].

SEQUELAE OF THE TRENDS PREDISPOSING TO COMPLICATED MOURNING

As a result of all the aforementioned sociocultural and technological trends, there have been changes in three main areas which have significantly increased the prevalence of complicated mourning:

1. the types of death occurring today
2. the characteristics of personal relationships that are severed by today's deaths
3. the personality and resources of today's mourner.

Each of these adversely impacts in one or more ways upon one or more of the high-risk factors for complicated mourning, thereby increasing its prevalence.

TYPES OF DEATH OCCURRING TODAY

Contemporary American society is witnessing the increase in three types of death known to be at high risk for complicated mourning: 1) sudden and unanticipated deaths, especially if they are traumatic (i.e., characterized not only by suddenness

and lack of anticipation, but violence, mutilation, and destruction; preventability and/or randomness; multiple death; or the mourner's personal encounter with death [20]; 2) deaths that result from excessively lengthy chronic illnesses; and 3) deaths of children. Each of these deaths presents the survivors with issues known to compromise the "R" processes of mourning, hence each circumstance is a high-risk factor for complicated mourning.

Sudden and Unanticipated Traumatic Deaths

Sudden and unanticipated traumatic deaths stem primarily from four main causes: 1) accidents; 2) technological advances; 3) increasing rates of homicide and the escalating violence and pathology of perpetrators; and 4) higher suicide rates. Although mortality rates for children and youth in the United States have decreased since 1900, the large proportion of deaths from external causes—injuries, homicide, and suicide—distinguishes mortality at ages one to nineteen from that at other ages; with external causes of death accounting for about ten percent of the deaths of children and youth in 1900 and rising to 64 percent in 1985 [21].

Current trends reveal that "accidents"—a term covering most deaths from motor vehicle crashes, falls, poisoning, drowning, fire, suffocation, and firearms—are the leading cause of death among all persons aged one to thirty-seven and represent the fourth leading cause of death among persons of all ages [22]. On the average, there are eleven accidental deaths and approximately 1,030 disabling injuries every hour during the year [22]. Accidents are the single most common type of horrendous death for persons of any age, bringing deaths which are "premature, torturous, and without redeeming value" [23].

Technological advances simultaneously have both decreased the proportion of natural deaths that occur and increased the proportion of sudden and unanticipated traumatic deaths. For instance, substantial improvements in biomedical technology have culminated in higher survival rates from illnesses which previously would have been fatal. This leaves individuals alive longer to be susceptible to unnatural death. Additionally, the increase in unnatural death is due to greater current exposure to technology, machinery, motor vehicles, airplanes, chemicals, firearms, weapon systems, and so forth that put human beings at greater risk for unnatural death. For example, prior to the advent of the airplane, a crash of a horse and buggy could claim far fewer lives and be less mutilating to the bodies than the crash of a DC-10.

The third reason for the increase in sudden and unanticipated traumatic deaths stems from the increasing rates of homicide and the escalating violence and pathology of those who perpetrate these crimes upon others. The increase in actual homicide incidence; the rising percentage of serial killers; and the types of violence perpetrated before, during, and after the final homicidal act suggest that there are sicker individuals doing sicker things. More than ever before, homicide may be marked by cult or ritual killing, thrill killing, random killing, drive-by shootings, and accompanied by predeath torture and postdeath defilement. The increasing pathology of those who commit violent crimes may be seen as the result of the previously mentioned sociocultural trends, especially but not exclusively the individual's decreasing social connections and sense of power; fewer social prohibitions, and increasing societal violence. It reflects the increasing number of individuals with impaired psychological development, characterized often by an absent conscience, low frustration tolerance, poor impulse control, inability to delay gratification or modulate aggression, a sense of deprivation and entitlement, and notably poor attachment bonds and pathological patterns of relationships.

The fourth reason for the increase in sudden and unanticipated traumatic deaths follows from the higher suicide rates currently found in Western society. As above, these types of death appear to derive from all of the aforementioned trends contributing to complicated mourning in general.

The reader will note that most of the sudden and unanticipated traumatic deaths in this category also are preventable. Given that the perception of preventability is a high-risk factor predisposing to complicated mourning, to the extent that a mourner maintains this perception as an element in his or her mourning of the death that individual sustains a greater chance for experiencing complications in the process.

Long-Term Chronic Illness Death

This type of death is increasing in frequency because of biomedical and technological advances that can combat disease and forestall cessation of life. Consequently, today's illnesses are longer in duration than ever before. However, it has been well-documented that there are significant problems for survivors when a loved one's terminal illness persists for too long [24]. These illnesses often present loved ones with inherent difficulties that eventually complicate their postdeath bereavement and expose them to situations and dilemmas previously unheard of when patients died sooner and/or without becoming the focus for bioethical debates around the use of machinery and the prolongation of life without quality. With the increase in the Human Immunodeficiency Virus (HIV) and Acquired Immunodeficiency Syndrome (AIDS), significant multidimensional stresses arise which engender those known to complicate mourning in anyone (e.g., anger, ambivalence, guilt, stigmatization, social disenfranchisement, problems obtaining required health care, and so forth). The fact that an individual may be positive for the HIV virus for an exceptionally long period of time prior to developing the often long-term, multiproblemic, and idiosyncratic course of their particular version of AIDS, with all of its vicissitudes, gives new meaning these days to the stresses of long-term chronic illness.

Parental Loss of a Child

In earlier years, by the time an adult child died, his or her parents would have been long deceased. Today, with increases in lifespan and advances in medical technology, parents are permitted to survive long enough to witness the deaths of the adult children they used to predecease. Clinically and empirically, it is well-known that significant problematic issues are associated with the parental loss of a child—issues which when

compared to those generated by other losses appear to make this loss the most difficult with which to cope [25]. These problematic issues and complicated mourning are now visited upon older parents who remain alive to experience the death of their adult child. There is even some suggestion that additional stresses are added to the normal burdens of parental bereavement when the child is an adult in his or her own right [26]. It is a uniquely contemporary trend, therefore, that associated with all of today's deaths are a greater percentage of parents who, because of medical advancements, are alive to be placed in the high-risk situation for complicated mourning upon the death of their adult child. This is a population that can be excepted to increase, and consequently swell the numbers of complicated mourners as well.

CHARACTERISTICS OF PERSONAL RELATIONSHIPS SEVERED BY TODAY'S DEATHS

As a consequence of societal trends, there has been an increase in conflicted and dependent relationships in our society. Both types are high-risk factors when they characterize the mourner's premorbid relationship with the deceased [1]. With more of these types of relationships than ever before, there is a relative increase in the prevalence of complicated mourning, which is predisposed to develop after the death of one with whom the mourner has had this type of bond.

In 1957, Edmond Volkart offered a classic discussion of why death in the American family tends to cause greater psychological impact than in other cultures, specifically causing the family to be uniquely vulnerable to bereavement [6]. The reasons he delineated are even more salient today, and are part of the trends already cited above. Among other trends, he noted that the limited range of interaction in the American family fosters unusually intense emotional involvement as compared to other societies, and that there is an exclusivity of relationships in the American family. Both trends breed overidentification and overdependence among family members, which in turn engender ambivalence, repressed hostility, and guilt that create greater potential for complications after the death. Adding fuel to this fire is the societal expectation that grief expression concentrates on feelings and expression of loss. There is a failure both to recognize and to provide channels for hostility, guilt, and ambivalence.

Problematic relationships are on the rise in our society for other reasons as well. Quite importantly, there is an overall increase in sexual and physical abuse of children, as well as other adults. Research repeatedly documents the malignant intrapsychic and interpersonal sequelae of abuse and victimization [27, 28]. This leaves the victim susceptible to complications in mourning not only because of the myriad symptomatology and biopsychosocial issues they caused, but typically with significant amounts of the anger, ambivalence, and/or dependence known to complicate any individual's mourning. In addition, the victimization may interfere with the mourner permitting him or herself to mourn the death of the perpetrator—an often necessary task that many victims resist because of inaccurate beliefs about mourning in general and/or misconstruals of what their specifically mourning the perpetrator's death may mean [1]. This only further victimizes the person through the consequences of incomplete mourning.

These forms of victimization are not the only experiences which give rise to the conflicted and dependent relationships identified as predisposing to complicated mourning. Individuals raised in families with one or more alcoholic parents or a parent who is an adult child of an alcoholic (ACOA), or with one or more parents who are psychologically impaired, rigid in beliefs, compulsive in behaviors, codependent, absent, neglectful, or chronically ill are vulnerable too. As sociocultural trends escalate these scenarios, relationships characterized by anger, ambivalence, and dependency will become prevalent, and complicated mourning will, in turn, become more frequent.

THE PERSONALITY AND RESOURCES OF TODAY'S MOURNER

Current trends suggest that the personality and resources of today's mourner leave that individual compromised in mourning for three reasons. First, given the trends previously discussed, the personalities and mental health of today's mourners are often more impaired. These impaired persons—who themselves frequently sustain poor attachment bonds with their own parents because of these trends—typically effect intergenerational transmission of these deficits via the inadequate parenting provided to their own children and the unhealthy experiences those children undergo. Clinically, one sees more often these days impaired superego development, lower level personality organization, narcissistic behavior, character disorder, and poor impulse control. Given that one's personality and previous and current states of mental health are critical factors influencing any mourner's ability to address mourning successfully, a trend towards relatively more impairment in this area has implications for greater numbers of people being added to the rolls of complicated mourners.

Another liability for a mourner is the existence of unaccommodated prior or concurrent losses or stresses. In this regard, a second reason for the increased prevalence of complicated mourning comes from the presence of more loss and stress in the life of today's mourner as compared to times in the past. To the extent that contemporary sociocultural trends bring relatively more losses and stresses for a person, both prior to a given death (e.g., parents' divorce) and concomitant with it (e.g., unemployment), today's mourner is relatively more disadvantaged given his or her increased exposure to these high-risk factors.

The third reason for increased complications in mourning arises from the compromise of the mourner's resources. Disenfranchised mourning [29] is on the rise, and the consequent perceived lack of social support it stimulates is a high-risk factor for complicated mourning. It is quite evident that conditions in contemporary American society promote all three of the main reasons for social disenfranchisement during mourn-

ing, i.e., invalidation of the loss, the lost relationship, or the mourner [29]. Examples of unrecognized losses that are increasing in today's society include abortions, adoptions, the deaths of pets, and the inherent losses of those with Alzheimer's disease. Cases of the second type of disenfranchised loss that are on the increase include relationships that are not based on kin ties, or are not socially sanctioned (e.g., gay or lesbian relationships, extramarital affairs), or those that existed primarily in the past (e.g., former spouses or in-laws). Increasingly prevalent situations where the mourner is unrecognized can be found when the mourner is elderly, mentally handicapped, or a child. The more society creates, maintains, or permits individuals to be disenfranchised in their mourning, the more those individuals are at risk for complicated mourning given that disenfranchisement is so intimately linked with the high-risk factor of the mourner's perception of lack of social support.

PROBLEMS INHERENT IN THE MENTAL HEALTH PROFESSION WHICH INTERFERE WITH PROPER RESPONSE TO COMPLICATED MOURNING AND TO ITS ESCALATION

There are three serious problems inherent in mental health today that interfere with the profession's response to complicated mourning and its escalation. Each one contributes to increasing the prevalence of complicated mourning either by facilitating misdiagnosis and/or hampering requisite treatment. The three problems are: 1) lack of an appropriate diagnostic category in the DSM-III-R; 2) insufficient knowledge about grief, mourning, and bereavement in general; and 3) decreased funds for and increased restrictions upon contemporary mental health services.

In the DSM-III-R, there is the lack of a diagnostic category for anything but the most basic uncomplicated grief, with the criteria even for this being significantly unrealistic for duration and symptomatology in light of today's data on uncomplicated grief and mourning. If they want to treat a mourning individual, mental health clinicians are often forced to utilize other diagnoses, many of which have clinical implications that are unacceptable. Other diagnoses that clinicians employ to justify treatment and to incorporate more fully the symptomatology of the bereaved individual frequently include one of the depressive, anxiety, or adjustment disorders; brief reactive psychosis; or one of the V code diagnoses.

The second area of problems in the mental health profession is the shocking insufficiency of knowledge about grief and bereavement in general. Mental health professionals tend, as does the general public, to have inappropriate expectations and unrealistic attitudes about grief and mourning, and to believe in and promote the myths and stereotypes known to pervade society at large. These not only do not help, but actually harm bereaved individuals given that they are used to (a) set the standards against which the bereaved individual is evaluated, (b) determine the assistance and support provided and/or judged to be needed, and (c) support unwarranted diagnoses of failure and pathology [30]. Yet, the problem is not all in *mis*information. Too many clinicians actually do not even know that they lack the requisite information they must possess if they want to treat a bereaved person successfully. Without a doubt, the majority of clinicians know an insufficient amount about uncomplicated grief and mourning; and of those who do know an adequate amount, only a fraction of them know enough about complicated mourning. Clinician lack of information and misinformation is the major cause of iatrogenesis in the treatment of grief and mourning.

An overall decrease in funds permitted and an increase in third-party payer insurance restrictions mark contemporary mental health services and constitute the third problem in the field adding to the prevalence of complicated mourning. These changes occur at a time when it not only is becoming more clearly documented that uncomplicated grief and mourning is more associated with psychiatric distress than previously recognized [31] and that it persists for longer duration [32], but precisely when the incidence of complicated mourning is increasing and demanding more extensive treatment for higher proportions of the bereaved. Consequently, at the exact point in time that the mental health community will have more bereaved individuals with greater complicated mourning requiring treatment for longer periods of time, mental health services will be increasingly subjected to limitations, preapprovals, third-party reviews by persons ignorant of the area, short-term models, and forced usage of inappropriate diagnostic classification. This scenario demands that the mental health professional working with the bereaved find new policies models, approaches, and treatments which are appropriate to these serious realities. Failing to do so, the future is frightening as the current system simply is not equipped to respond to the coming onslaught of complicated mourners.

THE PITFALLS FOR ADDRESSING COMPLICATED MOURNING RESIDING IN THE FIELD OF THANATOLOGY TODAY

It is unfortunate, but true: Thanatologists are contributing to the rising prevalence of complicated mourning as are contemporary sociocultural and technological trends and the mental health profession. While it is not in the purview of this article to discuss at length the myriad problems inherent in our own field of thanatology that contribute to complicated mourning, it must be noted:

- A significant amount of caregivers lack adequate clinical information about uncomplicated grief and mourning, e.g., the "normal" psychiatric complications of uncomplicated grief and mourning.
- Many thanatologists, in their effort to promote the naturalness of grief and mourning and to depathologize the way they construe it to have been medicalized, maintain an insufficient understanding of complicated grief and mourning.

- There is nonexistent, or at the very least woefully insufficient, assessment conducted by caregivers who assume that the grief and mourning they observe must be related exclusively to the particular death closest in time and who do not place the individual's responses within the context of his or her entire life prior to evaluating them.
- The phenomenon of "throwing the baby out with the bathwater" has occurred regarding medication in bereavement. Out of a concern that a mourner not be inappropriately medicated as had been done so often in the past, caregivers today often fail to send mourners for medication evaluations that are desperately needed, e.g., antianxiety medication following traumatic deaths.
- The research in the field has not been sufficiently longitudinal and has overfocused on certain populations (e.g., widows), leaving findings that are not generalizable over time for many types of mourners, especially complicated mourners.
- Caregivers do not always recognize that any work as a grief or mourning counselor or therapist must overlay a basic foundation of training in mental health intervention in general. While education in thanatology, good intentions, and/or previous experience with loss may be appropriate credentials for the individual facilitating uncomplicated grief and mourning (e.g., a facilitator of a mutual help group for the bereaved), this is not sufficient for that person offering counseling or therapy.
- Given that thanatology itself is a "specialty area," thanatologists often fail to recognize that the field encompasses a number of "subspecialty areas," each of which has its own data base and treatment requirements, i.e., all mourners are not alike and caregivers must recognize and respond to the differences inherent in different loss situations (e.g., loss of a child versus loss of a spouse or sudden and unanticipated death versus an expected chronic illness death).
- Clinicians working with the dying and the bereaved are subject to countertransference phenomena, stress reactions, codependency, "vicarious traumatization" [33], and burnout.

This constitutes a brief, and by no means exhaustive, listing of the types of pitfalls into which a thanatologist may fall. Each "fall" has the potential for compromising the mourning of the bereaved individual and in that regard has the potential for increasing the prevalence of complicated mourning today.

CONCLUSION

This article has discussed the causes and forms of complicated mourning, and has delineated the seven high-risk factors known to predispose to it. The purpose has been to illustrate how current sociocultural and technological trends are exacerbating these factors, thereby significantly increasing the prevalence of complicated mourning today. Problems both in the mental health profession and in the field of thanatology further contribute by preventing or interfering with requisite intervention. It is imperative that these grim realities be recognized in order that appropriate policies, models, approaches, and treatments be developed to respond to the individual and societal needs created by complicated mourning and its sequelae.

REFERENCES

1. T. Rando, *Treatment of Complicated Mourning,* Research Press, Champaign, Illinois, 1993.

2. T. Rando, *Grief, Dying, and Death: Clinical Interventions for Caregivers,* Research Press, Champaign, Illinois, 1984.

3. American Psychiatric Association, *Diagnostic and Statistical Manual of Mental Disorders,* (3rd ed. rev.), Washington, D.C., 1987.

4. H. Feifel, The Meaning of Death in American Society: Implications for Education, in *Death Education: Preparation for Living,* B. Green and D. Irish (eds.), Schenkman, Cambridge, Massachusetts, 1971.

5. R. Lifton, *Death in Life: Survivors of Hiroshima,* Random House, New York, 1968.

6. E. Volkart (with collaboration of S. Michael), Bereavement and Mental Health, in *Explorations in Social Psychiatry,* A. Leighton, J. Clausen, and R. Wilson (eds.), Basic Books, New York, 1957.

7. Federal Bureau of Investigation, U.S. Department of Justice, *Uniform Crime Reports for the United States,* U.S. Government Printing Office, Washington, D.C., 1990.

8. Violent Crimes up 10%, *Providence Journal,* pp. A1 and A6, April 29, 1991.

9. National Victim Center, *America Speaks Out: Citizens' Attitudes about Victims' Rights and Violence,* (Executive Summary), Fort Worth, Texas, 1991.

10. Bureau of Justice Statistics Special Report, *The Risk of Violent Crime,* (NCJ-97119), U.S. Department of Justice, Washington, D.C., May 1985.

11. Killing by Kids "Epidemic" Forecast, *APA Monitor,* pp. 1 and 31, April, 1991.

12. National Victim Center, *National Victim Center Overview of Crime and Victimization in America,* Fort Worth, Texas, 1991.

13. Violence in Our Culture, *Newsweek,* pp. 46–52, April 1, 1991.

14. J. Patterson and P. Kim, *The Day America Told the Truth,* Prentice Hall Press, New York, 1991.

15. National Victim Center, *Crime, Safety and You!,* 1:3, 1990.

16. Children's Defense Fund Memo on the Family Preservation Act, Washington, D.C., July 2, 1991.

17. E. Bass and L. Davis, *The Courage to Heal: A Guide for Women Survivors of Child Sexual Abuse,* Harper and Row Publishers, New York, 1988.

18. A. Brown, *"Women's Roles" and Responses to Violence by Intimates: Hard Choices for Women Living in a Violent Society,* paper presented at the conference on "Trauma and Victimization: Understanding and Healing Survivors" sponsored by the University of Connecticut Center for Professional Development, Vernon, Connecticut, September 27–28, 1991.

19. R. Gelles, *The Roots, Context, and Causes of Family Violence,* paper presented at the conference on "Trauma and Victimization: Understanding and Healing Survivors" sponsored by the University of Connecticut Center for Professional Development, Vernon, Connecticut, September 27–28, 1991.

20. T. Rando, Complications in Mourning Traumatic Death, in *Death, Dying and Bereavement,* I. Corless, B. Germino, and M. Pittman-Lindeman (eds.), Jones and Bartlett Publishers, Inc., Boston, (in press).

21. L. Fingerhut and J. Kleinman, Mortality Among Children and Youth, *American Journal of Public Health, 79,* pp. 899–901, 1989.

22. National Safety Council, *Accident Facts, 1991 Edition,* Chicago, 1991.

23. M. Dixon and H. Clearwater, Accidents, in *Horrendous Death, Health, and Well-Being,* D. Leviton (ed.), Hemisphere Publishing Corporation, New York, 1991.

24. T. Rando (ed.) *Loss and Anticipatory Grief,* Lexington Books, Lexington, Massachusetts, 1986.

25. T. Rando (ed.), *Parental Loss of a Child,* Research Press, Champaign, Illinois, 1986.

26. T. Rando, Death of an Adult Child, in *Parental Loss of a Child,* T. Rando, (ed.), Research Press, Champaign, Illinois, 1986.

27. C. Courtois, *Healing the Incest Wound: Adult Survivors in Therapy,* Norton, New York, 1988.

28. F. Ochberg (ed.), *Post-Traumatic Therapy and Victims of Violence,* Brunner/Mazel, New York, 1988.

29. K. Doka (ed.), *Disenfranchised Grief: Recognizing Hidden Sorrow,* Lexington Books, Lexington, Massachusetts, 1989.

30. T. Rando, *Grieving: How To Go On Living When Someone You Love Dies,* Lexington Books, Lexington, Massachusetts, 1988.

31. S. Jacobs and K. Kim, Psychiatric Complications of Bereavement, *Psychiatric Annals, 20,* pp. 314–317, 1990.

32. S. Zisook and S. Shuchter, Time Course of Spousal Bereavement, *General Hospital Psychiatry, 7,* pp. 95–100, 1985.

33. I. McCann and L. Pearlman, Vicarious Traumatization: A Framework for Understanding the Psychological Effects of Working with Victims, *Journal of Traumatic Stress, 3,* pp. 131–149, 1990.

Children Grieve Too

Lessons in how to support children through a normal, healthy grief process

by Linda Goldman

Certified Grief Therapist and Grief Educator
Center for Loss and Grief Therapy
Kensington, Maryland

Learning how to deal with grieving children will help parents, teachers, and students exist in a more healthy living and learning environment. The complex relationship between loss issues and a young child's ability to function in and out of the classroom needs to be addressed in a new and fresh way. We need to see children's grief, and our own, as on ongoing life process that is approachable through words, activities, and nonverbal communication. This understanding can enable Head Start centers to create a safe environment for parents, teachers, and children to acknowledge and process difficult feelings.

The prevailing myth that Head Start children are too young to understand grief and loss issues seems outdated. If children are capable of love, they are certainly capable of feeling grief. We, as Head Start parents and educators, can model our own grief as a teaching tool for young children, allowing them to express thoughts and feelings of sadness, anger, fear and frustration. As role models, we need to be in touch with our own grief in order to help grieving children heal.

Young children continually process and incorporate a large part of their physical world. They are influenced by how adults around them act and react to this world. Children will process and incorporate the reactions of

From *Children and Families*, Spring 1997, pp. 22-31. Reprinted by permission of the author and the National Head Start Association. © 1997.

Drawing is a great way to relay unacknowledged feelings. This picture was drawn by 7-year-old Sara who has AIDS. This picture illustrates her hope that after she dies, she can be in heaven with her mother, who also has AIDS.

Head Start parents and teachers into their own grief. The Head Start community serves as a model for the children when it expresses sadness that a teacher died, anger that a friend has cancer, fear that a school was vandalized, and frustration that there is no cure for AIDS.

This article will show you how to help a grieving child, and in turn help Head Start educators create a more effective learning environment for the entire school community. Grief issues can create trauma in children that can inhibit learning and development, resulting in larger numbers of our children having social and academic difficulties in and out of school. Children's experiences in the pre-school years lay the foundation for their ability, openness, and readiness to learn. School systems need to identify, work with, and meet the needs of children faced with these life-changing situations.

Normal grief symptoms

Before we can help children with their grief issues, we need to understand how grief affects all of us. The death of a parent, sibling, friend, or teacher greatly impacts kids and grownups. Shame and guilt often ac-company the death of a loved one, with adults and children fearing they in some way caused the death. Isolation and loneliness sometimes follow a death. People who are grieving often feel that they are not understood and that they are different from others.

In addition to death, members of the Head Start community may grieve losses in other life circumstances. Moving to a new state, learning that a beloved teacher is retiring, or losing a favorite doll are typical examples of nondeath losses that can create great stress and anxiety. Normal grief may involve feelings of numbness, rage, deep sadness, overwhelmed states of emotion, regression, panic, and difficulties eating and sleeping. Time appears to stand still, and adults and children experience forever the loss of life as they knew it before the grief experience.

Normal signs of grief for children

In addition to normal grief issues,

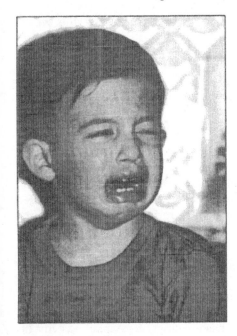

It's healthy for a grieving child to cry. Children need to feel their sadness and feel free to express it.

there are special considerations that apply specifically to kids. Understanding their unique method of grieving can enable Head Start personnel to gain a greater depth of understanding for a grieving child. There appears to be a direct relationship between the intensity of children's grief and loss issues and their ability to learn and grow. Children experience decreased capacity to concentrate if they experience an extreme trauma, such as witnessing their mom's murder. If they cannot or will not speak about this event, the trauma begins a long episode of blocked energy, and this block often results in an inability to learn.

A grieving child often is misdiagnosed as learning disabled or as having Attention Deficit Disorder. The unresolved grief continues and grows unaddressed throughout the child's education. Children may become hyperactive, easily distracted, or impulsive. These behaviors are often misinterpreted as emotional or learning problems instead of being viewed as a cry for help. Head Start teachers and educators need to become familiar with normal grief symptoms in order to more accurately identify problem areas.

Young children are often preoccupied with death, and they worry excessively about their own health and the health of those around them. Four-year-old Tommy, whose baby sister Ann had died, asked his mom every night, "Am I going to die too?" "If our baby Ann went to heaven, can I go with her?" The young child often speaks of the person that died in the present and maintains a continuous and ongoing relationship with the deceased. Alice, a 6-year-old, used her toy telephone to call her mom who had died and tell her about the school day. "I miss you, Mommy. I'm showing you my art project while we talk. I love you!"

Adam, a 5-year-old, began imitating his dad's gestures after he died. Adam patted his dog, Muffin, saying, "You're a good girl, Muffin" just the way his dad used to do. Imitating a loved one who died is a normal sign of grief. Children often feel the presence of a mom or dad who has died. Mary, a 4-year-old preschooler, told me she felt her mom was with her whenever she saw a butterfly and that the butterfly was a messenger saying, "I love you."

Parents, teachers, educators, and caring adults can reduce anxieties for children and their families by normalizing common thoughts and feelings. For example, adults can assure children that it is a normal grief response to worry about their own health after a loved one dies. It's normal to fear death after a parent dies in a car crash. And it's also normal to want to seek revenge after the

Normal Signs of Grief

Adults and children need to be aware of normal signs of grief. When educators and parents see signs of grief, they can ensure that children get the help and support they need. And when children learn normal signs of grief, they can share similar ways of expressing thoughts and feelings with other grieving children. The following are common responses to grief. Children may:

- Tell and retell their stories.
- Become preoccupied with death or their own health and that of a surviving parent or guardian.
- Speak of dead loved one in the present.
- Feel the presence of a loved one.
- Imitate and idolize a loved one who died.
- Become the class clown or the class bully.
- Withdraw from other children.
- Show an inability to concentrate and have a tendency to daydream.
- Experience nightmares, manifest bedwetting, or regress and become clingy.
- Complain of stomachaches and headaches.

murder of a family member. Normalizing grief responses will help minimize the stress level that often accompanies these new and scary feelings.

The young child's view of death

Piaget, a French educator whose thoughts have greatly influenced the world of grief therapy for children, explains that young children between the ages of 2 and 7 are categorized as part of the preoperational stage of cognitive development. This state is marked by magical thinking, egocentricity, reversibility, and causality.

Kids imagine their words have magical powers, and so they often feel that they are in some way responsible for tragedies. Ashley and Roxanne are sisters, ages 4 and 7. After a tremendous argument over a stuffed animal, Ashley screamed at her sister, "I hate you, and I wish you were dead!" She tore Roxanne's stuffed toy to bits. The next night, Roxanne was killed in a car accident. Ashley blamed herself, saying over and over that she knew her words made her sister die.

In a similar example, Charlie yelled at his older brother, "I hate you. I wish you were dead!" Charlie was haunted with the idea that this wish created his brother's fatal ski accident. Charlie's egocentric perception made him see himself at the center of the universe, capable of creating and destroying the world around him just by willing it.

Molly, a 6-year-old first grader whose dad died in an automobile accident, visualized death as reversible and believed that her dad was going to come back. She wrote a letter to her dad, addressed it to heaven, and put it in the mail. She waited and waited to receive a letter back, even though she knew her dad was killed in a car crash. Her age-appropriate belief in causality caused her to question in her mind: "Is Dad not writing back because I didn't get a good report card?"

Brian was a 3-year-old whose thinking convinced him that he had killed his dad. When he confided these feelings, he explained why he thought that he had murdered his dad. "My dad picked me up the night he had his heart attack. If he hadn't done that, he wouldn't have died. It's all my fault." Brian needed to understand that his dad's heart attack was caused by being overweight and smoking cigarettes, not his driving to pick up Brian.

Clichés that inhibit the grief process

Many times, children take language literally. They need direct and simple language explaining death. When defining death for the young child we could say, "Death is when the body stops working. Usually people die when they are very, very old, or very, very, very sick, or their bodies are so injured that the doctors

DRAW YOUR FAMILY AFTER DAD DIED

OK

Look at me

This is Mom & John Watching me at the playground.

Memory books are a collection of drawings and writings that allow a child to re-experience memories and share thoughts and feelings in a safe way. This picture is from the memory book of Tommy, a 5-year-old. The large figure in the center is his Uncle John, whom Tommy had not seen in three years. The picture helped Tommy's grief therapist realize that the child had been lacking male support since his father's death four years earlier.

and nurses can't make their bodies work again." The following examples show how children misunderstand clichés:

- "Mom said they put our dog Lucky to sleep. Will I die when I go to sleep too?" questions 4-year-old Sam.
- "Grandpa went to heaven." Alice thought, "Why can't I go too?"
- "Do you think Dad is watching over me?" Kevin asked. "I hope not. That's too embarrassing."
- Five-year-old Mary wondered, "Grandma said God loved Grandpa so much he took him to heaven. Doesn't God love me that much?"

Children take these clichés so literally that sometimes their limited understanding can produce tragic events. Tanya was a 6-year-old whose mom had AIDS. Tanya heard adults repeatedly say her mom was "going to be with the angels," Tanya decided she wanted to be with the angels too and, so, after telling her older cousins she was "going to be with Mom," she walked in front of a moving train. Experts debate whether this death was suicide. The sad truth is that Tanya probably took the cliché literally, thinking that she would be with the angels and her mom. Like most children her age, she also probably assumed that her and her mom's deaths would be reversible.

Letter writing is an excellent activity to help grieving children express unrecognized feelings. This letter by 5-year-old Ashley clarified her perception that her mother was buried in the ground, but she was still alive.

Ways to help the grieving child

Grieving children must feel heard and understood. Many sensitive issues will arise, and feelings of worry, sadness, rage, terror, shame, abandonment, and self-hatred will emerge. The Head Start community needs to create a safe environment to meet the needs of all grieving children. Children must feel secure and free to express their thoughts and feelings, and feel listened to in the process.

Amy, who was a 5-year-old client in grief therapy, expressed great anger at her teacher Mrs. Jones for failing to acknowledge the death of Amy's dad. After her first week of school, Amy had bravely told Mrs. Jones that her father had died of cancer. Mrs. Jones never responded to her, and Amy waited and waited for a reply.

Every child is unique, and so is their grief. Too often, adults try to prescribe to children what they should think and feel, instead of allowing

children to tell us what they think and feel.

Usually, it is a good idea to encourage children to share pictures of deceased loved ones in order to open a dialogue and allow the expression of memories. Adam refused to bring into grief therapy a picture of his dad after he died, but he said he would later. Six months later, when he was ready, Adam appeared with a picture of his dad and him playing baseball. This behavior is typical, and it shows how important it is to respect a grieving child and wait until the child is ready to show a picture and share memories of a loved one who has died.

When children can express previously hidden emotions, they gain a greater understanding of themselves and allow adults to be more in touch with what is going on in their grief process. So often, children need to tell their story over and over. Using tools such as drawing, writing, role-playing, and re-enactment, children can safely project feelings and thoughts about their loss.

Grief feelings and thoughts are continual and ever-changing. Sometimes, they arrive without warning, and children may feel unprepared for their enormity in a school setting. Create an understanding with the grieving child that allows her or him to go to a safe place outside the classroom when these unexpected situations occur, without needing to explain why in front of classmates. Also, allowing visits to the school nurse reassures children that they and their family are okay.

Memory work is used in grief therapy to enable children to tell about a person who died and open discussion. Memory books are a collection of drawings and writings that allow a child to re-experience memories and share thoughts and feelings in a safe way. Kids can tell about how their family was before their dad died, and how their family appears to them after dad died.

A 5-year-old named Ryan created a page in his memory book explaining feelings before his dad died. He drew and wrote about his dad yelling at him to "Go to bed!" and wrote his response of "Help me." Ryan used his memory book page as a tool to understand his relationship with his dad, discovering the anger and fear he felt toward his father before he was murdered. These unresolved feelings had made the grief process more difficult by stifling feelings. This page in his memory book allowed Ryan to discover hidden feelings, see his grief, and bring his difficult relationship out in the open.

Tommy was another 5-year-old whose memory book revealed a great absence of men in his life. When asked to draw his family now (four years after his father's death), he drew his Uncle John in the center of his picture watching him play on the playground. Tommy's mother was shocked by the placement of Tommy's uncle, because Tommy hadn't seen his Uncle John for almost three years. The loss of any significant men since his dad's death

---

Do's and Don'ts
for Adults Responding to Grieving Children

How parents and educators respond to a child's grief has a great impact on the child's ability to heal. Maintaining direct, honest, age-appropriate communication allows children to process thoughts and feelings at their own rate and comfort level.

Do:
- Keep the sense of security real for children.
- Maintain consistent routines.
- Prepare children for what will come (death, funeral, feelings).
- Use age-appropriate, clear, truthful language, because young children take words literally.
- Familiarize yourself with the normal symptoms of grief.
- Become a role model for grieving children.
- Validate children's feelings.
- Promote continuing communication with family.
- Allow children to call home if needed during the school day, and allow them to leave the room without having to give explanations.
- Create a safe person or place for children to go to during the school day to discuss feelings comfortably.
- Keep explanations brief and to the point. Repeat if needed, and ask the children to repeat what they think they heard to verify their understanding.
- Remember that children grieve differently.
- Realize many children grieve through play.
- Encourage children to say good-bye to a loved one who has died.

Don't:
- Force or expect children to verbalize feelings about their loss.
- Use clichés that children could take literally.
- Tell children their feelings are wrong.
- Suggest to children that they will get over their grief.
- Assume that children are not grieving if they don't show their feelings.

Phone play is one of many tools adults can use to encourage children to say good-bye to a loved one who has died.

emerged as a central issue for Tommy through the use of his memory book. With this knowledge, a new support group of men could be formed in Tommy's life. This male support group included a Big Brother, a coach as mentor in sports activities, and more frequent visits with Uncle John.

Another memory book page illustrates the worries in words and drawing of 6-year-old Alice. She explains that she worries about her family and that they are sad. "This is a picture of what I worry about," she says and shares a drawing of her family at the grave of her father. When questioned, she explained that one of her worries was that her surviving family wouldn't have enough money to stay in their house and they may have to move. This memory book page served as a vehicle to establish that Alice was worrying and to explore what those worries were.

Letter writing is another tool that allows children to express unrecognized feelings. Ashley, a 5-year-old kindergartener, came into grief therapy on Mother's Day, very angry that no one had mentioned the death of her mom. She was encouraged to write a letter to her mom. The letter clarified Ashley's perception that her mom was still alive but buried in the ground. In the letter, Ashley maintained an ongoing relationship with her mom, wondering what she would buy her for Mother's Day. Children's magical thinking can hold two contradictory concepts together. Ashley knew that her mom's body was no longer working, yet she believed that her mother would be coming back.

Drawing is a great way to allow small children to relay unacknowledged feelings. Kids can draw pictures of how they visualized their loved one dying, the hospital or fu-neral scene, or their image of where their loved one is now. Seven-year-old Sara has AIDS and so does her mom. Sara drew a picture of herself and her Mom in heaven, expressing her own and her mom's imagined death, and the hope they could be together in heaven.

Remember, it's healthy for a grieving child to cry. Children need to feel their sadness and feel free to express it. So often, well-meaning adults tend to inhibit tears, perhaps because we feel helpless when we see a young child cry, or perhaps it reminds us of our own sadness. Children are given messages such as "Don't cry, you need to be grown up!" "Boys don't cry, you need to be the man of the house now," and "Your dad wouldn't have wanted you to cry." These messages shut off tears and halt the natural grief process. Tears may be upsetting for an adult to see, but healthy for the child to experience.

Grief Activities for the Young Child

Following are hands-on activities that parents and teachers can use with grieving children to help them express their grief and ultimately heal.

- Use puppets and dolls to role-play, act out feelings, or act out the funeral or death of loved one.

- Use a sandtable or a dollhouse to re-enact the death or funeral of a loved one.

- Make memory books or memory boxes to allow children a physical way to store and hold memories.

- Use a tape recorder or punching bag as a vehicle to release feelings.

- Draw pictures that describe stories, dreams, and happenings surrounding a death.

- Use clay as a vehicle to re-create feelings and also as a means to work through feelings kinesthetically.

- Play music such as Hap Palmer's feelings song to open discussion about how kids feel.

- Read books about death (see the Books about Death and Grieving sidebar with this article).

- Display props such as toy telephones, ambulances, baby bottles, sunglasses, and doctor kits to promote creative fantasy for the young child.

- Have children draw their bodies and show where they feel happy, sad, angry, worried, or scared. Choose colors to tell about feelings.

- Have children write letters to a loved one who has died in order to understand their age-appropriate beliefs and perceptions.

What we can mention . . .

Too many children face losses in the form of sudden fatal accidents and deaths due to illness, suicide, homicide, and AIDS. There are also many nondeath related issues that have a similar or same effect on children. Loss of family stability from separation and divorce, violence and abuse, unemployment, multiple moves, parental imprisonment, and family alcohol and drug addiction are a few of the many grief issues impacting young children. In forming an open Head Start environment for exploring these life circumstances, it is helpful to remember that what we can mention, we can manage. If we, as caring and educated adults, are incapable of discussing an important and universal life issue, how then are children to learn what to think? Who will model such thoughts for them?

If Head Start professionals and parents can provide grief vocabulary, resources, and crisis and educational interventions, they will create a loss and grief program for young children that allows a safe experience of these deep and difficult life issues. Head Start centers can become a bridge of communication between the world of fear, isolation, and loneliness to the world of truth, compassion, and dignity for grieving children.

Linda Goldman specializes in working with children and grief. She is the author of two books on helping children with grief issues, Life and Loss: A Guide to Help Grieving Children *and* Breaking the Silence: A Guide to Help Children With Complicated Grief: Suicide, Homicide, AIDS, Violence, and Abuse. *Goldman is a consultant to Head Start, and she conducts workshops for school systems and universities to educate caring adults to respond to children's loss issues. Write her with questions or comments at the Center for Loss and Grief Therapy, 10400 Connecticut Avenue, Suite 514, Kensington, MD 20895. FAX: 301-656-4350.*

Photographs and illustrations are reprinted from Life and Loss: A Guide to Help Grieving Children *and* Breaking the Silence: A Guide to Help Children with Complicated Grief: Suicide, Homicide, AIDS, Violence, and Abuse *with permission from Taylor & Francis, publisher.*

Books about Death and Grieving

For teachers and parents:

Breaking the Silence: A Guide to Help Children With Complicated Grief: Suicide, Homicide, AIDS, Violence, and Abuse by Linda Goldman. 1996. Washington, DC: Taylor & Francis. A clearly written guide for adults to help children with complicated grief issues. It includes guidelines for educators, national resources, and an annotated bibliography.

Death in the Classroom by Kathleen Cassini and Jacqueline Rogers. 1990. Cincinnati, OH: Griefwork of Cincinnati. An informative teacher's textbook and resource guide that sensitively confronts ways to work in the classroom with death.

Grief Comes to Class by Majel Gliko-Braden. 1992. Omaha, NE: Centering Corp. A practical book designed to help teachers and parents assist bereaved children.

Life and Loss: A Guide to Help Grieving Children by Linda Goldman. 1994. Washington, DC: Taylor & Francis. A resource for working with children and grief. It provides practical information, resources, hands-on activities, a model of a good-bye visit for children, and an annotated bibliography.

For children:

About Dying by Sarah Stein. 1974. New York: Walker & Co. (ages 3-6). This book contains simple text and photographs to help young children understand death and provide ways to help them participate in commemorating.

The Frog Family's Baby Dies by Jerri Oehler. 1978. Durham, NC: Duke University Medical Center (ages 3-6). A coloring book explaining and answering questions about death for the young child.

When Someone Very Special Dies by Marge Heegaard. 1988. Minneapolis, MN: Woodland Press (ages 4-7). An excellent workbook for young children that uses artwork and journaling to allow them to understand and express their grief.

Where's Jess? by Joy and Marv Johnson. 1982. Omaha, NE: Centering Corporation (ages 4-6). A book for young children that answers their questions and expresses their feelings when a sibling dies.

LIVING WITH LOSS: A GROUP FOR BEREAVED COLLEGE STUDENTS

SHARON M. JANOWIAK
RENA MEI-TAL
and
RITA G. DRAPKIN

Indiana University of Pennsylvania, Indiana, Pennsylvania, USA

The college atmosphere is not one that is conducive to grieving. Students who are faced with the challenge of coming to terms with a loss bring unique concerns and difficulties to this task. A seven-session bereavement group run under the auspices of a college counseling center is described. The rationale for the group is discussed, and the planning and implementation of the group are described.

Students who come to college counseling centers present with a wide variety of problems. They may be dealing with loss issues resulting from graduating from high school, being separated from loved ones and familiar places, dealing with academic failure, or breaking off a romantic relationship (LaGrand, 1986). Grief issues are not often a presenting complaint, but they often surface when background information about the individual is obtained (Aubrey, 1988). Students dealing with grief may be only beginning to cope with the earlier death of a parent, now that they are away from home (Silverman, 1987). There are also students who experience the death of a loved one for the first time while they are in college.

Whatever the nature of the student's loss, the college atmosphere is rarely conducive to grieving. Campus life is geared primarily toward academic and social activities, leaving little room for bereaved students to get the support and understanding they need to make it through the grieving process. Individuals soon realize that it is easy to feel isolated on a college campus (Corey & Corey, 1992). Even well-meaning students may not know what to do to help a bereaved friend. They may avoid contact with the student who is grieving the loss of a parent, for example, in order to escape the uncomfortable knowledge that their own parents will someday die. As Silverman (1987) noted, "The college community, on the whole, mirror[s]

the attitudes and values of the larger community in its inability to deal with grief" (p. 393).

According to Erikson's (1963) theory of development, the typical college student is faced with the developmental task of intimacy versus isolation. College students are struggling with breaking away from their families of origin and developing independent identities. It can be especially difficult for these young adults to cope with the loss of a loved one at the same time they are attempting to become autonomous individuals. As Berson (1988) noted, "If a parent dies at the time when a student is physically and emotionally pushing that parent away, the student's guilt feelings may be significantly increased, especially when the student realizes that all the 'unfinished business' can never be accomplished" (p. 102). These young adults face a continual process of integrating the impact of their parents' death into their own identity as adults (Silverman, 1987). LaGrand (1986) noted "Young adults are caught between the pressures of dependence and independence and the establishment of a basic human need—identity. The establishment of one's identity is itself problematic and tends to exacerbate the resolution of the loss" (p. 17). Thus, for the college student, the process of self-definition may include the integration of past and present losses into a new definition of the self.

Bereaved college students face a number of difficult and painful tasks in a setting that is not conducive to, or

even tolerant of, the resolution of grief issues. On college campuses, where there are often waiting lists for individual counseling, a group for bereaved college students can be an asset. Such a group can provide validation of students' feelings and experiences. It is a place where they can realize that they are not going crazy and are not alone in their grief. Yalom (1985) referred to this concept as "universality." Observing the groups he led, Berson (1988) noted that "in terms of helping students accomplish their grief work, participation in the group helped them maintain attention to the reality of their losses and prevented the all-too-easy delaying or distorting of the mourning process" (p. 106). A bereavement group for college students gives its members the opportunity to set aside time to talk about the person they have lost. It also brings together individuals who are struggling with the same issues of identity and independence and who can turn to each other for support and understanding.

Living With Loss

The bereavement group "Living with Loss" was run under the auspices of the Counseling and Student Development Center at Indiana University of Pennsylvania (IUP). The center is the site for professionally facilitated therapy and support groups on campus, providing services to a wide range of students. Other groups held at the center include a women's group; interpersonal aware-

Address correspondence to Sharon M. Janowiak, Department of Psychology, Clark Hall, Indiana University of Pennsylvania, Indiana, PA 15705.

From *Death Studies*, Vol. 19, 1995, pp. 55-63. © 1995 by Francis & Taylor, Inc., 625 Chestnut Street, 8th Floor, Philadelphia, PA, 19106. All rights reserved. Reprinted by permission.

ness groups; and a group for gay, lesbian, and bisexual students. This site was selected primarily because of its group program, which provided an existing system for advertising, recruiting, and screening; a private meeting space; clerical support; a reputation on campus for offering confidential services; and supervision for the group leaders. Thus, having this framework already in place had both practical and clinical advantages. The motivation for running the bereavement group grew out of the interests of one of the co-leaders. In addition, on the basis of their experiences, the center's faculty believed that a group format would be an excellent means for addressing the concerns of bereaved students. These concerns included the difficulty in obtaining support and understanding from friends, roommates, or family members; doubts as to whether they were "doing grieving right," especially in light of the implicit expectations of peers and professors that they "get over it"; and a hunger of guidance and advice from peers who were experiencing similar difficulties. The rationale for a bereavement support group was both pragmatic, in that the group format would enable more clients to be seen by fewer therapists, and therapeutic, in that the group format provided advantages that were not likely to be present in individual therapy.

Personnel

The co-leaders were both students in the doctoral program in clinical psychology at IUP. The decision to hold [a] professionally led group, rather than a member-facilitated or self-help group, was based on a variety of factors. First, the graduate student co-leaders had initiated the group and were seeking experience as group facilitators. Second, the counseling center offers only groups that are professionally led for various reasons, including clinical efficacy, the provision of group training to doctoral students, and liability. Prior to the actual running of the group, the co-leaders completed a long planning period during which they were able to share their perspectives and develop an understanding and appreciation of each other's goals and interpersonal styles.

The leaders received weekly supervision from one of the licensed psychologists on the center's faculty (the third author). The supervision process included discussion and feedback of is-

sues that arose during each phase of the group process, from planning through termination.

Format

On the basis of their clinical experiences, the co-leaders and supervisor decided to incorporate a psychoeducational and interpersonal process approach in the group sessions. The leaders were prepared to share information on such topics as the stage theories of the grieving process and cultural issues related to grief and mourning. At the same time, the leaders were cognizant of the benefits inherent in the group process itself, including universality, altruism, interpersonal learning, catharsis, and the sharing of personal information (Yalom, 1985).

The co-leaders decided to limit the group's size to eight members, because the format was not to be purely psychoeducational and a high degree of emotional intensity was expected.

Although we had originally planned to have 10–12 weekly sessions, each 90 min in length, difficulties recruiting members and coordinating the schedules of group members and leaders caused a delay in the start of the group, restricting its duration to 7 weekly sessions and limiting the length of each session to 1 hr. The brevity of the group mitigated against the acceptance of new members once the group began. At the first session, the members decided to close the group.

Recruitment and Screening

Recruitment of group members proceeded along two avenues: in-house referral (i.e., referral of clients who came to the center seeking counseling and were deemed appropriate for the group by the intake therapist) and external referral. The latter included self-referral of students, who read about the group in advertisements in the student newspaper and in fliers posted around campus, and referral of students by faculty and staff.

The screening procedure consisted of a screening interview, a half-hour in length, during which the candidate for the group met with one of the two group leaders. The purpose of the meeting was twofold: (a) to see if there was a match between the individual and the group and (b) to prepare the potential member for the group experience. If there was some question regarding the match between a candidate and the group, the

candidate was referred to the second group leader for an additional interview, after which the group leaders conferred together with the supervisor before making a final decision.

The only inclusion criterion with regard to the candidates' loss was that someone significant to them had died; neither the nature of the relationship to the deceased nor the length of time since the death was dictated. Exclusion criteria were the standard exclusion criteria for short-term groups and included suicidal/homicidal ideation; the existence of hallucinations, delusions and/or loose associations; vegetative signs including severe sleep and appetite disturbances; and a history of multiple losses. In addition, the therapists screened for outliers (i.e., persons who differed significantly from the remaining group members on any one variable, such as age, to the degree that it might be difficult for them to feel comfortable in the group).

Two candidates (one female and one male) were deemed inappropriate for group membership and were referred for individual counseling. Two other females initially expressed interest in the group and later opted not to attend. One of them was looking for a group that offered structured lectures and was not receptive to the notion of active participation in a group.

The final composition of the group included 4 female college students. Two of the students had lost a parent; one, a brother; and another, an ex-boyfriend. The length of the time since the deaths ranged from a few months to 3 years.

Implementation

Over the course of the seven group meetings, the group evolved from a highly structured and leader-directed entity to an unstructured and member-directed, leader-facilitated entity. The greater structure of the opening sessions was necessary so that the groundwork for a safe and productive group could be done (Corey & Corey, 1992). This initial phase included a discussion of confidentiality as well as structured activities in which members exchanged information and formulated personal goals for their work in the group. From the first session and throughout the life of the group, the leaders stressed the participants' responsibility in moving toward their own goals.

The group members were quick to establish bonds of caring and support; the passing of a box of tissues from one to another as needed became symbolic of the participants' acceptance of one another's pain. As the group progressed, less "acceptable" feelings began to surface; members dared to express feelings of guilt and selfishness, as well as envy of those who had moved on with their lives and anger at family members who pretended that everything was okay. Despite the sadness and despair that members touched on during these meetings, all voiced the conviction that sharing these feelings was helpful. However, some ambivalence about the grieving process may have been reflected in the suggestion, made by one group member, that every session should end with members sharing something positive that had happened to them during the week.

During this middle stage of the group's life, the leaders were faced with a decision regarding the balance between the psychoeducational and process components in the sessions. Whereas the leaders had presumed that members would be interested in some structured information giving, by the third session the group members were initiating personal material without waiting for the leaders' presentation, and so the facilitators decided to follow the members' lead. Thus, educational material was presented only when the members requested it, and the degree to which this occurred decreased steadily over the life of the group. This shift seemed to reflect the members' realization that there was not one right way to grieve, but that, instead, their task was to find their own ways of coming to terms with their losses.

Given the autonomy to set their own agenda, the group members moved into new areas. In particular, they began to examine how their losses had affected their interpersonal patterns, such as their ability to share feelings and to let others do so as well. These patterns were examined in the here and now.

The final stage of the group was marked by an increasing number of references to the imminent end of the group and a growing sense of frustration on the part of members that they did not have enough time to achieve all they had hoped they would achieve. The members also acknowledged the particularly difficult nature of endings for them. The final session closed with a ritual suggested by the leaders in which the members expressed their appreciation of and hopes for one another.

Evaluation

An evaluation questionnaire was administered at the end of the final group session for two reasons: to provide feedback to the co-leaders and to assist the members in consolidating their discoveries about themselves and integrating the group experience into their lives (Corey & Corey, 1992). The evaluations indicated that the participants found the most valuable aspect of the group to be the opportunity to have been with others who were grieving. This experience gave the members the chance both to share feelings about the person who had died and to hear from others about their own grieving process. The members indicated that they thought differently about themselves and behaved differently with others as a result of having participated in the group.

Discussion

The number of students who expressed an interest in the group was small, given the extent of unsupported grief in the college community (the group had a total of 4 members at the end of the screening procedure). This discrepancy can be accounted for in at least three ways. First, students who are grieving are likely to be more withdrawn from campus activities and may not have read the campus newspaper in which the group was advertised. Second, there may have been students who were aware of the group's existence but who were not emotionally ready to engage in grief work at the time. Third, there may have been students who were considering the possibility of doing grief work but were ambivalent about it; even those students who did attend the screening interviews were highly ambivalent about participating in a group experience. During the screening process, most candidates said they would like to listen to others but preferred not to talk about their own experiences and expressed fears about being emotional in front of other members. This ambivalence was a consistent thread throughout the life of the group. Other students for whom the group might have been appropriate may have been deterred from participating by similar fears.

Summary

Just as there is not one right way to grieve, so there is not one right way to run a bereavement group. We have offered herein an account of one type of group that, according to their evaluations, participants found helpful. In general, we tried to be open to group members' needs and used our clinical expertise to provide information (when desired) and validation of members' perceptions and experiences. Our goal was to create a group setting that (a) provided members with support and understanding of their grieving process and (b) respected their developmental tasks by affording them a way of interacting with others that safeguarded their autonomy. Although the losses experienced by the participants in our bereavement group were not all the same (e.g., loss of a parent), the grief processes of all our group members consisted of common threads that held the group together, regardless of the type of loss.

As group leaders, we learned the importance of being aware of our own attitudes regarding the grieving process and of being sensitive to our own personal experiences of grief and loss. We can provide for our group members a sense of hope, an appreciation of the dignity and courage they bring to their struggles, and a renewal of their determination to integrate their losses into the tapestry of their lives.

References

Aubrey, R. (1988). Separation and loss in university mental health work. *Journal of the American Academy of Psychoanalysis, 16,* 221–234.

Berson, R. J. (1988). A bereavement group for college students. *Journal of American College Health, 37,* 101–108.

Calvin, S., & Smith, I. M. (1986). Counseling adolescents in death-related situations. In C. A. Corr & J. McNeil (Eds.), *Adolescence and death* (pp. 215–230). New York: Springer Publishing Company.

Corey, M. S., & Corey, G. (1992). *Groups: Process and practice* (4th ed.). Pacific Grove, CA: Brooks/Cole.

Erikson, E. (1963). *Childhood and society.* New York; W. W. Norton.

LaGrand, L. E. (1986). *Coping with separation and loss as a young adult.* Springfield, IL: Charles C. Thomas.

Silverman, P. R. (1987). The impact of parental death on college-age women. *Psychiatric Clinics of North America, 10,* 387–404.

Yalom, I. D. (1985). *The theory and practice of group psychotherapy* (3rd ed.). New York: Basic Books.

Grief & Depression

ARE INTIMATE STRANGERS

THE DEATH OF A LOVED ONE CAN BE ONE OF THE MOST DIFFICULT EXPERIENCES A PERSON FACES.

JUDITH LARSON, PH.D.

Dr. Larson is a Research Associate in the Psychology Department at Stanford University and has a private practice in Menlo Park, CA.

Everybody says, "Well, give it a year or two and you'll start to feel better." But I haven't noticed that I feel any better yet. I've considered going to a support group, but I just don't have the energy. I wonder how long I'm going to have these feelings. I think what I feel is normal. I don't have any states of depression or guilt. I miss her a lot, but that's to be expected.

The death of a loved one can be one of the most difficult experiences a person faces. For some, the loss results in a long and protracted period of grief—the normal human response to loss. Symptoms of grief include sadness, longing, appetite and sleep disturbances, memory and concentration impairment, and diminished interest in activities. These symptoms are also symptoms of depression. While some bereaved people experience the symptoms mildly and with decreased intensity over time, other bereaved people experience them to such a degree that they qualify for a diagnosis of clinical depression.

We know that bereaved people grieve in their own time and in their own way, but what accounts for the differences?

Social Support

PEOPLE WHO ARE ISOLATED ARE MORE LIKELY TO BE DEPRESSED than people who have a support network and someone in whom they can confide. However, the benefits of such support may be compromised by other factors, including conflict. Arguments among family members about settling an estate, for example, may contribute to depression rather than relieve it. Reactions of friends and acquaintances are also important. The widow who says, "My friends tell me it's been six months, so I should be over this by now" is more likely to be depressed than the person whose feelings are accepted as normal.

Practical support may be as important, if not more important, than emotional support. If a bereaved person is overwhelmed by legal matters or insurance hassles, having a caring friend who listens may not, by itself, alleviate the depression. Grief can compromise a person's ability to cope with even the most routine tasks. The friend who comes to clean the house or mow the lawn may provide as much or more support as the friend who lends a shoulder to cry on.

Concurrent Stressors

BEREAVEMENT DOES NOT OCCUR IN A VACUUM. FOR EXAMPLE, in one study of 360 recently-bereaved people, researchers found that 3.5 percent were also coping with marital separation, 15 percent did not have enough money to live on, and 8 percent were deeply in debt. In addition, 11 percent had experienced the death of another immediate family member or close friend within the previous six months, 24 percent were themselves seriously ill or injured, and 16 percent had legal problems. The more additional stressors a bereaved person faces, the greater the risk of depression.

Coping Style

EVERYONE COPES DIFFERENTLY WITH STRESSFUL EVENTS. THOSE who feel helpless, pessimistic, and isolated have a harder time coping. Those who ruminate about their feelings of sadness and depression are more likely to remain depressed than those who find activities that re-engage their attention and give them a sense of accomplishment. Similarly, people who try to avoid feelings associated with their bereavement have a harder time adjusting. Some activities that people engage in to avoid their feelings, such as drinking heavily or working excessively, can lead to additional problems.

But what about the people who do not seem to have a difficult time coping with bereavement? Early theorists believed that a period of depression was a necessary part of the grief process and that, if a person did not experience depression, he or she would be unable to reach a state of resolution. However, there are people who do not become seriously depressed following the death of a loved one and are able to accept and resolve their loss.

People who cope well typically have an optimistic, positive outlook on life. They view upsetting events as isolated occurrences, rather than evidence that "bad things are always happening." These people have confidence in their ability to cope. They may have a life philosophy or spiritual practice that gives them comfort. They are able to make sense of the death, and to find some meaning in it. Many such people report that they learned something about themselves or about their loved one. Many say that they discovered they were stronger or better at caregiving than they thought they could be. People who cope well do not deny their feelings of sad-

ness, but regard them as a natural part of the grief process and express them.

When a death occurs, many people do not know what to expect. They may turn to books, friends, relatives, counselors, and therapists for guidance. As a result of the messages they receive, many people feel judged or criticized for not "doing it right." Common statements made to bereaved individuals include "You should be over it by now," "You're just in denial," "You should put it out of your mind," "It must be so hard for you" and "Just try to think happy thoughts." As if that weren't enough, many people judge and criticize themselves for failing to grieve according to their own expectations. One woman said, "There must be something wrong with me. My sisters are crying their eyes out, and I just don't feel like I need to cry." A young widower said, "I haven't felt angry yet, but I guess I will at some point, because I read in a book that anger is always part of the grieving process."

It is important for professionals, family members, friends, and the bereaved themselves to understand and remember that everyone has his or her own style of grieving. This style may not match preconceived notions about grief. It is also important to know the factors that may contribute to serious depression in the bereaved. Recognizing depression and providing assistance early can help promote a more positive outcome.

GriefTips
Help for Those Who Mourn

Following are many ideas to help people who are mourning a loved one's death. Different kinds of losses dictate different responses, so not all of these ideas will suit everyone. Likewise, no two people grieve alike—what works for one may not work for another. Treat this list for what it is: a gathering of assorted suggestions that various people have tried with success. Perhaps what helped them through their grief will help you. The emphasis here is upon specific, practical ideas.

Talk regularly with a friend.

Talking with another about what you think and feel is one of the best things you can do for yourself. It helps relieve some of the pressure you may feel, it can give you a sense of perspective, and it keeps you in touch with others. Look for someone who's a good listener and a caring soul. Then speak what's on your mind and in your heart. If this feels one-sided, let that be okay for this period of your life. Chances are the other person will find meaning in what they're doing. And the time will come when you'll have the chance to be a good listener for someone else. You'll be a better listener then if you're a good talker now.

Walk.

Go for walks outside every day if you can. Don't overdo it, but walk briskly enough that it feels invigorating. Sometimes try walking slowly enough you can look carefully at whatever you want to see. Observe what nature has to offer you, what it can teach you. Enjoy as much as you're able the sights and the sounds that come your way. If you like, walk with another.

Carry or wear a linking object.

Carry something in your pocket or purse that reminds you of the one who died—a keepsake they gave you perhaps, or a small object they once carried or used, or a memento you select for just this purpose. You might wear a piece of their jewelry in the same way. Whenever you want, reach for or gaze upon this object and remember what it signifies.

Visit the grave.

Not all people prefer to do this. But if it feels right to you, then do so. Don't let others convince you this is a morbid thing to do. Spend whatever time feels right there. Stand or sit in the quietness and do what comes naturally: be silent or talk, breathe deeply or cry, recollect or pray. You may wish to add your distinctive touch to the gravesite—straighten it a bit, or add little signs of your love.

Create a memory book.

Compile photographs which document your loved one's life. Arrange them into some sort of order so they tell a story. Add other elements if you want: diplomas, newspaper clippings, awards, accomplishments, reminders of significant events. Put all this in a special binder and keep it out for people to look at if they wish. Go through it on your own if you desire. Reminisce as you do so.

Recall your dreams.

Your dreams often have important things to say about your feelings and about your relationship with the one who died. Your dreams may be scary or sad, especially early on. They may seem weird or crazy to you. You may find that your loved one appears in your dreams. Accept your dreams for what they are and see what you can learn from them. No one knows that better than you.

Tell people what helps you and what doesn't.

People around you may not understand what you need. So tell them. If hearing your loved one's name spoken aloud by others feels good, say so. If you need more time alone, or assistance with chores you're unable to complete, or an occasional hug, be honest. People can't read your mind, so you'll have to speak it.

Write things down.

Most people who are grieving become more forgetful than usual. So help yourself remember what you want by keeping track of it on paper or with whatever system works best for you. This may include writing down things you want to preserve about the person who has died.

Ask for a copy of the memorial service.

If the funeral liturgy or memorial service held special meaning for you because of what was spoken or read, ask for the words. Whoever participated in that ritual will feel gratified that what they prepared was appreciated. Turn to these words whenever you want. Some people find these thoughts provide even more help weeks and months after the service.

Remember the serenity prayer.
There is a prayer attributed to theologian Reinhold Niebuhr, but it's actually an ancient German prayer. It has brought comfort and support to many who have suffered various kinds of afflictions. Perhaps it will help you. The prayer goes, God, grant me the serenity to accept the things I cannot change, courage to change the things I can, and wisdom to know one from the other. Great truth is contained here. Call these words to mind when you need their direction.

Plant something living as a memorial.
Plant a flower, a bush, or a tree in memory of the one who died. Or plant several things. Do this ceremonially if you wish, perhaps with others present. If you do this planting where you live, you can watch it grow and change day by day, season by season. You can even make it a part of special times of remembrance in the future.

Plan at least one thing you'll do each day.
Even if your grief is very painful and your energy very low, plan to complete at least one thing each day, even if it's a small thing. Then follow through with your plan, day after day. Don't feel you have to keep busy all day long; that can become awfully tiring and even counterproductive. Just help yourself feel that you're not entirely at the mercy of this overwhelming experience—there are some things you can do to help you through this time.

Spend time in your loved one's space.
If it's what you want to do, you may sit in the other's favorite chair, or lie in their bed, or just stand in their room or among their possessions. Do this if it brings you comfort. But don't do it if it feels too awkward. You'll know quickly enough what's right for you.

Journal.
Write out your thoughts and feelings. Do this whenever you feel the urge, but do it at least several times a week, if not several times a day. Don't censor what you write—be just as honest as you can. In time, go back through your writings and notice how you're changing and growing. Write about that, too.

Rest.
Grieving is hard work. So do what's best for you: get your rest. Take naps if you wish. Lie down from time to time. Relax in a comfortable chair. Pace yourself so you have interludes in which you can replenish yourself. Give yourself plenty of permission to take things easy.

Purchase something soft to sleep with.
A teddy bear is a favorite choice for some. But there are other options. Select something that feels warm and cuddly. Then, whatever your age, cuddle it.

Write the person who died.
Write letters or other messages to your loved one, thoughts you wish you could express if they were present. And who knows but what they're not present in some way? Preserve what you write in your journal if you wish, or on stationery, or on your computer. Or, if you wish, discard what you've written after awhile. You'll find this urge to write the other will eventually leave you, but for awhile it can be a real release for you, as well as a real connection.

Get a physical.
It's wise to get a physical examination within a few months after the death. But it's also an assuring thing to do. Chances are good you'll experience various physical reactions when you're grieving. It's helpful to make sure that your body is acting normally, whatever normal may be for you. Your physician can be an important ally at this time of your life.

Get physical.
Exercise. Flex your muscles. Stretch your body. Expand your lungs. It will help you feel better. It really will.

Consider a support group.
Spending time with a small group of people who have undergone a similar life experience can be very therapeutic. You can discover how natural your feelings are. You can learn from the experiences and the ideas of others. You can find backing as you make the changes you must. Support groups are not for everyone, of course. But many people have come to swear by them. You won't know unless you try.

If you're alone, and if you like animals, get a pet.
The attention and affection a pet provides may help you adapt to the loss of the attention and affection you're experiencing after this significant person has died. Pets can also be fun to play with. Certain pets offer you a sense of personal security, too, if that is important to you.

Light a candle at mealtime.
Especially if you eat alone, but even if you don't, consider lighting a taper at the table in memory of your loved one. Pause to remember them as you light it. Keep them nearby in this time of sustenance. You might light a candle at other times as well—as you sit alone in the evening, for instance.

Donate their possessions meaningfully.
Whether you give your loved one's personal possessions to someone you know or to a stranger, find ways to pass these things along so that others might benefit from them. Family members or friends might like to receive keepsakes. They or others might deserve tools or utensils or books or sporting equipment. Philanthropic organizations can put clothes to good use. Some wish to do this quickly following the death, while others wish to wait awhile.

Create a memory area at home.
In a space that feels appropriate, arrange a small tableau that honors the person: a framed photograph or two, perhaps a prized possession or award, or something they created, or something they loved. This might be placed on a small table,

or a mantel, or a desk. Some people like to use a grouping of candles, representing not just the person who died but others who have died as well. In that case, a variety of candles can be arranged, each representing a unique life.

Drink water.
Grieving people can easily become dehydrated. Crying can naturally lead to that. And with your normal routines turned upside down, you may simply not drink as much or as regularly as you did before this death. Make this one way you care for yourself.

Use your hands.
Sometimes there's value in doing repetitive things with your hands, something you don't have to think about very much because it becomes second nature. Knitting and crocheting are like that. So are carving, woodworking, polishing, solving jigsaw puzzles, painting, braiding, shoveling, washing, and countless other activities.

Give yourself respites from your grief.
Just because you're grieving doesn't mean you must always be feeling sad or forlorn. There's value in sometimes consciously deciding that you'll think about something else for awhile, or that you'll do something you've always enjoyed doing. Sometimes this happens naturally and it's only later you realize that your grief has taken a back seat. Let it. This is not an indication you love that person any less, or that you're forgetting them. It's a sign that you're human and you need relief from the unrelenting pressure. It can also be a healthy sign you're healing.

See a grief counselor.
If you're concerned about how you're feeling and how well you're adapting, make an appointment with a counselor who specializes in grief. Often you'll learn what you need, both about grief and about yourself as a griever, in only a few sessions. Ask questions of the counselor before you sign on: What specific training does he or she have? What accreditation? A person who is a family therapist or a psychologist doesn't necessarily understand the unique issues of someone in grief.

Begin your day with your loved one.
If your grief is young, you'll probably wake up thinking of that person anyway. So why not decide that you'll include her or him from the start? Focus this time in a positive way. Bring to your mind fulfilling memories. Recall lessons this person taught you, gifts he or she gave you. Think about how you can spend your day in ways that would be in keeping with your loved one's best self, and with your best self. Then carry that best self with you through your day.

Invite someone to be your telephone buddy.
If your grief and sadness hit you especially hard at times and you have no one nearby to turn to, ask someone you trust to be your telephone buddy. Ask their permission for you to call them whenever you feel you're at loose ends, day or night. Then put their number beside your phone and call them if you need them. Don't abuse this privilege, of course. And covenant that someday it will be payback time—someday you'll make yourself available to help someone else in the same way you've been helped. That will help you accept the care you're receiving.

Avoid certain people if you must.
No one likes to be unfriendly or cold. But if there are people in your life who make it very difficult for you to do your grieving, then do what you can to stay out of their way. Some people may lecture you, or belittle you, or antagonize you, either knowingly or unknowingly. Take care of your health during your grief, including your emotional health. If that means protecting yourself from others for awhile, then do so.

Structure alone time.
You may have your full share of alone time, in which case you'll want to ignore this suggestion. But if you're often among family, friends, and colleagues, make sure you also have time all by yourself. A large part of the grieving process involves what goes on inside yourself—your thoughts, your feelings, your memories, your hopes and dreams. So allow yourself the opportunity to go inside so you can grow inside.

Listen to music.
Choose music you believe will help you at a given moment, whether it's contemporary or ancient, instrumental or vocal, secular or religious. Let the sounds surround you and soothe you. Take this music with you, if you wish, as you go about your day.

Create your own music.
Play an instrument. Sing a song. Or just hum. Use your music to express what you feel, to unite you with others, to focus on your hope.

Do something your loved one would enjoy.
Remember the one who died in your own unique way. One widowed woman has a special sourkraut meal once a year. She doesn't like this tangy dish herself, but it was her husband's favorite, and she finds solace in remembering him in that way. There are probably a hundred different things you could do that once brought meaning or satisfaction to the one you loved. The meaning and satisfaction don't have to end with the death of that person.

Write stories about your loved one.
Recreate those events you don't want to forget. Write them out in detail—when and where they occurred, who was there, what happened, what the results were. Describe everything as well as you can. Add dialogue if you wish. Make an entire collection of stories. It will help you today and it will become a valuable resource for yourself and others in the future.

Screen your entertainment.
Some TV shows and movies are best not viewed when you're deep in grief. The same goes for certain books or articles. If

you have any question, do a bit of research before you find yourself in the midst of an experience which brings up too many feelings for you to handle comfortably. For example, if your loved one recently died of cancer, you can do without reliving that experience on a 30-foot movie screen.

Read practical books and articles on grief.
Reading is a great way to find your way through this round-about experience. Steer clear of those books that are like textbooks for professionals. They won't offer you the undergirding you need. Go for the ones that speak to you directly and honestly as a person in mourning. It will probably help to read shorter books and more succinct articles—your power of concentration is likely to be diminished.

Engage your soul.
You'll want to do this your own way. Some people meditate, some pray, and some spend time alone in nature. Some worship with a congregation and others do it on their own. Many grieving people begin to sense that all of us, living and dead, are connected on a spiritual level in a way that defies easy understanding. Include your soul as you grow through your grief.

Change some things.
As soon as it seems right, alter some things in your home to make clear this significant change that has occurred. Rearrange a room or replace a piece of furniture or give away certain items that will never again be used in your home. This does not mean to remove all signs of the one who died. It does mean not treating your home or your loved one's room as a shrine which cannot be altered in anyway.

Plan ahead for special days.
Birthdays, anniversaries, holidays, and other special events can be difficult times, especially for the first year or two. Give thought beforehand to how you will handle those days. Do things a little differently than you used to, as a way of acknowledging this change in your life. But also be sure to invoke that person's presence and memory somehow during the day. If you don't include that person in some way, you'll spend too much of your energy acting as if nothing has been changed with that day, knowing full well that much has changed.

Allow yourself to laugh.
Sometimes something funny will happen to you, just like it used to. Sometimes you'll recall something hilarious that happened in the past. When that happens, go ahead and laugh if it feels funny to you. You won't be desecrating your loved one's memory. You'll be consecrating their love of life, and your own, too.

Allow yourself to cry.
Crying goes naturally with grief. Tears well up and fall even when you least expect them. Subdued sniffles can become racking sobs on a moment's notice. It may feel awkward to you, but this is not unusual for a person in your situation. A good rule of thumb is this: if you feel like crying, then cry.

If not, then don't. Some grieving people seldom cry—it's just their way.

Talk to the other one.
If it helps, you might talk with the one who died as you drive alone in your car, or as you stand beside the grave, or as you screw up your courage to make an important decision. This talking might be out loud, or under your breath. Either way, it's the same: you're simply wishing the other was with you so you could talk things over, and for the moment you're doing the best you can to continue that conversation. This inclination to converse will eventually go away, when the time is right.

Donate in the other's name.
Honor the other's memory and spirit by giving a gift or gifts to a cause the other would appreciate. World hunger? A favorite charity? A local fund-raiser? A building project? Extend that person's influence even farther.

Create or commission a memory quilt.
Sew or invite others to sew with you. Or hire someone to sew for you. However you get it completed, put together a wall hanging or a bedroom quilt that remembers the important life events of the one who died. Take your time doing this. Make it what it is: a labor of love.

Take a yoga class.
People of almost any age can do yoga. More than conditioning your body, it helps you relax and focus your mind. It can be woven into a practice of meditation. It's a gentle art for that time in your life when you deserve gentleness all around you.

Plant yourself in nature.
Dig a flower garden and keep it in color as long as possible. Dig a vegetable garden and stay close to it until frost. Walk in forests and put your hands on trees. Collect leaves and wildflowers. Watch firsthand how rivers and lakes and oceans behave. Look up at the stars and don't just wonder—hope.

Connect on the Internet.
If you're computer savvy, search the Internet. You'll find many resources for people in grief, as well as the opportunity to chat with fellow grievers. You can link up with others without leaving your home. You'll also find much more to expand your horizons as a person who is beginning to grow.

Speak to a clergyperson.
If you're searching for answers to the larger questions about life and death, religion and spirituality, consider talking with a representative of your faith, or even another's faith. Consider becoming a spiritual friend with another and making your time of grieving a time of personal exploring.

Read how others have responded to a loved one's death.
You may feel that your own grief is all you can handle. But if you'd like to look at the ways others have done it, try C. S. Lewis's *A Grief Observed*, Lynn Caine's *Widow*, John Bram-

blett's *When Good-Bye Is Forever,* or Nicholas Wolterstorff's *Lament for a Son.* There are many others. Check with a counselor or a librarian.

Learn about your loved one from others.
Listen to the stories others have to tell about the one who died, both stories you're familiar with and those you've never heard before. Spend time with their friends or schoolmates or colleagues. Invite them into your home. Solicit the writings of others. Preserve whatever you find out. Celebrate your time together.

Take a day off.
When the mood is just right, take a one-day vacation. Do whatever you want, or don't do whatever you want. Travel somewhere or stay inside by yourself. Be very active or don't do anything at all. Just make it your day, whatever that means for you.

Invite someone to give you feedback.
Select someone you trust, preferably someone familiar with the workings of grief, to give you their reaction when you ask for it. If you want to check out how clearly you're thinking, how accurately you're remembering, how effectively you're coping, go to that person. Pose your questions, then listen to their responses. What you choose to do with that information will be up to you.

Vent your anger rather than hold it in.
You may feel awkward being angry when you're grieving, but anger is a common reaction. The expression holds true: anger is best out floatin' rather than in bloatin'. Even if you feel a bit ashamed as you do it, find ways to get it out of your system. Yell, even if it's in an empty house. Cry. Hit something soft. Throw eggs at something hard. Vacuum up a storm. Resist the temptation to be proper.

Give thanks every day.
Whatever has happened to you, you still have things to be thankful for. Perhaps it's your memories, your remaining family, your support, your work, your own health—all sorts of things. Draw your attention to those parts of life that are worth appreciating, then appreciate them.

Monitor signs of dependency.
While it's normal to become more dependent upon others for awhile immediately after a death, it will not be helpful to continue in that role long-term. Watch for signs that you're prolonging your need for assistance. Congratulate yourself when you do things for yourself.

Give yourself rewards.
Be kind to yourself in your grief. Do those things for yourself that you really enjoy, perhaps at the end of a long day, or in the midst of a lonely time. Treat yourself to a favorite meal or delicacy. Get a massage. Buy some flowers. Do something frivolous that makes you feel good. Then soak up those moments as fully as you can.

Eat healthy.
Your diet affects how you think and feel as well as how your body acts. Eat balanced meals. Eat even if you're not hungry. Eat regular meals rather than just snacking. Avoid too much fat.

Take up a new hobby.
Try something you've never tried before. Expand your horizons. Do what you want to do, not what someone else may have wanted for you. Learn. Be open to meeting new people. Associate this part of your life with who you're becoming, rather than who you've been.

Do something to help someone else.
Step out of your own problems from time to time and devote your attention to someone else. Offer a gift or your service. Do this for yourself as much as for the other. Feel good about your worth.

Honor your funnybone.
Watch a comedy on TV. View a funny movie. Read humorous books or articles. Savor jokes. When you're able to laugh, you encourage your healing.

Write down your lessons.
Your grief experience will have much to teach you. From time to time reflect upon what it is you're learning. State it as plainly as you're able. Carry those lessons with you as you go about your days.

GriefTips are intended for use by people in mourning. They're also intended to be the collected wisdom of people who have experienced mourning first-hand. I encourage you to add your own GriefTip along with any words of explanation you choose. Include your email address so I can show you the edited version of your idea before it's entered here as the latest GriefTip. Your name will appear if you desire. Just request it. (http://www.opn.com/willowgreen/tips.html)

James E. Miller

AE Article Review Form

We encourage you to photocopy and use this page as a tool to assess how the articles in **Annual Editions** expand on the information in your textbook. By reflecting on the articles you will gain enhanced text information. You can also access this useful form on a product's book support Web site at **http://www.dushkin.com/ online/.**

NAME: _____ DATE: _____

TITLE AND NUMBER OF ARTICLE: _____

BRIEFLY STATE THE MAIN IDEA OF THIS ARTICLE: _____

LIST THREE IMPORTANT FACTS THAT THE AUTHOR USES TO SUPPORT THE MAIN IDEA:

WHAT INFORMATION OR IDEAS DISCUSSED IN THIS ARTICLE ARE ALSO DISCUSSED IN YOUR TEXTBOOK OR OTHER READINGS THAT YOU HAVE DONE? LIST THE TEXTBOOK CHAPTERS AND PAGE NUMBERS:

LIST ANY EXAMPLES OF BIAS OR FAULTY REASONING THAT YOU FOUND IN THE ARTICLE:

LIST ANY NEW TERMS/CONCEPTS THAT WERE DISCUSSED IN THE ARTICLE, AND WRITE A SHORT DEFINITION:

ANNUAL EDITIONS revisions depend on two major opinion sources: one is our Advisory Board, listed in the front of this volume, which works with us in scanning the thousands of articles published in the public press each year; the other is you—the person actually using the book. Please help us and the users of the next edition by completing the prepaid article rating form on this page and returning it to us. Thank you for your help!

ANNUAL EDITIONS: Dying, Death, and Bereavement 00/01

ARTICLE RATING FORM

Here is an opportunity for you to have direct input into the next revision of this volume. We would like you to rate each of the 41 articles listed below, using the following scale:

1. Excellent: should definitely be retained
2. Above average: should probably be retained
3. Below average: should probably be deleted
4. Poor: should definitely be deleted

Your ratings will play a vital part in the next revision.
So please mail this prepaid form to us just as soon as you complete it.
Thanks for your help!

RATING

ARTICLE

1. The Facts of Death
2. Dealing with Death: A Culture in Denial
3. A Look at How Kentuckians in Knox County Once Treated the Dead
4. Death Be Not Painful
5. At Your Disposal: The Funeral Industry Prepares for Boom Times
6. The Death Poetry of Emily Dickinson
7. Putting Death on Ice
8. Is It Time to Abandon Brain Death?
9. Communication among Children, Parents, and Funeral Directors
10. Children, Death, and Fairy Tales
11. Failing to Discuss Dying Adds to Pain of Patient and Family
12. Older Americans in the 1990s and Beyond
13. Schools Struggle to Teach Lessons in Life and Death
14. Planning to Die
15. Attitudes to Death and Bereavement among Cultural Minority Groups
16. The Spiritual Needs of the Dying
17. The Request to Die
18. Quality End-of-Life Care
19. Maumee: My Walden Pond
20. Hospice Care for the 1990s: A Concept Coming of Age
21. Doctor, I Want to Die. Will You Help Me?

RATING

ARTICLE

22. The Supreme Court and Physician-Assisted Suicide: The Ultimate Right
23. Competent Care for the Dying Instead of Physician-Assisted Suicide
24. A Conversation with My Mother
25. Euthanasia: To Cease upon the Midnight
26. Attitudes toward Suicidal Behavior: A Review of the Literature
27. The Contemporary American Funeral
28. Psychocultural Influences on African-American Attitudes towards Death, Dying, and Funeral Rites
29. How Different Religions Pay Their Final Respects
30. Burying the Ungrateful Dead
31. We Can Help Children Grieve: A Child-Oriented Model for Memorializing
32. A Do-It-Yourself Funeral
33. A Time to Mourn
34. The Grieving Process
35. Learning to Mourn
36. Disenfranchised Grief
37. The Increasing Prevalence of Complicated Mourning: The Onslaught Is Just Beginning
38. Children Grieve Too: Lessons in How to Support Children through a Normal, Healthy Grief Process
39. Living with Loss: A Group for Bereaved College Students
40. Grief and Depression Are Intimate Strangers
41. GriefTips: Help for Those Who Mourn

(Continued on next page)

ANNUAL EDITIONS: DYING, DEATH, AND BEREAVEMENT 00/01

BUSINESS REPLY MAIL
FIRST-CLASS MAIL PERMIT NO. 84 GUILFORD CT

POSTAGE WILL BE PAID BY ADDRESSEE

Dushkin/McGraw-Hill
Sluice Dock
Guilford, CT 06437-9989

NO POSTAGE
NECESSARY
IF MAILED
IN THE
UNITED STATES

I|I...|I..I.I..I.I.II.I..III.I.I.I.I.I..I.I.I..I.I.I

ABOUT YOU

Name   Date

Are you a teacher? ☐   A student? ☐
Your school's name

Department

Address   City   State   Zip

School telephone #

YOUR COMMENTS ARE IMPORTANT TO US !

Please fill in the following information:
For which course did you use this book?

Did you use a text with this *ANNUAL EDITION*? ☐ yes ☐ no
What was the title of the text?

What are your general reactions to the *Annual Editions* concept?

Have you read any particular articles recently that you think should be included in the next edition?

Are there any articles you feel should be replaced in the next edition? Why?

Are there any World Wide Web sites you feel should be included in the next edition? Please annotate.

May we contact you for editorial input? ☐ yes ☐ no
May we quote your comments? ☐ yes ☐ no